The Superior Wife Syndrome

Why Women Do Everything So Well
and Why—for the Sake of Our Marriages—
We've Got to Stop

Carin Rubenstein

A Touchstone Book
Published by Simon & Schuster

NEW YORK   LONDON   TORONTO   SYDNEY

Touchstone
A Division of Simon & Schuster, Inc.
1230 Avenue of the Americas
New York, NY 10020

First Touchstone hardcover edition September 2009

TOUCHSTONE and colophon are
registered trademarks of Simon & Schuster, Inc.

For information about special discounts for bulk purchases,
please contact Simon & Schuster Special Sales at
1-866-506-1949 or business@simonandschuster.com.

The Simon & Schuster Speakers Bureau
can bring authors to your live event.
For more information or to book an event contact
the Simon & Schuster Speakers Bureau at 1-866-248-3049
or visit our website at www.simonspeakers.com.

Designed by Ruth Lee-Mui

Manufactured in the United States of America

1   3   5   7   9   10   8   6   4   2

Library of Congress Cataloging-in-Publication Data
Rubenstein, Carin.
The superior wife syndrome: why women do everything so well
and why—for the sake of our marriages—we've go to stop / by Carin Rubenstein.
p.   cm.
"A Touchstone Book."
Includes bibliographical references.
1. Wives—Family relationships. 2. Husbands. 3. Marriage.
4. Sexual division of labor. 5. Households. I. Title.
HQ759 .R822 2009
646.7'8082—dc22x   2009021564

ISBN 978-1-4165-6678-6
ISBN 978-1-4165-6687-8 (ebook)

CONTENTS

Introduction

Something is rotten in the state of modern marriage: it's the common expectation that wives should be superior. Wives are supposed to do all, know all, fix all.

Take this regular exchange I have with my husband of several decades. While I'm putting away groceries or cooking dinner or doing laundry, or all three at once, I'll ask him to let the dog out.

"I have to do everything!" he'll answer, in a testy, melodramatic huff, as he reluctantly gets up from the living room couch to open the front door.

The joke is, of course, that *I'm the one* who does nearly everything, but he pretends to get upset if he has to do one tiny thing. There are several layers of meaning embedded in his banter. First, he's making fun of himself for being upset. Second, he's admitting that he doesn't do anything. Third, he's acknowledging that I am the one who does everything. Finally, he's apologizing for the situation but confessing that there's nothing he can do about it.

All in one brief punch line.

It's no secret that in our family I'm the one who takes on more responsibility. I do more tasks, I oversee more of the daily business of living, and I also work full-time. I'm the head of our family unit: he's one of my minions. In our marriage, for example, I am the only one who can cook a turkey and make mashed potatoes. I am the one who can bake a birthday cake, from scratch or from a mix. And I am the one who knows how to get a coffee stain out of a shirt and where we keep the good glue. I'm also the one who knows how to replace the fill valve and flapper in the toilet tank so it will flush properly. I know how to restore Windows on our home computer, how to troubleshoot the satellite television system, how to repair the wireless

Internet connection, and how to load the iPod. I research, plan, and arrange our family vacations; I pack the suitcases. I help our children decide where to apply to college, how to write the applications, and what to look for when we visit the schools. I hire the painters, the driveway repavers, the siding guys. I buy new sheets and pillows and bath mats, and I clean the carpet and comforter after every dog accident. I organize family get-togethers on major holidays, and I arrange dinners and movie dates with our friends.

My husband follows my lead, quite willingly, but he has no desire to be in charge. Going to work every day, washing two cars every week (even in winter!), and handling the family finances are the only jobs that he has signed up for. So, in his mind, every other family task is mine. Not long ago I planned a four-day celebration for our daughter's college graduation, one that was attended by our entire extended family. During our stay in Washington, D.C., an unfamiliar city, I asked my husband to pick up a cake from a nearby bakery. He was unenthusiastic, protesting loudly that he should not be the one to have to do this errand.

"I don't want to have to *think*," he declared, as if this were the perfect reason for not doing something he doesn't want to do. The implication, of course, is that I'm the one who's supposed to do all the family thinking. I think, therefore he doesn't have to.

With this attitude, it's no wonder that if I were hit by a truck tomorrow, he'd need lots of help to get by.

The truth of the matter is that I am not unique, nor am I alone. It turns out that a majority of married couples—about two out of three—are just like us: the wife is the one who can't get hit by a truck. She's the one who develops expertise in nearly all aspects of modern life; she becomes the de facto master of the marital domain while also earning a significant part of the family income. It's as if by taking on a husband, a wife gains a dependent—not quite a child, but not quite a true partner either. She's Marge Simpson to her husband's Homer. This arrangement does not characterize every single married couple, of course, just a great many of them. While husbands may joke about wives being their "better half," quite often it's the literal truth. Wives *are* the better half—the ones who are capable and responsible, organized and efficient, caring and involved.

I don't mean to say that wives think of themselves as superior beings:

they do not. Most would never, ever call themselves better or more mature or more capable than their husbands, even if they are. Instead they might view themselves as the family manager. They might concede that they give more to the marriage. They might view themselves as being in charge. But few would ever use a word like *superior,* because it implies dominion over their mate. Also because it sounds snobbish and condescending and bitchy. And the bitch factor—the fear of being perceived as mean and nasty and fearsome—is what keeps superior wives from admitting their status. No wife wants to be seen as a bitch on wheels, as the Wicked Witch of the West, as the Cruella de Vil of the neighborhood.

The superiority of wives has become the only remaining fact of modern life that dare not speak its name.

We've come a long way since the early 1980s, a time when there was serious speculation that women suffered from a secret fear of independence. This was the premise of a bestselling book called *The Cinderella Complex,* which held that almost all women long for and need to be cared for by a man on a permanent basis.[1] Today that notion seems quaint, even absurd, like a bad joke. The theory that women furtively yearn to be swept off their feet, adored, and treated like a princess seems as alien to many superior wives as the idea of opening a restaurant on Mars or living in an igloo. While some contemporary wives may harbor this kind of retro longing, few expect such wishes to be fulfilled, even if only for a few days or weeks out of the year.

Indeed, the cultural mood had shifted so drastically by the end of the 1980s that fiercely independent working wives—and not secret Cinderellas—had become the focus of attention in American domestic life. Suddenly the mass of working women, far from being afraid of freedom, were wallowing in it. They were the ones working for pay all day, then returning home to do domestic work all night. Because couples devalued women's paid work, many of them assumed women should be responsible for child care and domestic chores, according to Arlie Hochschild, who wrote *The Second Shift* in 1989. Women were victims of a "stalled revolution," she said, trapped in the old role of unpaid domestic servant while also leaping into a new one, of paid employee.[2] They were leaders of a work/family revolution, but their husbands were sleeping through the bugle call to action. And in those days, most families considered the husband to be the head of the household, even if he had a working wife. While many men began to feel social pressure to do more at home, few responded in a meaningful fashion.

Today superior wives are still stuck in the same prerevolutionary rut. They continue to work the second shift, only now they're doing even more. They're doing everything, and doing it better too. While second-shift wives put in more hours of work at home, superior wives do that and more. They run and manage their family, often because they have no other choice. Beyond second-shifters, they're expected to do all, be all, and know all, but with little or no credit for their sizeable effort. As a result, their superiority is often invisible, shrouded in silence and secrecy.

The recipe for concocting a modern superior wife is simple. First, take a husband who tries to do as little as possible, one who may even fake incompetence to avoid responsibility. Second, add a wife who steps into the breach and uses her natural ability to master most aspects of adult and family life. And third, stir in the complicity of both: a husband who avoids domestic effort, worry, and stress, and a wife who allows her husband to be an unequal partner. Let the mixture simmer, and eventually the result will be a marriage that includes a superior wife.

I'm not just saying this because my own marriage ended up this way: I've got solid, scientific proof that it's true. The Web research I conducted over the past few years provides strong and incontrovertible evidence that the superior wife syndrome is real. My research consists of several original surveys that I designed, posted on the Internet, and analyzed statistically, which I'll describe in detail in chapter 1. Using these surveys, I studied 1,529 wives and husbands from across the country and around the world. The wives and husbands who answered were mostly Americans and came from all fifty states. I heard from a husband in Hilo, Hawaii, and a wife in Kasilof, Alaska. My research included at least one wife from Delray Beach, Florida, and another from Athens, Georgia; one from Bismarck, North Dakota, and another from Cheyenne, Wyoming; and several from East Brunswick, New Jersey. I heard from husbands in Tuscaloosa, Alabama, and Houston, Texas, and Carlsbad, New Mexico. Although my focus is mainly on superior wives in the United States, I also heard from English-speaking spouses around the world. I had responses from wives in Istanbul, Turkey; Sydney, Australia; Bournemouth, England; and Bayamón, Puerto

Rico; I heard from husbands in Davao, Philippines; Riyadh, Saudi Arabia; Chiang Mai, Thailand; and Rio de Janeiro, Brazil.

In addition I conducted personal interviews with a large number of married women and men. I quote from them extensively here, both their written answers and what they told me on the telephone or in person. I've changed their names and some identifying details, since I promised them anonymity, although I've used their comments almost verbatim. I also pored over the latest social science research about marriage and relationships, divorce and femininity, household chores and dual-earner couples. All my research leads me to conclude that superior wives have emerged as the heads of the household, they make most of the family decisions, and they handle most of the family management tasks.

Indeed, when wives describe their situation, they use the word *everything* constantly. It's as if "everything" is their one-word motto: "I do everything" and "Everything is what I do" and "I have the most responsibility for everything."

Adelina, for instance, is a thirty-one-year-old office manager and mother of one from San Jose, California. She and her husband, Frank, work full-time, and both earn about the same amount. Here's how she describes her role in the family: "I do all of the financial planning, the long-term investing, the registering for work benefits at enrollment time, and the balancing of the checking account. Anything paperwork-related is me. I also do most of the clothes shopping, grocery shopping, and household shopping. I handle everything related to our daughter's school, her doctor visits, her friends. I handle our family calendar, I plan parties, I take care of correspondence. Frank calls me the CEO." There is, however, one thing that Adelina never does: "I don't take out the trash, ever."

Adelina could accurately describe her job in life as "Everything but the trash."

Although a majority of marriages may contain wives like Adelina, who are married to husbands like Frank, I am not saying that the male gender is comprehensively incompetent, nor am I taking a man-hating stance here. What I am saying is that after being married for a while, and especially after having children, a large number of husbands deliberately surrender family concerns and responsibilities and begin to expect their wives to take charge. And in many marriages, that assignment eventually includes nearly everything. It's as if husbands raise the art of oblivion to new heights; they can fiddle while wives burn through most of the tasks of adult life.

Some wives claim that they have taken control of family life because "it seems like I have no choice, it's just a natural occurrence," as a forty-two-year-old woman puts it. Others confess to being impressed that their husbands are able to function in the world at all, without their constant intervention. "I'm amazed he's still alive," says one such wife.

I don't believe that there are rigid gender differences that cause this phenomenon, although it's true that women have several biologically based advantages when it comes to being able to manage at work and to care for a family at home. (I'll provide evidence for this statement in chapter 2.) Instead, I think the process is insidious; responsibilities shift over time, until both partners simply accept the wife's superiority as a natural state of affairs. The husband of a superior wife has it easy, so why rock the marital boat if she has already agreed to do the rowing?

Another reason for the proliferation of the superiority syndrome is a growing sense of confusion about the definitions of masculinity and femininity, especially on the part of husbands. Wives have grown used to the idea that being feminine means being sensitive and caring, but now it also means being ambitious and strong. They are able to think and behave like a loving mother at home, yet act like a cutthroat competitor at work. Their notions about femininity have adapted to the era in which they live, and to their family and work situation. But it's much more difficult for men to separate their sense of masculinity into different compartments. They see a masculine man as one who is aggressive and competitive and strong, not as one who is nurturing, warm, and self-sacrificing. If he can earn a good living, a manly man can't also roast a chicken and soothe a screaming toddler. Some husbands simply can't reconcile two such dramatically different ways of being; it's too confusing for their one-track minds to deal with. (Yet there are rare exceptions to this rule, like Intersex husbands, as we'll see in chapter 7.)

In any given couple, then, the husband is more likely than the wife to be the one who is oblivious to the needs of others. He is the one who sees the world mainly from his own point of view. He won't visit a doctor until his wife makes the appointment. He is incapable of buying the children new shoes unless she makes him a list, one that includes sizes and color preferences. He won't accompany the family to see a movie unless she asks the children what they want to see, checks the movie schedule, arranges to buy the tickets, gets everybody ready, and announces their imminent departure. He is perfectly content to sit and watch football or basketball or baseball or ice hockey on television while family activity hums all around him, as oblivious as if he were sitting on the bottom of the ocean floor.

In marriages that include a superior wife, the husband also tends to revel in his aura of ignorance. He may not know how to cook a decent meal, but he brags about how well he can grill a premade hamburger or a previously marinated chicken breast. He may be unable to calm a cranky infant or to shop for his children's clothing, but he'll insist that that's because his wife knows how to do this stuff better. He may not be able to balance a checkbook or pay the monthly bills, but he believes that his wife has more free time to do such chores. He can't organize a dinner party or keep track of his own siblings' birthdays either, but he thinks that's not his job. And doing the weekly grocery shopping after putting in a full day of work is simply too much for him.

After all, a superior wife can manage all this just fine, so why shouldn't she?

In addition, a husband with a superior wife can't do more than one thing at a time. He can't chop carrots and keep track of a toddler; he can't organize the tax information while helping an eight-year-old with an art project. He can't watch a baseball game and also discuss the family's upcoming vacation. He'll get upset and angry if forced to multitask; it makes him irritable and resentful, which is why he tends to freeze during emergencies: there's too much to do all at once. In some ways, though, it's not his fault, because it turns out that men are not biologically equipped to do several things at once, as we'll see in chapter 2.

A superior wife, then, is left to deal with the broken furnace or the projectile-vomiting toddler. It is the superior wife who ends up doing two or three or four things at a time, usually because she must. She steps into the competence breach, cooking and supervising and shopping and organizing family life, while also holding down a job.

A superior wife's life is one big, supersized multitask.

Even when both partners work outside the home, it is quite often the husband who feels exempt from doing anything other than delivering the paycheck. It's as if nothing but the job is his job, the way it would be in a traditional marriage if his wife were a homemaker. It doesn't seem to matter if she works twenty or thirty or fifty-five hours a week. Even if the couple assumed they would share everything after they were married, they often abandon that assumption when life gets complicated by children and home owning and life managing. What were once *their* responsibilities become *her* responsibilities, and that's a very long list.

Take Sue, a New Yorker who at forty-five has been married to Bill for twenty years. Sue, who worked before she and Bill were parents, took only a brief maternity leave after each of their two daughters was born. Sue has always planned all the meals, cared for the children, paid the bills, arranged the vacations, organized the medical and dental care, figured out the social life, managed the household, and earned most of their income. Where she leads, Bill happily follows, she says.

This leaves Sue with a certain lack of respect for her husband, a man who is less than a partner, someone who "can't cope in an emergency. He freezes up, like he's terrified, and he can't even think or speak." Worse, he seems unable to manage even the most basic tasks. Sue explains, "My favorite is, he'll tie up the garbage and then he'll say, 'Can you take it out?'"

Sue has taken fond care of Bill, as if he were a large and balding third child, for decades, and that's what he's come to expect from her. If Sue dropped dead, she says, "My husband could probably not survive without me. And I'm pretty sure he'd live on pizza, take-out Chinese, and food in cans."

Many superior wives imagine the same if-I-dropped-dead scenario, usually with disastrous consequences for their clueless husbands, who would need to be on the market for another superior wife, and pronto.

Sherry, forty-two, a mother of two, can't imagine what her husband would do without her. She tells me that in her next life, "I want to come back as my husband, because his life never changes, no matter what happens." She does everything, she says, while he waits around to be told what to do and where to go. He expects her to take care of him, and she does. If she vanished from his life, she'd need to clone herself first.

Marge, thirty-nine, is a working wife from Connecticut who is also her husband's knight in shining armor. She says that she and her husband, a workaholic dentist who is rarely home, reached an agreement early on in their marriage. "I do everything inside, he does everything outside," she says. Because they live in the northern hemisphere and not in a palm-frond hut in Tonga, where life is lived outdoors, this means that she does the cooking and laundry, the child care and the pet care, the social arranging and the cleaning. He does the gardening, mostly because that's his hobby and that's the only chore he really wants to do. He considers this a fair deal. She considers it her lot in life.

Sandra, a twenty-nine-year-old newlywed from Great Britain, senses that her husband "feels better than me, because he earns so much and I don't earn anything." That's why "he never lifts a finger at home," she adds, despite the fact that she's in school to earn a graduate degree in counseling. Sandra has figured out that if she wants to get her husband to do anything other than work and sleep and eat, "I have to smile and ask him if he wouldn't mind doing it. But he usually forgets I asked. He'd rather go to the dentist than do anything that's helpful at home."

Finally there's Cindy, forty, who lives on Long Island in New York and works part-time as a physical therapist. She doesn't think her husband could manage without her, unless he found a replacement wife. Cindy expresses a nostalgic longing to be taken care of by her husband, only once a year, on their anniversary. But even then, she's the one who has to plan that special night, because, she says, her husband is "out to lunch" when he comes home from work and isn't capable of making such arrangements without her help. It's as if, she claims, his brain stops functioning the moment he leaves his New York City office.

All these wives agree that "what we're doing is keeping the world functioning."

Wives like these insist, whether they work for pay full-time, part-time, or not at all, that it's only through their efforts that their family stays together. This situation no longer disturbs or troubles most of them, simply because it seems inevitable, the way it has been since they said "I do" and will remain, at least until they say "I won't."

While I'd like to claim credit for the idea that women, or wives, may be superior to men, it's not a new one. Four hundred years ago, an Italian noblewoman, Moderata Fonte, wrote *The Worth of Women*, in which she stated that women would be much better off, in every way, if they could live "without the company of men."[3]

More recently, the Baltimore journalist H. L. Mencken wrote a book titled *In Defense of Women*, in which he explained the many reasons that women are better and smarter than men. He stated that "complete masculinity and stupidity are often indistinguishable" and claimed that women are much more perceptive and intuitive and intelligent than men, which, at the time, was probably a much more shocking and radical proclamation than it is now.[4]

Half a century ago, the anthropologist Ashley Montagu also expressed the view that women are naturally superior to men. He proposed a revolutionary idea for the time, that college-educated wives were wasting their lives as homemakers and that it was foolish for them to be subservient to their husbands. "It is the function of women to teach men how to be human," he wrote.[5]

My premise is similar, although I do not believe that women and men should live apart or that innate gender differences are an insurmountable problem. Instead I am proposing that the person in the husband role, usually a man, often exploits the one who is in the wife role, usually a woman. He will try to get away with doing and thinking and planning as little as possible, simply because he can. When he does, the person in the wife role takes over. Because women are better than men at many aspects of life crucial to a family's well-being, they are the ones who tend to end up as the more accomplished and the more efficient member of the marital union. *Being accomplished is a woman's default mode.*

Some husbands, though not all, are willing to admit that this has happened in their own marriage. Gerry, thirty-nine, confesses that his wife is superior in many ways but that this is to his benefit. "Because she's in charge, I don't have to be," Gerry says, quite happy and relatively unembarrassed about coasting through his married life.

Gerry eased himself into incompetence, he says, by not trying very hard, so that his wife does whatever he prefers not to do—which is a lot. But Gerry's conscious and deliberate inferiority strategy is highly unusual. More often, husbandly inferiority is not premeditated, it just seems to happen. It occurs when a husband tells his wife, "You do the dishes so much faster than I do," and so she does. Or when he admits, "I can't change the sheets by myself," and so never does. Or when he confesses that he doesn't feel clearheaded enough to pay the bills, and so she does. It's not that she thinks she does all of this better than he does; it's just that he wheedles his way out of being responsible, and she steps in to fill the vacuum.

This book will explore how the superior wife scenario arises. In chapter 1 I will define and describe the phenomenon and explain how I came to these conclusions. In chapter 2 I'll delve into the biological and social and psychological reasons for the existence of superior wives and describe how women's innate advantages make it relatively easy to fall into the trap of self-denying superiority. Wives are equipped with a biological advantage that makes them more empathic and gives them the ability to multitask. In addition they are saddled with dual social expectations, that they *should* be in charge of the family but that they *should* also work for pay. Women are also blessed with a psychological need to please others, no matter what. Thus, this triple-headed female blessing—of biology, culture, and psychology—acts as the catalyst that propels wives onto the path of superiority.

I'll also discuss, in chapter 3, the differences among wives' work situations as a function of the proportion of the family's income they earn. There are four types of wives, based on their monetary contribution to the marriage and family: the Captain and Mate wife, who stays at home while her husband earns the money; the Booster wife, who earns some of the family income; the Even-Steven wife, who earns about the same as her husband; and the Alpha wife, who earns all or nearly all of the family income. No one type of wife is more likely than any other to be superior; as we will see, wifely superiority is *not* based on who earns more money or who spends more time at home.

In addition, many couples don't see eye to eye about whether the wife is the superior one. When I mentioned the title of my book to several men, one responded that it would obviously be "a work of fiction." Another said that it was probably going to be "some kind of pamphlet." Neither of these men, by the way, has ever been married. But even married men are resistant to the idea that their wives may be much better than they themselves at modern domestic life. Their wives would say that the men say that because they are completely oblivious to what's going on, which their husbands emphatically deny. But if the men truly are unaware, then that's what they *would* say, no? Chapter 4 delves into the superior wife situation from the husband's point of view, exploring the reasons for male obliviousness. It also presents an encyclopedia of nagging, summarizing husbands' views and commentary on what their wives nag them about, from "A, Appearance" to "Z, Zoning Out," and everything in between.

In chapter 5, I look at the situation from the female point of view. As it turns out, superior wives are less happy about their lives than other wives, and they're more likely to believe that their marriage might have been a mistake. Half of them admit too that they are the family's "primary nagger," and they confess to their own nagging habits. They also comment on their husbands' favorite topics for nagging, which are not all that different from their own. Marital nagging hot spots, for wives and husbands, include laundry and socks, dishes and television, video games and money, money, money.

A great deal of marital nagging also revolves around the most incendiary topic in modern life, sex. Some wives make a habit of refusing sex; most husbands are the sexual initiators. In some marriages, however, the reverse is true, and wives initiate and husbands refuse. I explore both situations, as well as the top ten sex wishes of wives and husbands, which are more similar than you might expect. I also reveal the four types of married sex: Duty Sex, Old Shoe Sex, Hot Sex, and No Sex. The groups are not mutually exclusive, so you could have Old Shoe Sex, say, for years, and then suddenly tip over into Hot Sex. Still, many couples find themselves in one group or another most of the time. Chapter 6 will examine the ways in which a wife's superiority affects her sexuality.

Finally, as I've mentioned, *not all marriages include a superior wife*. I've examined nonsuperior wives and their husbands in great detail, using statistical methods, and in chapter 7 I explain how these couples manage to escape the superior wife trap. Somewhat surprisingly, these couples are either supertraditional or extremely egalitarian, at one extreme or the other. When partners are in agreement about how the marriage should be arranged, there's a better likelihood they'll be in a nonsuperior union. Wives in traditional marriages believe that the husband is the unequivocal head of the household, and thus they reject superiority out of hand. They tend to have mates I call Caveman husbands. Wives in egalitarian marriages have husbands who are truly committed to equality; they have a Team Player husband or an Intersex husband. Nonsuperior wives accept imperfection, and they don't need to have everything done their way all the time. They use an as-if operating system, which means they function as if they are not able to do all and be all for everybody, always.

Women who have already fallen into the superior wife life need not despair, however. In chapter 8, I advise wives on how to create a new and more perfect nonsuperior wife union. The key is to convince their husband of the importance of this step, to work on ridding themselves of their old habits, and to rehabilitate the marriage, as a team effort. I offer twenty-one suggestions and tips for how to do this. Making this change won't be easy and it won't be quick, but you can do it if you want it badly enough and if you can convince your husband that change is in his best interests too. The aim for wives is to lead a marriage rebellion, by redefining and reinventing modern marriage. They must strive to reshape their twentieth-century union by creating a new and improved conjugal partnership, one that includes not one but two "wives" in each marriage.

First, however, it's crucial to figure out what kind of marriage you yourself are in. Are you a superior wife? Or are you married to one? Here are a few signs that your marriage may be one that includes a superior wife.

In your marriage, does the wife

- plan the family vacations?
- remember when the children need their booster vaccines?
- decide where and how to spend holiday gatherings with other family members?
- nag or criticize a lot?
- know when the home owner's insurance payment is due?
- often seem reluctant to have sex?
- organize social events and get-togethers with friends?
- know the exact number of the husband's cholesterol level?
- decide what to do about a son's failing math grade?
- leave detailed instructions when leaving home for a few days, including everything from when to feed and walk the dog to when to take the children to music lessons and what to defrost for dinner?

In your marriage, does the husband

- expect the wife to remember his sister's birthday?
- forget to make his own doctor's appointments?

- not know the names of his children's teachers?
- rarely, if ever, make plans to see friends?
- seem absentminded about children's activities?
- often feel nagged?
- claim that he feels as if he has to beg for sex?
- get angry if asked to do more than one thing at a time?
- sometimes seem oblivious about other family members' needs?
- often seem befuddled at home, as if he's not sure he's in the right place?

If you answered yes to at least six in each of these two groups of questions, you may be a superior wife—or married to one. If so, then this book is your ticket for a tour aboard the good ship *Wifely Superiority*, with detailed instructions on how to disembark. It will explain why wives become superior, how their superiority works in the family, and how such wives and their husbands view their situation. It will reveal the many consequences of wifely superiority, describing the ways in which that situation harms the marriage, damages a woman's sense of self, and leads to long-lasting disappointment and unhappiness. Finally, this book will reveal several ways in which superior wives can ditch their superiority and transform their marriage into a mutually beneficial union.

There's no time to waste, so get on board. You've got nothing to lose—except your superiority.

I

Six Signs of Superiority

The fact that wives are superior to husbands is utterly, irrevocably true. But it's also disguised, supremely well camouflaged, like a patch of ice on a wintry road or the tip of a crocus poking through the ground in spring. We feel an understandable reluctance to accept the phenomenon as it really is, because to do so seems so harsh, so misanthropic, so mean. That's probably why no one has reported on it or studied it or attempted to explain it until now, because the subject of superior wives has been unmentionable.

Nevertheless, it is real.

In a majority of marriages, wives are, quite simply, more efficient, more decisive, more intuitive, and more competent than their husbands.

We've entered the age of the superior wife, a trend that is as common as it is uncharted. A majority of couples—about two out of three—now belong to a marriage in which the wife is superior, according to the results of my extensive research. Supreme matriarchy is the twenty-first-century family rule, and it transcends social class, race, culture, and religion. It doesn't matter if you are working-class or professional, black or white or Asian, Catholic, Protestant, or Jewish: whoever you are or whatever you believe or wherever you live, it's equally likely that you're either a superior wife or married to one.

The overwhelming superiority of wives is, I believe, the key to understanding what troubles many modern marriages. The fact of their superiority is growing increasingly apparent to wives, who complain about the helplessness of their husbands, men who seem to cultivate cluelessness as easily as they chill a six-pack of beer. When comedians describe marriage as an institution in which "a man loses his bachelor's degree and the woman gets her master's," it's no joke, it's reality. It's the reality of a widely circulated Internet joke about a woman who meets a man, refuses to marry him, and *only then* lives happily ever after. It's the reality of a *New Yorker* cartoon depicting a woman talking on a cell phone and explaining her marriage, saying "We divided it up so I do everything right and he does everything wrong."[1]

It's the reality of an anonymous Internet chain letter that was sent "to bring relief to tired and discouraged women." Wives who received the email were supposed to "bundle up" the man in their lives and send him to the name at the top of the list. If they did it correctly, the letter advised, they'd receive 15,625 men in the mail, one of whom "is bound to be better than the one you already have." The letter concluded with a stern warning that any woman who broke the chain might be unlucky enough to get her own husband back.

It's the reality of a popular email attachment titled "A Woman's Mind," which depicts a woman's brain as an incredibly complex system of pulleys and levers, tubes and chains, a mechanical masterpiece that juggles and transports dozens of balls at once. It moves superfast, all of the balls rising and falling and spinning in simultaneous and intricate patterns, in a hypnotic and endless loop. At the bottom of the page, there's a footnote that reads, "A man has only two balls and they take up all his thoughts."

And it's the reality of an Internet fantasy about a new version of a reality television show in which six husbands are dropped on an island with their three children for six weeks. They are in charge of everything, but there's no fast food, each child plays several sports and takes a music or dance class, and the dads are responsible for remembering birthdays of the entire extended family, as well as making and keeping the children's appointments at the doctor and the dentist and the barbershop. He has to care for the children, clean the house, help with homework and science projects, cook, do laundry, and pay bills with not enough money. In addition, "he must make one unscheduled and inconvenient visit per child to the emergency room." He has to decorate the house, plant flowers, hold a job, shave his legs, wear makeup and jewelry and uncomfortably stylish shoes, keep his fingernails polished and eyebrows groomed. At the end of the six weeks, the fathers will be tested on their knowledge of the three children's preferences—including favorite snack, song, drink, and toy—and biggest fear. The children get to vote the dads off the island, and the last man left wins, but only "if he still has enough energy to be intimate with his wife" with only "a moment's notice."

I've discovered the truth about the reality of wifely superiority through my research, which includes a comprehensive Web survey of more than 1,500 wives and husbands from across the country and around the world. In addition, I've examined social science research from the fields of psychology, sociology, economics, demographics, and anthropology, and almost all of it leads me to the same conclusion.

Wives are the alpha members of the marriage, the leaders of the family pack, the chief executive officers of the household. This is not misanthropy or man hating or bitter feminism, it's simple fact.

It's not just that wives do more of the chores and the errands and the daily work of domestic life; it's also that they are the ones who see the big picture, the ones who take charge. Wives have become the managers of the family, while their husbands are more like employees. In unprecedented numbers, women have even taken over formerly "masculine" domestic work, such as household repairs, bill paying, and the troubleshooting of electronic gadgets. Indeed, increasing numbers of wives view themselves as the family experts; they make most of the major family decisions; they do most of the family management tasks, including handling the finances; and a small but growing proportion outearn their husbands.

There are two distinct states of mind in superior wife marriages. In the mind of the husband, it's his job to be taken care of; in the mind of the wife, it's her job to do the taking care. This is despite the fact that a majority of married couples now expect both partners to earn a living, while also assuming that wives will be responsible for housekeeping, child care, and money management. It's almost as if *couples expect wives to be superior.* He gives up, she steps up, and their course is set for a one-way ticket to wifely superiority.

Not convinced yet? Then listen to the voices of just a few of the superior wives who were generous enough to describe their marriages to me in remarkably intimate detail.

- "It breaks my heart to portray my husband like this, but the truth is the truth. I know that I contribute more to our lives than he does."

- "I married a very sensitive guy, but I am the doer, the planner, the accountant, the organizer."
- "I feel I put more into our marriage and our family. Sometimes I feel that my husband is like a third child. I would love to feel that I'm the one being taken care of, from time to time, at least. But that never happens."
- "My role in this marriage seems to be to make it all work."
- "I truly love my husband, but I do need more from him. I am not Superwoman, though he thinks that I am, and it's so frustrating."
- "I am the glue that holds our family together, and I have definitely done the most work, made the most sacrifices, and accepted the most responsibility to keep our family going."
- "I am the detail/relationship/problem solver for our family—the logistician."
- "I am the master coordinator of everything; I run the master board for the entire family."
- "My brain function involves six people in every decision; his only involves one."
- "I am shouldering much more of what makes my marriage and family work."
- "I hate to say it, because I know marriage shouldn't be this way, but I am better than him in every way. I treat people better. I think of everyone involved when making decisions. I have a better job and I am respected in my field. I make and keep friends very easily. I can handle myself in any situation. He can do none of this."

Other superior wives use just a single word to describe themselves. They say that they are the instigator, the doer, the planner, the organizer, the manager, the CEO; they say they are the decider. In such marriages, wives insist that they are the family's only safety net. "If I do not do things, they do not get done," says Alice, a forty-five-year-old social studies teacher from Queens, in New York City.

Wives like Alice are sometimes aware of their superiority, but they often feel powerless to alter it. Peggy, a forty-eight-year-old guidance counselor from Boston, agrees that she's the superior spouse and adds, "I need to feel in control, and he likes to be taken care of."

That's precisely what happens in many families when husbands accept their wives' expertise and skills as a generous and selfless offering, one that they choose to accept with no strings attached. "His philosophy is that if he's got me, then he doesn't need to worry about things," says a twenty-nine-year-old Dunkin' Donuts franchise manager from Louisville, Kentucky, explaining her husband's logic.

The marital formula is simple: if she takes control, he doesn't have to.

Husbands with wives who take charge don't bother having too much anxiety or too much stress. After all, their better half will shoulder the burden, so why should they worry? One such husband describes his superior wife situation this way: "If it ain't broke, why would I fix it?" In this way, wives become the masterful leaders of the family, the ones in the know and in power. That's why a wife from California jokes that "the only thing he does better than me is pee standing up; he's much better at that!"

And while some superior wives may long to trade places with their husband, to lead his relatively carefree life, they realize that this life switch is not possible. "I sometimes think how nice it would be to be him," says Marla, thirty-two, a Texas mother of five who works full-time and is now married to her second husband. "When he clocks out, he comes home and has a meal waiting for him, he takes a shower and relaxes, and the day is over for him, but it has just begun for me," she says, adding that she can't figure out how to change her situation.

Because so many wives like Marla have become superior, they constitute a pervasive social trend, which has, in turn, begun to alter the way masses of women perceive marriage. Indeed, I believe that the superior wife phenomenon is the underlying explanation for women's increasing distrust of and disdain for marriage as a viable institution. The U.S. Census Bureau reported recently that slightly more than half of American women are now opting out of marriage completely, to live on their own, husband-free. While most women marry eventually, they also spend *at least half of their lives outside marriage,* either before they marry or after their first or second marriage ends. It's as if many women sense that life is easier and less stressful without a man around the house. Even the census researchers conclude that being married has become a voluntary state, one that is no longer usually a permanent part of a woman's adult life.[2]

These conclusions inspired an outpouring of cartoons and commentary, most of it depicting some variation on a beer-swilling, remote-clutching,

By permission of Mike Luckovich and Creators Syndicate, Inc.

unshaved husband who lazes around the house while ignoring his franti-
cally busy wife. Here is one of the best.[3]

As it happens, women around the world are also postponing or avoiding
marriage altogether, and marriage rates are declining in most industrial-
ized nations. This is true in Japan, as well as in almost every European
country, including Italy, Germany, Finland, Sweden, Austria, and the
United Kingdom, where the number of couples getting married has plum-
meted dramatically over the past few decades.[4]

As I see it, single women and divorcées everywhere are beginning to
understand that if they marry or remarry, it's probably their fate to become
superior. And a few are voicing these fears openly. "I doubt that any woman
should get married now," a sixty-year-old woman tells me. After being married for thirty-five years and drawing her own conclusions, she adds that
"a woman's development is hindered by marriage." It's as if a great many
women are figuring out that men may simply be more trouble than they
are worth.

More women are drawing this conclusion, apparently, and without
much difficulty or embarrassment. Among women without a college
degree, a large number no longer bother to marry even after they have a

child. And only about 65 percent of African American women will ever get married, perhaps because they have little tolerance for being the superior spouse.[5] This is why, for the first time, slightly more than one in four American households now consist of just one person.[6] It's not that these singles will never marry or haven't been married at least once. It's just that most don't want to be married at the moment. What's more surprising, though, is that they feel neither shame about being single nor intense social pressure to get married. Indeed, a majority of Americans believe that postponing marriage is a good thing and that it's possible to have a complete and happy life even if you never marry.[7]

Being unwed is no longer such a big deal.

This idea, that being married is not an essential part of being a well-adjusted grown-up, represents a breathtakingly dramatic social revolution. In 1976 a majority of Americans believed that married people were happier than singles.[8] But now, just 22 percent of men say that being married is one of the most important things in life, and even fewer women do—just 17 percent.[9] And this small minority tends to be over the age of sixty-five and more politically conservative.[10] For most Americans, then, marriage has become one of several options for living happily ever after. You could live with a lover, or play the field by dating, or have a series of intense love affairs—and none of these options would end in "I do." The bottom line is that love and marriage no longer go together like a horse and carriage, or even like a Toyota Prius and good gas mileage. In fact, a huge majority of American women—83 percent in one study—say that it is possible for a woman who never marries to have a complete and happy life.[11] Being a fish without a bicycle—as they used to say in the 1970s about a woman without a man—turns out to be a perfectly acceptable way of life. It's not as if these women are living like nuns, of course. They socialize with men, they have fun with men, they even sleep with men; they are just growing more reluctant to marry one.

I'd like to point out, though, that fewer women believe that it's possible for a single man to live happily ever after without a wife. Many women understand, intuitively, that men need wives more than women need husbands.[12] Generally speaking, when a woman lives alone, her life is pretty much the same as if she were a wife. She cooks, she cleans up after herself, she has work and friends and male lovers and an active social life. If a man lives alone, he's much more likely to get by as a marginally functional bachelor, one who eats pizza and frozen dinners and lives like a college boy. I'm not saying that *every* single woman is blissfully happy and secure or that *every* single man is a wretched mess. I'm just saying that, on average, women tend to get along a lot better without a husband than men get along without a wife.

And when they are married, of course, women are more likely than men to end up being the superior spouse. It's no wonder, then, that marriage loses its allure and its promise and its magic for so many women. It's no wonder too that marriage becomes more of a burden than a blessing for women, more of a step backward than a step forward. And it's no wonder that more and more of them are simply avoiding the institution of marriage altogether.

Remember the old query, the one that asks why a man should buy the cow when he can get the milk for free? Potential superior wives may be asking themselves a somewhat similar question: "Why buy the bull when you know you'll be getting the shit for free?"

A Really Brief History of Marriage

The fact that Americans view marriage as dispensable and no longer compulsory indicates that radical changes are taking place within the culture. Surely the meaning of marriage has been transformed more during the past century than it had for thousands of years previously. For hundreds of generations, women around the world viewed marriage as an obligation, a nonnegotiable and necessary life path. Girls were born, they grew up, they married; they gave birth, they raised children, they died. For women, marriage was the bridge between life as a child and life as an adult; it was how they crossed over from family of origin to newly created family. Few women, in any time or in any country, have refused to cross that bridge. In most cases, the idea would never have occurred to them, but even if it did, their families would have protested vigorously. In Western culture, rare exceptions to the women-must-marry rule were made only for women who joined a convent or a religious order, giving their lives to God. Otherwise, they were expected to give their lives to one mortal man.

There was never any question about *whether* to marry; it was only a question of *whom* to marry, and that decision was rarely left up to the bride.

Most of the time, communities joined couples in marriage for political, economic, or social reasons. The goal for a woman to become a bride was always to benefit the family in some way. The idea of something called a "love match" was unthinkable but also quite impractical, since fathers used their marriageable daughters to make deals for the purpose of enriching the entire extended family. Marriage was, in essence, a business transaction between the father of the potential bride and the father of the potential groom. It was a way for wealthy men to manage their landholdings and to consolidate their assets. When the father of a rich girl made a deal with the father of a rich boy, both families profited. His family gained land or cattle or money in a dowry, and hers got the prestige of a good match and a new batch of wealthy and influential relatives. Betrothing a daughter to a prominent family could fend off enemies and create new alliances; it could increase the family's prestige and power. Such a marriage was good for the brides' parents, sisters, and brothers, for her aunts and uncles and cousins, and for all her as yet unborn children. Even poor families could benefit from giving away a daughter in marriage, because the boy's family might gain a small dowry and, more important, an extra pair of hands. The new wife could work the fields, gather and cook the food, and produce more workers, if her children survived infancy. Her family would be allied with a family whose fortunes might improve and end up increasing their own. Rich or poor, love simply did not enter the marital picture; because making a good match was often a matter of family survival, the bride's feelings about the matter were irrelevant.

For hundreds of generations, then, families treated women as property, to be traded in marriage for political and economic advantage. You can almost hear the ancestral fathers bargaining with each other: "I'll give you my eldest, the prettiest girl I have, along with a dozen head of cattle, a flock of sheep, and I'll throw in some valuable silver goblets." The father of the potential groom might refuse the goblets and make a counteroffer. "I'll take five of your plowhorses too, and the twenty acres of land on the other side of the river," he'd respond. "And I'll settle for your second daughter, the one with the big nose." The brides' views on their intended husbands did not matter, though it might have been a small bonus if they felt any affection for or attraction to their intended spouse. In any case, wives rarely had much say or power after marriage: they married to serve. A wife was acquired to be obedient and humble, to nurture her husband, and to bear as many children as possible.[13]

Most of the historical record is silent about the existence of superior wives, although several exceptions emerge. The very first mention of a superior wife—almost the very definition of such a wife, in fact—appears in the Old Testament, in Proverbs.[14] The passage begins by asking, "A woman of valour who can find? For her price is far above rubies." The verse continues as a clever anagram containing twenty-one lines, the first beginning with A (alef) and the last with Z (taf), each line beginning with the next letter of the Hebrew alphabet, in order. The wife described is highly efficient, a woman who buys fields and plants them, who cooks the food she grows, who dabbles in real estate, who invests judiciously, who makes clothing by hand, who stays awake all day and all night, who is wise and kind, loyal and well dressed, "in fine linen and purple." She's always busy and "eateth not the bread of idleness" while managing the family; she "looketh well to the ways of her household." She's biblical superior—a combination ancient superwoman and primitive trophy wife. It's almost certain, though, that even a superior wife like this was not in what we think of as a traditional marriage, with one wife dutiful to one husband. In fact, many marriages in biblical times were polygamous, and each husband had two or four or more wives, a harem of superiority.

The one-husband, many-wife setup was probably not a foolproof formula for marital bliss, or even for wifely contentment, unless a group of sisterly wives formed their own family tribe. But then again, nobody cared whether women were happy or not, just that they were well married.

In the late sixteenth century, though, there is strong evidence that a few wives rebelled against marriage and may have even felt a sense of superiority. An Italian noblewoman from Venice, Moderata Fonte, wrote a book in 1592 in which she stated that women "are only ever really happy when we are alone with other women, and the best thing that can happen to any woman is to be able to live alone, without the company of men." Fonte's view of marriage was that women who are married, "or martyred, more accurately—have endless sources of misery."[15]

Her book was called *The Worth of Women: Wherein Is Clearly Revealed Their Nobility and Their Superiority to Men*. Moderata was the first self-declared superior wife.

According to Moderata's uncle, who edited Fonte's work after she died, she was "extremely good at running her household . . . her husband scarcely needed to give it a thought and confessed on several occasions that he had no idea what it felt like to have the responsibility of a home and family, for she took everything out of his hands and did it all herself, with extraordinary efficiency and diligence."[16]

Although Moderata's thinking was amazingly modern, she was born centuries too soon to embrace the concept of marrying for love or to realize that other wives may have felt as superior as she did. Long after she died, at least one tribal culture in the Americas recognized women's superior worth, telling fables about foolish men who were in desperate need of women to guide them. The Blackfoot Indians passed down a creation tale that includes the notion that men and women didn't live together at first. The women made lovely lodges and tanned buffalo hides for robes and prepared dried meat and gathered berries, and "their things were just as fine." But the men of the tribe were very poor and had no homes and wore raw skins. They were unable to shelter or clothe or feed themselves on their own.

"They did not know, how they should make lodges. They did not know, how they should tan the buffalo-hides. They did not know, too, how they should cut dried meat, how they should sew their clothes." These pitiful, decidedly inferior men were hungry and cold and desperate for wives to teach them how to live. Finally, the story goes, a female chief took pity on the men and decided to choose one as a husband. The rest of her tribe followed her lead, and, presumably, the Blackfoot husbands lived happily ever after, looked after by their superior wives.[17]

In most cultures other than the Blackfoot, however, it was taboo for a wife to question her husband's judgment or knowledge, let alone to believe in her own superiority. With no say about whom they were to marry, women were obliged to abide by their father's wishes and then by their husbands' demands. This situation changed drastically, however, as soon as the idea of marrying for love took hold. When a woman married for love, she gained the authority to participate in choosing the man she would wed; thus, the balance of marital power shifted from fathers to brides and grooms. With love came personal choice and control, a very simple alteration of the ancient marriage formula but one that revolutionized the way women functioned as wives.

It was near the end of the eighteenth century, in Western culture at least, that this marital transformation became widespread. Suddenly more families believed that couples could, and should, marry for love, so that they could live happily ever after. That's why authors like Jane Austen began to write with feeling about the pain of being forced into an arranged marriage, contrasted with the bliss of one based on love. "Oh Lizzy!" Jane Bennett declares to her sister Elizabeth in Pride and Prejudice, "do any thing rather than marry without affection."[18] Both sisters, of course, end up marrying for love, unlike Jane Austen herself, who never married at all.

This attitude—a refusal to accept a loveless match—is what changed old-fashioned marriages into modern ones. The idea that a woman should love her future husband gave women a sense of control and influence in the process of betrothal and marriage. It was empowering, because it allowed women to decide for themselves whether marriage was worth the effort. Eventually, it became their right to choose to stay married or to divorce, to remarry or not. The ability to marry for love, and not for the family's benefit or convenience, was a first step in liberating women from the indentured servitude of old-style marriage. More important, it allowed women to view marriage as a personal option, one that they could choose or forgo.

Even when women married for love, though, they often entered a paternalistic relationship, one in which the husband reigned supreme. He was supposed to earn the money; she was supposed to keep house and defer to his will. The idea that she might be superior would hardly have been considered in private, let alone spoken aloud. For several generations, beginning after the turn of the twentieth century, many American wives lived under the feminine mystique, as Betty Friedan later put it, and were trapped in unhappy, dysfunctional marriages from which there was little possibility of escape. Their frustrated desires were captured early on in a 1915 novel, Herland, written by Charlotte Perkins Gilman. Gilman was a social activist whose book contains extremely bizarre feminist fantasies, so weird that they now seem drug-induced. At that time, most women in America could not vote, and the notion that women would someday become doctors and lawyers, senators and presidential candidates, would have been considered either science fiction or wildly deluded fantasy. Yet Gilman's novel imagines, with great yearning and desperate hope, a country she describes as "a strange and terrible Woman Land," in which all the men have slowly died off and all the women have gained the ability to bear children asexually. In this female paradise, most women give birth to five babies, all girls, of course. The place is discovered by three astonished young men, one of whom narrates the story, providing a man's view of the place. The interlopers are horrified when they realize that these husband-free wives are vastly superior women, with no need of men whatsoever.

"These stalwart virgins had no men to fear and therefore no need of protection," because men had been rendered superfluous, Gilman writes.[19] In this strange place, the male explorers realize, women are brave and strong and without wiles, and they have no need to be protected or worshipped. The women of Herland are superior beings with nothing to prove and without the burden of incessant sexual demands by desperate husbands. In fact, Gilman seems thrilled by the idea of a life without sexual intercourse—it's what makes the superior ladies of Herland so carefree and contented. There are no sexually demanding husbands around to ruin the day!

In 1918, three years after Gilman's novel was published, the journalist and satirist H. L. Mencken wrote *In Defense of Women*, a very different book but one with somewhat similar views about women's superiority. "A man's women folk, whatever their outward show of respect for his merit and authority," he wrote, "always regard him secretly as an ass, and with something akin to pity."[20] He describes most men as "shallow and pathetic," adding that while women may envy their husbands' power and freedom, they never envy men's "puerile ego" and rampant helplessness and "touching self-delusion." Clearly trying to be provocative and confrontational, Mencken expressed a view that women were less prone than men to fall in love and were actually the more intelligent and sensible gender: "They see at a glance what most men could not see with search-lights and telescopes; they are at grips with the essentials of a problem before men have finished debating its mere externals."[21]

His contemporaries thought that Mencken was joking, that he was writing satirically, for a laugh. But we know better; he was telling it like it was, and is.

In the mid–twentieth century, anthropologist Ashley Montagu wrote *The Natural Superiority of Women*, in which he claimed that women are biologically, socially, and emotionally better than men, despite the common assumption in the early 1950s that the male of the species was the rightfully dominant gender. He explained that "woman is the creator and fosterer of life; man has been the mechanizer and destroyer of life."[22] For this and many other reasons, he argued, women, not men, are the superior gender. Even then, a half century ago, most people viewed such an opinion as an amusing but meaningless affectation, like speaking with a British accent or wearing a beret.

Today, though, we've arrived at a point at which it no longer seems whimsical to assert that wives are better than husbands. The notion has become, quite obviously, a clear and simple fact.

Modern Marriage

American women's lives have changed almost beyond recognition since Mencken accused the entire male gender of being asses in the early twentieth century. Back then, women had just gained the right to vote for the first time, and although they were marrying for love, they had little actual control in the marriage itself, since husbands were considered kings of the castle. Likewise, barely 10 percent of young wives worked outside the home in 1920.[23] Today, more than 60 percent of American wives work for pay, and only a minority view their husband as an all-knowing, all-powerful family patriarch. Women now earn college and professional degrees, of course, and they engage in lifelong careers. They postpone marriage and childbearing, but when they do marry, it's for love, although they almost always select a man from a similar social class and educational background, someone whom their father might have chosen. They also expect husbands to share the domestic burdens, to care for children, and to do chores. And when women are unhappy in marriage, they just say no and file for divorce, instead of suffering for decades in a lifeless and miserable union. Despite the common misperception that husbands are the ones who get cold feet about staying married, *it's wives who are most likely to file for divorce.* Research shows that between 60 and 70 percent of divorces in America are now initiated by wives.[24]

Indeed, over the past few decades, marriage has become more voluntary, less rigid, less permanent, and even less essential than before. As I mentioned earlier, most Americans now feel that both women and men can be perfectly happy if they remain single. Thirty years ago, very few Americans thought this could be true, and most disapproved of cohabitation.[25] But half of couples now live together before they marry, and just about all of them have sex before they marry too.[26] Since close to half of marriages end in divorce, it seems reasonable to take a practice run at marriage before making it official. That's why American women marry for the first time, on average, shortly after their twenty-fifth birthday, and men don't tie the knot until the age of twenty-seven.[27] This is the longest Americans have ever waited to marry, at least since the Census Bureau began collecting such information in 1890.

But really, the *expectations* that wives and husbands have for married life are what have changed most drastically, according to recent research, including my own. Now, more than ever before, many couples expect to share both the breadwinning and the household chores, to be soul mates, and to reap essential emotional benefits from wedded bliss. They expect marriage to fulfill all their needs and wishes and deepest desires, while also expecting to split all the domestic responsibilities right down the middle. These expectations are so high, and in some ways so unrealistic, that it's almost guaranteed that women will be disappointed with married life. It's as if they started a diet assuming they'd lose twenty pounds in the first week or got a haircut imagining that it would instantly make them look ten years younger.

As for breadwinning, a growing number of Americans, as well as adults around the world, believe that both husband and wife should contribute to the family income. When pollsters at the University of Wisconsin asked this question in 1994, 59 percent of Americans agreed that couples should share breadwinning. By 2005 many more, 70 percent, agreed.[28] Worldwide, slightly more than eight in ten adults say that both partners should work for pay, according to a massive, eighty-country study spanning Asia, Africa, North and South America, and Europe.[29]

In my research too, most wives and husbands say that when they were first married, they expected that both partners would work and that both would share household chores as well. Their lives, they predicted, would be even-steven, all the way. As newlyweds, apparently, wives and husbands tend to be cockeyed optimists, though they end up facing a less-than-perfect reality in the long run. Still, a majority of Americans say that sharing chores is "very important for a successful marriage"—even more than the number who say that children are important![30] Most recently, three-quarters of Americans are adamant that if a wife works full-time, both partners should share household chores equally.[31]

What couples *believe* will happen and what they *hope* will happen after they marry are rarely the same as what *actually* happens, however. The problem is that brides, especially, have incredibly high standards for marriage. Women hope and expect to find a partner who will be a soul mate: someone who is their other half, a lifelong friend and lover and supportive partner, an eternal heart's companion. This belief, that a spouse should be the only person in your emotional universe, is held by just about all single twentysomethings. (Only a few of these youngsters, however, feel that the main purpose of marriage is to have children.)[32] While nobody knows the exact number of wives and husbands who feel they have found their soul mates—especially five or ten or fifteen years after the wedding day—it's clear that American wives assume that marriage will be the Yellow Brick Road to their Oz of personal gratification and fulfillment. It's as if, along with a wedding ring, women assume that marriage will provide them with a sense of security and contentment and delight that they won't find anywhere else in life.

Guess who's bound to be disappointed?

Perhaps that's the reason women are especially troubled when they find themselves the superior member of the marriage. If, in addition, they don't receive even a small portion of the love and intimacy they long for, or the chore sharing they expect, they grow increasingly frustrated and cantankerous. I'm not saying that no couples share household responsibilities or that none remain soul mates after the honeymoon is over, it's just that not nearly as many wives end up that way as the number who originally hoped and assumed they would.

What happens instead is that wives fall into a superiority habit, and their marriage suffers for it. They grow apart from their husbands, they become dissatisfied and unhappy, and they come to regret their decision to marry in the first place. I know this happens, at least in part, because several marriage researchers have discovered that spouses are now highly self-sufficient and independent. They report that they engage in fewer activities together and have fewer friends in common than couples did just several decades ago.[33] It's almost as if wives and husbands outgrow their desire to be soul mates, becoming more like congenial housemates, the researchers say, because each partner is always darting off to do his or her own thing and the two come together only to have an occasional meal and to sleep.

"Spouses do more separate activities and have more separate friends than they used to," says Stacy Rogers, one of the sociologists involved in this research. Although tied by marriage, more and more wives and husbands are pursuing their own interests and finding their own friends, separately and not as couples. "Women have become more independent within marriage too, economically, socially, and psychologically," she notes. Because superior wives do so much for their husbands, many come to realize that they don't really need him all that much.

Indeed, Rogers and her colleagues, who study how marriage has changed over the past twenty years, find that couples argue more often than they used to and are less satisfied with marriage. Overall, the researchers find that *only about one in three marriages is stable and harmonious.* And it's not husbands who are most agitated and disappointed with their relationship: it's wives who are more disgruntled with life as a wife. Wives are less happy with marriage than husbands are, they feel they spend less time talking to and being with their spouses, they believe they argue and fight more often, and they are more likely than husbands to have thought about divorce.[34] Their perception of marriage reality is different and much more pessimistic.

Other research confirms the existence of wives' massive marital disillusionment, along with the female tendency to suffer from depression and anxiety. In a recent Internet poll, ironically in honor of Mother's Day, half the mothers surveyed said that they were *the least happy person in the household.*[35] In another study of couples in unhappy marriages, the wives had higher rates of depression and were more likely to abuse alcohol than unmarried women were. The unhappy wives were even more than twice as likely as other women to be at risk for heart attack or stroke.[36] Finally, there is a large and disturbing happiness gap between women and men. Over the past several decades, American women have grown increasingly less happy, while men have become much happier.[37]

I believe that the superior wife phenomenon is the most central and important explanation for this drastic decline in women's happiness levels. Simply put, wives become unhappy when they are forced to become superior. Most superior wives admit that it's draining and debilitating and depressing to be the one in charge of everything all the time. Furthermore, as I'll demonstrate, wifely superiority can often mean marital misery and discontent.

"I run circles around my husband," says Kelly, forty, a nurse from Loxa-hatchee, Florida. "Working full-time, taking care of the kids, taking care of the house, cooking, cleaning, and being a Brownie leader is exhausting." Kelly works twelve-hour shifts but earns less than her husband, whose only responsibility at home, she says, is maintaining the cars. She does everything else, including managing the finances and the health care and dealing with their three-year-old son's refusal to sleep through the night. She makes time to see her close friends, and she values these private nights out, which comprise the only bright spots in Kelly's sleep-deprived life, she says.

Likewise, Aimée, twenty-seven, lives a relatively independent life as a wife in Ontario, Canada. Her husband works midnight to noon, while she works days and also takes care of their three children. "My husband could do at least a little something to make my life easier," she says, "but he chooses not to. Also, he doesn't have a strong bond with our kids, so it's almost as if we're separate people who accidentally live in the same house."

My Superior Wife Research

My exploration of the superior wife took more than two years to complete and involved far-reaching interviews, careful pilot testing, a massive Web survey, and a wide-ranging review of academic research on marriage and relationships. In the first wave, I interviewed several large groups of women about their marriage, their husbands, and the way they live their lives at home and at work. After collating and analyzing their responses, I designed a pilot survey that I posted on the Internet. About one hundred husbands and wives answered this preliminary marriage poll. I used these responses to refine and improve my basic assumptions and survey questions. Next I created two versions of a final Web survey, one for wives and a separate one for husbands. While both partners could answer the survey, it was *not* a re-quirement, because I did not want couples collaborating on their answers. Thus, this is not a study of couples; instead, it focuses on the answers of married women and married men gathered in identical ways and coming from very similar backgrounds. Although I did not ask couples if they answered together—for reasons of privacy and anonymity—I believe that about one in four did so, based on their answers to several essay questions. Still, my results are based not on the way individual couples answered the survey but rather on the way wives and husbands answered on their own.

The survey contained thirty-eight questions, some multiple choice and others requiring answers to be written in. I was very careful to present the Web survey *only* as a research study about marriage, or what I called "Life in the Married Lane." I appealed to women and men to reveal "Who does what at home?" "Who's in charge?" "Who's the family expert?" and "How does your marriage work?" I was quite deliberate about *not* prejudicing the responses, so I never used the word *superior* or made any mention of my superior wife theory. I did not want to bias my results by attracting wives who view themselves as superior. In fact, I think that a large number of the wives and husbands who answered the survey would be shocked to learn the central hypothesis of my research.[38]

I began to gather my main sample of wives and husbands in midsummer of 2007. I had aquamarine-colored business cards printed, with my Web address and logo and this message: "Husbands and Wives, Answer My Marriage Survey" and "You could win a Wii or an iPod or other great prizes!" I gave away these cards at lectures and at personal appearances, so that I could gather subjects in person.[39] I also posted notices on Internet message boards and on various motherhood and fatherhood Web sites, as well as on marriage Web sites, including MayasMom.com, About.com, TheMotherhood.net, iVillage.com, and Eons.com. By the time I had appeared on the *Today* show to publicize another book I'd written, and spoken on several dozen radio shows nationwide, hundreds of spouses had answered my survey.[40]

I also advertised the survey on search engines, including Google and MSN. In addition, I placed sponsored advertisements on Facebook. These tiny ads, just over one inch high, were visible only to men and women who had registered with the social networking service as being married and over the age of twenty-one. (As it turns out, other researchers from universities across the country have begun to use Facebook as a method for gathering data as well.)[41] As a result, most of the wives and husbands who responded were people I didn't know, people who'd never seen me or heard me speak.

By the end of the fall, I had my complete sample, 1,529 spouses, drawn from a wide variety of sources and sampling techniques. These married women and men are by no means a random sample—after all, they had access to the Internet and volunteered to answer the survey—but because I found them in so many different ways, from so many different sources, I believe that they are fairly representative of Internet-using, middle- and upper-middle-class wives and husbands. Thus, the women and men I studied represent a wide range of currently married people.

In conducting my data analyses, I excluded young people, since I wanted to hear from experienced marriage partners, not those who had just embarked on their marriage journey. For this reason, I limited my sample to wives over the age of twenty-five and husbands over the age of twenty-seven, the average ages at which American women and men marry for the first time.[42] Likewise, few of the spouses who answered my survey were over the age of sixty-five. As a result, the wives and husbands in my sample are, on average, forty-one or forty-two years old and have been married an average of about fourteen years. Most, about eight in ten, are in a first marriage. They have, on average, about two children. The vast majority, about 85 percent, are white; 6 percent are Hispanic and 5 percent are African American. One-third are college graduates, and another third have done some graduate work or have a graduate degree. Finally, slightly more than half of the wives work full-time, about one in four of the wives does not work outside the home, and 23 percent work part-time. Nearly nine in ten of the husbands work full-time.[43]

These people tend to have slightly higher household incomes than couples nationwide. The average income for married-couple families in the United States was about $91,000, according to 2007 figures gathered by the Census Bureau.[44] Among my respondents the average household income was $96,000. My sample does not include low-income and very poor couples, nor does it include the very wealthy. Still, when I look at the four different types of marriages, based on the relative income of the wife and the husband, I find that my income distribution is almost identical to that obtained from recent census figures, which I discuss in chapter 3. In my opinion, then, the wives and husbands who answered my Web survey are representative of most middle-class Americans between the ages of twenty-five and sixty-five.

As I mentioned earlier, couples responded from all fifty states and from places around the world, including the Philippines and Thailand, Australia and Germany. Among the wives are homemakers and hairstylists, pharmacists and insurance agents, nurses, truck drivers, chefs, innkeepers, and at least one "bindery machine helper." There are a mortician, an executive nanny, a certified legal interpreter, a ranch worker, a microbiologist, and a life coach. One wife described herself as a "domestic goddess," and many others called themselves at-home moms. The husbands have equally varied jobs. There are a federal prosecutor, a guitar instructor, a plumber, a police officer, an executive pastor, a pawnbroker, a bicycle builder, a bartender, a firefighter, a Coast Guard officer, an airline pilot, a rural letter carrier, an auto mechanic, an installer of "medical gas piping," and a podiatrist. There are also at-home dads.

In some ways, my Web sample of married women and men is a *more* accurate and reliable way to get at the truth than other national surveys, in which people tend to respond the way they believe they are supposed to answer, regardless of what they really think and feel. This is called *social desirability*, and it's one of the major problems plaguing psychologists who try to understand how people feel by posing personal questions on the telephone or in person. Most people try to provide what they think are the "right answers," even when there really aren't any, so the trick is to pose neutral questions, in a neutral setting, with no hint of right or wrong.[45]

Thus, in my survey, I offered simple choices, like "Which partner is usually the one who can do more than one thing at a time?" or "In your marriage, who is the primary nagger?" and spouses could respond with "the husband," "the wife," "both," or "neither one." I also asked ten questions in which I encouraged couples to write essay answers. For instance, I asked, "What does your spouse nag or criticize you about most often? Also, what do you nag or criticize your spouse about most often?"[46] (You can see the entire Web survey beginning on page 309.) Women and men answered these write-in questions in amazingly open and honest ways, providing most of the stories you'll be reading here. Because I promised anonymity to my respondents, I have changed their names, but they are all real and all drawn from my Web survey and personal interviews.

In fact, I read through every one of the written responses, thousands of them, no matter how lengthy or circuitous or distressing. The wives confessed their marriage stories to me the way they'd talk to their hairdresser or best friend or sister. Some of their answers were long enough to fill nearly a whole page in *The New York Times*; others were much briefer. The husbands wrote at length too, boasting about their understanding wives, their biblical-style marriages, their best-friend wives. Women and men discussed their complaints and their annoyances. Answering personal questions at home, anonymously, makes it that much easier to tell the truth than having to confess such things in person or to a telephone interviewer.

The answers were both honest and heartfelt, I believe. Several wives and husbands confessed that they had never thought about their marriage in this way before or revealed their feelings or concerns or doubts about the marriage to anyone. Others mentioned that they appreciated answering the survey because it gave them a chance to view their marriage in a new way, as they'd never done before. A woman from Iowa said that she had been considering divorce and that answering the survey convinced her that things were really as bad as she'd thought. Another concluded the opposite—that her marriage was actually much better than she'd assumed. A young mother from Ohio commented that she usually doesn't like surveys, but answering this one was like being awarded a free session of marriage counseling.

In any case, the Web surveys led to many startling and unexpected discoveries.

Who Is a Superior Wife?

My research exposed the superior wife syndrome for what it is: alive and well and living in the twenty-first century. Superior wives are in the majority, and so many of them sing the same theme song, it's as if they're all tuned in to the same broadcast. Listen to their voices.

"My husband may think he's the head of our house, but I am the neck that controls that head," says Mia, a thirty-two-year-old Kansas wife and Web designer, who considers her marriage a traditional one. Aileen, forty-four, a full-time medical records administrator in Houston, is on the same wavelength as Mia. "I've always felt that I'm expected to do more than my husband," she says. In the fourteenth year of her second marriage, Aileen says, "I am the one responsible for the kids, the house, the laundry, and I am also expected to keep a full-time job. He used to handle the finances, but now I have to do that too." Nora, a part-time art teacher in Chicago, has been married for twenty-six years, and she too chants the same melody: "I feel that I take more responsibility and I do more work to sustain our lives. I don't make much money, but I have a job and I also have an organized and emotionally fulfilling life on my own. My husband's life would dissolve into utter chaos without me. He truly seems to believe that his only responsibility is to do the very best at work that he can. He's very good at his job, but he is awful at home. It never occurs to him to also work at being a good husband or a good household manager."

Superior wives like Mia, Aileen, and Nora refer to their husbands, with some despair, as second, third, or fourth children, because the men seem so dependent and needy. Their mates are less adult partner and more major responsibility. What they are saying too is that while they could survive very nicely on their own, their husbands probably could not. Like the Blackfoot Indian wives, they must rescue their helpless husbands.

"Mike needs me more. If I die first, he might be able to survive, but just barely," says Tracey, forty-six, who hosted a group of six wives in her home, at my request, for a lively, early evening discussion about marriage and husbands and life in the crazy lane. Tracey is energetic and vibrant, a domestic whirlwind who has two teenage children, works full-time, and is head fund-raiser for her local high school. A nonstop talker, she has never met a silence she didn't fill with chatter. In her spacious home just north of New York City, she and her friends are cackling over their husbands' occasional ineptitude.

"My husband, Jay, is in charge of dinner only on Friday night," explains Toni, forty-two, who works a fifty-hour week as an accountant. "And every single Friday night, he calls me and says, 'What do you want me to order for dinner?' But I just want my dinner to appear. I don't ask him what he wants every night; his dinner just appears. So I say, 'Please surprise me,' but he never does." She sighs. "I am not subtle, but he just doesn't get it."

Seated on a plush couch, drinking herbal tea from a pale blue mug as the sun sets over Tracey's heavily wooded backyard, Toni laughs. "I just want him to be able to take charge of one very simple thing, and that's Friday night dinner. There are only three choices for take-out, either Chinese or Mexican or Greek. But he can't decide; it's like he's paralyzed!" Toni adds that she works longer hours than Jay and earns more than he does too. She figures that Jay could survive her death, "but he'd have a totally different life, and I don't know how he would eat."

It's relatively easy to figure out which wives are superior if you listen to them discuss their marriages long enough. But with an anonymous, remote Web survey, it's important to ask one or two simple questions that will reliably determine which wives fall into the superior category. I asked several such questions and eventually combined the answers to figure out which wives are superior.

First, I asked people to tell me "Which spouse has the most control over and responsibility for the family's needs and problems?" Here's how wives answer:

- 75 percent of wives say that they are in control, and
- 25 percent of wives say their husbands are in charge.

I also asked a more complex, six-part question as a second method of measurement, to ensure the reliability of my results: Which partner is the one who

1. can do more than one thing at a time?
2. organizes and plans most family events and schedules?
3. makes most of the family decisions?
4. is the most efficient person in the marriage?
5. shows the most support and affection to family and friends?
6. is likely to sacrifice his/her own needs for others in the family?

These questions tap into what I call the six signs of superiority, and each one is crucial to defining and explaining what it means to be a superior wife. I did a simple statistical calculation to count how many of these six key life tasks each wife had mastered. The figures for this count ranged from none, or zero, to six, for all of them. I found that

- almost no wives—*not even 1 percent*—say that they have mastered none or just one of these six areas.

- 40 percent of wives say they have mastered all six tasks, and
- 23 percent say they are best at five of them.

Thus, 63 percent of wives consider themselves superior by this measure, meaning that in their judgment they have acquired five or six of the signs of superiority. When I average this figure with the 75 percent from the first question, I conclude that slightly more than two-thirds of wives believe that they are the superior partner in the marriage.

Let's look at that figure again: *two-thirds of wives say that they are the superior spouse.* That is an impressively large number.

The obvious question, though, is how men answer these two questions about their wives. Few husbands agree that their wife is the superior one in the marriage: just 24 percent of husbands say that their wives have five or six of the signs of superiority. (Again, remember that many of these wives and husbands are not married to each other.) Likewise, fewer husbands say that their wives are in control of the family universe, just 55 percent. But they describe their situation with apparent honesty, like this twenty-nine-year-old California man, who uses John Wayne logic, terse and to the point: "She calls the shots, I just supply the bullets."

Others express similar sentiments:

- "She definitely assumes the lion's share of the work."
- "She does a better job at taking care of our family with everything."
- "I am the king, she is the prime minister. I may look like I am in charge, but she is the one calling all of the shots."
- "I've seen her job. I don't want it."
- "I am along for the ride. She is driving the car."
- "She runs the show. I just get in the way."
- "She's the boss. She's the planner/organizer/socializer. She reminds me which chores I agreed to do."
- "Without my wife, I'd be a sunken ship."
- "She's the voice of God."
- "Without her, I would be friendless, living in languid squalor."
- "My wife is the sandpaper of life that rounds out my rough edges."
- "My wife does it all: she is a monster. She goes to work, cleans, cooks, handles the finances, takes dance and guitar classes at night, organizes and

maintains the family, and she also has to live with me: a beer-drinking, video-game playing slob who is the King of Procrastination."

What is disturbing, though, is that insightful men like these are few in number. Not nearly as many husbands as wives are conscious of the wife's superiority. There's a gender gap on this issue of between 20 and 40 percent, depending on which question I focus on. A few husbands even express hostility about these questions, perhaps because it disturbs them to think too deeply about female superiority. More than a few husbands object to having just two choices in deciding who has the most control over the family's wants and desires. They want to be able to say that *both* partners share responsibility. They fume over my method and even my integrity. "This is a false option," one says, "since there is conflict for control and we have domains of competence, some overlapping." Another claims that he doesn't understand the question about who has the most control over the family. A few insist that I am cheating by asking the questions the way I did.

But I designed these questions deliberately to be *forced choice*, which means that they compel people to choose one way or the other, with no third alternative. I wanted to force this either-or choice on wives and husbands, because I didn't want them to evade the issue by giving the politically correct or socially desirable answer, as so many would be tempted to do. That answer, of course, would be that "both partners share," even if that is *not* the most accurate or truthful one.

I used a third question to explore the extent of superior wives' mastery of modern life, both at home and out in the world. Given a list of ten tasks, wives say they have mastered seven, on average, while their husbands have mastered three. Again, the items posed forced choices: respondents could say that the wife is the family expert on each one or that the husband is the expert, but not that both are.

In your marriage, who is the family expert on

1. cooking a decent meal?
2. earning money?
3. maintaining cars?

4. managing finances?
5. managing health care?
6. taking care of the house?
7. talking about feelings?
8. seeing relatives?
9. socializing with friends?
10. supervising children?

As it turns out, a majority of wives say they are the expert on supervising children (93 percent), talking about feelings (89 percent), taking care of the house (85 percent), managing health care (83 percent), seeing relatives (82 percent), cooking a decent meal (81 percent), socializing with friends (75 percent), and managing finances (55 percent). A majority of wives believe that their husband is the family expert on two of these tasks: maintaining cars (81 percent) and earning money (77 percent).

As I've said, it doesn't matter what race or religion couples are: all are equally likely to include a superior wife. In addition, in determining who is a superior wife, it doesn't seem to matter how many hours wives work or how much money they earn. (For more about superior wives and their work situation, see chapter 3.) Let me clarify, again, that I am not saying that all marriages include a superior wife: they do not. In fact, I discuss the dramatic and important exceptions to the superior wife rule in chapter 7. Still, the majority of marriages include a superior wife.

Toni, the New York wife whose husband balks at deciding what to order for dinner on Fridays, glances at the family expert question and says, "Read me anything on that list, and the answer will be 'me.' I do the cooking and cleaning and laundry and shopping and kids. I also pay all the bills. My husband has no idea what is a good electric bill and what is a bad electric bill. I could say it was four thousand dollars, and he'd say, 'Oh, okay.' He has no idea how much money we have or where I keep all the statements," she says, laughing and grimacing at the same time. She looks at her friends, pauses, and states with heartfelt sincerity, "I want to be my husband when I come back," presumably meaning that she'd like to be reincarnated as the man she married. "I will walk in the door and my dinner will be ready, my clothes will be clean, and my kids will be taking a bath!"

"My husband is comfortable with me handling everything, and he actually prefers it," agrees Chloe, forty-two, a mother of three and full-time project manager who earns slightly more than her second husband. "He can completely disassemble and reassemble a car engine, but he can't tie a bow in our daughter's hair." In Chloe's mind, though, both jobs are equally important—though the bow tying might be slightly more useful, since it's required a lot more often than the car dismantling.

Six Signs of Superiority

Chloe is a superior wife—*though she doesn't think of herself as one*—because she has all six of the essential characteristics of superiority. These traits, like cogs in a complex and well-oiled machine, work together to become more than just the sum of their parts. These six signs of superiority define and explain a superior wife. I chose these six signs after a great deal of research and testing in my pilot study. They are drawn from management theory

The Six Signs of Superiority

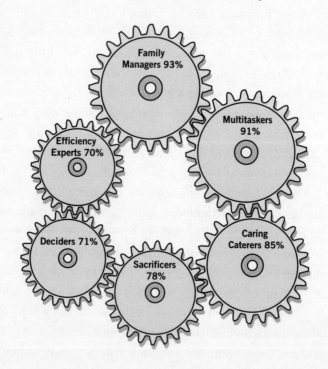

and organizational psychology research, as well as from simple common sense.

The six signs are managing the household, being able to multitask, caring for and supporting loved ones, sacrificing one's own needs, making decisions, and being as efficient as possible. A majority of wives say they possess five or six of these traits.

First Sign: Family Managers. Ninety-three percent of wives say they are the one who is best at organizing and planning for the family. This is not just a matter of mastering the cooking and the kids, or the birthday parties and the Thanksgiving plans. Being the family manager means being in charge of everything, from overseeing health care to juggling the credit card bills to giving the dog a monthly heartworm pill. It means being able to keep everything that matters in your brain, then figuring out what's most important and needs to be done right away, what can wait, and how to get all of it done eventually. And it means doing this mostly without help.

"I feel as though I have way more on my plate to deal with than he has on his," says Betty, forty-four, an office manager from Pennsylvania, referring to her husband. "I am always doing, doing, doing, and there is always something not yet done, when it comes to working full-time and taking care of my family. My husband does help out, but he also makes sure he gets 'his time' to relax or work out. It does not bother him that laundry is piling up, or that the house needs to be vacuumed, or that we need groceries," she adds. After all, that stuff is her responsibility, so why should it bother him?

Some wives—those with disabled husbands, say, or with husbands who work nights—believe that the fact that they've had to become the family manager is the exception, when, in fact, it's the rule. Sheila's third husband has a back injury and can no longer work as a mason. Sheila, forty-six, a real estate broker in West Virginia, thinks that's why she's become the sole breadwinner and household manager, although she recalls that this was also her role in her first marriage and the second as well. She figures that her life would be easier if only her husband were healthy.

Maybe yes, but probably not.

Marla is in a similar situation, but she thinks it's because her husband works nights. "I handle the money and I see that the bills are paid," says Marla, a Missouri wife and cashier whose husband has the midnight shift as a deputy in the county jail. "But any kind of housework, he won't touch," she says. It's not so easy for her to be the family manager, though, because she's had knee replacement surgery and can't move around very well. If her husband only had a day job, her life would be easier, she guesses.

Maybe yes, but probably not.

Wives like Sheila and Marla are the family's chief executive officers, the bosses, the ones who run the show. For them, this situation seems due to life circumstances, but for many others, it has become a habitual way of life for no apparent reason. And it's a habit that they can't, or won't, break. These wives feel they have no choice but to be the manager, because their husband is lazy, or an immigrant, or not interested, or just can't cope. This is willful ignorance on the part of some men, a refusal to take on any family responsibility other than working for pay, and it afflicts many husbands. Some even admit their slackerdom and credit their wives for being the one who fills in the large gaps.

"I make most of the money, but my wife is the one who manages everything else," says Bobby, a twenty-nine-year-old physical education teacher from Royse City, Texas, who admits his wife's superiority. "She's really good at figuring out how much to spend and where to spend it, and keeps immaculate records, way better than I ever could. I think that my wife is, without question, the better spouse," he concludes.

Plenty of wives agree that they have superior management skills, including Susan, twenty-seven, a mother of three who works full-time as a clerk near her home in Fort Worth, Texas. Susan's husband, whom she describes as "pretty lazy," gets home from work and flops down on the couch for the rest of the evening. The cooking and the cleaning and the kids and the finances and the cars and the yard are hers to manage or to ignore, her choice. He surely won't interfere, she says. So far, Susan has opted to take charge. The same goes for Deb, forty-six, a disability claims examiner in Wisconsin who is in a second marriage to a resident alien. He's an alien, but he's not from Mars, he's from the United Kingdom. Still, "He thinks he can't do anything in this country. So he is responsible for creating most of our problems, and I am the one who has to fix them." He doesn't even have the excuse of a language barrier, she points out, though sometimes he piles on the British accent pretty thick.

A Los Angeles wife who works in human resources has a husband whom she calls "a couch potato," a guy who has to be prodded to do anything at all. Another wife, Margie, thirty-eight, from Canton, Ohio, says, "I have one of those good ole boys who works, comes home, has a few beers, and goes to bed." While Margie is busy managing the family and the outstanding bills and the medical insurance forms, she's also fantasizing about "becoming intimate with the Swedish massage guy." Not that she knows such a man, Margie admits, but she's allowed to dream, right?

Stories like these vary by detail and small degree, but the outcome is the same: wives have no choice, so they become the family managers. It's not a matter of pushiness or being a control freak or wearing the pants, it's simply a matter of doing what needs to be done. Somebody has to steer the family vehicle, and if the husband is asleep in the shotgun seat, then it's the wife who has to get behind the wheel and start the engine.

Liza, forty-three, a life coach in Winston-Salem, North Carolina, is in the driver's seat, for sure. While her husband is "supportive and appreciative" of her efforts in finding therapy for their autistic son, she says, "Sometimes I wish I didn't have to do it all, and I also wish that I didn't have to be the manager of the family. I schedule and supervise all work to be done on the house, and I plan all social events. I make sure the bills are paid on time and that there are clean clothes and food to eat. If I oversimplify, all he does is earn part of our living, take the trash out when I remind him, and take care of the cars. I do all the rest. He will help me with things when I ask, but I wish he would do more without my having to ask."

That's the sticking point: the having to ask. Superior wives who become the family managers often end up not bothering to ask, because it seems like too much effort for too little in return.

"Women are still the orchestrators of family life, even though it's more egalitarian today," agrees Suzanne M. Bianchi, a social researcher who specializes in the study of gender and work issues. "Women feel responsible for having lots of balls in the air, for arranging their own schedules and everyone else's schedules. When women speak about this, they talk about having to be on top of everything."[47]

Bianchi studies how wives and husbands spend their time, and she asks people what they do every minute during a twenty-four-hour period. She says that mothers spend much less time than they used to doing chores like vacuuming and dusting and cooking, but they spend just as much time with their children as mothers did twenty years ago, even if they work. And although some husbands do housework and help out with children, it's usually the wives who are assigning the duties and checking to see that everything gets done on time, Bianchi notes.[48]

Superior wives do most of the managing.

Second Sign: Multitaskers. Being able to multitask is almost synonymous with being ultrafeminine, since it has become so much a part of what it means to be a modern wife and mother. Indeed, 91 percent of the wives in my Web survey say that they are the person in the marriage who can do more than one thing at a time. Multitasking is part of being a successful manager—figuring out the most efficient way to finish the largest number of tasks in the shortest time period. That's true in an office or on a construction site, or at home. Wives who can multitask are able to avoid feeling overwhelmed by the sense that they have too much to do all at once. As long as they can pay enough attention to each of the things they are doing simultaneously—like watching three or four or five juggling hoops fly through the air—then they won't mess up too badly. Thus, a multitasking wife can concentrate on several things at once, without being distracted by any one of them. She can make a pot roast while helping a ten-year-old with homework while also paying the bills. And she won't dry out the meat or forget to sign the checks. She is the one who answers the telephone, no matter what else she is doing, since her husband is too busy to bother. She's the one who can drive two daughters to volleyball practice, do the grocery shopping, drop off the dry cleaning, buy food for dinner, then pick up the girls and be home in time to cook the meal and feed the family. She can be talking on the telephone while watching television with the kids and stroking the dog. And she's paying attention to everything, all at once. This is why American wives buy microfiber cleaning slippers in lime green or pink, so that they can mop the floor while walking around the house doing seventeen other chores: it's the epitome of a multitasking household product, available online and at local big-box stores.[49]

"Most women are good at multitasking, and so am I, but it means that I have to keep an enormous amount of stuff in my tired brain," explains Sally, forty, an evangelical Christian wife from Massachusetts who expected to work full-time throughout her marriage but is now homeschooling her three children instead. "I also think I am the smarter spouse. I am a much faster thinker, and by being a mommy, I'm trained to see things coming, so I can anticipate and therefore avoid disasters. Whereas my hubby will have the kids for half an hour, and two of them will end up bleeding!"

It's a given that being able to think about, and act on, several things at once is useful in emergencies. That's why multitasking superior wives must take charge when minidebacles strike. "We don't tell my husband much, because he gets hysterical and he worries," says Tracey, the wife who hosted the gaggle of New York superior wives I interviewed. "He's no good in an emergency, that's for sure. A few years ago, we went on vacation for a week and a pipe broke in the basement while we were gone. When we got home, I heard water running and I figured out right away what had happened, mostly because there was a foot of water in the basement. But Mike didn't know which place to go first; he was frantic and totally overwhelmed. So I wrote a grocery list, and I said, 'You leave with the boys and buy some food.' After I kicked him out of the house, I turned off the water, I called up the insurance company, and I got somebody in there to pump everything out. By the time Mike got back, it was all done. He gets hysterical if there are too many things to think of at once, but I calm down almost to a stand-still."

Social scientists who study minute-by-minute details of people's daily activities find that wives are outstanding multitaskers, regardless of where in the world the women live. In a recent British study of how people spend their time, women are much more likely than men to say they multitask often, especially in the morning and at mealtimes.[50] In a similar study conducted in Finland, three-quarters of wives say they multitask while doing housework, both on weekdays and on weekends. Not even half of Finnish husbands do the same.[51] In the United States, nearly seven in ten married moms feel as if they are multitasking most of the time, compared to four in ten married dads. Just as many mothers say they have little time for themselves, and four in ten constantly feel rushed.[52]

"Women practice multitasking because they allow themselves to be interrupted more than guys do, even when they are adolescents," explains Suzanne Bianchi, who conducted the American multitasking research. "Guys like to focus on one thing at a time much more often than women do," she adds, mostly because men are so bad at multitasking.[53]

Moms who multitask—it sounds like the start of a nasty tongue twister—are often in a hurry and usually feel somewhat besieged, even as they are superefficient. In some cases, they may feel trapped and despondent. "I take care of the basic needs of the children after working an eight-hour day," says Connie, twenty-six, who is a loan officer at a bank near her home in upstate New York. "I do all the household chores for the family on a daily and a weekly basis. My husband comes to me with all of our financial problems, and for his wants and needs, and our three children come to me for their wants and needs. I constantly feel used and unappreciated. My children are the only ones who show me any affection at all," she explains. Married just three years, Connie has become a whirling dervish of a multitasker, because she feels she has no other choice. But, she adds, "I sometimes wonder if I had married somebody older and more mature if I wouldn't have to do so much all the time, and if I'd get more help from my husband."

Maybe yes, but probably not.

Probably not, according to Melanie, forty-eight, who did marry a man ten years older when she was in her twenties. As it turned out, though, he cares about nothing other than his work. "My husband can only do one thing at a time," Melanie says, "while I am just overloaded. Household things, like keeping clean and doing chores, painting the house and mowing the lawn, don't mean very much to him. So I've pretty much got to do it all." With three children and a full-time job, she's living proof that working mothers constantly feel pressed for time, take no personal breaks for themselves, and almost never have the true luxury of doing just one thing at a time—and also that an older husband doesn't necessarily mean a better husband. Melanie spends her days, she says, multitasking her brains out.

Superior wives are the majesties of multitasking.

Third Sign: Caring Caterers. The main reason that most superior wives become family managers and masters of multitasking is that they care so much. They care about their marriage and their children; they care about their in-laws and their friends; they care about their neighbors and their relatives. Such wives suffer from a common case of overcare. Indeed, 85 percent of wives say they are the person in the marriage who shows the most support and affection to family members and friends, according to my Web survey.

Amy, a sixty-year-old wife from Minneapolis, compares herself to her husband: "I am just more tuned in." Wives like Amy are tuned to an emotional wavelength—receiving transmissions right to the heart from children and friends and sisters and husbands and colleagues and neighbors—on a receiver that gets a much clearer signal than their husband's does. That's why wives suffer when a best friend's son has to go to rehab for drug abuse and why wives lose sleep when a niece flunks out of college. It's why mothers agonize over a son's inability to find a date to the prom and worry about a daughter's chronic headaches. This kind of superempathy seems to prevail, by the way, among wives who have a professional aptitude for emotional intelligence, like therapists and nurses, as well as among wives who work in more traditionally masculine jobs. That's why so many wives say, as thirty-four-year-old Wendy from Delaware puts it, "I am responsible for meeting my family's emotional needs and for helping to solve their emotional problems."

When wives do such "emotion work," it becomes another domestic job like child care and household chores, according to some sociologists. Even though there is no heavy lifting involved and you don't need rubber gloves to give comfort and encouragement, this work is far from effortless. Actually, wives and mothers *feel the pain* of those whom they love, so it's hard work that also has emotional consequences. It's a cliché that mothers are only as happy as their least happy child, but it's also true. In addition, wives are the ones who take the initiative to talk things over with their husband, who listen to him complain about his day, who do favors for him, who offer encouragement, who show appreciation for him, unasked.[54] Wives are the ones who insist that a couple spend time together and have meaningful conversations; wives enforce the rules of emotional engagement in marriage. Wives are the five-star generals of the family's emotional battlefield.

"I'm more emotionally involved than my husband and I take care of any problems that may arise," explains Krista, thirty-five, a psychotherapist in Kentucky and mother of a three-year-old daughter. With some disbelief, she adds that "my husband told me one time that he believes he's very ultramasculine, so he doesn't have feelings to hurt! I about cracked up. I have so many feelings, and I just couldn't believe he would actually think that he doesn't have any feelings."

"Needs and problems upset my husband, so I am the one who listens and empathizes," agrees Deborah, fifty-one, a mother of three daughters in Wyoming who is a global account executive for a telecommunications company. Deborah works a sixty-hour week, and she's also a marathon runner. While Deborah's work life is as masculine as can be—she's as cutthroat in the office as she is on the running trail—when she's at home, she's all heart. She too is tuned in to her family's emotional transmissions, much more so than her husband, she says.

Likewise, Marianne, thirty-five, says that her husband never shows any feelings at all. "I wish he'd get angry sometimes. Just tell me what he's feeling, how he's feeling. That would show some emotion, at least. I just wish he'd see how he comes across as not caring, not putting as much into our family as I do. I feel like I'm the one crying at night while he's watching television. He's always been a head-in-the-sand person, and he thinks if he pretends that it's not there, it won't be," Marianne says. "I don't feel like we're equals when it comes to the caring department. I feel as if I care much more, while he's content to just sit back and let life go by. I've explained this to him many times, but he just doesn't get it."

Marianne is not alone in the husband-doesn't-get-it department.

In many marriages—though not all—wives end up being starved for emotional support and comfort and affection from husbands. It's as if they are shipwrecked, all alone, on a deserted atoll, with no one to hear their cries. In fact, some research shows that many marriages are emotionally asymmetrical, with all the empathy and emotion emanating from the wife, who has to beg her partner to be more sympathetic and understanding.[55] Eventually such wives become disappointed by their marriage. Then, ironically, they end up *blaming themselves* for wanting too much or for being unrealistic or unduly demanding.

It's not that men don't have feelings; of course they do. It's just that their emotional radar is less fine-tuned and a lot more self- than other-focused. If forced, a husband can tell you exactly how *he* feels, but he may not be able to guess how his wife feels, simply because it doesn't occur to him to think about it. A large national study of Americans' inner feelings shows that women and men have the same number of emotions but that men have more positive ones than women. More men than women often feel calm or excited; more women than men say they feel anxious or sad. But women are also more likely to express their emotions readily; they don't hold back, the way many men do, when they are feeling anxious or worried, elated or pleased.[56]

Superior wives put their heart and soul into marriage and family.

Fourth Sign: Sacrificers. Wives and mothers often assume that it's their job to put themselves last. And that's the unspoken assumption in many marriages too. In my research, 76 percent of wives say that they—and not their husbands—are the ones who sacrifice their own needs and desires for the sake of the family. Wives give up spending time alone or getting some exercise to be with the children, while husbands are less likely to do so. Also, wives are the ones who believe that being self-sacrificing means being feminine. Nearly six in ten wives say it's feminine and ultrawomanly to sacrifice oneself.

"My family's needs are my purpose in life" is the way LouAnn, forty, from San Antonio, Texas, puts it. Married twice, she lives with her three children, an unemployed husband, and her seventy-five-year-old mother. With six people in her house, LouAnn always puts her own needs and desires in sixth place. That's because, LouAnn says, she's simply better equipped to give of herself than is her husband or anybody else. "I am better at keeping harmony and making our home a place every family member enjoys. I try to encourage family meetings and discussions, so blowups don't happen," she says. LouAnn organizes and manages all the chores and the duties at home, and she knows that nobody is putting her needs first. "My husband is one more person I have to care for, and my needs are not met by him very often," she says, "but that's a situation I've come to accept."

LouAnn is like many of the women I studied a decade ago for my research on sacrificial mothers. To conduct that pre-Internet survey, I mailed questionnaires to a random national sample of families with at least one child. I discovered that about nine in ten mothers say they often sacrifice their own needs and personal pleasures for their family, but only 16 percent believe their husbands do the same. When I presented wives with a list of twenty-three sacrifices, most say that they make at least four major personal sacrifices. The most common sacrifices for wives and mothers are giving up being alone as often as they'd like, spending money the way they want, reading for pleasure, getting enough sleep, and socializing with their friends.

Back then I designed a sacrifice test, so I could figure out how wives and husbands view what they give up. As it turns out, wives score significantly higher on this test than husbands do. Here's a modified version of that test: the more strongly you agree with these simple statements, the more sacrificial you are.[57]

    1. I often sacrifice my needs and desires for my spouse.
    2. I often sacrifice my needs and desires for my children.
    3. It's a mother's job to sacrifice for her children.
    4. Sometimes I think of my spouse as just another child.

Many wives might scoff at the idea of taking this kind of test, mostly because they automatically put themselves last, almost without thinking. Sherry, thirty-three, a Tennessee mother of three, says that "I never order anything for myself that my children can't have too, except a cup of coffee." But whenever she sends her husband out with the kids, the excursion invariably ends in tears, and he's not the one who's crying. "He is more thoughtless and selfish, in the sense that he will buy himself a doughnut and a Coke, but he doesn't understand that the kids will want to order the same thing. And we never let them eat that much sugar, and we never let them drink soda either. So it's scream, scream, whine, whine, until he finally gives in. I am used to sacrificing, but he is just clueless."

Lindsay, fifty-eight, agrees with the notion of spousal cluelessness. A legal editor who has been married to her second husband for twenty-five years, Lindsay says that she is absolutely the better partner in the marriage. "I am way more observant, sensitive, empathic, and willing to postpone or sacrifice my own gratification for his sake. I put a significant effort into using kind gestures and speaking to him carefully, and I am just generally more thoughtful about every single aspect of our life together," she says. "But I have made this choice, and no one forced me into it." Lindsay's not sure that her husband could be as sacrificial as she is, even if he tried.

Superior wives put their own needs and dreams on hold for the sake of their family.

Fifth Sign: Deciders. In every marriage, couples have to make small, everyday decisions, like what vegetables to buy at the grocery store or what color to paint the living room or whether to let the ten-year-old play tackle football. But they also have to decide more important issues, like where the children will go to school, whether the family should move, or when the hot water heater needs to be replaced. In terms of decision making, minor and major, it turns out that 71 percent of wives say that they are the ones who make most of the decisions.

"I have become very good at making good decisions fast, mostly because I have to juggle so many different things at once that I have no choice," says Sally, thirty-five. With two children and a full-time job, Sally says that she is the family's master decision maker, but only by default. "My husband will spend a long, long time mulling it over and still be indecisive. That means I get to decide again. My level of energy is much higher too," she adds. Sally's husband has opted out of making decisions, so she has had to opt in.

Wives like Sally, who are willing to be the family's decider, have the self-confidence and assurance necessary to be convinced that they know what's best for the family. They don't have the luxury of being anxious or insecure about their opinions: they just need to decide. A belief that the man of the house should make all the decisions has gone the way of black-and-white television sets and rotary telephones.

Some economists believe, however, that wives earn the right to make decisions only if they earn some of the family's income, especially if the decisions go beyond trivial ones, like whether to buy chicken thighs or ground beef for dinner. Their theory is that the more money a wife brings in, the more power she has in the relationship and, therefore, the more sway she will have in big decisions.[58] But it doesn't work that way in real life. In fact, very few Americans now believe that the partner who earns the most money should have the most say in family decisions.[59] And in my research, wives who don't work outside the home are just as likely as wives who work for pay to say they make most of the family decisions. *Being the one to make family decisions is not about being the one who makes the most money.*

Elizabeth, twenty-seven, is on maternity leave in Berlin while caring for her one-year-old son, a sabbatical funded by the German government. Her husband works part-time, she says, "but I am the one who makes most of the decisions in the house. I usually say when things should happen, and I start the ball rolling so that they happen. If I want something done, I either have to ask my husband, beg, or simply do it myself. And mostly I do it myself, because otherwise, it might never get done."

Elizabeth is irritated that her husband is not looking for a better-paying, full-time job, "and the longer he putzes around, the more upset I get," she says. If she sees that a decision has to be made, she just makes it, while he will postpone and postpone it, almost to the point of no return. "Having a baby and earning a master's degree have taught me that procrastination is evil, and I resent that my husband doesn't have my work ethic or my ability to decide," she explains. Elizabeth also manages the family's money and organizes their lives, and she has been doing so since the birth of her son.

"Before I got pregnant, I sometimes felt I could not make a decision and that the important decisions shouldn't be in my hands. Since then, though, I've had to decide what to eat when I was pregnant and how to raise the baby and how to care for him. Now my husband doesn't make a move without asking me first, and I decide almost everything. Still, I don't like to make a decision without knowing his position on the matter, even if I overrule his opinion," Elizabeth says.

Not thrilled about having to make all the decisions, Elizabeth nevertheless believes that she is the one who is best at it. Kim, forty-eight, an accountant with three children in Sacramento, California, is not happy about her own situation either. "I am tired of being the one who makes most of the decisions—about everything! I nag him to make decisions, hopefully thoughtful decisions, but I'm usually the one who ends up making all of the big and many of the small decisions, with no input from him," she says. "I am thankful that my husband helps with housework, cooking, and car maintenance, but sometimes I feel like I am the only adult in the house. I really, really would like him to take charge, at least once in a while," Kim says. "Somehow, though, we have morphed into our current roles, me deciding and him not."

If making decisions is, indeed, a way to wield power in marriage, then a majority of wives have marital power by the barrelful. On the other hand, some husbands, overwhelmed by the demands of daily life, *decide* not to decide. For them, that's the easy way out, but it's also a passive way of forcing their wives to shoulder more of the household burden. Eventually, being the decider becomes the wife's job, just like doing the dishes, helping with homework, and paying the bills.

Take Adela, twenty-seven, an African American clerical worker and mother of a six-month-old baby in Port Angeles, Washington. "I'm the one who makes all of the important decisions, because my husband leaves everything up to me. He doesn't want to know when or how I pay the bills, just that they get paid. It is awful, because I feel like I'm on an island, all by myself, waiting for someone to come and rescue me. I clean the house, make dinner, go to work, feed and bathe the baby. Sometimes I feel like I'm drowning, but if it were up to my husband, things just wouldn't get done," she concludes. Adela, too, longs to be rescued from the isolation of her superiority.

Maria tells the same story, although at fifty-five, she's decades older than Adela. Maria, a Mexican immigrant and social worker in Los Angeles, calls herself "the boss of the family. Since I am more verbal than my husband and I am not afraid of confrontation, I have found myself in the position of decision maker of my family. It was only when I began raising my four children that I had to be proactive in many areas, such as finding day care, making doctors' appointments, arranging for music lessons, and other things," she explains. "It is clear who rules the roost in this house. I most certainly do wish that my husband would step out of his box and try to be more engaged, but the kids see me as the one who is the decision maker, not their dad."

Many decision-making superior wives like Maria wish that the situation weren't so lopsided, but they feel they've fallen into an unbreakable habit. "My husband has some input, but he often feels too stressed to make any of the final decisions," says Carly, thirty-nine, a chef from Yonkers, New York, who has three children. "Unfortunately, the longer I take charge and the more complex our lives become, the harder it is to let go of these roles. When he feels unsure about a task or less competent, he relies on me to get it done. This is extremely frustrating and very unfair," she adds.

Superior wives decide.

Sixth Sign: Efficiency Experts. Because wives do most of the managing and the multitasking, the organizing and the deciding, it's no surprise that many also consider themselves to be the most efficient member of the family. Seventy percent of the wives in my Web survey call themselves the more competent partner. Being efficient is a matter of getting a job done with minimal waste, expense, and unnecessary effort, and that's exactly what these women do. They are reliably, consistently, amazingly effica-cious. Think of them as bionic women—only not so perfect and with fewer artificial body parts. In fact, being efficient, like being able to multitask, has become a supremely feminine characteristic.

"I make no secret of the fact that I would rather lie on a sofa than sweep beneath it. But you have to be efficient if you're going to be lazy" is the way Shirley Conran described the importance of female efficiency in her 1975 household advice book, optimistically entitled *Superwoman*. She declared that "life is too short to stuff a mushroom," during a time when many housewives thought mushroom stuffing a perfectly admirable domestic activity. Back then, mothers spent an average of more than twenty-five hours a week doing housework and chores, even the ones who thought of themselves as lazy. Today, though, mothers spend just fifteen hours a week doing chores, mostly because so many more of them are working outside the home.[60] That's why today's mothers and wives have learned to be even more fiercely efficient than Conran ever dreamed possible, as well as ruth-less about deciding what's important and what's not. For most mothers today, spending time with children is important; having a spotless house and impeccably ironed clothing and homemade chocolate chip cookies is not.

Many of the wives in my Web survey seem to take their efficiency for granted. They assume that their speedy and proficient dash through the daily marathon of duties at home and work and home again is natural, merely what must be done.

"I do the gift buying, the party planning, the meal planning, the doctor visiting, and the holiday event planning, and I make sure that everyone is clothed and in their right minds, most of the time," says Sasha, forty-seven, a mortgage broker in Nashville, Tennessee. "I feel like my husband is a good provider and it's in his heart to do the right thing, whatever that is, but he just has a hard time grasping it. Sometimes I feel like I'm a juggler and my entire family is standing on the sidelines, tossing me more and more balls. Somehow I manage to keep them all in the air, but one day I fear that they're all going to come crashing down. From the time I open my eyes in the morning, I'm planning everything that gets done around here and mak-ing sure it gets done and when and how it should be done."

Sasha continues, "I plan the meals, I cook the meals, and I clean up the kitchen after whoever 'sort of' cleaned it. I take care of the dogs, from walking them to feeding them to taking them to the veterinarian. Thank goodness my teenage daughters do their own laundry! I really wouldn't mind the fact that I have to get the cars serviced, if only my husband would help with some of the more 'womanly' chores. I don't care whether it's a guy thing or a girl thing, I'd just like some help," she says, in a blatant cry for, well, help.

But Sasha's efficiency pales next to Nancy's, a thirty-nine-year-old Korean American who lives in Chicago. Nancy and her husband built a company from scratch, which they recently sold for several million dollars, though they still manage the business. They have a five-year-old son, who fits into Nancy's superefficient, minute-by-minute plan for each and every day. "I take care of most of the family's needs, because I am type A and I love to take control. I wake up at five o'clock, my son gets up at six, and then I get him ready to take to our office. I make breakfast there, and my husband comes an hour later so he can drop our son off at school," Nancy says with great precision. "I am responsible for setting up my son's play-dates, and his after-school programs. I make sure he is in bed early, so he gets at least ten hours of sleep a night. I try to make dinner at home at least three times a week too. I also like to arrange our social schedule, so that we can have friends over for dinner parties and playdates. I don't feel complete or satisfied unless every aspect in my life is fulfilled," Nancy concludes. That's what I call a superior wife, squared.

Superior wives are superefficient.

These six signs of superiority are integral pieces of the superior wife puzzle. But there's a central mystery about these superior traits: why is it that nearly two-thirds of wives believe in their hearts that they have most or all of these aspects, but just one-quarter of husbands agree? Are the men being stubborn? Deliberately obtuse? Or do they really and truly not see what is staring them in the face?

The Great Big Wide Gender Divide

It's possible, I think, that some husbands live in a world of elaborate and intricate denial, a bizarro universe in which they are truly members of an egalitarian partnership, an equal legend in their own minds. The difference in superiority perceptions between wives and husbands is astonishing: almost three times as many wives as husbands view themselves as having superior traits. Ask wives how many of the six signs they have, and 63 percent answer that they have five or six. Ask husbands how many of the six signs their wives have, and just 24 percent agree that their wives have five or six. Ask wives how many of the ten household tasks they excel in, and they say seven, giving husbands credit for greater expertise in just three of the tasks. But ask husbands the same question, and they say the expertise is evenly divided: wives are the greater experts at five tasks, and so are husbands. More than simply a gender divide, these results reveal a comprehension chasm. These two realms—of female and male perception—simply do not intersect. This puzzling and disturbing disconnect between spouses is a beginning-of-the-millennium social and psychological mystery.

Why is this gender gap so wide?

In some cases, perhaps, it's because wives prefer to delude their husbands into believing they are in charge, to cushion the allegedly fragile male ego. "I make more decisions at home than he does," says Kit, forty-one, a customer service representative in Saint Louis. "But I do it in a way that he thinks he is really in on it! Because in the end, I know what I want and I almost always get it without hurting his pride." Another tactic in Kit's arsenal, she says, is "If I want something done around the house that he has been putting off, I will throw a party, and that gives him a deadline to get it done." Kit's methods are subtle and somewhat manipulative, but they are for her husband's benefit, since he never really knows he's being played.

Randi, forty-two, a stay-at-home mother of two from Michigan, agrees, noting that "I let him think he's got the bull by the horns," implying that he doesn't even know where the damn bull is. "You know that old saying, 'Behind every good man is a very good woman'? Well, it's true."

Another possibility, of course, is that each wife is much more aware of, and focused on, what she herself is doing than what anybody else is doing, so it's only natural that she believes she does more, knows more, cares more. (The same would apply to husbands too, of course.) This is exactly how Ellen views her situation. "Now that my husband has a higher-paying job and I'm able to work part-time, I feel as if we both think we contribute more than the other one does," the forty-seven-year-old nurse-practitioner in Sheboygan, Wisconsin, says. "I feel I do more, because I organize our lives, I keep the household running, I deal with the children, I take care of all the finances, and I do the best I can to keep up with the laundry and fit in some housekeeping while trying to keep myself healthy and also maintain a professional career." But Ellen says her husband believes he's just as involved, just as masterful, just as essential. It's just that, according to Ellen, *he's wrong.*

A third explanation for this gender abyss, among wives who've given the matter some thought, is that their husband is simply oblivious to what is going on around him. If it's not work-related, he just isn't tuned in. "He is consciously unconscious," explains Annette, fifty-five, a retired teacher in Los Angeles, about her oblivious spouse. "My husband has always had blinders on: if he pretends that something's not there, then it won't be," agrees Michela, thirty-two, an Atlanta mother of two young children who's also in law school. Her husband just doesn't understand the scope of her talents and responsibilities and signs of superiority, and he never will, Michela insists.

That's exactly how Regina, thirty-one, a Mississippi mother of three, feels about her husband. "He doesn't seem to notice if things are falling apart, both in the physical and emotional realms. I know he is a very sensitive guy, so I think he just tunes it all out to get out of responsibility for anything, just like my dad used to." Apparently, it's a multigenerational, surefire male tactic: Tune out, turn away, drop out, as Timothy Leary, the 1960s psychedelic guru, might have put it.

Clearly there is a pronounced level of male blindness when it comes to wifely superiority, as I'll discuss in chapter 4. But listen to how a few sensitive and appreciative husbands, those in the minority, recognize, acknowledge, and applaud their wives' superiority, all six signs of it. "Without my wife, I'd be broke and homeless at best, and quite possibly dead," says Grayson, forty-nine, an unemployed writer in Denver who occasionally does freelance work. Somewhat of a drama queen—or drama king—he admits that he needs his wife desperately. "I suffer from depression, and I was laid off in my midforties and I'm having trouble finding another job. These factors limit what I bring to the marriage, both financially and emotionally. My wife picks up the slack and has refused my offers to separate, even when it would have been to her advantage. She carries a much heavier burden than I do, and I don't know how or why she does it, but I'm very glad she does," he concludes.

I'll let Bill, from Wilton, Connecticut, have the final say on the matter, which he expresses in a fit of brutal and self-critical honesty. Bill admits that when it comes to family, and life in general, "I am clueless." Now fifty-three and in his second marriage, Bill is a well-paid financial consultant on Wall Street and a father of four. "Yes, my wife carries the weight of the family on her shoulders most of the time. She puts up with whiny kids, a selfish, spoiled husband, a messy dog, and a house that seems in a perpetual state of chaos. She is the warmest yet strongest woman I know and everyone loves her. If it weren't for her, I'm pretty sure I would have no friends at all. She attracts people, who open up to her, confide in her, and seek her friendship. Unless they want money, people run from me," he concludes, quite forthright about his ineptitude.

Though husbands may not realize it, superior wives are everywhere. But how did they get that way, and why? The next chapter addresses the biological, social, and psychological origins of the superior wife syndrome.

2

The Biology and Psychology of Wifely Superiority

To look at Peggy Jo, you'd never guess that she is a superior wife. A plump, curly-haired blonde, she was born and raised in Iowa, and her soft gaze seems content and comfortable. Now fifty-four, Peggy Jo is a hospital administrator with a master's degree, a mother of four, and earns almost twice as much as her husband, Ray, a middle school social studies teacher. She is a superior wife in a heartland marriage that is badly in need of repair.

"I work full-time, I pay the bills, I do the grocery shopping, I fix all of the meals, I get medicine for the family, and I take care of our aging parents," Peggy Jo says about her role in the family. "Ray spends his time at work or by himself, puttering around the yard and mowing the lawn." According to Peggy Jo, she's the one who has all six signs of superiority. Oddly, though, she claims that her husband is the family expert on earning money, despite the fact that she's earned substantially more than he has for the past fifteen years. It seems almost as if she feels she has to give him some credit, any credit, for doing at least one thing, whether it's true or not. That said, Peggy Jo admits that she's the family's culinary expert, the car maintenance expert, the health care expert, the emotion expert, and the financial management expert. She does all this, she guesses, because she's good at it and because she's always felt a need to please everybody, especially her family and friends and the people she loves.

"I am pretty much a get-it-done person," Peggy Jo explains. "I don't like to wait on Ray to do things, so I do them myself."

In the end, though, being a get-it-doner hasn't helped her marriage. Peggy Jo feels that she and Ray have grown apart since their children left home a few years ago. Ray is quiet, rarely speaks, and doesn't like to socialize, so Peggy Jo has to organize outings with friends and attend parties by herself, and she visits their children on her own. The disturbing truth, from Peggy Jo's point of view, is that "it would be nice for me to feel more love and support from him, but he is totally without insight into the fact that I feel this way. He thinks we are close, and that we support each other, and that life is good. Therein lies our problem."

He thinks everything is fine; she knows it is not.

This is a classic superior wife marriage, one in which the husband seems to have no idea that his wife might be superior, that she might also be miserable, or that he is not doing his share. Peggy Jo's story is not unusual; there are millions of similar, superior wife marriages, and the underlying, fundamental question about them is *why?*

Why are women the ones who take charge of the family? Why are women the ones who shoulder much of the responsibility for the household? Why are women the ones who juggle and manage and coax and soothe and organize? Why do they take on so much of the domestic and financial burden?

Why?

When I pose this question to wives, many confess that they just don't know the answer. It's simply a mystery; they honestly don't understand how it came to pass that they do so much. One in three wives in my Web survey says she has no idea how this happened; even more husbands, 45 percent, say they don't know either. Wives understand what their family life has become—she's in charge, he's not—but they have no clue how it got that way. Some wives, 28 percent, say that their mastery of the family is "natural, it's in our genes." It's as if this arrangement has become their fate, somehow, because it was preordained in an ancient past, beyond human memory. A few explain further, by saying that "I'm beginning to believe that this is just the way things are in nature, as far as *Homo sapiens* goes." Another agrees that "my being in charge seems only natural, like it happened automatically." Even more husbands, about one in three, agree with this point of view.

Two in ten wives believe that society has trained them to take the family reins, to steer the family ship, to be in charge. About one in ten wives feels that it is a woman's need to please that guides her onto a superior path, and almost as many say that it is related to whichever partner is the one who earns the most money. The biggest breadwinner, they believe, will be the one who does the fewest chores and handles the smallest amount of dirty work. That person is the one who sits in the most comfortable chair, the one who holds the television remote, the one who tunes out the rest of the world. That person is, of course, usually a man.

As it turns out, however, the cause of the superior wife phenomenon is not mysterious, nor is it simple. There are several persuasive arguments for why so many wives end up being the superior spouse. First, there are formidable biological reasons for the phenomenon. There are general, species-wide distinctions between the genders that apply to all human be-ings. A woman's brain is vastly different from a man's brain, and her female hormones offer a lifelong advantage in being social, in understanding emotion, and in being able to manage a complex life that includes bread-winning, child rearing, and household managing. Second, on a cultural level, social pressures reinforce these genetic tendencies and guide the ways in which women and men behave in the particular place and time in which they live. These forces also influence the way people think and behave within their own clan and in their own extended family. Third, on an individual level, there are essential psychological differences between wives and husbands—inspired and informed by biology and culture and

Causes of the Superior Wife Syndrome

family—that motivate each woman and each man to behave and to think in different ways.

The Brains of Superior Wives

Only a few decades ago, it was nearly taboo among scientists to talk about brain-cased gender differences; to do so was politically incorrect before the term was even invented. Just about everybody believed that men and women were more alike than not, and it was considered highly unacceptable, antifeminist even, to insist otherwise. But now the pendulum has moved in the other direction. It has swung so far the other way, in fact, that gender experts focus almost exclusively on a wide variety of innate, biological differences between women and men. They proclaim that neurobiology is destiny, that women have female brains, that men have male brains, and that never the twain shall meet. As one group of endocrinologists put it, "Female and male brains differ. Differences begin early during development due to a combination of genetic and hormonal events and continue throughout the lifespan of an individual."[1]

Other neuroscientists preach at great length about the differences between female and male brain structure, hormone levels, and neuron counts. The neurological reality, they say, is that women and men will always and forever be more distinct than alike. That fact, they insist, is owing to gender differences in the hardwiring of the brain, and there's nothing to be done about it.[2] It's not that biology is destiny, exactly, rather that biology is unavoidable, so get used to it.

For my purposes, the unique qualities of the female brain and the pervasive influence of female hormones provide strong confirmation of the existence of wifely superiority. And the issue is not as complex or as obscure as you might think. Once you begin to view life through a hormonal lens, you notice that a great deal of human behavior and feelings and relationships can be explained, at least in part, by brain chemistry. The brain helps determine how a good wife thinks and feels, how a decent mother behaves, how a reliable friend functions, how a loving daughter responds. If you have any doubts, think of an extreme premenstrual syndrome, with its wild mood swings, terrible anxiety, and intense feelings of anger or affection or sadness. That is estrogen gone wild. The calm and contentment a woman feels during the second or third trimester of pregnancy is also due to an infusion of a hormone, one called oxytocin. And the most common symptoms of perimenopause, the sweats and the moodiness and the insomnia, are all caused by a sudden loss of estrogen and progesterone, the consequences of a hormonal faucet that has been suddenly turned off. This is the power and persuasion of female hormones.

Indeed, the biological argument for female superiority is convincing, especially if you accept the fact that scientists have a lot more to learn about it. It's also true that a great deal of the research relies on evolutionary biology, a branch of science based on speculation and guesswork about the lives of our prehistoric ancestors who lived thousands or millions of years ago. We can never know, for sure, exactly how these protohumans lived, but that should not, and will not, prevent us from making provocative and creative suppositions about how they spent their days and nights.

"A million years ago ancestral men were building fires, chipping stone hand axes, and hunting big animals in East Africa," writes anthropologist Helen Fisher, to explain the reasons that men are so single-minded. "As they pursued these dangerous beasts, men had to concentrate. . . . Those who didn't pay strict attention were gored, trampled, or eaten." She concludes that men's brains therefore evolved "to screen out peripheral thoughts."[3] This certainly seems plausible, and it fits what we know about men's inability to multitask, so it's tempting to accept the tale as truth.

Neurological research conducted in modern laboratories also supports a biological explanation for superiority in wives. Indeed, there are at least six widely accepted gender differences in brain structure and hormone allotment that could account for wifely superiority. Current research on the brain and its neurochemicals reveals that, compared with men, women are more verbal, more sociable, more empathic, more organized, more able to multitask, and more eager to avoid conflict. Keep in mind that these are vast overgeneralizations that apply to whole populations, not to single individuals. Overall, *women as a group* have more of these qualities than *men as a group*. That does not mean, however, that any one woman selected at random will be more adept at language, say, than any one man. Having a girlfriend who can't string three sentences together or knowing a guy at work who discusses his feelings in great and intimate detail doesn't mean that these theories aren't true. It just means that there are exceptions to the rules. Looking at the big picture, these biological factors help explain women's mastery of the six signs of superiority.

Women are more verbal. Women's brain center contains more neurons for hearing and language, which is probably why women, on average, use twenty thousand words a day, while men use an average of seven thousand.[4] Like Peggy Jo's husband, many men don't say much, and when they do, they use fewer words. It's as if the male motto is Why use a paragraph when a sentence will do? This tendency shows up quite early in life, since girl toddlers speak at a younger age than boy toddlers do, and they use longer sentences. As they grow, girls have fewer language problems, like stuttering, and they use language in more sophisticated ways than boys do. Girls' speech is more reciprocal and more collaborative, because they use words to keep conversations going and to draw other people in.[5] Teenage girls around the world outscore boys on standardized tests for both writing and reading comprehension, and even on math concepts.[6] So the stereotype about women is true: they talk more than men, and they're better at it too.

Superior wives use their language skills to make choices and to think through important life issues, which also helps them make vital decisions about family and about work. They tend to excel at writing, so they are better equipped to handle work that requires written reports or oral statements. Wives who have to talk a lot, like teachers and counselors and sales representatives, will also thrive in their work.

Women are more sociable. Being able to use words better, and being more adept at language, means that women have an advantage when it comes to forming and maintaining social relationships. Women speak; therefore, women connect.

In general, women are fond of socializing and chatting and gossiping. They value keeping social harmony and preserving bonds with girlfriends and neighbors, sisters and aunts, colleagues and hairdressers. In general, they tend to be better at intimacy and friendship than men, in part because they care more about these aspects of life. There's evidence, in fact, that this ability is innate. Baby girls just one day old prefer to look at a human face, for example, while newborn boys prefer to look at a mechanical mobile. One-year-old girls make more eye contact than one-year-old boys, as do older girls and women, when compared to boys and men of similar ages.[7] This kind of behavior is what encourages and supports and solidifies intimacy and compatibility and friendship.

Some sociable and superior wives mourn their husband's lack of affability, seeing his social failings as a symptom of the marriage's flaws. "My husband prefers to be left alone to do his own thing," says Taruni, forty-nine, an Indian American mother of two from Connecticut. "I am the partner who is more verbal, more emotionally engaged, more interested in life." Taruni, who works full-time as a Web graphics designer, earns slightly less than her husband, but she takes responsibility for the social life of everyone in her family. "I deal with the children and issues of connection, relationships, emotions, gratitude, passing on family stories and memories, discussing ethical issues, talking about Indian culture and American politics," she explains. "He manages our money, but that's it." Taruni is a socially superior wife who yearns to have a partner who would be equally outgoing and lively. In her heart, though, she knows that this will probably never happen.

Women's gregarious nature becomes even more magnified and enhanced by pregnancy and motherhood, according to recent research. Mothers secrete high levels of oxytocin and prolactin right after they give birth and also when they are breast-feeding. Both hormones suppress anxiety and stress and act as opiates, a kind of natural "happy juice" that persuades a woman to bond with her infant by also encouraging physical contact. When scientists inject oxytocin into female rats, the animals become more curious and sociable. Virgin rats, who would otherwise have absolutely no interest in newborns, begin to lick, groom, and protect strange pups (obviously, not their own) after being given just a single dose of oxytocin.[8] It's like mommy medicine.

Baby love, it turns out, is triggered, in part, by neurochemicals. In fact, when scientists examine oxytocin receptors in the brain, they find that feelings of love for a child and feelings of love for a man show similar responses in the same small section of the brain.[9] Thus, oxytocin helps mothers to bond with their babies, but it also helps women to bond with their sexual and romantic partners. In fact, oxytocin is sometimes called the "cuddle chemical," because it encourages "love and social bonds, sexual relationships and friendships," according to Kelly G. Lambert, a professor of behavioral neuroscience at Randolph-Macon College.

Lambert believes that pregnancy and motherhood change the structure of a woman's brain, dramatically and forever. A pioneer in what she calls "mommy brain" research, Lambert insists that this makes evolutionary sense. "The mom is making a huge genetic investment when she gives birth, so she needs to take care, to make sure her offspring reach reproductive age," she tells me. One way for a mother to do this, she says, is to enlist close friends and neighbors, an entire social network, to want to help her.[10] Thus, it's in a woman's best biological interests to be sociable. It may take a village to raise a child, but it takes a mom to befriend the villagers first.

Wives and mothers are equipped by brain structure and hormones, then, to excel at caretaking and socializing. They are most likely, too, to become adept at family management, using their verbal skills to persuade and convince husbands and children to do what's best for themselves and for the family. In addition, their aptitude for intimacy means that they are the ones most likely to keep in touch with grandparents and aunts and uncles and cousins. They reciprocate dinner invitations from neighbors, they arrange to meet an unemployed friend for coffee and sympathy, and they organize family picnics and reunions and summer vacations.

Wives are especially good at doing these things. But, as we'll see, they also feel obligated, by family and society, to arrange such events, because all these tasks are considered women's work. It's their job, of course, because they tend to be naturally good at it, an infinite loop of somewhat flawed logic. It's her job, so she does it; she gets better at it, so she does it; she does it, so it's her job.

Women are wired for empathy. The part of the brain that registers gut reactions, feelings, and moods is larger and more sensitive in women than in men. As a result, perhaps, women have a much greater ability to read faces and tone of voice for emotional meaning and nuance. It sounds almost too corny to be true, but there may be a neurological basis for what is usually called "female intuition." Women have more "mirror neurons" than men do, and it is precisely this abundance that allows them to accurately read someone else's feelings and to feel other people's pain. Because this ability is hardwired in the brain, however, women who are very empathic are not conscious of doing anything out of the ordinary; they are, quite simply, adept at empathy.[11]

The area of a woman's brain that is wired for emotion and for memories of emotion is wide and efficient and fast, as if it were a ten-lane superhighway. In a man's brain, those emotional connections are small, narrow, and slow, more like a winding, two-lane country road, as neuropsychiatrist Louann Brizendine puts it. In addition, she says, "women use both sides of the brain to respond to emotional experiences, while men use just one side." Brizendine explains that researchers find that women remember first dates and big fights in greater detail and for much longer periods than men do.[12] Wives can hold serious grudges and harbor great waves of affection as well.

Indeed, some superior wives actually have to remind their husbands "to be more emotional." That's what Tiffany, twenty-five, a paralegal in Springfield, Illinois, does for her husband, a weekend rock musician. Tiffany likes that her man is so level-headed and good with numbers, she says, but she wishes that sometimes he'd express his feelings of love, or his anxiety about money, or his longing to be a father. Instead, she has to imagine all of that from the few words that do leak out of his mouth. "I just have to read into what he says and figure out what it really means," she says, "but I get so frustrated sometimes, 'cause I feel like a spy trying to decipher a code."

In fact, the British neurologist Simon Baron-Cohen has developed a gender-based theory of neurobiology based on differences in the ways in which women's and men's brains deal with empathy. Because women are so much more likely to prefer to take turns and to cooperate, to avoid physical aggression and hostility, even as very young children, they are type E, for empathizing, he reports. Men's brains are much more suited to analyze and to build, to compete and to fight, according to Baron-Cohen. This is because in the womb, before birth, boys receive a flood of fetal testosterone, which is what gives them an aversion to empathy. He calls the typical male brain type S, for systematizing, since they prefer structure, compartmentalizing, and attending to details.

"In one study, young boys showed fifty times more competition, while girls showed twenty times more turn-taking. These are everyday examples of large sex differences in empathizing," he writes.[13] Baron-Cohen goes on to describe several studies of toddlers, which show that even one-year-old girls feel more concern than one-year-old boys do for the distress of others, by giving more sad looks, making more sympathetic sounds, and patting and comforting a sad mother or a stranger.[14]

Baron-Cohen is also known for his research on what he calls "the Empathy Quotient." This is a test designed to detect subtle and not-so-subtle differences between women and men on how they figure out what other people are feeling. In other words, having a strong sense of empathy is not the same as being a sycophant or a teacher's pet. Empathic people don't necessarily yearn to be liked and to fit in; instead, they are somehow able to intuit other people's anxieties and joys and fears, and then they use that information quite naturally.[15] It may seem like a magical ability, especially to those who don't have it, but being empathic is really an innate talent, just like being able to run really fast or to sing with perfect pitch.

Not all wives are empathic, of course. But *generally speaking*, wives tend to have more empathy than husbands do. That's why so many superior wives say that they are the ones in touch with their family's needs and with their children's feelings, for instance. "I am the one who knows what's going on with our kids," says Kathy, a substitute teacher in Oklahoma. "I know when my two-year-old daughter is scared of the dark windows in her room, and I know when our little boy needs kisses before he goes to day care in the morning. My husband only becomes aware of these things through me."

Wives understand the importance of empathy, and they also realize when it's missing from their lives. "I worry that when my boys leave for college in a few years, I will feel even more disconnected from my husband than I do now," says Nellie, a forty-one-year-old wife from Arizona. "I need emotional support. I need closeness. I need tenderness," she says. "I need a shoulder to cry on. I need warm smiles and soft touches, but I don't get any of this from my husband."

Wives who are more empathic than their husband will also be better equipped than he is to care for the family and sacrifice their own needs for the sake of their loved ones.

Women are more organized. Girls do better than boys in school, from elementary grades right on through college, and one reason is that they are better organized. Girls also follow directions better than boys, and they spend less time watching television and playing video games. Boys are more likely than girls to be placed in special education classes, more likely to be held back a grade, and more likely to drop out of high school.[16] In the United States, as in several other countries, high school girls do better on standardized tests, and they get better grades than boys. More girls than boys attend college in the United States and in Canada, and their grades are better during all four years.[17]

Some education experts say that boys just don't try as hard as girls do, because they're naturally less organized and they seem to have a tendency to be selectively lazy. Boys do the work they really like to do, but they skip everything else. Indeed, private tutors thrive on helping boys do better in school, mostly just by organizing the boys' backpacks and subject binders. Girls understand how important it is to be well organized, one tutor says, but boys have to be reminded over and over again.[18]

Alima, twenty-seven, a Muslim American human resources officer from Long Island, always did well in school, in part because she is supremely well organized, she says. She works long hours in her job as a finance manager in Manhattan, and she also attends school at night, earning a master's degree in business administration. Her husband is currently unemployed and not really looking for work. "I make a significant salary, and I go to school part-time, so I am putting forth a tremendous effort for our future," Alima explains. "I also pay all the bills, I take care of anything that needs to be organized, and I spend a significant amount of time decorating our house. My husband runs errands during the day and drives me where I need to go, but I have to explain to him what to do and when to do it," she says. "I just wish he would take a more serious look at our future and get a job so we can save more money."

Being as organized as Alima is what helps superior wives become the most efficient member of the marriage, and it also permits them to make quick and reasonable decisions, an essential part of being a successful wife and mother and worker. It's also what makes them superior.

Women are better at multitasking. While American culture may persuade boys that it isn't manly to get good grades, that it's much better to be a basketball star or a lacrosse player than an A student, there may actually be another biological reason that boys struggle in school. Boys tend to have more trouble multitasking than girls do. This ability is crucial for academic

achievement, however, since students have to concentrate on several subjects in a day, and they have to be able to juggle homework and studying
with sports and social life and family obligations. It's really a matter of
being efficient at whatever you have to do, and girls are more likely to be
endowed with this kind of competence.

In addition, when women become mothers, whatever innate ability
they have to multitask increases dramatically. Some experimental neuroscientists have discovered that when rats become mothers, for instance, the
animals' multitasking abilities are significantly improved over those of virgin rats, because the mom rats can find a treat in a laboratory maze much
more quickly and efficiently. (The tastiest rat treat in the rat universe, it
turns out, is Froot Loops cereal. Mother rats find Froot Loops much faster
than virgin rats do, even when they have to do several things at once to
figure out the location.)

Again, although this is overgeneralizing, women's multitasking skills
allow them to become proficient at family management. "I think the maternal experience is itself a multitasking experience," agrees Kelly Lambert,
the Froot Loops experimenter. "Estrogen could play a role in learning and
memory, which would aid multitasking and make it easier, but it could also
be related to dopamine, which helps with focus, attention, and reward."[19]

Women avoid conflict. Because the female brain is soaked in estrogen and
not in testosterone, women are more likely than men to be focused on emotion and social communication and sustaining close bonds. They prefer to
avoid arguments and fights and rifts, in their family or with their friends
or lovers or even at work. The male brain, which is drenched in testosterone, tends to be much more fascinated by conflict and anger and contests
of comparison. Who is bigger? Who is stronger? Who is faster? Who is
longer? Any numerical contest fascinates those with male brains. In men's
brains, the amygdala, a regulator of fear, anger, and aggression, is larger
than it is in women's brains. This, along with higher testosterone levels,
means that men tend to be like a short fuse on a long stick. It's not manly
to duck a fight—and for good reason, since men are wired to want to tussle,
often with those sticks.

It comes as no surprise, then, that women and men might react to stress
very differently. Just a century ago, scientific wisdom had it that human

beings either fight or run away when under stress. This was called the *fight-or-flight* response, and aside from rhyming nicely, it seemed to make a lot of sense. But more recent research shows that this is the way that *men*, not women, react to threats. While men are likely to punch or lash out when stressed, women are much more likely to try to talk their way out of a problem, to use coercion and flattery and verbal stroking to avoid conflict. Instead of fighting or fleeing, they "tend and befriend."[20]

When threatened, both women and men undergo a powerful hormonal rush, but it is simply not practical for most women either to fight or to run away, especially if they have small children to protect. For men, the urge to fight is aided by an extra surge of testosterone, which men's brains produce in stressful situations. But under stress women's brains release oxytocin, a neurochemical that fosters bonding and tenderness rather than aggression and anger. Thus, it is to women's evolutionary advantage, and it is rigged into their hormonal guidance system, to seek help from other women, to care for those who can't care for themselves, and to try, if possible, to talk themselves out of danger.

Superior wives, then, use the gift of conflict avoidance to keep from being sidetracked from family organization and management. They can be more efficient and make better decisions if they are not distracted by disagreements and squabbles, resentment and angry feelings. It's not that such wives don't experience conflict or rage or irritation, it's just that they are better able than many men to put such sentiments into perspective and to avoid becoming derailed from their central purpose. And that purpose is to manage family life, and to manage it well.

The Social Rules of Superior Wives

If the brain rules the body, then family and culture propel people to behave within their neurochemical guidelines. It's true that social rules define our beliefs and attitudes and expectations about gender roles, but they do so in a way that is consistent with biology. Our feelings and thoughts and opinions are subject not only to social approval and current social trends but also to biological imperatives. The brain leads us along a culturally acceptable path.

In the United States, social expectations about the proper roles for wives and husbands have changed over the past several decades. Most newlyweds in 1950 or 1960 assumed that the husband would become the breadwinner and the wife would become the homemaker, and their behavior supported those beliefs. In the 1960s, 90 percent of husbands were in the labor force, compared to 30 percent of wives, most of whom were working-class or minority women. Back then, wives spent an average of forty hours a week doing housework and child care; their husbands spent an average of eleven hours. By 1985 more wives were working, but they were still doing about thirty hours a week of domestic work, compared to fifteen hours for husbands.[21] Couples were still following the old rules: the man's job was paid work; the woman's job was the home, even if she also worked for pay.

Today many newlyweds express very different beliefs, waving a banner of household equality. They expect to share household chores and also to share responsibility for earning money. Theirs is an everybody-should-do-everything ethos, although they are not quite practicing what they preach.

In my Web survey, for instance, six in ten wives say that when they first married, they expected to share household chores; even more husbands, seven in ten, thought they'd be doing the same. Likewise, eight in ten wives and husbands say they expected to share responsibility for earning an income when they were first married. The new "shoulds" are as clear, and as different, from those of the past as they could possibly be. National polls show that an overwhelming majority of Americans, both women and men, now agree that "a husband whose wife is working full time should spend just as many hours doing housework as his wife." Likewise, the vast majority believe that "both the husband and wife should contribute to the family income."[22]

This is what American wives and husbands *believe*, although it's not necessarily what they *do*.

Rebecca, twenty-six, a teacher from the progressive city of Eugene, Oregon, assumed when she married, two years ago, that both she and her husband would share all household responsibilities, the dishwashing and the money earning alike. Although she and her husband make about the same amount of money, she says, "I have a work schedule with more flexible hours, so I pay the bills and I do the budget and the housework more often than my husband. Generally, I am also the one to make plans with my family, write thank-you letters, correspond with friends and family, make appointments, pay the bills, and clean out the refrigerator. Despite the fact that my husband and I believe that the division of labor should be equal, he is still the first person to initiate a new electrical installation, and I will always make sure there is enough milk in the fridge. We gravitate towards the socially prescribed jobs for our respective genders," she adds. This upsets her, because she thought they'd be different, not tied to traditional gender chores. But it's almost as if they just can't help themselves, Rebecca says.

Indeed, Rebecca's situation is common in many marriages, since not nearly as many husbands share chores as they expected on their wedding day. In 2003 wives were doing thirty-two hours a week of child care and household chores, compared to seventeen hours for husbands, more than they used to do but still not nearly on a par with wives.[23] Even though the phrase "being a homemaker" now seems quaint and rather stale, like something out of a black-and-white movie, many wives are still doing that job—only they're working too. Fifty-nine percent of American wives are in the labor force, as are 75 percent of husbands.[24] This figure—the proportion of married men who work—has decreased significantly over the last few decades. Apparently, now that more wives are working for pay, fewer husbands are doing so.

In many cases, in fact, husbands have become "marital moochers," giving up work altogether when they can no longer find a job that's good enough or that pays well enough. One out of eight American men between the ages of thirty and fifty-four is *not working,* the largest number in at least fifty years. Most often these men have no college degree, and they end up either divorced or being supported by their wives.[25] Their number will surely grow whenever the economy weakens.

The all-American, wedding-day belief about gender roles in marriage— that everybody should do everything—has not caught up to domestic and workplace reality. In a way, life was easier and simpler a half century ago, when just about everybody in the middle class believed that men should be breadwinners and women should be homemakers, and that's the way almost everybody behaved too. Now that there's a chasm between what couples believe and what they actually do, that rift has forced women to become superior.

Superior wives must step in where husbands fear to tread, doing what needs to be done, because it's biologically easier for them and because the social "shoulds" require it. Most superior wives say they do more than they ever expected, both at home and at work. But men are aware of the new social rules, which dictate that that they *should* be sharing, so in their imagination, *they are sharing*. They are domestic legends in their own mind: every time they move a single load of laundry to the dryer, they are doing all of the laundry. Every time they read a bedtime story, they are always putting the children to sleep. Every time they scramble eggs on Sunday, they are cooking family meals. Indeed, men consistently overestimate their contributions at home in just about every study on the topic, including my own.[26] While 85 percent of wives in my Web survey say that they are the family expert on taking care of the house, 61 percent of husbands believe that they themselves are. Likewise, eight in ten wives say they're the ones who know how to cook a decent meal; but six in ten husbands believe that's their role. And while nine in ten wives say they're the spouse who is most adept at talking about feelings, seven in ten husbands insist that's their strength. For the most part, I believe the wives' side of the story, based on their lengthy, written explanations of how their families really work. (Don't worry, I allow men to tell their side of the story in chapter 4.)

This credibility gap exemplifies men's refusal to perceive how superior their wives really are. That reality simply doesn't jibe with their beliefs and expectations about what they should be doing, so they choose to ignore it. Although she hates to face this truth, that's what Angelica's husband, Charlie, does. "My husband comes from a family where the mom worked and still did all the cooking and cleaning," says Angelica, thirty, manager of an after-school program just north of Seattle, Washington. "Now when he comes home, he tends to take the fact that I do the same for granted. There are times when he doesn't think twice about what I do or the reason I do it. To Charlie, some things are just 'a woman's work,' like packing his lunch, doing his laundry, and making the bed." For Angelica, it is Charlie's definition of femininity and notion of womanly labor that are in need of repair, not her own insistence on overworking herself.

Like Charlie, many men have trouble ridding themselves of old-fashioned, outdated notions about gender roles, about what is masculine and what is feminine. Women are actually more open-minded and flexible when it comes to what social scientists call *gender identity*—the ways in which people think about what it means to be a man or a woman. In traditional thought, masculinity means being strong and aggressive and independent; femininity means being weak and submissive and compliant. These concepts are not written in stone, and they can change, depending on time and place and culture. Indeed, anthropologists often illustrate the flexibility of gender identity by using extreme, antithetical examples from obscure corners of the globe. Thus, they cite a small tribe in New Guinea, for instance, whose members are all uniformly passive and gentle and co-operative, both the men and the women. And they point to another tribe, equally small and remote, in which both genders are extremely aggressive and violent.[27] The experts conclude that being feminine doesn't have to mean being frail and delicate, nor does being masculine have to mean the opposite.

But usually it does.

Indeed, in most cultures around the world, most people believe in gender stereotypes; that is, they view masculinity as synonymous with being strong and aggressive and femininity with being weak and passive.[28] Social scientists first began to study such notions of gender identity in the 1930s. In those days, women were considered feminine if they liked "babies" and "charades" and the word "nursing" and agreed that they were "often afraid of the dark" and preferred "someone else to take the lead." Men were considered masculine for preferring "hunting" and people "with loud voices" and for saying that when young they were "extremely disobedient" and that they could "stand as much pain" as anybody else.[29] This neolithic test was used, in some form or another, for decades, eventually producing the following list, which was used in a widely circulated test to measure American standards of masculinity and femininity forty years ago:[30]

Feminine	Masculine
Difficulty making decisions	Make decisions easily
Not ambitious	Very ambitious
Very quiet	Very loud
Very submissive	Very dominant
Very passive	Very active
Very aware of the feelings of others	Not at all aware of feelings of others

This notion, that masculinity and femininity are mutually exclusive polar opposites, was sharply criticized in the 1970s, when researchers decided that the two categories should be inclusive, or at least more flexible. In response, psychologists decided to invent a third gender category, which they called *androgyny*. This was to be the future of gender identity in America; it would replace outdated notions of masculinity and femininity with a highly improved gender-neutral state. They dreamed of combining the best of masculine and feminine to produce androgyny, an ideal state of in-betweenness. They were hoping to discover this new truth:

$$M(asculine) + F(eminine) = A(ndrogyny).^{31}$$

The only problem, though, was that the formula didn't really work. The research showed that most American girls and boys, as well as American women and men, continued to feel that being masculine meant being aggressive and strong and that being feminine meant being soft and sensitive. People liked and approved of such predictable gender differences, in fact, because they didn't have to spend time figuring them out. Few people thought of themselves, or of anybody they knew, as being gender neutral. After a while, most social scientists gave up on the idea of androgyny, and almost no one studies it anymore. Androgyny research has become a relic of the 1970s, like macramé belts, hip-hugging bell-bottoms, and psychedelic rock music.

Today standards of masculinity and femininity survive, though in slightly more modern, more realistic forms. In my research, for instance, I find that wives tend to be more open-minded about gender than husbands are. A majority of wives in my research say that ambition and strength can be both masculine and feminine, but they are also more convinced than men that being emotional, self-sacrificing, and sensitive are feminine qualities. This is not surprising, since so many women are working, earning at least half, or more, of the family income. Such working wives have a need to consider themselves old-school feminine, but they also want to feel strong and ambitious and powerful in the world. They are flexible enough to be able to think of themselves as feminine at home, where they are warm and caring, but as masculine at work, where they are determined and driven. Wives can encompass two different worlds and two different ways of being and thinking rather easily. Husbands tend to have more difficulty doing so.

American husbands are much more likely than wives to view being aggressive, ambitious, and strong as solely masculine qualities, though some concede that being ambitious might also be feminine. In addition, the more money a man earns, the more likely he is to believe in traditional forms of masculinity. Men in my Web survey who earn more than seventy or eighty thousand dollars a year tend to say that someone who is aggressive and ambitious and strong is quite manly and that these traits are not feminine. Overall, it seems that men have an inability to compartmentalize their view of gender roles, either for themselves or for women. They have trouble viewing a man as masculine who is tender and sensitive at home, yet aggressive and dominant at work. Some do believe, however, that being self-sacrificing can be both masculine and feminine, in part because they view their own sacrifices as substantial. Wives are less likely to agree with this view, since they don't believe that masculinity requires much sacrifice at all.

The growing gap between wives' somewhat progressive views on gender identity and their husbands' relative rigidity about gender identity contributes to superior wives' sense of irritation, anger, and resentment. But

Gender Differences in Views on Gender

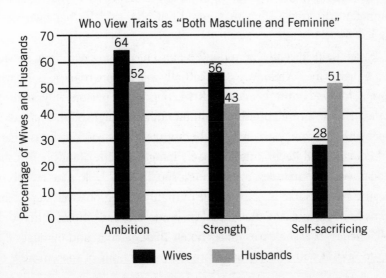

Who View Traits as "Both Masculine and Feminine"

superior wives have a serious gender issue problem, since they are more likely than other women to feel that being emotional, self-sacrificing, and sensitive are exclusively feminine traits. It's as if their inability to abandon a belief in stereotypical female roles gets in their way and drags them down, compelling them to become superior, even if it flies against many of their other beliefs. One wife tells me that she is incensed that her husband, who takes pride in his extreme and conventional manliness, "is so busy competing and running his daily rat race that he doesn't value our family." He can't turn off his testosterone flow when he gets home, she believes, so he's an aggressive, dominant male wherever he goes. Meanwhile, she's trapped by her belief that a feminine woman is one who sacrifices her own needs for the sake of her family, which is exactly what she does. Another typical working wife is infuriated by her husband's unspoken assumption that it's her job to have a job, but it's also her job to cook, her job to deal with doctors, her job to invite the family for his birthday. Meanwhile his only job is his job. His outlook reflects a male inability to adjust to different gender roles and rules when appropriate, to be flexible depending on the situation.

This is already Melody's problem, only two years after her wedding day. Thirty-two years old and a theater professor at a small college in central Vermont, Melody is married to another newly minted professor, also just out of graduate school. He is mired in student debt, a four-hundred-dollar-a-month tab that they can't afford. Melody hates dealing with money, so she lets her husband control it, although she's actually more financially competent than he is, having figured out how to defer her own student loans.

"Since he deals with the money, he also has more say in how it's spent, which upsets me," Melody says. "I actually make more than he does, which I suspect bothers him, because he's a very prideful person." She continues by saying that "our relationship is almost embarrassingly old-fashioned. He's good with cars and carpentry and computers. I'm good at housekeeping and cooking and decorating and socializing." Melody allows her husband to deal with the finances, even though she'd probably do a better job of it, because it seems like his last vestige of manly power, one that her husband seems to need, and one that would be borderline castrating for her to control. The fact that she earns more money than he does, and manages it better, doesn't fit with her husband's traditional notions of masculinity, even though that's the reality in their marriage. This bothers her, but Melody works hard at trying to disguise the truth, for her husband's sake.

Ideas about masculinity and femininity around the world are remarkably similar to the standard American model. Men and women in twenty-five countries, including the Netherlands, Germany, Venezuela, Pakistan, India, Japan, and Bolivia, rate being active and strong and dominant as masculine traits and being passive, weak, and nurturing as feminine traits.[32] These are stereotypes for a reason: they are wild generalizations that everybody can agree upon, even if nobody actually behaves that way. It's the *ideal idea* of gender, rather than the *actual reality* of gender.

The reality, in many of these countries, is that women have, in fact, adopted masculine traits, like independence and assertiveness, in their everyday lives. That's because women have been forced by social circumstance to become more traditionally masculine, in places as different as the United States, Brazil, and Chile, for example. In many parts of the world, women are working full-time, they are living in cities, and they are actively participating in politics, all of which help to expand women's traditional views on femininity. After a military coup in Chile, for example, the government allowed only women to gather in public places, foolishly assuming that such meetings would not be threatening. As it turned out, though, women were the ones who led the country's successful resistance movement. As a result, perhaps, Chilean women now say that feminine women can have masculine traits, like being competitive, daring, and courageous.[33]

If women around the world have expanded their views about what it means to be a woman, and if they recognize the ways in which men have not caught up to them, then there should be a growing number of superior wives around the world, not just in the United States. That's certainly true in Latin cultures. In Brazil, for example, the rule of masculinity, or *machismo*, is prevalent and extreme, a concept that emphasizes male power, dominance, and sexual aggression. A corollary, sometimes known as *marianismo*, holds that women should be pious, submissive, self-sacrificing, and obedient wives and mothers.[34] These gender roles seem as if they would not be open to change, but that's dead wrong. Both are cultural masks, and they hide a new reality that lurks just beneath the surface: wifely superiority actually thrives in places like Brazil, even though it may be barely acknowledged.

How many Brazilian wives are superior?

"Oh, it's like ninety percent," says Silvia Koller, a psychology professor at the Federal University of Rio Grande del Sul, only half joking. "Women are in charge, and it's changing our society. More women work, and we are also keeping up the traditional roles. We are stronger and more powerful than any man," she tells me, "and in the end, we take care of everything."

Perceptive Brazilian men agree. A fifty-four-year-old truck driver from Rio de Janeiro told me that this is certainly true in his family. "My wife has always been the head of our house. We men don't admit that toward the friends, but this is the truth!" he said, in accurate but irregular English, about his twenty-five-year-long second marriage.

"It's a very *machista* society in Brazil, so this man would never admit to his friends that his wife dominates him," Koller comments. "Inside the house, though, women rule."[35]

Brazilian wives like Luzia concur. Luzia, thirty-eight, is a cheerful, hefty woman, with big, curly hair and huge, dangling silver earrings, so long that they rest on her shoulders. She has a broad, dark face and wears skin-tight, calf-length jeans. Luzia works two jobs as a housekeeper in Rio de Janeiro, supporting her two sons and a second, common-law husband, who is unemployed. She met him ten years ago at a neighborhood barbecue in the favela where she lives and liked him right away, she says, because he didn't seem like so many other men, whose only goal in life is chasing women. She calls such men *conquistadores*, which is Portuguese for men who consider it their duty to chase and subdue women, regardless of whether they are married or not.

"In my first marriage, my husband did *nada, nada, nada*, for five years," Luzia says. "He had a good job, but our marriage did not work out. He was very *machista* and thought that I should be responsible for cooking and cleaning and working. Women do everything because they are good at it, and they do things out of love. The difference between men and women is that women are more willing to learn something new, they're more adaptable. Men have a job, they learn how to do it, and that's all they want to have to do. Men think that on the weekends, it's their right to play cards, watch soccer, and drink beer."

Luzia stayed married to the card-playing, soccer-watching, beer-drinking husband just long enough to have two sons, and then she left. "Now it takes me two hours to get to work and two hours to get home every day, and I work five days, eight hours a day," she explains. Because he is jobless, her new man cooks dinner during the week, and she cooks on weekends. Even that concession, she says, took a great deal of persuasion, and he gets teased by friends, who say, "If you're a man, why are you doing all that?"

That, of course, is the public stance in Brazil, but in the privacy of the home, many superior wives are like Luzia, in charge of the family and angry about the situation. "I buy the children's clothes and I get their school supplies and I take them to the dentist and doctor and I deal with all the medical bills," Luzia says. "When my husband was working, we split everything equally, but now I am responsible for paying for everything. He goes to pay the bills, though, with my money, because everything is in his name," she adds, slightly annoyed by the situation. In Rio, where Luzia lives, residents have to pay bills in person, not by mail, and only the person whose name is on the account can pay.

Multitasking is Luzia's middle name, and she does it "*sempre, sempre!* I never do just one thing at a time. I have no washing machine, so I have the food on the stove, and I go outside and do my cleaning in a tank, by hand. My husband can only do one thing at a time. If he's cooking, he gets nervous if the children are even in the house," she says, laughing. "And he can cook chicken, but only if I take the whole chicken and cut it up for him," she adds.

The fact that gender stereotypes are somewhat similar almost everywhere in the world implies that these characteristics must be partly hardwired into the brain, by hormones and by neurochemistry. Cultures and countries enhance and embellish these differences, of course, imposing their own distinct attitudes and feelings about masculinity and femininity. Eventually, these views are absorbed and internalized by individual women and men, wives and husbands. It is in this way—with a triple play of biology, sociology, and psychology—that superior wives are fashioned.

The Inner Lives of Superior Wives

Most women don't really think of themselves as being controlled by hormones or neurons, or even by the invisible social rules and regulations that actually govern modern life. They believe that their actions and feelings are based on the way they were raised and on their own unique "personality." If they bother to think about it at all, women who are superior wives probably think it's because they have a "superior wife personality."

Despite what many people may believe, however, personality is almost always influenced by both biology and culture. It is shaped and molded by these powerful forces, then transformed into something that becomes personal and unique. It's like what happens when you mix flour, eggs, sugar, and butter, put the batter in the oven, and end up with a warm, freshly baked cake. The cake is similar to every other cake made with the same recipe, only it is also slightly distinct, depending on how well you creamed the butter and sugar and how much vanilla you added and how far above sea level your oven is. Likewise, superior wives become who they are by a complicated combination of neurochemistry and culture, family and society, as well as individual personality.

Superior wives are mostly alike, having very similar personality traits, but each is also slightly different in her own way.

Personality is certainly complex, but psychologists have been studying the issue for decades, and many have concluded that there are at least five basic personality traits. These traits are present at birth and last a lifetime, although they are influenced somewhat by how people are raised and the environment in which they grow up. The attributes are universal around the globe, and they are distributed differently in men and women no matter where they live, according to a comprehensive study conducted in twenty-six countries.[36] The five fundamental personality traits are *neuroticism, agreeableness, openness to experience, conscientiousness,* and *extraversion.* It turns out that women score higher in neuroticism than men do, in countries as diverse as the United States and Zimbabwe, India, Norway, Croatia, Peru, Spain, and Malaysia. Women are more prone to be anxious, depressed, self-conscious, and vulnerable, and that's true no matter where they live. Women score higher on agreeableness too, a mouthful of an awkward word that means they are more likely than men to show trust, altruism, compliance, and modesty, and to be forgiving and straightforward. Finally, women score higher on extraversion, which means that they are warmer and more gregarious than men and more likely to express positive emotions. If these traits sound familiar, that's because they are: many of these attributes correspond to the biologically based gender differences that

I mentioned earlier, including being more social, more verbal, and more empathic.

These particular personality traits seem ideal for producing superior wives, women who are worried about doing what's best for their family and who act as the emotional caretakers for everybody they love. Not all women are extremely extraverted, for example, but in general, they tend to be the spouse who is the caring caterer, squared. Perhaps that's why, in fact, women actually feel more distress than men do: not only are they better able to talk about and mull over their bad feelings, *they actually feel unhappy or sad, worried or anxious, more often than men do.*[37] We know that women speak the language of anguish and despair quite well: they can articulate these feelings as fluently as a United Nations translator can speak English and French and Spanish. But it seems that the reason they are so conversant in sorrow and regret is that the feelings are familiar to them. Women are experienced at mining their misery.

But women are also more likely than men to feel angry, despite the gender stereotype that it's women who get depressed and men who get angry. Not so, according to one study that finds that women feel irritated and angry more often than men do and are more likely to yell at someone when they get angry. "Depression is anger's companion," the researchers say, "not its substitute."[38] As we'll see, superior wives are angry wives, although many try to suppress or ignore their feelings of hostility and irritation.

Superior wives are particularly adept at recognizing their own distress, especially when their need for warmth and companionship is thwarted. "My husband is an excellent father and friend, but he does not know how to support me emotionally," says Tanisha, twenty-five, who works full-time as a paralegal and goes to law school at night. "He just doesn't pay attention, and he's very immature. He's like the class clown, impulsive and selfish, but I think things through. I always feel like I need more from him than I get."

Tanisha and her husband earn about the same amount, but she does all the family's organizing and planning, child rearing and relative visiting, cooking and cleaning, and she also manages their finances. She desperately needs support and kind words from her husband, especially when she's taking exams or writing papers, but he is deaf to her pleas. "Sometimes I sit him down and say, 'Baby, I could really use your help right now,'" she says, "but that rarely works."

Superior wives who've been married much longer than Tanisha sing the same song of woe. "It's the same old story" is the way Lois, forty-six, of Cincinnati, Ohio, puts it. Married for twenty-two years, Lois says that she just naturally talks more than her husband, "and I think sometimes he tunes me out. He tries to listen when I am upset, but most of the time he doesn't bother, so I have learned to talk to my mother or to my sisters if I need to get something off my chest." Lois makes excuses for her husband's emotional distance, saying that his family business is demanding and at the end of the day, "he's all 'listened up.'" Anyway, she says, it's her job to take care of him, now that their children are grown, so that's exactly what she's doing, while ignoring his inability to meet her emotional needs.

Both Tanisha and Lois would probably score high on the agreeableness test, and on extraversion too. And both believe that they give more than their husbands, as do more than half the superior wives from my Web survey. Indeed, only 16 percent of husbands believe they are the ones who give more to the relationship. Many superior wives who give more are tired of doing all the work, of carrying the conversation, of trying so hard, of being the one who does the encouraging and the supporting and the expressing of feelings. After a while, all that exertion—while getting so little in return—becomes exhausting. It feels unjust, like taxation without reciprocation.

"It seems to me that I work hard at our marriage, and he just sort of expects everything to come to him in a pretty package," explains Lily, twenty-nine, a pharmacy technician from St. Louis, Missouri. "I am taking eleven credit hours at college, while working full-time and maintaining the house," she says, adding that she also pays the bills, buys the groceries, cleans the house, cares for the cat, does the laundry, cooks, and washes the dishes by hand. "I love him," Lily says, "but I don't understand how we ended up this way, after being married for four years."

Another central personality issue for some superior wives is the overwhelming power of their need to please. In American society, little girls are often raised to be "sugar and spice and everything nice," no matter how smart or ambitious or athletic they are. Even when wives try to fight their impulse for niceness, they are often unable to resist it. It's as if they were bewitched, under some kind of "Please Everybody" magic spell, a siren song that enchants them to believe that their primary goal in life should be to make everybody else happy. Maybe that's why one in ten wives in my Web survey are convinced that their family situation is a result of their own need to please.

This kind of thinking, by the way, could be why women are more likely than men to be depressed. Cue the chorus of neuroticism here: it heralds the grand entrance of sadness, self-pity, and gloom. Researchers say that women who are highly dependent—who rely on others for their sense of self-worth and well-being—are also the women most prone to depression. You are overdependent if you tend to be clingy and submissive, if you are in constant fear of separation, if you are desperate to be physically close to your man, and if you yearn to be protected by him. Overdependent women are also desperately afraid of being criticized or disapproved of, by him or just about anybody else they know.[39] A dependent woman, basically, is one who is extremely needy, whose longing for closeness is so strong that she often drives away the very people she wants to keep nearby. It's as if she yearns to maintain an irresistible attraction, only she's got the polarity all wrong, so she keeps repelling her man instead of attracting him.

Wives who, desperate to please, love their husbands more than they are loved in return actually produce more stress hormones than other wives when they have a marital spat. Women who feel this kind of possessive, all-consuming love—if it keeps them awake at night, or if it gives them stomach pains, or if they can't concentrate or relax when they're not with their lover—are much more likely to be stressed and are prone to getting physically sick after a marital spat. A group of psychologists proved this by studying seventy-two newlywed couples, questioning them about their love for each other and testing their blood for stress hormone levels. The less emotional power a wife has in her relationship, the researchers say, the sicker she gets when things aren't going well at home.[40] It's as if the fact that her relationship is unbalanced makes her more vulnerable to physical problems.

It's probably not surprising that such depressed wives are more likely to be in unhappy marriages, but it's also true that unhappy wives are more likely to be depressed. It's not clear, though, which comes first—the chicken of depression or the egg of unhappy marriage—since the two can operate in an endless, no-exit cycle. She's depressed, so her marriage seems bad, which makes her depressed. What happens in such marriages— many of which include a superior wife—is that wives eventually silence themselves to save the marriage. They keep their thoughts and despair to themselves, losing their own voice in the process. Or they try another approach, confronting their husband, to demand changes and improvements. Quite often, though, that's when husbands withdraw.[41] So when a superior wife wants to talk about the reasons she's unhappy and how she and her husband might become closer or how he might do more around the house, he becomes desperate to avoid the confrontation and shuts down completely by clamming up, leaving the room, going to sleep, or turning on the television. She persists in trying to entice him, to engage him in serious conversation, and he persists in deterring and avoiding. This cycle is quite common in American marriages, with the wife as the demander and the husband as the avoider, but it is equally widespread among couples in countries as diverse as Brazil, Italy, and Taiwan.[42] (I discuss this dynamic in greater detail in chapter 5.)

Zahira, thirty-one, a Muslim immigrant from India, is an example of a superior and depressed wife. She lives in rural Maryland, and although she has a master's degree in nursing, she stays home with her two children because her traditional husband prefers it this way. Meanwhile, she is lonely and bored, and her husband does not respond to her pleas for relief. "As a wife, I think we should be equal, but I am frustrated being at home all the time with the kids and having to do everything he tells me to do," she says. "He is so into his work all the time, and he does not understand the depression that has hit me," Zahira says. "He says, 'Well, this is your job, and this is what I want for a wife, so deal with it.' I can cry, shout, or scream, but nothing changes his mind."

Zahira has little leverage for her demands, since she has no income of her own and the family is in the United States on her husband's work visa; she's at his mercy. He gets to decide who does what when, he has the right to evade her pleas, and he decrees that she should stay at home while he goes to work. It's no wonder that Zahira is depressed, since she'd rather be out of the house and working. Because she is an at-home wife, not by her own choice, she's miserable.

Although Zahira's situation as an immigrant wife in America may be unusual, her situation as a financially dependent wife is not. In fact, I find that the more money a husband earns, the more likely it is that his wife will be superior. Superior wives are married to men who earn significantly more money than the husbands of wives who are not superior. It's as if men who earn big bucks feel exempt from doing anything other than bringing home a paycheck. Indeed, the size of that paycheck is a marker of marital power for men, but not for wives. To many husbands, the larger the number behind the dollar sign, the more manly they feel, since their self-worth is based on how much money they bring home. It's not as if most men have reasoned this out: it's an unconscious assumption, one that is expressed through their attitudes and behavior at home. They delude themselves into feeling in control, because they view it as a right, because "I'm the bread-winner" or "I supply most of the income." They don't really need to think about the symbolic meaning of money, in the same way that they don't need to think about being a football fan or a fantasy baseball addict. It's simply a given to them that more money means more control.

Wives don't usually base their feelings of self-esteem on how much money they earn, however. Being a superior wife is *not* related to a woman's own income, and most wives do not view their earnings as a mirror of their value as a human being. They bring home the bacon, and they move on. Try as I might to find a connection between women's salary and their superiority, there just isn't one. Money simply doesn't matter to wives in the way it does to husbands. But it does play an important role in the nature and form their marriage takes. There are four types of modern marriage, based on how much money wives earn relative to their husbands' income, as we'll see in the following chapter.

3

The Four Marriage Types

Superior wives are born, biologically endowed with natural abilities, but they are also made, by cultural expectations and by personal circumstance. Superior wives are blessed with special talents, which they are proud to use every day. A wife does not become superior by accident or aberration; she's designed by biology and influenced by the circumstances of her life, which include the place and time in which she lives, as well as her education and social class.

Now that a vast tidal wave of wives has entered the workforce, many superior wives are also working wives. More wives are now working outside the home than at any time since the turn of the last century, in the year 1900.[1] (Women have always worked inside the home, of course, and they still do: that's part of what makes them superior.) Because more wives are working, more are earning their own money for the first time. And the money is complicating their lives somewhat, since money is a hidden source of marital power and a potential cause of marital conflict. In addition, there is now a widespread American expectation that wives *should* work for pay, that both wife and husband *should* share the responsibility for breadwinning. Thus, when wives don't work, some feel grateful that they can be home with their children, while others feel guilty for not working. Among wives who work for pay, some feel resentful about having to leave their children every day, while others feel relieved about being able to escape. The variations on how wives react to working or not working are almost endless, but it's surely a given that all wives have strong feelings about their work status.

"I have a lot of guilt that my husband is the only breadwinner, though I am the one most emotionally tuned in to my sons, and I put their needs before my own," says Vicky, forty-one, a Florida wife who expected to continue to work when she got married eighteen years ago but who, instead, quit her job after her children were born. "I feel bad that I do not contribute, because I do not make a salary," she adds. Her husband, who earns more than $100,000 a year and travels four days out of every fourteen, is often condescending and critical, she says, because the floors are not as spotless as he would like and the rugs not as steam-cleaned perfect. If only she had her own paycheck, Vicky believes, he wouldn't be so annoyed about her housekeeping skills. As it is, though, she doesn't feel that she has a right to protest about his criticism.

Husbands like Vicky's seem to resent their wife for not bringing home a paycheck. "I work and she plays, and she's got a cushy life and she knows it," says Tony, thirty-seven, a medical device salesman whose wife stays home with their two children. Though he got married expecting that his bride would always have a paying job, she quit work and now spends her days "doing things she wants to do," Tony says. "I do the have-tos and she does the want-tos" is how he puts it, his resentment profound and undisguised.

You might expect that wives like Tony's would not be superior, since the home is their only domain. But this is not true, according to my research. It turns out that superior wives are equally likely to be at home as to work; they can earn less than, as much as, or more than their husbands. Thus, there's no way to predict whether a woman will be a superior wife based on her income.

Superior wives run the gamut, from earning no income on their own, to being the supplementary earner, to being the only breadwinner. Wives are all equally likely to be superior, *no matter what their work situation or their income.* The superior wife phenomenon is *not* about disgruntled and angry housewives who pour all their pent-up frustration into taking charge. Nor is it about frantic working wives who try to assuage their feelings of guilt about not being at-home moms. The trend is much more complicated and much more pervasive.

There is, however, a relationship between wives' superiority and their *husbands'* income. *The more money a husband earns, the more likely his wife is to be superior,* according to my Web survey. Superior wives are married to men who earn on average about 11 percent more than do husbands married to nonsuperior wives, I find. It's as if men who earn a hefty wage are convinced that this fact exempts them from any and all other family responsibility, no matter how much their wives also earn. In this passive yet antagonistic way, they are compelling their wives to become the expert at every domestic chore and household task and parental responsibility they refuse to master. They're doing the only job that matters to them, which is bringing in the big bucks, according to their way of thinking. As far as they're concerned, they don't have to sweat the small stuff, since they have a wife to do that. For many high-earning husbands, then, a woman's job includes everything but bringing home the big bacon.

High-earning wives, however, don't abdicate their superior status, nor do they use their financial prowess to bargain themselves out of doing chores and making domestic decisions the way high-earning husbands do. Wives in the top income brackets, those who earn more than fifty or seventy-five thousand dollars a year, are no less likely to be superior than wives who earn much less, according to my research.

Quite simply, money matters more to men.

While it may sound like a banal fortune cookie sentiment or maybe a clichéd tee shirt slogan, the fact that men revere money is the most important rule of modern marital life. While women also care about money, and worry about it, men are especially enamored of obsessing over their earnings. Any figures following a dollar sign are almost guaranteed to fascinate men. Because of their systematizing brains, men are drawn to the structure that numbers provide, which is why they love competitions that count goals, runs, baskets, time in milliseconds, and touchdowns, or any outcome of any contest that has numbers attached. That's why men are so passionate about baseball and hockey, football and basketball games, race times and poker hands, stock market prices and the history of their own take-home pay. Anything related to figures and decimal points and rankings turns men on; it's a brain-given fondness, generally speaking. Wives may feel this way too, but it's less important for them, since keeping score with dollars and cents doesn't entrance them as deeply.

Although work and income do not influence wives' marital superiority, their work status strongly influences how they live their lives. There are four basic variations on the working wife theme, and each one includes a different way of life for the wife. The proportion of women in each type of marriage will fluctuate according to a particular country's economic situation, birthrate, and incidence of divorce, but these four marriage types are here to stay. Wives will not be quitting their jobs en masse and returning to the kitchen anytime soon. Likewise, there will never be a day when every single American wife will feel compelled to find a full-time job. There will always be wives who don't work for pay, while there will always be others who earn varying portions of the family income.

This wide range of work options for wives—from all to nothing at all—is relatively recent. Just a few generations ago, the only job that many women would ever have was to be a wife. "Marriage offers the best career that the average woman can reasonably aspire to" is the way H. L. Mencken put it, ignoring all women who were not middle- or upper-class. The sardonic newspaperman's view, presumably quite common in the early 1900s, was that it would be pointless to hire a woman for any real job, since "no sane man, seeking a woman for a post requiring laborious training and unremitting diligence, would select a woman still definitely young and marriageable." He added that the only women who could possibly be decent workers were those too old to marry, with no hope of snaring a bridegroom. They worked because they had no other choice, he said.[2]

If Mencken could witness the number of wives who have jobs today, well paid and not, his mind would be utterly boggled. A majority of wives and single women now have careers that require extensive training and diligence. And they're doing rather well too, since they no longer have to rely on a husband for economic security. The care of a husband is no longer a wife's primary or only job. It's possible that Mencken would have approved of this new reality, since he also believed that women were far superior to men. Every man needs a woman, he said, "to rule him and think for him" because man is "a truly lamentable spectacle: a baby with whiskers."[3]

Married to a bewhiskered infant or not, six in ten American wives were working in 2007, as were 71 percent of wives with children under the age of eighteen, according to the Bureau of Labor Statistics. Although women still don't earn as much as men do, their relative income has been creeping up, slowly and surely. Thirty years ago, in 1979, women working full-time earned 62 percent of what men did. Today they earn 80 percent of men's income. Both Asian women and white women make more than the median weekly income of $614, at $731 and $629, respectively. Black women and Hispanic women earn less than that, $533 and $473, respectively. What would probably shock the shorts right off Mencken, though, is that among working wives whose husbands also work, about *one in four now earns more money than he does*.[4]

Breadwinning is no longer just a manly thing, it's a family thing, though wives tend to be the ones who earn less and who work less. "The overwhelming majority of couples still include wives who work fewer hours and whose career is secondary to their husbands'," agrees Sara Raley, a sociologist who has done extensive research on dual-earner marriages. But the days when most wives stayed at home and their husbands won the bread are not only gone, they are gone forever, she believes. "There is an economic incentive for wives to work, to raise the family's standard of living," she argues. "Wives need to be able to support themselves too, in case some economic shock happens to the family, like divorce or death. And there is the intangible fulfillment that comes from work, which has more social status than staying at home, and one that makes women feel that they are contributing to society."[5]

Even when wives earn their own income, money is still one of the primary sources of contention and tension among married couples. Now that so many wives are working, more of them wield the financial sword of marital power, which is based on who manages the family money and who earns more of it. Fifty-five percent of the wives in my Web survey say they manage the family finances, which seems to have become a social norm, since several other recent studies reveal similar findings. In a *Money* magazine survey of five hundred wives and five hundred husbands, for instance, 57 percent of wives say they pay the bills, 59 percent say they do the family budget, and 64 percent control the day-to-day spending.[6] In another national study, this one conducted over several decades and including thirty-three thousand Americans, wives say they pay the bills 61 percent of the time.[7] Even an international study finds that the more women earn, the more control they have over the money and the less likely husbands are to manage it. This pattern is common in the twenty-one countries the researchers studied, which include the United States, Great Britain, Canada, Hungary, Italy, Japan, Bulgaria, the Czech Republic, and Russia.[8]

But what's most remarkable about married couples and their money—and also somewhat comical—is that, apparently, almost none of them can agree on exactly *how much money* they earn or have. The precise amount seems to elude both women and men. Wives say they earn more than their husbands say the wives earn; husbands report that they earn more than their wives say they do. Thus, neither group agrees on how much the other one makes. Not only that, but half of couples disagree, by a large margin, about their assets. Wives estimate the family assets to be at least 10 percent smaller than their husbands' guess, an average difference of between twelve thousand and thirty-six thousand dollars.[9] Husbands say they've got more; wives believe they have less.

Who's right? It almost doesn't matter, since a person's *perception* of how much money she has is more important than how much she *actually* has, according to Boston University economist Jay Zagorsky, who conducted the research on what he calls "wealth misperceptions." If you feel rich, you spend money; if not, you don't, he says. In fact, that's the main reason so many couples disagree about money. "It's when couples have mismatched perceptions about their money that they get angry," he tells me. The husband goes out and buys a flat-screen television set because he feels flush, but his wife has a fit, because she doesn't see it that way at all. "Couples who have bigger differences in their estimates of how much they are worth are more likely to end up divorced," he says. For this reason, he urges couples "to work through their financial numbers together" at least once a year, so they'll have a more accurate idea of where they stand financially.[10]

Now that a majority of couples have two incomes, such calculations are more complicated, and more fraught with hidden meaning too. Just a generation or two ago, many middle-class couples viewed the wife's income as "pin money," pocket change to be used for special treats, not the serious funding necessary for a family's survival. In those days, it was mostly husbands who had marital power and the final say in major decisions, because they were the ones who supported the family. Most couples considered it natural for the family power to be in the man's hands and for him to share it with his wife, but only at his discretion. Husbands tended to manage the finances, often giving an allowance to their wives, enough for food and children's clothing but little else. The only couples who managed money jointly were those in which the husbands were more educated, held less traditional views on gender roles, or had wives working full-time. But such husbands were in the minority back then, researchers say.[11]

Now, though, men who cede control of the family finances are no longer

The Four Marriage Types

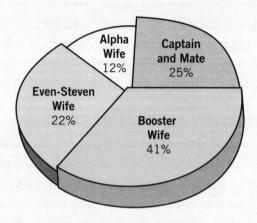

in the minority. Today it's superior wives who wield the family power, and it's their decision to share that clout or not. To better understand the most common patterns of breadwinning in American culture, I've divided marriages into four types, based on the relative income of each spouse. The *Captain and Mate marriage* is one in which the husband works and the wife stays home. In my Web survey, about 25 percent of marriages fall into this category. In the *Booster Wife marriage,* the wife contributes to the family income but earns less than her husband. This type includes about 41 percent of marriages. The *Even-Steven marriage* occurs when the wife earns about the same as her husband; it comprises about 22 percent of marriages. The *Alpha Wife marriage* is one in which the wife earns all or most of the family income; it makes up 12 percent of marriages, according to my Web survey.

The percentages of couples I've found in each of these four marriage types are almost identical to those in a recent study based on national census data. That research was restricted to couples between the ages of twenty-five and fifty-four, because they are the ones most likely to be finished with school but not yet retired.[12] My Web survey, although far from a random sample, includes a group of couples between similar ages, so I believe it is fair to use them as a model for the majority of American marriages.

Dividing couples this way, it's clear that a couple's breadwinning type determines their relative financial standing. Captain and Mate marriages in my survey have the lowest household income among all four, about $76,000. These couples make an economic sacrifice by having just one income earner. Eighty-four percent of Captain and Mate wives are in first marriages, the largest proportion of all four types. Alpha Wife marriages have the second-lowest household income, about $95,000 a year, probably because the wives tend to be the sole earners. These wives, the most educated, are most likely to be in second or third marriages. Even-Steven couples have an average annual household income, in my Web survey, of about $102,000. Finally, Booster Wife marriages have the highest average household income, about $112,000 a year. The census study discovered the same income patterns among these four marriage types, with Captain and Mate marriages the lowest earners and Booster Wife marriages the highest. (The census researchers did not use these labels, however, which are mine.) Thus, it's clear that couples with only the husband working—the so-called traditional breadwinner marriages—are also those with the least financial resources.

Although the four marriage types earn significantly different incomes, the actual amounts don't seem to make a difference in the emotional and psychological lives of wives. Here's one of my most important findings about the four marriage types: *women and men in every marriage type are as happy, or as unhappy, as those in any other type.* When I compare the relative happiness of wives, based on these four types, women in one type are no more satisfied with their marriage or with their lives than women in any other type. Likewise, men in any one type are no more content than those in any other. So it doesn't really matter how much money they have or who is earning it; there is no magic formula, no single *best* way of arranging work and family life, one that will provide an ideal solution to the "How should we live?" question. That's because women's feelings about work and family are based on a wide variety of factors, not just on how many hours a week they work or how much money they earn.

How women feel about being in a particular type of marriage depends on at least four factors. First, has the wife arrived at that type by choice? A Captain and Mate wife who would prefer to work, for instance, will not be nearly as pleased about being at home as will a nonworking wife who chose that state. Likewise, an Even-Steven wife who'd rather be at home may be disgruntled no matter how much money she earns.

Second, how much support does a woman receive from her husband, compared with how much she expected to get? Almost all wives have a mental picture of an ideal marriage, and almost all those pictures, as I've said, involve some variation on an equal partnership. What ends up being the real marital arrangement, though, may be very far from that image. This discrepancy will influence how a wife feels about her breadwinning situation, since many wives expect more evenly balanced chore sharing than they actually get, researchers say. Wives almost always say that their husbands are less involved with the children than the men believe they are, for example. Women who don't get as much help from their husband as they expect or want tend to feel more stress and are more likely to harbor a sense that their marriage is unfair, according to recent research.[13] In my view, this frustration is what riles up superior wives of every stripe.

Third, how does the wife feel about her paid work? Wives with menial, low-paying jobs may view their work differently from wives who have demanding and challenging jobs for which they are well paid. Wives who hate their work will, of course, be much more unhappy than those who either love their work or don't despise it all that much. It's simply a matter of meeting Monday. Do they dread that day, do they look forward to it, or do they fall somewhere in between?

Finally, what is the wife's stage of life? It's a lot easier to go to work every day if the only person you leave at home is your husband and not a precious six-month-old baby or teary toddler. It becomes somewhat easier too once those babies have become teenagers who no longer care where you go every day, just so long as you're not in their face. But many mothers have to work, even when their children are babies, so this fact will influence how they feel about their work situation.

How wives feel about their marriage type matters, because it also influences the ways in which they deal with money, housework, child care, and just about every other crucial aspect of modern married life. Overall, a majority of wives say that they are the ones who manage the money, no matter what type of marriage they are in. But even more Alpha wives—74 percent—do so than any other type of wives. More Alpha wives—87 percent—also say they have the most control over the family, not only over the finances but over everything else too. But while many of these wives may have taken on the formerly masculine task of being sole breadwinner, they haven't ceded control of the domestic domain. In fact, they seem to adhere to a bend-over-backward rule, trying very hard to master both the formerly masculine domain of breadwinning and the formerly feminine domain of domestic toil. Nearly as many Alpha wives as others, for instance, say they are the family's culinary expert, as well as the one who is best at supervising children. Nearly as many Alpha wives as others are also the family expert when it comes to arranging social outings with friends and relatives. As we'll see, these wives try especially hard not to emasculate their husbands any more than they feel they already have by earning most of the family's income. So they try hard to Martha Stewart their way through life, attempting to present a reasonable facsimile of one domestic goddess or other.

Let's examine the four marriage types, in greater detail, from the most traditional type, the Captain and Mate, to the least traditional, the Alpha wife.

The Captain and Mate Marriage

When I think of wives in Captain and Mate marriages, I almost always think about Polly, who was my inspiration for the name "Captain and Mate." Now forty-five and living in New Jersey, Polly hasn't worked since she was first married, at the age of twenty. She earned a high school degree in Ireland, where she grew up, but has never been to college. She feels somewhat embarrassed about her lack of education, since most of her American friends and neighbors have college degrees, but she is also somewhat smug about the fact that she doesn't have to work. Proud of being in a Captain and Mate marriage, Polly is petite but endowed with a large bosom and full curves. She wears her blond hair short and has an engaging, cheerful attitude. Her nails are always painted, her clothes are always clean and carefully coordinated, and her teenage children are painfully polite. Her husband, Nick, rugged but dour, speaks in a gravelly voice and is used to being obeyed. It's his job to earn the family income, and it's Polly's job to do everything else, including the lawn mowing and the garbage removing. This is what Polly wanted and expected from marriage, so she's content with the way things turned out. She is quite happily subservient, deferring to Nick's decisions and wishes, his needs and desires. It never occurs to Polly to question her husband's authority, because that's not part of their agreement. She even calls Nick her "captain," an apt metaphor in her family, since Nick is an avid sailor. In the summer, when they go out on their ten-foot sailboat, Polly is, in fact, Nick's mate. He trims the sails, handles the rudder, sets the course; she climbs aboard and follows his orders. He makes most of the family decisions, and she goes along. Their roles are clear-cut and well defined, and she would never, ever, in a million years, consider herself superior.

His commands are what she wishes for.

"I'm his mate, and that's how it has always been," Polly says. She doesn't even mind cleaning her house, she adds, because she feels "that's how I earn my keep."

Polly is one version of a Captain and Mate wife, but Peg is a completely different, much less self-satisfied version. Instead of feeling pride about her marital setup, Peg feels embarrassed, ashamed of the pact she's made to stay home, as if it were a top secret deal with the devil. A compulsive swimmer who is built like a Popsicle stick and looks as if she would displace no pool water whatsoever, Peg rarely misses a day of exercise. She and her second husband, Phil, have been married for nearly twenty-five years and have no children. When I meet her for coffee, fifty-year-old Peg is wearing what she always wears, sweatpants and a plain, long-sleeved tee shirt. She dresses like a twelve-year-old on the way to gymnastics class, but it suits her, because from a distance she could almost pass for a sixth grader. Peg is grateful for the skim milk latte I buy her, since she rarely treats herself to high-priced caffeinated beverages. Until a few years ago, Peg had always worked, at least part-time, and felt she could spend her own money on whatever she pleased, even the ultrafrivolous. She taught a Shakespeare course at a small, local university; before that she was a clerk in a bookstore, and before that she was a writer for a cheesy fan magazine. Then Peg decided that she really wanted to write poetry full-time and not have to worry about going to a semicrummy job every day. So she made an arrangement with Phil: He'd continue to work, and she'd be the wife. She promised to take care of the house, but she'd spend most of her day focusing on her poetry, which meant that she would have to avoid luxury spending of any kind.

"I tell my husband that I won't spend money and that he's in charge.

I decided that if I want to be supported financially, I'd have to let him do what he wants. So if we decide to move, he says where. If we decide to buy something big, he says what. We have a weird conventional deal where I do all of the feminine things," Peg says, almost disgusted by her own behavior. "I clean, I do all the shopping, and all that stuff. It's quirky, because I'm not terribly efficient. Actually, I'm really bad at it. I'm a poet, so I'm not a home-maker, except by obligation."

She explains, "In certain ways, I have abnegated all responsibility, and that's become the best thing for me, although it appalls my sister. But I get what I need, because I gave up a lot of worries and duties. I don't want to learn practical things, like doing the finances, so I let him run the show. We talk openly about our deal, and I'm trying to do more of the practical things. But I failed to learn about finances and investing. My interest is really low and I'd rather clean toilets, so that's what I do," she concludes, laughing.

Peg expected to work all her life, which is why she feels so odd and so guilty about no longer earning her own paycheck. Still, she's not a superior wife, simply because she's only going through the wifely motions. Her heart isn't in domestic bliss; it's in her sonnets about nature and love.

Most Captain and Mate wives fall somewhere between the two extremes of smug Polly and horrified Peg. They are somewhat proud or slightly re-lieved that they do not have to work, or they are grateful to be at home with their children, or they are appreciative of their husband for excusing them from work, or they are convinced that this is a temporary phase in their work life. Indeed, when Captain and Mate wives were first married, two out of three expected that both partners would always work for pay, so many of these wives are defying their own expectations, at least for the moment.

There is no evidence that traditional gender roles in marriage encour-age better or longer-lasting or more secure marriages. Just because she keeps house and he earns money, a marriage isn't thereby happy or failure-proof. This is, in fact, the most impractical kind of marriage, since it's ut-terly inflexible. If the husband dies, who will earn a living? If the wife gets sick, who will take care of the children? Nonetheless, this is the marriage we think of as traditional, mostly because a majority of middle-class mar-riages were like this for a brief period in the middle of the last century.

Husbands in so-called traditional marriages, particularly those who are working-class, view their situation as prestigious, because having a wife who doesn't work means that you are a man capable of supporting a family, an increasing rarity in today's world. I heard this from many American husbands who answered my Web survey, like Mark, fifty, a Captain and Mate husband from a small city north of Atlanta, Georgia. "My wife is the Proverbs thirty-one wife," Mark says, referring to the Old Testament passage about the superior wife, whose price is "far above rubies." He's pleased that his wife has never had to work during the nineteen years they've been married. "I'm the breadwinner, and she does the shopping and cleaning and cooking, and that's what I always wanted in a wife," he explains. He also classifies her as superior, since she's the one who manages the money, runs the household, and deals with insurance issues. She even makes most of the important family decisions, Mark admits, although he claims to hold veto power.

I hear the same sentiments from husbands I interviewed in Rio de Janeiro, Brazil, where I traveled to see if I could find superior wives on the other side of the equator. In fact, I could and I did. "I joined the Army because I knew I would always have a job and that my pay would be safe and regular," says Artur, fifty-three, an army officer in Brazil who is married to his high school sweetheart, Fabiana. "I never wanted my wife to work, and I'm glad she never had to," he adds.

"Sometimes I am annoyed that I never got to finish college, but it's a luxury for me not to work," agrees Fabiana, forty-nine, who had three children with Artur. "Military men get a salary that's livable enough so the wife doesn't have to work," she explains, adding that most of the Army wives she knows don't work either. "The wife's job is changing a lot, but people from my generation, especially the men, believe that everything to do with raising the children is something the women should do," which makes it difficult to have a full-time job. "My niece, whose husband is also in the Army, is much younger, and she divides the child rearing more with her husband. She also works too," Fabiana adds, with some envy in her voice.

Fabiana is a typical Captain and Mate wife, and she's also superior— because she's the one in charge of the household and the finances, the cars and the health care. Artur earns the money, but Fabiana does everything else, including making most of the decisions about how to spend it. Indeed, among Captain and Mate wives, 62 percent are superior, according to my research.

Other husbands in Captain and Mate marriages believe that the man is the natural leader, that it is "his place to be the head of the household," as a young Mormon husband from Utah puts it. Another Mormon husband, who works as a groundskeeper at a golf course while his wife stays home with their first baby, says that "both of us are pulling our weight for the family." And it's a bonus that they're doing it in what he considers the right way, one in which he's proud to be sole breadwinner.

It's not just Mormon couples who feel this way either. Soledad, twenty-nine, is a Captain and Mate wife and a devout Catholic. An Ecuadorian immigrant who lives fifty miles north of Detroit, Michigan, she prefers to stay at home with her children. "My husband has all responsibility for earning the income," she says, "but I have all responsibility for everything else. All choices, all errands, all bill paying and banking, cooking, cleaning, taking the children to appointments, doing yard work, taking out the trash; you name it and it is my job," she says. That's why she considers herself superior. Her husband, Javier, unloads trucks at a warehouse, earning about fifty thousand dollars a year. Soledad never finished high school and always expected to be in this kind of traditional marriage. Still, she resents her husband's lack of involvement with the family.

She says he always "plays the Hispanic card," refusing to take their three children out on Halloween or to go to their school events, "because he is not from here and everyone is white and he doesn't fit in." Soledad observes, "I wish I could take the financial burden off of him, because his job takes a lot out of him. But then I think, well, I do everything else around here, and I do not feel appreciated at all. Sometimes I think he feels he is better than me, because what I do is no big deal and not as important as earning the money."

Soledad is in an old-school, traditional marriage, one with very gender-specific divisions of labor: he works for money, she works at home. Indeed, wives who don't work outside the home end up spending more time on housework than other wives, though they're doing a lot less of it now than housewives did just thirty years ago. While working wives do about sixteen hours of housework each week, Captain and Mate wives do twenty-five hours of domestic chores each week, not including child care, according to a major national study. (In 1975, though, Captain and Mate wives were doing even more housework, twenty-nine hours a week.) The researchers asked wives and mothers to keep daily time diaries to record the number of minutes they spent doing everything, from brushing their hair to eating snacks to listening to music. Captain and Mate wives, it turns out, get more sleep than working wives—fifty-eight hours a week, compared to fifty-three. They also spend more time watching television—about sixteen hours a week, compared to ten hours for wives who work for pay. Finally, they spend just slightly more time taking care of their children but no more time alone with their husband or with friends and relatives.[14]

There are dozens of reasons, at least, that wives end up being in a Captain and Mate marriage, some by choice, others not. From my point of view what's more important are the ways in which Captain and Mate wives also become superior wives. How do these traditional women reconcile their apparently submissive status with a secret show of strength and superiority?

First, most of these superior wives did not expect to end up as a Captain and Mate wife. Before they were married, only two in ten expected to stay home and be supported by their husband. Perhaps that's why so many of these wives feel conflicted and a bit defensive about their situation. It's also why some of them feel guilty for not earning any money and believe that they have no right to make important decisions about spending it. "My husband is king of this castle, because he works and I don't," says Josie, forty-five, a Massachusetts wife and mother of three. A high school graduate married to a police officer, Josie sees herself as the superior spouse, despite the fact that she is dependent on her husband's income, at least for now. "He reminds me constantly how lucky I am to be a stay-at-home mother, which makes me feel guilty about not having a job," Josie says. "But he doesn't want me to work either." Josie feels both grateful and guilt-ridden for being supported by her husband.

Like Josie, many other superior Captain and Mate wives expect their situation to be temporary. That's true for Amelia, thirty-one, who lives in Tucson with her second husband of four years, an Air Force officer. They live with their four-year-old daughter and Amelia's twelve-year-old daughter from her first marriage. Amelia is a high school graduate, a somewhat reluctant at-home wife and mother who thinks of herself as superior. "I don't love housework, but it's part of my 'job' as the housewife," she says. "I make more of the home-related decisions, and I run the finances and pay the bills, even though my husband is bringing home the figurative bacon." This will all change when her youngest daughter starts kindergarten, since Amelia plans to go back to college and get her degree. She considers an education her reward for being at home for so long, and for being so superior.

Second, a great many superior Captain and Mate wives justify their secondary status through their religious beliefs. Some accede to the view that the husband is the head of the household, while also taking on a subtly superior role in the family. In fact, the largest proportion of Captain and Mate couples—about 30 percent—are evangelical Christians. Because they hold strict and traditional views about the husband's role in the family, many have opted for a marriage in which the husband is ostensibly the chief. "According to Scripture," says a forty-nine-year-old youth pastor from a small town in rural Alabama, "my wife is submissive and obedient to my authority."

Presumably, his wife agrees with Carlotta, a twenty-six-year-old wife from Georgia, who says that "as Christian believers, my husband is the biblical head of our household. It's his responsibility to earn a living, to manage our finances, to make final decisions, to take out the trash, and to mow the yard. It's my responsibility to clean and straighten the house and to take care of everything else." Although most evangelical wives support this male-dominant view, just as many of them as other wives see themselves as superior.

"As Christians, we believe that the husband is the head of the household and has the final word on things," says Kendra, fifty, an evangelical from a small town in East Texas who dropped out of college to get married. "I gladly do my duties at home while my husband is at work, and I also homeschool our five children," she explains. Although she defers to her husband, there's no question that she runs the family or that her husband always turns to her for advice. He may be the head of their family, but she's the brains.

Finally, a great many superior wives in a Captain and Mate marriage see the situation as temporary, one that will last only as long as their children live at home. Before Kendra was married, for instance, she expected to be working outside the home and earning a living, along with her husband. The day after her youngest child leaves home, she says, she'll be out the door looking for work, her Captain and Wife status gone with the wind.

Likewise, Rebecca is a twenty-nine-year-old Captain and Mate wife from Ohio who is adamant about her choice to stay home with her two preschool children. "My husband and I are both doing what we want to do, and we are both very happy with our roles," she says. "I grew up with a group of well-educated women who would never give up their money-earning careers for family life. If my husband didn't work outside the home, there is no way I'd be able to live this life that I love so much, to have enough time with our children to raise them in the manner that I prefer." Rebecca is a superior wife too and confesses that she does "ninety-nine point ninety-nine percent of everything around the house. I make the doctors' appointments, I deal with the insurance companies, I do most of the automobile maintenance and the yard work, and I do the cooking, cleaning, laundry, and housework. I handle the child care and the library trips and the nursery school accounts, and I am the one who plans all of our social activities." She's a superior Captain and Mate wife, and she's proud of being both. But as soon as her children are in high school, she says, she'll be looking for a job on the Internet.

Even some extremely well educated wives with professional careers end up in a Captain and Mate marriage because they want to stay home with their children. Charlotte, forty-three, is an obstetrician who used to work long hours in a solo practice in Maryland, almost always ending up at the hospital on evenings and weekends. But after she had her own two children, late in life, "I felt it was morally reprehensible to be away so much. I loved my patients, but I loved my children more. It's a thankless and mundane job being a housewife, but this is my choice. I want to raise my own children, not pay someone else to do it." A self-described superior wife, Charlotte plans to go back to work full-time when her children are older.

Ronit, too, is a forty-four-year-old superior wife in a Captain and Mate marriage, though not by choice. Her nine-year-old son is autistic, so she homeschools him, handles all the family finances, does all the housework, and takes care of pretty much everything else except bringing home a paycheck. "My husband and I agreed that it would be best for me to educate our autistic child at home, instead of fighting the Los Angeles school system year in and year out. I am the one best suited and qualified to educate and supervise therapy for our son. My husband is supportive and understands our son's issues, but he admits that he doesn't have what it takes to get through the day," she explains. Ronit does not earn any income, for now, but she longs for the day when she will give up her Captain and Mate status.

The Booster Wife Marriage

Most American wives go along with the working woman tide. It has now become the social standard—what's approved and what's expected—that both spouses will work for pay. The "What do you do?" cocktail party question is usually asked of wives and husbands both, and at-home moms often feel compelled to justify their unemployed status. Indeed, the largest proportion of American marriages—about four in ten—are Booster Wife marriages, those in which the wife works but earns less than her husband. About eight in ten of these wives are in first marriages, the second-highest proportion after Captain and Mate marriages. On average, Booster wives work fewer hours than other working wives, about thirty-two hours a week, compared to thirty-nine hours a week for Even-Steven wives and forty-three hours a week for Alpha wives.

Because so many Booster wives are part-timers, some view their income as secondary to their husband's, and a few even think of their job as a kind of frivolous pastime. For others, though, it's a lifeline to essential extra income. And for many, it involves the pursuit of a profession and is part-time only temporarily.

Joni, fifty-three, who calls herself a superior wife, is on the less serious end of the Booster wife spectrum. Living in the suburbs of Philadelphia, Pennsylvania, Joni describes her four-hour-a-day position in a trade publishing company "a hobby job which keeps me sane and active." She and her husband, Frank, who works ninety hours a week as a caterer, have two sons in college. Although Frank is a professional chef, "when he comes home, he cannot find the refrigerator or the remote control," so she's in charge of everything on the domestic front. And that's not necessarily a good thing.

"For years, my children thought the smoke alarm was the dinner bell," she explains, since her cooking almost always involved something burning or charring. "To this day, my children won't go into a restaurant that advertises 'home cooking'!" she says with a laugh. Because she's married to a well-paid workaholic, Joni has never taken her career seriously. It's a distraction, a lark, and she doesn't do it for the money, she works for pure enjoyment. She doesn't take that luxury for granted either. "I'm glad I don't have to help support my family, though I do provide for my close-knit family in a nonfinancial way, one that my husband deserves for all of his hard work," she says. Her work as the family's emotional center, Joni believes, is more important than any work she might do to earn more money.

Other Booster wives are more focused on their paid work, in part because they need the money, even if they don't bring in as much as their husbands do. Katarina, forty-eight, is a third-grade teacher in Connecticut with a master's degree in education who earns less than half of what her husband does. Because of that imbalance, and the greater flexibility of her schedule, Katarina has always been the one "who makes sure that there are groceries in the house, that the kids are picked up from school or practice, that they visit the doctor and the dentist, that their homework is done, that their clothes are clean, and that the cars are serviced. And I'm the one they come to for advice," she adds, referring to her four teenage children. When it comes right down to it, Katarina views herself as a superior wife who sacrifices and puts the most effort into her family. "I am willing to give up my hobbies, doing things with my friends, and having time to myself to help my children with anything they need," she explains. "But my husband puts an extraordinary effort into making a good living for his family, putting up with difficult bosses and clients, long hours, and lots of travel. But he also gets a sense of self-worth and appreciation that a stay-at-home mom never gets, which is why I went back to work after my children started middle school." Her work is a lifeline to feelings of confidence and responsibility that staying at home with her children didn't offer, Katarina believes.

Wives like Katarina work for the money, but they also work for personal fulfillment, for the feeling that what they do is worthwhile and has an impact outside their own family. But they feel an equal and just as powerful obligation to their family. They try even harder, perhaps, than Captain and Mate wives to be all things to their children and husband, because they often feel guilty for spending time at work, no matter how few hours they actually put in. Compared to other wives, more Booster wives say that they are the ones who are best able to organize the family, to show affection, and to sacrifice their own needs. Almost all of them agree too that they're the family expert at talking about feelings, caring for the house, socializing with friends and family, and cooking a great meal, according to my Web survey.

It's as if Booster wives are afraid that their work time will interfere with their ability to be perfect wives and mothers, so they overcompensate by trying even harder at home. Again, I call this the bend-over-backward rule, and it applies even more to Even-Steven and Alpha wives, as we'll see.

Many Booster wives, 64 percent of whom are also superior wives, find themselves bending over backward to be perfect wives and mothers and workers, although they get much less cooperation and support than they expected from their husbands. In fact, if you had a time machine and could go back to the wedding day of each and every Booster wife to find out their expectations, you'd get an enormous show of hands proclaiming an optimistic faith in a future filled with egalitarian marriages. Eighty-five percent of Booster wives assumed back then that both partners would work, and 56 percent imagined that both partners would share domestic chores, according to my research. But these egalitarian views and expectations—more like dreams and fantasies, actually—far exceed the reality of actual husbands. When that discrepancy becomes clear, wives express their dissatisfaction with the situation by complaining to their husbands about getting less support and affection than they need and want. She complains, he shuts down, and thus begins a downward marital spiral. The more wives expect to share responsibilities, the more disappointed they are when they don't share and the more the marriage suffers, according to researchers at the University of Virginia. These social scientists studied five thousand couples from across the United States and concluded that there's a widespread increase in marital misery nationwide, in part because wives' expectations of sharing and equality are rarely met.[15] In addition, many wives feel dismay and disappointment at being the one who has to run the family.

Again, this is why the proportion of superior wives does not vary from one marriage type to the next. No matter how much money wives earn, their husbands' beliefs about domestic and financial "shoulds" rarely match their wives' more progressive views. In fact, the chasm between wives' open-minded, sharing-based "shoulds" and husbands' narrowly focused, traditional "shoulds" is a Grand Canyon–sized abyss that is causing a crisis in the marriage market for eligible singles.[16] There are, quite simply, way too many egalitarian-minded future brides for the number of future grooms who believe in share and share alike. Today's brides anticipate liberty, equality, and sorority; today's husbands look forward to liberty, inequality, and traditional fraternity. Most husbands no longer "mind" if their wives work—a quaintly horrible way to put it—since they like the idea of a Booster income. But they still expect their working wives to be old-fashioned wives at home.

Many Booster wives have solved this nearly universal dilemma by working less than full-time so they can put in a second shift of work after work. About half of Booster wives work part-time so that they can be home to go to teacher conferences, attend recitals, and cook family meals. They've tried to solve the wifely time bind—the uncomfortable sensation of always being in a rush, never having enough time for anything—by working reduced hours. Thus, some Booster wives are less likely to feel heartburn and Friday afternoon anxiety than wives who work full-time. That still leaves the other half of Booster wives, the ones who work full-time and still try to do it all. Indeed, a large number of Booster wives fight a constant battle between family and work priorities. It's like trying to cram a few giant, overfilled balloons into a too-small car trunk without popping any.

Carrie, forty-seven, was a television producer in Miami, Florida, until she got pregnant with her daughter, now fifteen. She tried working full-time when her daughter was a baby, but she quickly cut back her hours when it became clear that her husband was "climbing the ladder of success," as she puts it, and had no intention of helping to manage the household. In addition, she was consumed by baby love. "I was glad to be home with my daughter, and she is a better person because of my ability to be there for a few years," Carrie says. Now that her daughter is a teenager, Carrie is putting in more hours at work, she says, but she's still not working full-time, "so I can be home when she gets out of school and so I can take her to after-school events." Carrie's husband works eighty hours a week to her twenty-five, and she knows "he sometimes wishes I made a full-time salary, but we do get by comfortably. Our common goal is that I'll be able to contribute more financially when our daughter reaches maturity."

Some Booster wives and their husbands harbor an unconscious assumption that earning more money buys domestic liberty. Men who earn more than their Booster wives often feel that they have a right to do less around the house; in their minds, they've bargained their way out of household responsibility by bringing home the bigger check. It's as if husbands adhere to an unspoken formula that goes like this:

If his total income > her total income, then her domestic responsibility > his domestic responsibility

This mathematical rule could be seen as an oversimplified explanation of the superior wife phenomenon; he does more financial supporting, so she does more of everything else, becoming the überwife and -mother and -worker and –human being. "I'm very organized and very focused at work, so when I get home, I want to physically and mentally relax and unwind," explains Frank, forty-three, a lobbyist in Washington who earns three times as much as his twenty-nine-year-old Booster wife. "But she wants to clean and do chores, which drives me crazy, because I'd rather she keep me company and do all that stuff on Saturdays," he complains. Frank's wife is superior, and that's the way he prefers it. "She's better than me about organizing our finances and doing housework, and she tends to make decisions without my input, though I insist on being consulted," he adds. The May-November couple don't have children yet, but Frank hopes that when they do, his wife will continue to work a bit, because he thinks it's good for her self-confidence. But of course he will expect her to be the one to organize and manage their growing family too.

Aaron, twenty-nine, is a college administrator at a state university in upstate New York who's also in a Booster Wife marriage. "Since I am making the most money, I should make a lot of the decisions," he says. But in his deepest heart, Aaron knows that this is not how his marriage really works. His wife does all, manages all, decides all; he blusters and avoids. Their only serious argument occurs when his wife accuses him of not paying enough attention to her when she speaks. "I really do listen," Aaron says, defending himself, "but she has a tendency to talk to me when I'm watching television or playing video games and I can't really concentrate on her."

Many Booster wives, like Frank's and Aaron's, are troubled by their superiority, though they can't quite put their finger on exactly what feels so wrong. "I really want to say my husband and I are equals, because I am an avid feminist and I believe it should be this way, but right now, I can't honestly say that," says Barbara, a thirty-seven-year-old superior Booster wife from Michigan. She earns about fifty thousand dollars a year working three days a week as a nurse-practitioner, but her husband earns almost twice that. Barbara has two children, eight and ten, and says that she's the one who supervises them and makes appointments for everyone's dental, health, and eye care visits, for haircuts and for orthodontia. She also arranges the veterinary care for two dogs, a cat, and an iguana. She mows the lawn and does most of the cooking, cleaning, grocery shopping, dishes, and car repairs too. She also decides where to go on vacation, what car to buy, which insurance policy to get, and where to put their savings. But plenty of domestic duties fall through the cracks, and Barbara is the first to admit it. "My husband nags me about our messy house, which drives him crazy. But I'm doing so much other stuff that I don't have much time to clean," she adds. Barbara could learn from Randy, another Booster wife, who used to fight bitterly with her husband about whose job it was to clean the house. "We were killing each other about who should clean the house, because his standards were so much higher," Randy says. "He wanted a perfectly clean house, but he wouldn't do any of the actual work, so we sought counseling." Randy, fifty, an occupational therapist in Massachusetts, explains that "the social worker said we did not need her, that what we needed was a good cleaning lady." Randy and her husband have employed a twice-a-month cleaning service ever since.

Much more troubling to Barbara than her filthy house, though, is how disturbed and upset she is by the way her superior, Booster Wife union has turned out. "Some days I can't believe that as a feminist with the ideals I had in college I am actually in this kind of a marriage," she says with disbelief. That feeling of astonished incredulity at how unfair and imbalanced married life has become is widespread among Booster wives, especially those who work as hard as their husbands but who earn much less. Grace is fifty-two and works forty-seven hours a week as a technology coordinator for a school district near her lakeside home in a tiny town in Missouri. Her husband works fifty hours a week and makes exactly twice what she does. A superior wife, Grace works six days a week and spends her day off cleaning her large house, doing laundry, and shopping for groceries. "My husband spends so much time at work that he comes home tired and he doesn't speak very much. He thinks he makes most of the decisions about purchases, though I really do, and I also pay the bills and feel pressure to be sure that we have enough money in our accounts," Grace explains. "He doesn't have time to keep Quicken updated, so that's my job," she says, adding that their division of labor seems about as unfair as does her relatively low income.

Wives like Grace are sometimes disgruntled about their marriage, though they don't necessarily know why. That's because wives whose husbands don't appreciate their contributions, financial or domestic, tend to be much less happy about their marriage than wives whose husbands express a sense of gratitude and respect, researchers say. In addition, wives need to feel a general sense of fairness about their lives, to believe that both partners are contributing equally. Wives who are convinced that they have a just partnership also tend to feel they can challenge their husband and can talk to him openly about what's bothering them. In contrast, wives who feel their arrangement is unfair are also likely to feel that they have to shut up and make the best of a not-great situation, according to a study of two-earner couples.[17]

Thus, it's better to marry a man who voices his respect and admiration than one who doesn't feel it or doesn't express it. Unfortunately, by the time most wives realize how important this is, it's too late: the faulty hubby has already been chosen. A short-term solution to the problem of an ungrateful or less-than-generous husband is to keep a private cash stash, as Isabel discovered several decades ago. Isabel, a sixty-year-old secretary from St. Louis, has earned less than her husband for most of their twenty-nine years together. "I keep my own separate checking account, with some of the money I've earned, to use at my own discretion and without discussion with my husband," Isabel confesses. She used to be a superior wife, but no longer: she quit doing all the household chores she never liked, including cooking, when her children left home. Now her husband does all the cooking and all the grocery shopping too. "After cooking two dinners every night, due to scheduling problems, for twenty years, I don't want to cook anymore, except for dinner parties," Isabel says. "So we share all of the home chores now, only he does more, and he even manages it all. It has been a successful marriage because of this," she adds.

Isabel is the rare wife who has extricated herself from a superior wife marriage without getting a divorce. (That's a feat I'll discuss in chapter 8.)

The Even-Steven Marriage

Twenty-two percent of marriages are Even-Stevens, in which wives and husbands earn about the same income, within 15 to 20 percent. The Even-Steven marriage has the potential to be the fairest marriage, since both partners pull equal financial weight. The question is, of course, whether they do so at home too. As we'll see, the answer is mostly no. In many families, Even-Steven wives are doing more than an even-steven share at home.

More than half of Even-Steven wives work full-time, and two-thirds of them are superior. This is how most marriages used to be: centuries ago, both partners shared the labor and income from working a small farm or running a family business. That kind of marriage is not the norm now, but as women's wages continue to rise and as more wives join the workforce, it's only a matter of time until the largest proportion of couples will again be Even-Stevens.

"Such marriages are the future for most Americans," agrees Steven Nock, a professor of sociology at the University of Virginia. In Nock's research on Even-Stevens, whom he calls "equally dependent spouses," he studied thousands of couples over a five-year period, tracking fluctuations in their income. He also asked both husbands and wives to imagine how much their lives would change, for better or worse, if they left their mate, in terms of their standard of living, their career, their sex lives, and their overall happiness. He finds that Even-Steven husbands remain equally committed to the marriage even after their wives begin to earn as much as they do, but when wives become equal earners, they begin to feel less committed to the marriage. As wives enter Even-Steven territory, some believe that their lives would be better, and they'd be happier, if they were no longer married. In addition, Nock reports that a few wives are actually more likely to divorce after they start earning about the same amount as their husband.[18] This makes sense, since wives who earn enough money are more able than other wives to leave a bad or even a mediocre marriage.

In my Web survey, I find that Even-Steven wives include the second-highest percentage of those who have divorced and remarried—about 22 percent. (As we'll see, the highest proportion is among Alpha wives, the ones who earn more than their husbands do.) They are equal earners because they've already lived on their own and they had to be earning enough to support themselves and their children. Take Diane, forty-nine, who's an Even-Steven wife in a second marriage. A nurse who lives in a Wisconsin village about a hundred miles southeast of Minneapolis, Diane was a superior wife too, at least until her recent split from her second husband. This happened, she says, because "we have different views on most of the things we hold dear." That wasn't the worst of it. "I worked full-time, but I also did the shopping, the cooking, and the cleaning, and I paid my half of the bills, which we split. He didn't want to take any responsibility for my two daughters or be a father to them or to his own two children from his first marriage. He is a kind and friendly man, but I guess when the wife makes the majority of the decisions, has all the family responsibility, does all of the inside-is-for-women work, and makes as much money, there is bound to be a problem," she explains. Diane got fed up with being a superior wife, and since she has a well-paying job, she asked her second husband to move out. Until their divorce is final, he's living in an apartment above the garage.

Why do Even-Steven wives like Diane put up with doing so much for so long for so little reward? Perhaps many wives, no matter how much they earn, can't help being superior, as if it's some kind of neurological necessity. Sociology professor Sara Raley agrees that this could be true. "All women are subject to the same kind of social norms and social expectations about what it means to be a wife and mother," she tells me. "Even if we're equal earners or main breadwinners, we still carry around the expectation that women are supposed to be self-sacrificing and nurturing, the primary caregivers and kin keepers, the family's emotional support, the one the kids want when they're sick," she explains. "That doesn't change if you're working outside the home; in many ways it might be intensified, because you're trying to compensate for the potential loss of your husband's masculinity," Raley concludes.[19]

Indeed, experts have been trying to figure out for years why working wives—especially those who earn as much as or more than their husbands—still do the most child care and household dirty work. Sociological theory says that spouses abide by unwritten rules of negotiation: whoever earns the most money buys his or her way out of unpaid domestic labor. If both partners work, then whoever earns less money does more at home. It's straightforward and simple; it's also not fair. But that logic doesn't hold when wives are equal earners or better earners. In fact, there's growing evidence that the more wives earn, the more domestic work they insist on doing.[20] This is the bend-over-backward rule I mentioned earlier, one that means wives must try to prove that although they're supersuccessful breadwinners, they're also hypercompetent mothers and Suzy Homemakers. Psychologists guess that high-earning working wives do so much domestic work to neutralize the *nonnormative* (very unusual) financial situation they find themselves in. Because it's so odd and still somewhat abnormal for a woman to earn as much money as her husband, or even more, she has to assuage her own discomfort, as well as her husband's, by excelling at home too.[21]

One such wife is Shatoya, thirty-two. A superior wife who lives in a suburb of Columbus, Ohio, Shatoya earns about the same amount as her husband, around thirty-two thousand dollars a year. But she is the one who balances the family budget and makes most of the family decisions. "I work long hours and still have to go home to five children who talk to me nonstop while I prepare dinner and help with homework, do laundry, wash dishes, and give baths," she says. "I have no time for myself, and I have worn the same clothes for four years, although I did just purchase a new pair of tennis shoes for myself. I'm afraid to lose weight, because I wouldn't be able to afford new clothes that would fit me," she adds. As a customer service representative for a credit card company, Shatoya works eight hours a day, then rushes home five days a week to do nearly everything for her large family. Her husband works eight hours a day and then rushes home so he can be home.

If Shatoya bent over backward any further, she'd be a human pretzel.

Like Shatoya, many wives with full-time jobs spend as much time as humanly possible with their children, often at the expense of everything else. Researchers find that employed mothers do less housework, sleep fewer hours, spend less time doing things for themselves, and even spend less time with their husbands than do nonworking moms. In fact, the only time at home they are reluctant to sacrifice is time with their children, which they consider to be sacred.[22]

"There's no question that there has been a dramatic increase in the number of mothers working outside the home," says sociologist Suzanne M. Bianchi. To compensate, working mothers cut back on the hours they spend doing nearly everything else, she says, so as to avoid neglecting their children. "They do less cooking, less cleaning, less laundry, and less yard work, but they don't give up child care." In her research, Bianchi finds that working mothers spend just five fewer hours a week with their children than nonworking moms, or about forty-three minutes a day.[23]

Joann, for example, is a forty-three-year-old Even-Steven wife who works full-time as an office manager near her home in Beaumont, Texas. She's also a superior wife who goes out of her way to spend time with her teenage daughter. "My husband is very supportive and sometimes does dishes," Joann says. "He'll do almost anything I ask, except bathrooms," she adds. "He allows me to work as much as I want and to throw myself body and soul into our daughter. This means I can be a good mother and raise a wonderful child, who gets to see that a man should respect, love, and share with his wife," Joanne says. But she's imagining much of that sharing, since she confesses that her house is never really clean and the laundry piles up into small mountains, since that's her responsibility. Joann makes sure to spend at least an hour every day with her daughter, but her husband doesn't really notice how much time he's spending either with her or with their daughter.

A few husbands are less than thrilled by how focused their Even-Steven wives are on the children. "Sometimes I feel like my wife is so passionately in love with our baby that her love for me is diminished," complains Jed, thirty-two, an Even-Steven husband from State College, Pennsylvania. Jed is a technical writer who earns slightly less than his real estate broker wife; he works forty-eight hours a week, while she puts in sixty hours a week. "My wife is definitely the more responsible of the two of us, as far as paying the bills, looking into financial investments, getting loans, and clearing debts. If it weren't for her, we would probably still be renting an apartment, owning the same old car, and have no furniture. I just don't have the financial savvy and confidence that she does, but I do all the yard work and all of the manual labor around the house," he says, which explains why he classifies her as a superior wife. Still, he can't figure out why she's peeved if he gives their son a peanut-butter-and-jelly sandwich for dinner, instead of the baked chicken legs and string beans she has prepared in advance. "It's not like I'm giving him cookies and Coke for dinner, and I think it's better for him to eat something rather than nothing at all," Jed adds. For his wife, though, what's upsetting is that it's her husband who's making the decisions about what their son eats for dinner, not she. He doesn't understand why that should bother her; she gets teary-eyed just thinking about it.

"I teach a martial arts class in the evenings and often get invited to go out and have a few beers with my students after our workout sessions," Jed says. "I usually convince myself it's no big deal, since nothing tastes better than a cold beer after hard training. But sometimes I come home to find my wife waiting up for me, angry that I didn't call and accusing me of preferring to spend time with the guys rather than with her and our son. I don't understand why it matters, since if I'd come home, we'd have just gone to sleep anyway, and there'd be nothing sexual involved," Jed concludes.

As far as Jed is concerned, the only good reason for him to rush home is sex on the horizon. Otherwise, he doesn't really see the point.

The Alpha Wife Marriage

The natural financial progression after Even-Stevens is Alpha wives, women who earn all or almost all of the family income, as do about 12 percent of wives, according to my Web survey. These wives work the most hours, forty-three per week, and they earn on average about ninety-five thousand dollars a year, more than most male breadwinners who are sole earners. This is probably because Alpha wives are highly educated: 40 percent have a graduate degree, and another 10 percent have had at least some postgraduate education. They're also most likely to be remarried: one in three has been divorced at least once, the highest proportion among all four marriage types. Alpha wives are accustomed to supporting themselves after a first, or even a second, divorce, and they don't get out of that habit just because they remarry. For them, earning a reasonably good living is a fine habit, one that they don't intend to break.

In fact, as the number of remarriages grows, so too do the number of Alpha Wife marriages, according to census researchers, who say that the proportion of wife-as-sole-breadwinner unions tripled between 1970 and 2001. That's because so many wives, especially well-educated ones, are finally being given a real chance to earn real money. Between those years, the income of such wives increased by 78 percent, a whopping figure, since husbands' income increased by only 26 percent during the same time period.[24] Alpha wives are women who tend to earn more than other women, and they work full-time, no matter what else is going on in their lives.

If you're assuming that Alpha wives are exotic creatures who carry Prada bags and wear designer shoes and get their hair and nails done every week, think again. It's true that Alpha wives are often the focus of magazine stories and newspaper articles and television shows. In those stories, Alpha wives are almost always highly paid lawyers or successful doctors or well-traveled corporate executives. It's even true that the first time the Census Bureau studied wives who earned more than their husbands, back in the early 1980s, the statistician who examined the numbers called these women "superstars" because they seemed so rare and so heroic.[25] But today they're neither unique nor glamorous.

In real life, most Alpha wives are working wives who are struggling to get by, and often they are married to men who can't or won't find a job. "The alpha title is a bit of a misnomer," explains Sara Raley, "since a lot of the wives who outearn their husbands are actually in very low income brackets. They earn more because their husbands have some kind of problem in their earning capability."[26] Many Alpha wives earn more simply because their husbands barely earn anything at all.

That's the reason that Mei Wei, twenty-five, earns more than her husband. She earns thirty thousand dollars a year doing telephone sales; her husband, who is blind, works just two hours a week as a massage therapist. "My husband is incredibly smart and uses a computer very well," she argues. "Employers are prejudiced against him because they are not convinced that he can do the tasks they need him to do. In interviews, they ask questions like 'How can you use a keyboard if you can't see the keys?' instead of 'How fast can you type?'" She doesn't mind being the sole breadwinner, in part because she got her way when she insisted that they move from Chicago, where they met, to southern California, where they now live. "He criticized our decision to move here and my selfish desire to stay in my home state," Mei Wei says. Still, he does many of the chores at home, other than grocery shopping, which is much easier for a sighted person, she points out. They don't have children yet, though, and their lives will become infinitely more complicated when they do.

Peggy Sue, forty-five and living with her second husband and her three children, also earns the family's income, about thirty-two thousand dollars a year, caring for developmentally disabled adults in a halfway house. Her husband has medical issues, she says, but "he cannot or will not hold a job. He has a silver tongue and can get along with anybody, but he's outspoken in his opinions of people, especially those who don't know as much about computers, even if they're his boss. One time, I looked at his résumé, and he had written that he had a bachelor's degree in theology," Peggy Sue says, exasperated. "He has no college degree at all. There's a lot of pressure on him that as the man, he should be the breadwinner and provide for his family, though I don't feel that way. Still, I do resent him a little bit, since I've had to be the only breadwinner and I have missed my children growing up. I feel like I have the heavier family load on my back," she adds, not proud of being an Alpha wife but resigned to it.

Many Alpha wives, like Peggy Sue, are sole breadwinners not by choice but by necessity. Marilyn, thirty-two, is in a second marriage and works as a research assistant in a hospital near her home in Raleigh, North Carolina, earning about thirty-five thousand dollars a year. She's also a superior wife and resents it. "I provide the steady income and the health insurance, and I feel like I make a lot of the decisions, since I earn twice as much money as my husband," Marilyn says. She suffers from chronic back pain, commutes about an hour each way, and would prefer to be an at-home mom. "But I have come to the realization that this will never happen for me. I make good money at my job, provide great health benefits, and I do not expect my husband to be able to get a job that will allow this to change," she says. So she puts up and shuts up.

There are, of course, Alpha wives who are superstars and proud of it. Louisa, fifty, for example, is a graduate of Duke University Law School and has her own law practice in St. Louis, Missouri. She is not, however, a superior wife, since her husband is the one who's efficient, affectionate, and sacrificing, she says. He earns about seventy-five thousand dollars a year at his job, but she earns more than triple that amount. "I've ended up being the spouse with the higher earning capacity," Louisa says, "but I only reached this point with his support and encouragement. I'm aware that he curtailed his own career advancement opportunities because of the demands of mine, by turning down a promotion that would have required us to relocate to another city," she explains. "Unconditional love means not keeping score, because in the end, what we've each contributed to the marital equation, whether or not it was equal, has returned to each of us individually and to us both, as multiples of joy." Louisa is pleased to be an Alpha and grateful that her husband has supported her all the way there.

No matter why they end up earning more than their husbands, I find that there are five basic categories of Alpha wife reactions to their work situation. Alpha wives run the emotional gamut of each of these categories. Either they are proud of their achievements, or they are ashamed of the way things have turned out. They are grateful that they've been given the chance to excel or resentful of the financial burden placed upon them. They are happy to provide or angry that they've been forced to provide. They feel a sense of power and control in their marriage, or they feel weak and defensive. Finally, they feel feminine in their capability, or they feel that their femininity is tainted by being the sole breadwinner.

Likewise, husbands of Alpha wives have similar reactions to being the one who is supported. Some husbands of Alpha wives are like Louisa's husband, grateful to have found such an ambitious and successful wife. Some at-home dads, like a thirty-five-year-old aspiring actor from Connecticut and a forty-one-year-old prematurely retired teacher from Henderson, Tennessee, are relieved to be the one who stays home with the children. They're fed up with the rat race and thankful to be the one driving car pools, fixing spaghetti with homemade sauce, and cleaning the toilets. Others feel somewhat ashamed that they aren't pulling their financial weight, like Jack, twenty-seven, who's married to a superior wife who earns most of their income. Jack builds bicycles for a living, and he's also a graduate student at Illinois State University. "I show flashes of brilliance, but mostly I forget to do important things, like picking up my check from work, scheduling my college classes on time, or answering when somebody speaks to me," he explains. "Right now, my wife does more for the family. If I were the man I'm capable of being, I'd do more. But I'm in a constant battle with myself, trying to understand why I can't do better."

Not all Alpha wife husbands are quite so despairing, of course, although some express discomfort about the situation, even if it's temporary. "My wife does more work, makes more decisions, and takes more responsibility for our shared life," admits Keith, twenty-nine, who attends college in Kansas City while his wife earns about forty thousand dollars a year working fifty hours a week. "I regret that my wife must do so much more around the house and to maintain our relationship, and it breaks my heart that she works so hard on my behalf," he confesses. "She works two jobs to put me through school and has to do the overwhelming majority of the housework, and she's a fantastic person," Keith continues. "Am I ever going to be able to repay her for all that she has done? That question weighs on my conscience more than any other, and I wonder whether I am worthy of all that she does for me." According to Keith, his wife is superior and does everything around the house, "because I'm away from home fourteen hours a day, and even when I'm at home, I have to be studying or trying to accomplish important goals." But Keith also admits that "I am fundamentally bad at most forms of housework. I am significantly less efficient at, say, washing the dishes, which takes me an hour and a half to complete, which she can do in fifteen minutes, and the dishes are cleaner when she does them." Keith's got a whopper combo, a superior wife who's also an Alpha wife, one who relieves him of any and all family responsibility. Keith has a sugar mommy; she's called his wife.

Other husbands who depend on Alpha wives aren't nearly as tortured about the situation. Marlon, thirty-seven, is unemployed, and his wife supports their family of five on her income of sixty thousand dollars a year. "Even though I am not working, I am the head of the home, and all financial decisions are discussed but finalized through me," he says. Marlon, an African American and former union man who lives in western Pennsylvania, doesn't view his wife as superior, and he believes that the key to his success is that "I am laid back. I don't worry or stress like most folks would about bills, though my wife can't take it and throws a fit." Marlon is cool with having an Alpha wife, and while he doesn't believe the situation is permanent, he's also not pressuring himself about looking for work.

Husbands who feel strongly that their manliness is defined by being the breadwinner tend to be the most distressed and unhappy if their wives earn more, since their beliefs are contradicted by their marital reality. It hurts their masculine pride to have a wife who earns more, even though they're the ones who benefit. My research shows over and over again that wives have an easier time defining femininity as including ambition than husbands have defining masculinity as including dependency. For men, there is inherent power in being the moneymaker, and many are unable to shake the moneymaker notion, even when they benefit by being the recipient of female-earned income. Many of the men who answered my Web survey admit this, either openly or in slightly disguised form. It's why they get "peace of mind" from paying the bills, as one Alpha Wife husband says, and why they believe that since she's the one who "cares that the house is clean and the clothes are folded," she's the one who ends up doing domestic chores, as another explains.

When wives begin to outearn their husbands, the men become uncomfortable, according to a psychological study of about three hundred dual-earner couples. The same does not apply to wives, who adjust rather quickly when they begin to earn more than their husbands. The researchers examined how couples feel about their marriage in great detail, asking fifty-two questions about the possible rewards and costs of marriage, all the good things you can imagine and all the bad, and then a little bit more. The couples had to answer questions like "Is your partner easy to get along with? Does your partner make you feel physically attractive? Does your partner encourage you? Do you do things together for fun? Do you fight about money? Is your partner too self-absorbed? Does your partner often criticize you? Does your partner take you for granted?" It is fairly obvious, they concluded, that being the family provider is a lot more important for a husband's sense of well-being than it is for a wife's.[27] Husbands whose wives significantly outearn them begin to see flaws in the marriage, slightly more of the bad and slightly less of the good. But wives in happy marriages who outearn their husbands don't suddenly perceive their good marriage in a harsher light after theirs becomes the biggest paycheck.

Still, Alpha wives are not exempt from superiority. Alpha Wife marriages include just as many superior wives as do other marriage types, I find. Alpha wives are the family expert in seven out of ten tasks, like cooking and getting together with relatives and supervising children, just like other wives. However, their areas of expertise expand into the more so-called masculine areas too, such as earning money, maintaining the car, managing finances, and dealing with health care. Compared to the other three marriage types, slightly fewer Alpha wives say they are the one who's best at feminine jobs, like taking care of the house, expressing their feelings, and keeping in touch with friends. But that's only by a small margin, since a majority of Alpha wives insist that they are best at doing these things too. Thus, Alpha wives, like their Even-Steven sisters, abide by the bend-over-backward rule: they may earn the most money, but they also insist on doing the most for their family.

Some Alpha wives deliberately defer to their husband and try to ignore the financial elephant in the room—the fact that their larger income makes their family female-powered. They usually do so gently, tactfully, and in a way that high-earning men almost never do. "I earn more than three-quarters of our total income," explains Liza, fifty-one, "but we are co-equal partners as much as possible in sharing the 'control' of family needs and problems. Most men in my position hold that fact as a trump card over their wives in decision making, as my own father did over my mother, but I've tried hard over the years to make sure that my husband doesn't feel that I veto his decisions based on the disparity in our incomes." A radiologist in Kansas City, Liza has two children, and she's not a superior wife. Sometimes, though, she wishes she were married to a man who, as she puts it, "would provide me with more leisure time and plenty of money." It's not that she doesn't want to be an Alpha, just that sometimes she'd like a vacation from being so Alpha and from trying so hard to pretend that she's not.

Tami, twenty-five, also tries not to emasculate her husband any more than her double salary already does, but that's not so easy, since she's in the military, where rank and status are openly displayed and celebrated. Tami is a commissioned officer on active duty with the Army. She works fifty hours a week, and her husband had to quit his job to move to Germany with her. "He is willing to give up so much for me to follow my dream, and he is okay with me earning more money," Tami says. "I try to do the majority of the housework, and I take care of most of our responsibilities, because I feel I really owe him." Still, "sometimes I get overwhelmed, and I want to scream," Tami adds. Married about eighteen months, Tami and her husband have a long way to go before they adjust to being in an Alpha Wife marriage.

The key to Alpha Wife marriages is that the balance of power and status has been subtly reversed, from husband to wife, whether the couple is willing to admit it or not. Because this reversal makes some wives uncomfortable, they go out of their way to pretend that it doesn't exist. What's troubling, though, is that many of these wives actually *feel guilty* for not doing enough around the house or with the children. "They seem to feel that supporting the family does not compensate for the household labor that their husband performs," says Veronica Tichenor, a sociologist who has studied Alpha Wife marriages. She finds that such wives do not wield more power in the family, on purpose, although they do act as gatekeepers of the family money.[28]

In my Web survey too, it's clear that Alpha wives are most likely to take control of the family money. About three out of four of them say they are the ones who manage the money, making investments and planning budgets, compared to about half of other wives. Half also say that it's their job to keep track of the family finances by paying bills, compared to just 24 percent of Even-Steven wives. Take Anne, forty-eight, an Alpha wife who says her unemployed husband simply doesn't care enough about the family money to deal with it. "It falls to me to assure that all my family's needs are met," says Anne, a nursing supervisor in suburban Chicago. "I pay the bills, invest our money, buy the insurance, and borrow for our son's college tuition," she explains. "I resent him for not stepping up to the plate, but that is his way of being." She's a superior wife as well as an Alpha, and she's bitter about having to do everything. But she's also not embarrassed or intimidated about taking the reins of family power.

Like Anne, six in ten Alphas are superior wives. But I'm fairly sure that most of them would never say that out loud. Or even whisper it in private. Wives who are sole breadwinners go out of their way to avoid even the appearance of being bitchy or domineering or unlovable. There is a potent bitch taboo in our culture, one that's most obvious among Alpha wives but exists among other superior wives as well. No woman, no matter how much of the family income she earns, or how much of the family power she wields, wants to be seen as a power-hungry, man-eating, fire-breathing, pants-wearing demon. Alpha wives are the ones most likely to be seen as just that, but they're also the ones most likely to go out of their way to avoid all appearances of bitchiness.

If wives in all four marriage types are equally likely to be superior—which they are—then how do their husbands view the situation? Do men view their superior wives as bitchy and controlling? Are they grateful for being exempted from responsibility by their all-doing wives? Are they even aware of their mates' superiority? In the next chapter, I'll look at wifely superiority from the male point of view.

4

What, Me Oblivious?
How Husbands See (or Don't See) Wifely Superiority

The real question is not, as Sigmund Freud famously put it, "What do women want?" The truly slippery and formidable question is *"What are men thinking?"*

Right now they're probably thinking that the superiority of wives is the most ridiculous, the most absurd, the most asinine idea they've ever heard. I can hear the roars of masculine protest, even before they are uttered. I don't believe that many husbands will countenance the superiority of wives, and the very word *superiority* is bound to offend a great many of them. Indeed, although I was scrupulous in my Web survey about never using that word, some husbands even objected to a relatively innocuous question about which spouse is "better" than the other. They didn't like it at all when I asked who's the one who does more work, makes more decisions, and takes on more family responsibility. Many voiced the opinion, with great fervor, that this question was unfair and inappropriate and just wrong. "We share everything," some responded. "We're a team," others insisted. "We cooperate and we communicate," a few husbands boasted. "There's no such thing as one being better in our marriage," they maintained.

Fine.

But if that's true, then why do two-thirds of wives classify themselves as superior, the ones who are efficient and organized, caring and self-depriving, the deciders and multitaskers? Are these women delusional? Are they boosting their own ego for the sake of their sanity and self-confidence? Are they ignoring the marital reality that surrounds them every day and every night of every week?

No, they are not. It's their husbands who are deceived. I believe this wholeheartedly, mostly because my research strongly supports this intuition.

First, a small minority of insightful husbands—24 percent—consider their wives to be the superior member of the marriage. They have no problem calling their wife superior, and it's not because they are "henpecked" or "whipped" or any other derogatory term that describes browbeaten men. It's not because they are wusses who "let their wives wear the pants" in the family. (At this point in American culture, nearly all wives wear pants nearly all the time.) Instead, these husbands are the only ones who are able to see reality with clear and accurate vision; it's as if they're the only men who wear glasses with the right prescription. Other husbands, who don't recognize their own wives' superiority, are farsighted or astigmatic, and unable to see what's in front of their noses.

The clear-eyed husbands, the ones who recognize their wives as superior, are also more likely than other men to say that their wives are in charge of the family, according to my Web survey. And they are significantly more likely than other husbands to agree that she's the one who gives more to the relationship. Finally, these husbands are much more likely than others to say that their wife is the one who's the expert at supervising the children, seeing relatives, taking care of the house, cooking a decent meal, and expressing feelings. They're not ashamed that their wife is master of the family domain; they've come to accept it as the way things are.

Trevor, twenty-nine, is his wife's biggest cheerleader, and he has no doubts about her superiority. "My wife is great at knowing what needs to be done and figuring things out," says this doctoral candidate in chemistry who works sixty hours a week at a Maryland university. "We are living in a nice apartment for a cheap price because she did her research and got us into a program that allows low-income earners to live in nice areas. She clips coupons and only buys something if it is on sale, even if it means going to three stores for all her needs. She does our taxes on time, which I never did when I was single. She takes care of the car registration too. She knows when our daughter needs to see the pediatrician, and when we moved, she arranged for the telephone transfer, the Internet transfer, the cable transfer, and got us a better auto insurance rate for living in a safer neighborhood," Trevor recalls. "She even ordered the moving truck. She is definitely the queen of responsibility and decision making in our family."

Husbands like Trevor who say their wives are superior differ from other husbands by how much money they earn. They are about the same age, on average, as other husbands, and they have been married about as long. Like other husbands in the survey, nearly 70 percent have at least a college degree, and they are no more likely to belong to one religious group than another. But those who admit to having a superior wife earn slightly more than other husbands, by about 11 percent, and they work longer hours, forty-six hours a week compared to forty-two, according to my research. It's possible that husbands who confess to having a superior wife delegate more family work to her as a deliberate tactic. Anton, thirty-nine, is aware that he does just that. He's a technician in an electronics plant near his home in Marietta, Georgia, with an Even-Steven wife whom he designates as superior. Because Anton's wife works at home, "she's there when our two children come home from school, and she gets them started on their homework and takes care of any pressing issues they might bring home," he explains. He calls her level of family commitment "incredible," adding that "she plans most of the meals, takes care of the domestic things, does the doctor visits, the family calendar, and the social coordination, all while working full-time and rarely taking time for herself." Plus, he says, "dealing with me is never a cakewalk. So she is doing a much better and much more important job than what I do most of the time." It's her obvious superiority, in fact, that makes him feel somewhat inadequate. "There are times that I feel that I am not as good a husband, father, or lover as I want to be," Anton confesses. "I try my best to supply the love and support my family needs, but I do fall short on occasion."

Unlike Anton, Larry is not at all embarrassed by his wife's superiority. A forty-six-year-old evangelical Christian minister in Urbana, Illinois, Larry has a Booster wife who went back to work part-time two years ago. He hasn't quite gotten used to taking more initiative at home, now that she's working, but he knows that he should, since she's gone most of the day and they have four high-maintenance children. "She carries an inordinate amount of the daily responsibility that it takes to run our family, and by far, she makes more of the decisions," he says. "I really need to pay attention to the wear that takes on her, and to pitch in and help her with things as much as I can, because I know that it's clearly my wife who does more." Perhaps it's his strong faith that keeps Larry so utterly and unabashedly honest.

Husbands who classify their wives as superior are no less happy about their marriage or their sex life, and they are not more likely than other husbands to believe that their marriage might have been a mistake. So don't feel sorry for these honest, highly perceptive men; their wives' superiority is not a matter of their discontent, it's just a matter of fact.

It's obvious to Shane, twenty-seven, that his Booster wife is the superior one, mostly because he's never home. Shane works eighty-four hours a week on an offshore oil rig, and he's away from home eight months out of the year. His wife is a teacher who works forty hours a week and lives in Lafayette, Louisiana, waiting for Shane to show up like a traveling salesman who makes an occasional conjugal pit stop. Shane's wife is superior, he says, simply because she has to be. "When I'm at home, I don't feel like doing much," Shane says. "While she's at work, I go to sleep or relax, and then when she gets home and asks me what I did all day, I can only answer, 'Nothing!'" They don't have children yet, so their lives aren't complicated by the constant demands of a crying infant or a teething toddler. Right now, in fact, their only problem, according to Shane, is being able to save up enough money to buy a high-definition plasma television set, for him, and a new living room couch, for her.

Explaining the Great Divide

Why are husbands like Larry and Shane, who openly admit their wives' superiority, so rare? Why is it that nearly three times as many wives as husbands believe they are superior? In this chapter, I try to figure out the answers to these questions, by giving husbands a voice and by allowing them to express their beliefs and feelings about marriage and life, the joys as well as the irritations and fears. I confess, however, that I believe most husbands simply do not comprehend their wives' level of superiority. The men aren't lying, they just don't get it. I can't offer definitive proof of wifely superiority, with objective measures like grade point averages or height in millimeters or speed in miles per hour. But I can offer logical interpretations of my research, which provides strong signs that wives are *not* mistaken about their superiority and that wives view marriage in a more accurate light than do husbands.

First, let's look again at additional evidence that supports wives' superiority. Faced with a list of the ten most common family duties, from cooking a decent meal to maintaining cars and managing finances, wives say they have mastered, on average, seven of the ten and that husbands are the expert, on average, of three of the ten. Husbands disagree, however, saying that they are expert at five of these tasks, two more than their wives give them credit for. Likewise, more wives than husbands believe they are the one who gives more in the marriage: 37 percent of wives say so, compared to just 18 percent of husbands. Compared to husbands, twice as many wives feel that organizing the family and supervising the children are their responsibility. It makes sense, then, that more wives than husbands sometimes feel that their marriage was a mistake and that their marriage is less than happy. Wives perceive the reality of their superiority, and that makes them more upset than husbands about their marital status quo. Husbands, however, view family life and marriage through their own male-centric lens, which blinds them to certain truths about their own shortcomings.

Husbands tend not to see how much more their wives do, or how much more their wives sacrifice, or how much more peeved and distressed their wives feel. They see what they have been raised and trained to see: just the male facts. They see the external details of family life but not the complexity and demands of its internal mechanisms; it's as if their eyes can't focus on the small stuff, only on what's large and really obvious.

I'd like to point out, however, that it's not as if all wives disagree with everything their husbands say. Many wives and husbands agree, for example, about whose job it is to earn money: half say it's up to both partners, according to my Web survey. In addition, half of wives and half of husbands agree that the wife is the primary nagger in the family. As long as husbands aren't being asked to confess how much they pitch in at home, or how much family responsibility they are taking, or anything that they feel remotely guilty about, their answers are much more in line with those of their wives. When I ask couples how many hours a week their spouse works outside the home, for instance, the answers that husbands and wives give are almost identical. Likewise, when I ask husbands to describe their marriage type, based on their wives' comparative income, the proportion of men in each marriage type is about the same as the percentages according to wives. So men are reliable when reporting objective family facts and figures.

It's only the subjective, emotion-tinged details that men muddle, apparently. As a result, husbands misinterpret, misreport, and misunderstand their wives' superiority. There are at least four reasons for this. First, *men are in the habit of exaggerating to themselves* about how much they do around the house. It's not that they are lying; far from it, since they sincerely believe that what they report is accurate. The only problem is that it's usually not. Second, *some men are deliberately obtuse*, avoiding responsibility by pretending to be less capable than they really are. Third, *some men may be really and truly oblivious*, completely unaware of how their wives manage and maintain the family. And finally, it's possible that *some husbands feel threatened by their wives' superiority* and so refuse to accept or even acknowledge it.

Men exaggerate. Men, and husbands in particular, have a tendency to exaggerate just how much they do at home, research shows. This is what I call the *over/under problem*, and I'm not talking about sports gambling. Men are constantly overestimating what they do at home and underestimating what their wives do. Sixty-nine percent of wives say they do all or most of the housework, while only 29 percent of husbands believe their wives do that much, according to a random national survey conducted in 2004 by pollsters at the University of Chicago.[1] There's a clear difference between what men *say they do* and what they *actually do*, according to just about everybody who's ever studied domestic life. It turns out that on any given day, eight in ten married fathers do no housework at all, according to a massive study of seventeen thousand Americans. Yet on any given day, seven in ten married mothers who work full-time engage in some kind of housework, according to a study conducted between 2003 and 2005 by the Bureau of Labor Statistics.[2]

When sociologists try to figure out who's really washing the dishes and cleaning the house, doing the laundry and the cooking, the shopping and the paperwork, they find that their results vary dramatically, depending on whether they ask husbands or wives. Husbands are almost delusional in the amount of housework they claim to do, most likely because they answer the way they know they *should* answer. It's a matter of social desirability, which means that men feel a great deal of peer pressure to say that they contribute a fair share at home. A great many men succumb to this force and offer answers that are politically correct, rather than responses that are accurate and honest.[3] Researchers conclude that husbands are proud of expressing what they realize is the correct attitude—"I do as much as my wife, aren't

I terrific?"—although their actual behavior may be as politically incorrect as possible. In one study, wives estimate that they do about thirteen more hours of housework each week than their husbands, but husbands say the gap is just half that size. In addition, these social scientists find that wives spend more time than husbands thinking about what they have to do every day and planning for it. Thus, wives do at least one hour more each week of so-called mental labor.[4] As a result, wives are not only doing more of the nitty-gritty work for their families, they're also doing more of the organizing and preparing and hashing out of game plans and schedules.

Men play dumb. A second possible explanation for the perception gap is that men are deliberately obtuse, playing dumb to evade responsibility as well as to avoid facing the truth about their wives' superior skills and talents. Asking about this issue in my Web survey, I discovered that three in ten husbands say that they sometimes play dumb, pretending not to know how to do something to avoid doing it. Even more wives—four in ten—believe that their husband plays this little conjugal trick.

Playing dumb in marriage is certainly not a new idea. During the 1950s, a marriage counselor writing for *The Ladies' Home Journal* advised wives to bolster their husband's ego by pretending to be incompetent. The expert suggested that wives should make a husband feel needed by playing cards poorly or acting unable to balance the checkbook, so that hubby can be the one who takes charge. The author even lauded one wife who admitted that she had deliberately frayed a lamp cord so that her husband could step in and fix it, thereby becoming a do-it-yourself hero.[5]

Nowadays, though, it's more likely that the husband is the one sabotaging the electrical appliances. "My wife is very handy about the house, so I make a point of being hopeless with tools and crafty things," says a forty-one-year-old husband and father who owns a boutique winery in Northern California. Another says, "I don't do cell phones." Some husbands are downright cheerful about their adamant refusal to learn how to do domestic stuff or, as a sixty-one-year-old Connecticut banker puts it, "When asked to do things that are clearly 'wifely' in nature, I dummy up out of resentment."

Some husbands admit outright to playing dumb: they explain that "I am a champion avoider," or they admit that they simply don't complete chores and tasks, having learned to wait long enough for their wives to give in and do it themselves. Here are the most common chores that many husbands say they avoid: laundry, which is almost universally despised; cooking dinner; cleaning bathrooms; dusting anything; changing diapers; and paying bills. "I am not so much 'playing dumb' as momentarily overcome by male blindness, like the inability to see things in the refrigerator, not out of laziness but out of some temporary and bizarre electrochemical disability," explains a fifty-two-year-old entertainment lawyer and father of six from Beverly Hills, California. His method usually works, he believes, because it has helped his marriage thrive. Many husbands admit that if they really don't want to do something, they make sure to do a really bad job of it, "because if I do something badly enough times, I'm not asked to do it again," one such husband confesses.

A like-minded husband agrees that he loves playing dumb. "I am a deliberate underfunctioner," Mark explains, proud of inventing a word that describes his domestic undeeds. A tall, square-jawed, thirty-eight-year-old writer and father of three, Mark loves his wife, but he especially hates doing laundry and cleaning the kitchen. "When my wife and I moved in together, before we got married, I'd play incompetent around the house. Like, I'd mix colors in the wash when I tried to do the laundry. In my home, any job you flub gets taken away from you, so it works quite well," he says, adding that this scheme doesn't work at work, where it can get you fired. "Women just can't resist helplessness," he believes, so he gives his children what he calls "crappy baths" and he doesn't wipe the crumbs from underneath the toaster, because he knows his wife can't stand the mess. "But I don't mind," he concludes, "because mess is my natural state."

Playing dumb seems related to *learned helplessness*, a state in which people believe they are unable to overcome repeated failures. This happens when, no matter how hard you try, you can't control what happens, so eventually you give up trying completely. During the 1970s, social scientists used this term to explain all kinds of problems, from depression and low academic achievement to mortality rates among the elderly and even battered-wife syndrome, in which abused wives refuse to escape their tormentors.[6] When husbands play dumb, though, it's more like *self-taught helplessness*, a deliberate attempt by men to train themselves to be dependent on their wives.

Husbands like Mark, who's an expert at self-taught helplessness, rationalize their dumb-and-dumber strategy as something that all men do or that they practice only when necessary. A few also tell themselves that "there are some things that a woman should do for a man." Thus, they justify their helplessness as a natural response or as a temporary glitch. Whatever their rationale, though, they believe that helplessness is justified. Then there are a few men like the thirty-five-year-old music professor from Kansas who believes, "I actually *am* dumb."

I do not mean to assert here that most husbands are dumb and proud of it or that all of them play it that way. Not at all. Husbands who play dumb are in the minority. Men who would never do such a thing tell me that the concept is "lame," "offensive," "childish," "dishonest," and even "ridiculous." Another husband confesses that once burned by pretend dopiness, twice shy. "I tried that once, and it backfired," this twenty-nine-year-old husband and father of two toddlers confesses. "When my wife feels she is doing all the work, my life can get much harder than if I had just helped out." Husbands like this insist they don't pretend, that they prefer honesty and openness; as a fifty-one-year-old father of six says, "I am a worker bee: I just do it."

Men are oblivious. It's highly possible that some men are oblivious to their wife's superiority, that their self-involvement and egocentric view of the world simply does not allow them to recognize just how much more their partner does. They aren't pretending stupidity or ineptitude, and they aren't lying when they fail to acknowledge the extent of their wives' superiority. They simply don't notice what's going on around them. Such men live in an exclusive place, in the World According to Me, in which there is little wiggle room for reality. In some ways, this apparent handicap works to male advantage, allowing them more serenity and inner peace, albeit somewhat blinkered. Thus, fewer husbands than wives perceive their marriage as possibly a mistake, according to my Web survey; also, more husbands than wives describe their marriage as "very happy." Although a bit twisted and distorted, the masculine view of reality can be a much more cheerful and optimistic point of view than the feminine one. As a big-nosed man says to his big-haired wife in a *New Yorker* cartoon, "I've tried a lot of life strategies, and being completely self-serving works best for me."[7]

This attitude could explain, for example, why working husbands spend half as much time doing child care as working wives do. They have simply convinced themselves that there's not all that much to do. Married mothers who work full-time spend sixty-two minutes a day taking care of a child under the age of six; married fathers who work full-time spend twenty-seven minutes a day dealing with their young child, according to the Bureau of Labor Statistics.[8] The same study also finds that married moms with children under the age of eighteen spend forty-seven minutes a day cooking and cleaning up the kitchen; married dads with children that age spend seventeen minutes a day. And that's just two examples of how husbands manage to secure time for themselves, by wriggling their way out of responsibility and doing a bit less of everything. These numbers reveal how much more time wives spend with children and doing chores at home as compared to husbands, and they are repeated in every time-use study conducted during the past several decades. No matter how researchers ask the question, the results are the same: wives do more, husbands do less.

It's not surprising, then, that husbands have significantly more free time every day than wives do. Sociologists say that husbands have from thirty minutes to an hour more of free time each day than their wives. In addition, this free time tends to be what experts call "pure" free time, which means men aren't spending their time watching television with their children. Instead, husbands are just relaxing, chilling, and having fun *on their own*. In fact, as amazing as it may seem, husbands and fathers have the *same amount* of free time every day as single men do, according to Suzanne Bianchi's daily time diary studies. That's right, married dads have just as much time to play video games and watch television as do men with no wife and no kids. "The presence of young children is not a significant predictor of free time experiences for men," says Bianchi in the dry style of social science. The same is not true, of course, for married mothers, who have at least *one hour less* of free time than single women. And if married moms have at least one child under the age of six, they have even less leisure time: an hour less than other mothers and two hours less than single women.[9]

This is probably because wives and moms tend to be driven, sometimes obsessively so, to do whatever they can for and with their children. It's almost as if they believe that taking time for themselves is a sin, a terrible character flaw that they have to avoid at all costs. If they do happen to take time for themselves, they are stricken with guilt for hours and days. Most husbands don't feel that way, nor do they understand this way of thinking. Men feel utterly entitled to snag time for themselves, with no guilt strings attached, which is why they can relax so easily. Many wives tell me that their husband comes home, eats dinner, and plops down on the sofa, as if that's the only item on his agenda for the evening. Meanwhile, she's cleaning up the kitchen, giving baths, reading stories, doing laundry, and performing any one of thirty-seven other household tasks that have to be done before midnight. Some wives are angry about having a husband who doesn't notice that he's the only spouse with the leisure to unwind; others are mystified about "his loads of free time," as one wife puts it. Wives report that husbands chill using any number of methods, from the boring to the sublime to the ridiculous. They retreat to their home office; they go on the computer; they disappear into the basement; they turn on the television; they take a nap; they go to Home Depot; they have Internet sex.

One of the most popular ways in which husbands use their precious and guilt-free free time is to exercise. They go out for a run or a bike ride, they go rock climbing or to the gym. If it matters enough to them, they don't neglect their fitness level for anything or anyone. Married fathers spend two hours and eighteen minutes a week doing active sports, according to one of Suzanne Bianchi's studies. Married mothers who work full-time spend much less time, about one hour and twenty-four minutes a week, working out.[10] Men discover vast quantities of free time that allow them to play games like basketball and volleyball, tennis and golf, to run or to swim, to weight lift and to bike.[11]

It's as if male free time is a birthright, one that cannot and will not be denied. Meanwhile, female free time is taboo, a rare and extraordinary thing.

At fifty, Craig is a father of five from Missoula, Montana, with a great deal of birthright time. He spends almost two hours a day at the gym, lifting weights, biking, running on a treadmill, and taking spinning classes. Craig is in a second marriage, works forty-five hours a week, drinks one beer a day, and views his gym time as sacred. In addition, Craig feels that staying in shape means that someday his sex dreams will come true, including his detailed fantasies about an erotic life that would include "oils and lotions, vibrators and other sex toys."

However husbands use their abundant free time, either exercising like Craig or snoozing in front of the television, many seem oblivious to what's going on around them at home. Or at least they pretend to be oblivious. "If my children want a cup of juice poured for them, they have to ask my husband three or four times before he even hears them," says Shelly, thirty, a superior wife in White Plains, New York, who's also an Alpha wife. "They get tired of asking him and they come find me, usually. Does he not hear them because he does not care? I doubt it. I think he's just used to me taking care of these things, so he literally doesn't hear what's going on, because he doesn't have to."

This kind of self-absorption, deliberate or not, is more typical of husbands than of wives, and it's superior wives who zoom in while their mates zone out.

Men feel threatened. Some husbands truly believe that they belong to the superior gender and feel threatened by any hint otherwise. Rich, a fifty-year-old husband and father of two from a small town in Michigan, has been unhappily married for almost thirty years. He says his wife has "a histrionic personality disorder" and that she was traumatized by sexual abuse during childhood. Whatever the reason, Rich is bitter and resentful about the way his marriage has turned out. Here's how he puts it: "Today's liberated women are the most evil. They draw us in with sex, suck the life out of our bank accounts, and coldheartedly walk away. They are Satan's army elite." His wife may, in fact, be deeply troubled, but Rich himself seems scarily disturbed by the notion that his wife may be the one in the marital driver's seat.

In addition, some husbands may feel resentful of their wives because of women's greater latitude of choice. It's more socially acceptable for a woman to be able to choose to stay home, to work, or to do a bit of both, depending on the family's economic circumstances. Husbands tend to be locked in to the full-time work scenario, unless they are unconventional or less tied than most men to traditional definitions of masculinity. Their gender jealousy emerges in many different ways. One husband, a forty-eight-year-old consultant in a second marriage, lives in New York City and is bitter about supporting a wife he considers lazy and ungrateful. "My wife does the shopping, using Fresh Direct, the cleaning, by hiring a maid, the laundry, by sending everything to the cleaner, and the cooking, by picking up ready-to-serve meals at Whole Foods," he explains. "She is in charge of home furnishing, by hiring an interior decorator, takes our children to and from school, writes the monthly checks, balances the checkbook, badly, and does a lot of other administrative work. I am the 'soccer dad,' I bring home the bacon, and I have veto authority over most household decisions," he notes, "but my wife has more day-to-day control and responsibility for our family's needs and problems." Although he's the more efficient and organized spouse, his wife is superior, he says, because he works long hours and travels frequently, so she's the one who gets to be home more often. And he's envious of her at-home status too.

A few husbands confess that they've had a strategy in mind all along, which is to let their wives believe the wives are in charge, although the reality is otherwise. It's a husbandly indulgence, like letting a toddler believe that he's the one who's driving when he's really sitting in a merry-go-round race car. It's also a passive-aggressive way of demeaning a wife without her knowledge. Finally, it's a way to assuage feelings of impotence and resentment about a wife who's supercompetent.

"My wife has larger control needs than I do, so I let her feel that she is 'in charge,' though many times I am the one in control," explains Oliver, thirty-two, a nursery manager on Cape Cod, in Massachusetts. Oliver doesn't realize that this reaction reflects just how threatened he feels by his wife's abilities. "I have a carefree personality, so her being the boss does not infringe on me much," he says, unaware of his own sense of insecurity.

Are Men Incompetent?

It's certainly plausible that many husbands do not recognize their wives' superiority, because men exaggerate, men play dumb, men are oblivious, and men feel threatened. But another possibility exists, and there is no tactful way to put it, so I'll just state it outright. It could be that *some men actually are incompetent*. Some husbands, for example, do not have finely tuned social and emotional skills and are not very good with people. These men force their wives to deal with neighbors and relatives and friends, stepping

aside and letting the women arrange dinners and parties and holiday cel-
ebrations. They're the ones who can spend two hours watching sports on
television with a troubled teenage son and never talk about anything other
than the game. As I mentioned earlier, brain research shows that women's
prefrontal cortex is larger than men's, which allows women to excel at social
interactions like these and to be more mentally flexible than men. Women
think in more elastic ways, taking into account many different points of
view; men tend to think in more rigid ways, using a one-at-a-time form of
cogitation.[12] Whatever the reason, husbands may explain this kind of social
ineptitude to themselves by saying that emotional niceties are women's
work, traditionally feminine tasks that do not concern real men. In this
way, they protect and propagate their own emotional unintelligence.

But potential male incompetence encompasses more territory than just
the social and emotional. Some men really don't know how to do laundry
or dishes, they can't bake cookies or assemble a tray of lasagna, and furthermore, they have no desire to learn. They have mastered a small, very
specific skill set—their work and their basketball game, for example—and
that's all they care to conquer. Nothing else matters, because why do the
grunt work if someone else is willing to do it for you? That's what a superior
wife is for.

Male incompetence may therefore be more common than many men
realize, along with their *inability to recognize that incompetence.* Men's
failure to view themselves accurately is in line with the theory of some psychologists that many people are unable to form accurate self-impressions.
While men may be convinced that they know themselves really well, the
truth is that they don't. Experts say that people of all ages are far from exact
in judging their own abilities and shortcomings, their own talents and
flaws. Men are especially likely, researchers say, to be prone to unrealistic
optimism about their capabilities. Far more often than women, it's men
who hold outlandishly inflated views of their own skills, being unreasonably
self-aggrandizing and self-confident. Men tend to attribute their successes
to innate aptitude, a very self-assured though sometimes inaccurate stance.
Women, though, are more likely to explain their successes by quirks of fate
or luck, an approach that emphasizes women's vulnerability and insecurity.

The male tendency to self-inflation is the very essence of macho manhood, an attitude defined by an unduly optimistic view of one's self-worth.

This type of irrational and egocentric perception is caused by very common and very deeply flawed beliefs, according to psychologists. Most people, for example, rate themselves as "above average," which is, of course, a statistical impossibility. (If everybody were truly above average, then the average would no longer be the average.) People also overestimate the likelihood that great things will happen to them, like winning the lottery or picking a growth stock or becoming a music star, according to recent research. Finally, many people think they know more than they actually do. As a result, they are overconfident in their ability to make reliable judgments, about their own health, say, or about how much new material they have learned in school or how well they function at work.[13]

It makes sense, then, that many husbands fail to recognize their own incompetence. Because wives are less likely to be incompetent in family affairs, they are better able than husbands to recognize incompetence when they see it. This insight is more than a century old, at least. "To be ignorant of one's ignorance is the malady of the ignorant," wrote Amos Bronson Alcott, a nineteenth-century philosopher and the father of the author Louisa May Alcott.[14]

Exactly.

Psychologists at Cornell University demonstrated Alcott's point by conducting a series of studies showing that incompetent people are usually ignorant of their own ignorance, clueless about their cluelessness. Such incompetents fall under the "double curse" associated with incompetence, they say. "If people lack the skills to produce correct answers, they are also cursed with an inability to know when their answers, or anyone else's, are right or wrong," the researchers assert.[15] In other words, incompetent people lack the insight to know what they don't know. In addition, "the stereotype suggests that men wouldn't admit it even if they know they don't know what they are doing," says Joyce Ehrlinger, one of the researchers and now an assistant professor of psychology at Florida State University. Generally speaking, she tells me, "men are more overconfident than women."[16]

That's probably why husbands with superior wives simply don't understand how much less adept they are than their wives. In addition, "top performers," people who actually are competent, tend to overestimate everyone else's ability, because they assume everyone else is as competent as they are, the researchers find. That's why superior wives may not realize

The Gender Gap on Family Expertise

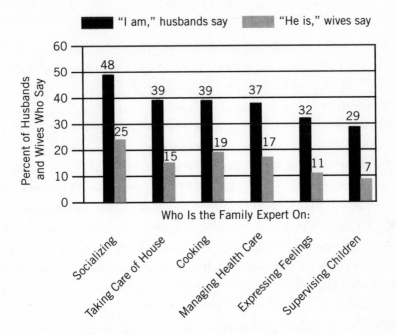

just how much more able they are than their mates, and it's why they may be naive about how much less capable their own husbands are, both at home and in the world.

This theory explains husbands' dramatic underestimation of their wives' superiority, as well as their overestimation of their own expertise. Forty-five percent of husbands believe that they are the one in the marriage with the most control and responsibility for the family; only 25 percent of wives agree with this assessment. In addition, between two and three times as many husbands as wives say they themselves are the family expert on socializing with friends, taking care of the house, cooking a decent meal, managing health care, talking about feelings, seeing relatives, and supervising children.

They just don't see that none of this is true.

Husbands clearly suffer from a failure to recognize their own incompetence on a much grander scale than wives do, which is why they are often wildly, even comically, misinformed about their own skills and expertise.

The more certain they are of their own capabilities, the greater the odds that they are utterly, entirely wrong. And the paradox is, of course, that *the less they know, the more they think they know,* since it's the most incompetent husbands who believe they know the most. In my Web survey, 35 percent of wives put their husband in the incompetent category, saying that he has mastered none or just one or two of ten areas of family expertise. Among husbands, just 7 percent admit to being that inept.

Although the Cornell researchers have never tried to pin down exactly how many men are truly incompetent, I am willing to make a guess. If two out of three wives are superior, then it's probably true that nearly that many husbands are closer to the incompetent end of the spectrum. To illustrate the point, let's look at the rare exceptions to the incompetent husband rule, the few who actually *are* at the superior end of the scale. A very small number of husbands—about 7 percent—characterize themselves, and not their wives, as the superior member of the union. These men insist that they have five or six signs of superiority, an exact parallel of the standard I've defined for superior wives. Most of these men are, indeed, superior husbands and have accurately judged themselves to be the more efficient, more decisive, more self-sacrificing, more caring, and more organized spouse. They are the only husbands who actually are top performers, a select few who are, indeed, above average. The fact that there are so very few superior husbands, a statistically negligible number, in fact, demonstrates just how rare that situation is.

Many of these husbands seem to have become superior through no choice of their own, but due to circumstances beyond their control. They are in a second or third marriage and struggling to raise their biological children with a wife who's a stepmother, for example. Or their wife is physically ill or emotionally troubled. Or they are at-home fathers married to Alpha wives and proud to be able to take on the wife role.

Mack, forty-two, is one of the rare superior husbands. He's an advertising man from Lansing, Michigan, and a newlywed in a second marriage with four children, all of them from his first marriage. "I'm the 'good cop' with the kids, and my wife is the tyrant about wearing shoes in the house, playing loud music, leaving drinking glasses on coffee tables, and eating in the living room," Mack says. "The main friction is between my wife and my thirteen-year-old daughter. They basically hate each other," he says. Not only is Mack the peacemaker, he's also the food maker, the laundry doer, and the yard worker. Although he works sixty hours a week, when he's at home, "It's usually 'tag,' I'm it," he says. "I end up with about eighty percent of the household burden on my shoulders." This is probably because his new wife believes that the children, meaning *his* children, are not her responsibility. So he picks up all the slack.

Likewise, Ryan is an Asian American superior husband because he has an emotionally fragile wife. She had twin girls a year ago, and she's still suffering from a mild case of postpartum depression. "As the only one working, I make most of the decisions when it comes to the budget and the way the house is run," says Ryan, thirty-five. "We just moved into a new house, and along with the babies, my wife faces challenges on a day-to-day basis that are very stressful and draining. She takes on too much and always feels overwhelmed." Ryan admits that his marriage is going through a rough spot, but he's hoping that will change when the babies get older and his wife gets happier. As Ryan sees it, his superiority is a temporary solution to a short-term problem.

Finally, there's Dwayne, forty-nine, a husband with an Alpha wife, from Bellingham, Washington. "I am the at-home dad and I know what the home and family needs are," he says, adding that "marriage is about love, faith, trust, and being best buddies and listening to each other." Having taken on the role of the traditional wife, Dwayne is glad that his more-educated wife is earning a living, since she makes so much more money than he ever could. "My wife is better at taking care of our financial needs, and she has had a remarkable career," he explains. "She has never once made me feel guilty about not being able to earn as much as she does, and it's only natural for me to be the one who stays home."

If it's true that most husbands are unlike Mack and Ryan and Dwayne and nowhere near as competent, then it's also logical that husbands need wives more than wives need husbands. This is not a new idea either. Benjamin Franklin, a pre-Revolutionary fount of American wisdom and invention, once referred to a single man as "an incomplete Animal," adding that such a fellow "resembles the odd Half of a Pair of Scissors," owing to his lack of a wife.[17] Several decades ago social scientists agreed completely, convinced that marriage was highly beneficial for men but mostly detrimental for women. Today that view has changed slightly, and many experts are now persuaded that marriage is a boon to both men and women in terms of finances, psychological well-being, and health, though to different degrees.[18] Married men are better off than single men, earning more money and enjoying better emotional and physical health. The same is true for married women, when compared to single women. Still, the benefits of marriage for men turn out to be much more pronounced and much more dramatic than those for women. Married men earn much more than single men, a larger difference than the one between married and single women. Husbands also live longer than never-married men, and the difference is much more significant than the one between married and single women. In part, that's because husbands take many fewer risks than single men do. They have lower suicide rates, they are victims of fewer accidents, they are less likely to smoke and therefore less prone to lung cancer, and they are less likely to become alcoholic and to die of cirrhosis of the liver. In addition, husbands are more likely than single men to use seat belts, they visit the doctor more often, and they see friends and socialize on a more regular basis. These medical and social advantages occur because husbands, unlike single guys, have someone who monitors their health, even if it is a nagging superior wife. The differences between wives and single women are somewhat similar but not nearly as dramatic.[19] So there's clearly an advantage for men in being married—in particular, in being married to a superior wife, a woman who is not ashamed or afraid to take charge of her mate's health and well-being and sanity.

Why is it, then, that so many husbands complain about their wife's nagging, when that could be what's saving their lives? It's part of the male refusal syndrome: the stubborn rejection of anything that's in their best interests if it's even remotely related to their wife's being right about something. It's similar to the way a two-year-old responds when you tell him that he has to take a bath or use the toilet or eat his dinner: "No, no, no!" A toddler doesn't call those constant reminders of what's best for him nagging, but many husbands do.

An Encyclopedia of Nagging

Husbands have a somewhat predictable view of nagging: they hate it.

Indeed, many married couples engage in nagging on a regular basis, as a kind of marital mental exercise. When I asked wives and husbands in my Web survey about who nags whom about what, I received a torrent of responses, literally a tidal surge of topics from A to Z, which I present here as an encyclopedia of nagging, from the husbands' point of view.

Wives are the primary naggers in about half of marriages, according to both wives and husbands in my Web survey. This finding is in line with the gender stereotype that says wives nag, husbands suggest; if it comes out of a woman's mouth, it's automatically nagging, but if he makes a naglike comment, it gets a more positive spin. That's probably why just 10 percent of couples say that it's the husband who does most of the nagging. Another 15 percent of both wives and husbands admit that both partners do the nagging. Finally, one in four wives and husbands claim that neither partner nags, that theirs are nag-free marriages. Such spouses even refuse to use the expression, insisting that the word *nag* is simply not part of their marital vocabulary, since it unfairly suggests the wife is a bitch and a harpy. They point out that *nag* has "negative connotations" and that the wife in their marriage doesn't nag; instead, she makes "suggestions," offers "friendly reminders," or "fusses" at her spouse. Occasionally, though, these wives can be "bossy" or "overbearing," spouses say.

"There is nothing to nag or criticize about," explains a forty-nine-year-old grocery store cashier from Florence, Kentucky. "We have been married so long that we have learned to live with everything." Another claims that "we have come to a point in our marriage where we allow each other to be who we are." Finally, one husband says quite simply that "life is too short to nag and argue." These husbands are the lucky ones, and part of their secret is related to superiority, I find. Couples are most likely to say that neither partner nags if they do *not* include a superior wife. (I'll discuss this in greater detail in chapter 7.) Nagging may in fact be a symptom of dissatisfaction and frustration lying just beneath the surface of a superior wife marriage, as we'll see. It's a subtle hint, a tell, that having a superior wife may not be in a husband's best interests after all.

It's certainly true that some husbands believe that their wife nags simply because she wants everything to be done the way she wants it done. She nags no matter what he does or how he does it, some men say. "My wife overrides my authority to have control: right or wrong, it must be her way, or else," says an engineer from Illinois who is now separated from his controlling wife. Even a retired seventy-year-old husband, happily married for thirty-eight years, says that his wife's method of control "is to publish a set of ironclad decrees. She nags to get me to do something she wants, and she never lets me forget."

These men are in the minority, however, since most husbands agree that their wives nag with a specific goal in mind. "Many women think that they have to nag their husbands just to get them to take care of things," according to Gordon, a thirty-four year-old husband in a Captain and Mate marriage from Lynnwood, Washington. "It's almost as if they think we can't function without them," he adds, nailing a common wifely sentiment right on the head. Gordon is married to a superior wife, so it's highly probable that he's right—that's exactly what she's thinking.

Many superior wives nag because their husbands do not, in fact, manage well without their help and advice and gentle suggesting. Call it nagging, call it reminding, but whatever you call it, superior wives tend to be on their husband's case for an almost infinite number of reasons.

As for whether nagging ever works, the male consensus is that no, it does not, even when they know it is justified. "I am quite forgetful, and I also tend to procrastinate," confesses a twenty-eight-year-old Boston husband. "I usually deserve the nagging, but typically, it is not effective," he adds. Another says that "my wife nags me continually about the tasks she has asked me to take care of but that I haven't yet completed." He tries to wangle his way out of it by not giving her a "timeline for completion. If I tell her I'll get something done by Saturday, she expects it to get done by Saturday, but if I leave the end date open," he confesses, "I can always tell her that I just haven't gotten to it but that I haven't forgotten it, even if I have." Likewise, a twenty-seven-year-old husband from Baltimore explains that his wife "only nags about things I don't want to do, because I don't like them and want to avoid doing them until the last possible second." But he doesn't really mind, he says, because he realizes that she's reminding him of stuff he really *should* be doing.

"The majority of nagging comes from a place where the husband pretends to forget something that he was secretly hoping she would forget as well" is the way a thirty-six-year-old librarian from New Jersey views it. Finally, a thirty-one-year-old new father from Minneapolis confesses that he most definitely needs to be nagged. "I'm fairly forgetful, so I admit that

I require some nagging to function effectively in society." Just because nagging might or might not work doesn't mean that wives or husbands won't try it anyway. And they do, they really do.

Men get nagged about "every thang," as a twenty-seven-year-old car detailer from Alabama writes. To include a truly comprehensive list of marital nags would be impossible, since the varieties are as myriad as grains of pollen on a spring morning. I believe it's safe to say, however, that there would be much less nagging in America if three things vanished from the face of the earth: dishes, socks, and video games. (If the first two never needed washing and the third never needed playing, husbands would almost never need nagging.)

Here, then, is a brief and far from complete alphabetical summary of what modern husbands say they get nagged about by their wives.

A, Appearance: Wives nag their husbands about losing weight, both for health reasons and for cosmetic reasons. One husband says that his wife repeats it over and over again, like a mantra: "Lose weight, lose weight, lose weight." A thirty-six-year-old husband from Raleigh, North Carolina, explains that "when we got married, I had been lifting weights religiously for nine years, but since we graduated from college and began working real jobs, I haven't been able to work out and I have terrible eating habits these days. Thus, my weight has increased. She's still smoking hot, so I guess it's not really fair, but she loves me anyway." Another is nagged about his posture, told by his wife every other day to "stand up straight." Husbands get nagged about not getting their hair cut often enough to "maintain a put-together look," about wearing dirty clothes, and about "not washing my face and getting blackheads." Several say they get nagged about not clipping nose hair or not getting rid of back hair. They are also gently reminded, or nagged, that their wives don't like what they are wearing, whatever it is that they may be wearing.

B, Bathroom: It may be the smallest room in the house, but it's the biggest source of nagging. The bathroom is a hotbed of nags, those that range from not replacing the empty toilet paper roll to leaving wet towels on the floor to not cleaning the toilet to "lack of aim when it comes to urination," as one husband confesses. There's also the problem of "leaving caps off things," like toothpaste tubes, which are located in the bathroom, and "leaving beard hair in the sink." One husband confesses that he has a habit of "leaving my towel bunched up," and that always gets him nagged. Another says he forgets to wipe up the dirty water he leaves on the floor, and his wife nags him about the puddle. A third gets nagged about "leaving my razor, toothpaste, and other bathroom items sitting on the sink. She won't pick them up, but she'll make sure I know I left them out where they don't belong." Then, of course, there's the leaving up of the toilet seat, a global problem, one that remains uncorrected by modern science to this day.

C, Cooking: A twenty-nine-year-old Kansas husband in an Even-Steven marriage says that his wife "nags me to have a hot meal made for her when she has to work late, but I rarely ever make a meal. We go pick up some fast food when she gets home." Another says that his wife nags him to cook dinner at least once a week, "but I pretend I'm not a very good cook," he confesses. A forty-five-year-old husband in New York complains because his wife nags him not just about cooking but about not thinking about what to cook. "She says it would help her if I could just decide what we should have for dinner, but I have no idea and I really don't care," he says. "I just don't ever like to think about what I'm going to eat, I just want to be able to do it."

D, Dishes: Husbands get nagged about not doing the dishes, but they also get nagged about not rinsing them, about leaving them in the sink, about not paying any attention whatsoever to them, and about "not cleaning up the kitchen often enough," as one says. Another confesses that his wife "nags me about not doing dishes when I don't have to go to work until the afternoon, or about not loading the dishwasher correctly." A Florida husband says he washes the dishes but can't be bothered "to figure out where they go," so he gets nagged about not putting them away. Undone dishes are an eyesore and an obvious symbol of a chore that needs to be completed, so they are a constant source of nagging tension. One husband is sheepish about "leaving dirty dishes stacked in the sink for a week and unwashed pans on the stove," because it's his responsibility to do them. It's just that, well, he doesn't want to do the dishes. Ever.

E, Ego: "I am often criticized about my antisocial behavior or about not speaking up when I have something to say in professional or social situations," says a twenty-seven-year-old husband from Florida who is married to an Alpha wife. A forty-one-year-old teacher from Oregon admits that his wife "reminds me to break out of my self-centeredness at times, since I tend to focus only on my own need for lots of quiet time. I will wrap myself up in a movie or a book, when I should be spending time with my family." These nags are focused on the husband's personality traits, on trying to change or fix who he is as a person. Husbands get nagged about "being boring and not liking to go places," as one says, or for "not being aggressive enough in seeking advancement opportunities at work." Another explains that "she gets on me about thinking of myself first, rather than anyone else's needs." Sometimes, but not always, husbands realize that their wives' critiques are on target. As one admits, "She gets frustrated at me, and she's right, because if I were her, I would call me lazy and stubborn and argumentative too."

F, Fixing things: While a traditional man used to be one who could fix a leaky pipe or a broken bicycle, such manly mechanical skills are on the wane. Even when husbands are capable of doing such work, they often fall short and therefore get zinged by wifely nags about repairs. A professional plumber even admits that he hasn't had time to put handles on his own home shower faucets, so his wife has to use a giant wrench every time she wants to turn on the hot water; she nags him about it every single day. Other husbands are given to-do lists by their wives, sometimes with deadlines that they invariably miss. Another says he gets nagged "about my incomplete projects around the house." Husbands also get nagged about stuff they are supposed to fix but never actually do.

G, General gripes: An all-purpose nagging category, this is for husbands whose wives nag them for "biting my nails" and "for putting on cologne, because she says it gives her a headache." It's for the husband who gets nagged for "the manner in which I take off my socks." And it's for the husband who eats pizza and wraps with a knife and fork, which drives his wife crazy. It's for a thirty-year-old youth pastor in Kansas, whose wife does not approve of his snacking habits. "An extra serving of cottage cheese here, a little too much peanut butter there, maybe a few fig bars, like a package at a time, and that nasty, dirty-water coffee that costs eight dollars a bag, it all adds up! Where I come from," he explains, "the purpose of food is eating. But in my wife's book, food is a garnish, a luxury item, an ornament. But I have more body mass and I require thirty-two percent more fuel," he says, admitting that "the science of my argument is a little shaky, but it sounds justifiable to me. Also, is having a highly refined palate such a crime?" An artist in Atlanta, thirty-five and a father of two, says his wife nags him about "my inability to make simple, quick decisions, like what to eat, whether to go to Target or Wal-Mart, and which tool to use in the kitchen." She's also on his case about his forgetfulness, "about statements she's made that were important but that didn't register in my memory." That's also a problem for Isaac, twenty-nine, a graduate student in Indiana, who claims that he often doesn't even know what his wife is nagging him about because "if I listened to her better, she wouldn't need to nag me as often. She has a habit of asking me to do something and assuming that I understand what she wants, that I will remember what she tells me, and that I agree to do the task. Generally, at least one of these assumptions is inaccurate, since I usually don't hear her, can't understand her, and have a memory like a sieve for things I don't care about." Isaac is clearly a guy who likes lists—just not lists about stuff he's supposed to do.

H, Health: This category includes nagging about bad habits that lead to bad health, like smoking, "dipping Skoal," not taking vitamins, and drinking too much. It's also about "not going to the doctor or dentist when I need to," as one husband says. It's about "smoking cigars and pipes," says another. And it includes nagging about bad eating habits, which are legion across American maledom. "I have a killer sweet tooth, and my wife nags me about eating too much ice cream," says one fellow. Another says his wife nags him about "eating correctly, choosing appropriate foods and serving sizes," and that he really needs these constant, though annoying, reminders. One husband's wife nags him about "taking out my contacts before bedtime," a personal chore that he can't seem to remember to do, just like the guy whose wife nags him "to brush my teeth and floss regularly." Finally, one man says his wife nags him because "I may be an alcoholic."

I, In-laws: "She nags me about seeing her parents, because we see mine more often," says a thirty-six-year-old Even-Steven husband from Pennsylvania. Another gets nagged because "she says I don't connect with her family enough," that he doesn't make an effort to talk to them or to get to know them. Yet another says his wife nags him that "my parents are intolerable, and I agree that they are, but they're still my parents." At the other end of the spectrum, a fifty-four-year-old father of four in Colorado says his wife nags him to call his own mother. "I am happy to do this once or twice a month, but my wife thinks I should call my mom every day." Many studies about marital harmony, by the way, reveal that arguments about in-laws are as common as tiffs over money and sex.[20] Not only that, but the less often couples argue about in-laws and the better their relationship with the other's family, the higher the quality of the marriage.[21] So interfamily harmony is essential in fostering a good marriage. It's a matter, perhaps, of love your mate, love his or her mom and dad.

J, Judging: In a nutshell: "She always tells me what to do and how I can do it better," says a twenty-nine-year-old Even-Steven husband from an outer suburb of Chicago. Other husbands say that their wife nags "like an overbearing boss instead of a partner" or that "she is a real complainer, very picky, moody, rarely satisfied, and with no sense of humor." It's just that she's so judgmental about whatever is relevant, or not. So one husband says, "She nags me about not reading my Bible daily," while another says, "It's because I don't know the difference between a dish-drying towel and a hand-drying towel, or the difference between a dust rag and a glass-cleaning rag. To me, a towel is a towel and a rag is a rag." An insurance underwriter from Arkansas says that his wife deems him socially inept and "nags me a lot about social obligations, from calling our son or my parents, to getting cards to celebrate an engagement or giving a gift to someone who bought a new house." One husband, a teacher in Missouri, summarizes the judging nag with a classic joke: "If a man says something in the forest and his wife is not there to hear it, is he still wrong?"

K, Kids: Husbands get nagged about spending more time with their children and paying more attention to the kids. They get nagged too about "teaching them to do things like ride a bike, tie their shoelaces, whistle, read, and pray," says a father of five in Iowa. A twenty-nine-year-old chef in Missouri complains, "It's not fair to expect me to come off an eight- or nine-hour work shift and take over, just because she has been with the babies all day." Another resents it when his wife "nags me to watch the baby while she is cooking, which I might not want to do, since I just got home from a long day at work." A father of three gets nagged about "not stepping up to the plate when it comes to the kids." Husbands are criticized for yelling at the children, for disciplining them too harshly or not enough, and for their inability to "put the needs of our children first and to take responsibility for them," as one father says. "She says I am not strict enough with the kids, that I let them watch too much television," says another. Finally, one exhausted father of one-year-old triplets gets nagged for not spending enough time with his baby boys, though he works six days a week as a teaching assistant in a college art department. "Unfortunately, there's only one of me, three of them, and twenty-four hours in a day," he says.

L, Laundry: This is the bane of husbandly existence, and it's also the most relentless, unforgiving, and unwanted chore of all. If rocket scientists could focus their attention on rendering the doing of laundry obsolete, they'd be doing mankind—husbandkind in particular—a great service. Husbands get nagged about washing the clothes, about folding the laundry, about putting their clothing in the laundry basket and not on the floor. "I don't know how to do the laundry, and I'm not too interested in learning, though my wife bugs me about it," one husband says. Another admits that "I can't stand folding laundry and I have trouble figuring out her system of where all the kids' clothes go," so he doesn't do that either, making for another ripe nagging nugget. Several husbands admit to "turning occasional pairs of socks the wrong color" by overenthusiastic laundering or shrinking their wife's clothes by overenthusiastic drying. In both cases, the result is enthusiastic wifely nagging.

M, Money: Husbands are nagged about spending too much on their children, about not paying bills on time, and about not spending wisely, which includes buying rounds of drinks at happy hour, going on shopping sprees in electronics stores, and buying all kinds of car gadgets. They are nagged about not earning enough or not earning more than their wife or about being in debt and living "check to check," as one husband puts it. One husband confesses that he never writes down the amounts he charges on his debit card, "and she hates that." A father of four in Greenville, Illinois, says, "She nags about our financial woes and about how I don't make enough and she has to work to make up the difference." He doesn't refer to this as nagging; he calls it "being criticized." A Muslim husband in California says his wife nags him about money "because she is frugal. But it's also difficult because she's the one who earns most of the money, and I'm the one who determines how to spend it."

N, Nagging: Husbands are nagged to stop nagging, in a kind of reverse metanagging. This works both ways, since husbands admit that they also nag their wives to stop nagging them. "I criticize her about being criticized," says one man. An at-home dad with an Alpha wife notes the irony in the way that he has become the family nagger. "I love raising my kids, but when you take over the house, you become the nagger," he says, adding, "Now I know how my mother felt!" It's like an infinite loop of nagging, with no beginning and no end in sight. Which is exactly the way a twenty-nine-year-old church youth director in Branson, Missouri, sees it. "She nags me about my nagging about her, and it's a vicious cycle," he says.

O, Organized or not: "She's organized, I'm a slob," admits a forty-two-year-old husband in Fort Lauderdale, Florida, a difference that makes for constant spousal nagging. Indeed, the issue of messiness is among the most common reasons for nagging on the part of wives. "She nags me to put my shoes in the closet," says another Florida husband, "because she's a little clumsy and doesn't watch where she puts her feet and she tends to trip over my shoes due to their size. This always upsets her." It's not that he's leaving his size-fourteen sneakers in the middle of the floor, it's just that she's uncoordinated and prone to stumbling.

P, Procrastinating: "I'm lazy, and I don't do things in a timely manner," says a forty-six-year-old mail carrier in Flint, Michigan, "and my wife gets irritated with me when I don't do the things she has asked me to do." A Pittsburgh husband agrees, saying that his wife's only real discontent is "related to my procrastination and my lack of follow-through on completion of projects." There are plenty of procrastinators, apparently, and most seem to receive wifely nagging on the issue. "I am by nature a procrastinator," says a thirty-three-year-old marketing executive in Gainesville, Florida, "but I do keep an eye on deadlines," which doesn't prevent his wife from nagging him about projects he hasn't finished. A computer programmer from Hixson, Tennessee, admits that "I put things off, like having the deck refinished or cleaning the siding, closing our pool for the winter or helping her with paperwork that I've promised to look over. My wife criticizes this and says it shows a lack of responsibility," he adds, not necessarily disagreeing with her. A fifty-year-old husband in Georgia says, "I don't always read my mail right away, so the letters and magazines and catalogs pile up and she lets me know about it." Not only that, but "she's always nagging me to 'Please clean up your pile,'" he adds. A forty-seven-year-old father of two in Texas is ashamed of being a die-hard procrastinator. "I have a number of unfinished home improvement projects like painting and remodeling that I haven't gotten done. She is ticked off and I have no excuse, guilty as charged. I need to step up and do more," he admits. The problem here, many husbands say, is that they agree to do things around the house and then never quite get around to doing them. Why not put off until tomorrow what you really, really don't feel like doing today?

Q, Quality of affection: "I get nagged about not being romantic, not getting her flowers and stuff more often," says a twenty-nine-year-old husband in Covington, Kentucky. Another says his wife is on him about "not saying I love her, or that she's beautiful, or that I want her." Husbands say that their wives get upset that they don't spend more time together, that there's no romance in the marriage, or that he's insensitive to her feelings. A few mention that their wives nag because they never go on dates together, the way they did before they got married. One husband calls this "being a victim of you-do-not-show-me-enough-affection nagging syndrome, a well-known condition that has caused many a man to consider consuming massive amounts of vodka." Another says his wife nags him about "how I behave around other women," because she doesn't approve "any time I have conversation or interaction of any type with another female." Finally, one husband is trying to give his wife a single red rose every month as a token of his affection, but he doesn't always remember to buy the dang flower.

R, Rides: This is about driving: husbands' driving style drives their wives crazy. One says his wife criticizes him for being too aggressive every time he makes a left turn into dense oncoming traffic. Another complains that she nags him about going too slowly and too fast. Husbands get nagged not only for how they drive but for which way they go when driving. "She nags me about the speed limit and where to turn and the best way to get somewhere," one husband says. Another claims that his wife tells him, "Your driving sucks," and won't get into the car with him unless she's driving. Another explains that his wife nags him about his "inattention to what she calls 'road dangers,' and also that I leave the garage door open." A twenty-nine-year-old minister in Columbus, Ohio, says that his wife has gotten on his case about driving only since they had their first baby. "I think it's probably a mother thing, because it only happens when the baby is in the car. I am not a bad driver, though, and she's the one who got a ticket, while I have a perfect driving record," he says. "I do drive fast, on occasion, and I don't always signal a lane change or a turn, but I would say I'm a better driver than she is."

S, Smells and Snores: Husbands are nagged about their bodily expulsions, about "bad farts," about "bodily function noises," and about their snoring. They get nagged about "being uncouth," about "not changing the cat litter box," and about belching at inappropriate public moments, all of which fall into this malodorous category. "She hates my snoring and my farting, and she tells me my poop smells," says a thirty-five-year-old physician assistant in rural Pennsylvania. A twenty-eight-year-old husband in Nebraska is even more specific. "She nags about my stinkiness and my back hair," he says. "But I think males have a stronger natural body odor than females. Either that, or we just don't take the necessary steps to eliminate the stink. I manage a fast food restaurant, so I probably don't smell all that great most of the time. Also, I'm a hairy beast." A twenty-nine-year-old computer technician from Colorado agrees. "My wife has the nose of a bloodhound, so it doesn't matter that I brush twice a day, floss, shower daily, and wear clean clothes. I smell funny to her." Another says his wife nags him about his "bad breath from garlic and coffee, and about stinking up the bathroom and not spraying air freshener."

T, Television: Husbands are nagged about spending too much time on the Internet or on the computer or on the Wii or the PlayStation or the Xbox. "She's jealous of how much I play video games" is the way a twenty-nine-year-old husband in Tomball, Texas, explains his wife's nagging. Another says his wife's view is that "I play way too many video games," though he doesn't see it that way at all. Wives also nag their husbands about watching too much sports on television, in any and all seasons. A twenty-eight-year-old husband in Illinois says his wife nags him, quite specifically, "about watching football and ice hockey on television instead of watching something 'mutual'" that they can both enjoy. Another says his wife nags him about his newly minted interest in watching football on television, "because you were never into football before we got married, blah, blah, blah," he says. One husband admits that he doesn't pay much attention to his wife when she's talking, "but that's because she only seems to talk to me when I'm watching television." Finally, one admits that "I watch TV late into the night, instead of going to bed with her, so she nags me about it." There are even high-tech TiVo nags, according to at least one husband. "She says I fill up the TiVo with things she doesn't want to see."

U, Unfair behavior: Wives nag their husbands about socializing for work while they're stuck at home with the children. "My wife is resentful that my job lets me go out and do things and that my job requires some necessary socializing," says a thirty-one-year-old contractor in Cincinnati, Ohio. He doesn't view this as unfair, but his wife sure does. Another has a wife who nags him because he travels overseas for business and she doesn't get to go along.

V, Very messy: The definition of *mess* depends on your point of view, of course, as one husband points out. "I see things as clean that she sees as messy," he claims. Untidy clutter drives some wives around the bend, and so they nag. Many husbands realize this but seem powerless to prevent the situation from occurring day after day after day. "She nags me about the amazing and ever-growing mess on my side of the bedroom," says a football coach in Vancouver, Washington. Another confesses that "when I come home from a long day at work, I leave a trail of clothes lying around the house, and my wife is constantly on me about that." "I don't always put things back where they are supposed to go," admits a thirty-year-old husband from Ohio. "I will drop my coat on the couch, and I leave my dishes in the living room. I put the food packaging on the kitchen counter, and I don't properly seal up items that go in the refrigerator. I leave my shoes in random places, wherever I kicked them off the night before. My keys are always in different locations too," he concludes. None of this bothers him, particularly, but his wife nags him about it constantly, and "recently she asked me if I thought I was a bachelor."

W, Workaholism: "The only thing my wife ever really nags about is that I work too many hours and I don't spend enough time with the family," says a father of four in Indianapolis, Indiana. Another claims that he spends fifteen hours a day at school or at work and just can't manage to be home except to sleep. His wife, though, doesn't understand his need to overwork or his belief that the situation is temporary. An entrepreneur in Washington who is beginning a start-up company says his wife doesn't understand how much potential is there or how much time it takes to build a new business. "Even though I'm spending a great deal of time and energy at work, we aren't seeing the financial rewards just yet. To my wife, it's not worth my being away from home all the time unless she's seeing that money coming in," he explains.

X, X-rated: Some wives nag their husbands about not having sex often enough. "She nags me about giving her attention after the children are all in bed, about massaging, having sex, snuggling, praying," says a father of four from Illinois. Other wives, upset that he wants it too often, nag him to shut up about it already. "I don't like asking anymore," says a thirty-year-old husband from Vancouver, Canada, "because I feel bad when I get turned down, so I make veiled comments and suggestions, which bug her no end." A twenty-seven-year-old husband from Austin, Texas, agrees that his wife nags him about wanting sex too often, since "she's tired all the time."

Y, Yard: "She says I don't take the initiative to do yard work unless she tells me," says one husband. Many husbands get nagged about letting the grass get too high. "When she wants something done in the yard, she will repeatedly mention it in a subtle way until I do it," says a twenty-nine-year-old Army officer from North Carolina. He's not upset about it, because she's somewhat tactful, unlike another guy's wife in Indiana. "She once criticized me for showing a little crack while I was hunched over in the front lawn, trying to fix a problem with the lawn mower," says this twenty-seven-year-old Web developer. "I felt it was justified, since I was working on my own property, and it isn't as if I run around with my crack showing all the time. We're talking thirty seconds of crack, tops, plus how she managed to notice it from inside the house, I'll never know."

Z, Zoning out: "I'm mainly nagged about being 'zoned out' at the end of the day," says a thirty-three-year-old pediatrician from Tennessee. "If I'm watching television and someone speaks to me without getting my attention, I'll miss the first few things they say. My wife calls me her 'little space cadet,' but I argue that it's normal not to be able to hear the first few sentences of someone who's speaking to me if I'm watching TV." Other husbands get nagged about spending too much time alone and too much time on the computer. "I am prone to periods of relaxation, where I lay on the couch and watch television or I get on the computer, because I feel I earned some downtime," says a thirty-seven-year-old attorney from Greensboro, North Carolina. "But when she gets it in her mind that she wants something done, she wants it done right then and there, like installing a new light fixture at eleven thirty at night when the old one still works." Then she keeps a mental tally of who does what, so we get into an argument over who did a certain chore last, and she'll launch into a diatribe about the last thirty times she did something that I didn't do."

• • •

So there it is: a nagging compendium, from A to Z, which does not, however, cover the true scope of wifely nagging. The topic could easily be expanded into its own book, albeit a somewhat repetitive and boring one. (In the next chapter, I'll explore what husbands nag their wives about, and how women react to these spousal reminders.)

His Marriage Mistakes

Despite this alphabetical litany of nagging, which seems somewhat disheartening when taken in all at once, a majority of husbands do *not* regret their decision to marry their current wife. This is true, by the way, regardless of whether they view their wife as superior or not, according to my Web survey. Overall, about six in ten husbands, 62 percent, say that they have never thought that their marriage might have been a mistake. By contrast, just half of wives, 51 percent, think the same way, a statistically significant difference. *Husbands are much less likely than wives to question the validity of their decision to marry.* It's almost as if husbands are under the protection of a cloud of naiveté, a haze of obliviousness, that allows them to view their marriage in a more optimistic and generous light than their wives do. Or maybe it's just that their expectations for what makes a good marriage are much lower than their wives' expectations, as we'll see in chapter 5.

Husbands who have an unwavering faith in their marriage, as do the majority of men, offer at least four different explanations for that sentiment. They say that their wife is a soul mate, that they work hard at the marriage, or that their marriage continues to improve over time. Or else—and a great number of husbands fall into this category—they just don't think about it all that much.

Soul mate husbands are like José, who says, "She is my best friend, she is the first person I want to talk to in the morning and the last person I want to speak to at night." At twenty-nine, José is a romantically inclined graduate student who has been married to a superior wife for three years. "She is everything to me," he says, adding that "it's a cliché, but my wife is my better half." Likewise, Guillermo, twenty-seven, an evangelical Christian car salesman in Gettysburg, Pennsylvania, has been married for three years and has never regretted it. "I married my soul mate and my best friend. I love the idea that she is the one with whom I will share the rest of my life," he says. Finally, Tom, forty, is an at-home father of two and has been married for ten years to a high-earning Alpha wife. He says that they are soul mates and that their relationship is based on "total disclosure of feelings and expectations. Not everyone could have a marriage like we do, but the proof is in the pudding, which I have several delicious recipes for, by the way!" Please note, however, that I couldn't find any husbands in soul mate marriages who'd been together longer than a decade. It's possible that spouses mature beyond the need to call each other soul mates; it's also possible that soul mate marriages don't last beyond the ten- or fifteen-year mark.

Other husbands say that they work hard to keep the marriage in good health and therefore rarely regret their decision to marry. "We both work at our marriage, and we try to balance control and responsibility between us," says Sean, fifty-three, a software developer in Dallas, Texas. "I've never regretted our marriage, and I sometimes think how wrong things would have been had I married someone else," he adds. Another Texas husband, a Protestant minister who's been married for twenty-seven years, admits that he and his wife had some bad times when their children were babies, a long stretch during which neither was able to get a good night's sleep. "But you never let the fact that marriage is difficult make you think that you have made a mistake," he explains. "Just because something is tough doesn't mean it is wrong."

There are also some husbands who say they have never sensed that they made a marital blunder, because their relationship seems to improve over time, like fine wine or smelly cheese. "We have issues, but my wife is able to forgive even the most egregious and stupid stuff I do," says Sam, sixty-five, an evangelical Christian from San Jose, California. "Even at our age, we have a great sex life and lots of laughs together, and we both share our love of Jesus," he explains. "I love my wife more than ever," adds Sam, who has been married for thirty-seven years. Another marital long-termer, a fifty-seven-year-old airport security officer from Canton, Michigan, has been married for twenty-four years. He says, "Our relationship is maturing, and she is wise and I am brave. We both apologize frequently to each other, and we consider each other to be our best friend." Some of these husbands clearly rely on strong religious conviction to pull them through tough times; others never lose that loving feeling, even across many, many years.

Finally, a great many husbands choose not to reflect too much on the wisdom of their decision to marry. A twenty-nine-year-old software engineer from Hurst, Texas, isn't certain about his marriage, but only because "if I was ever one hundred percent sure about anything, it'd be a sure sign of insanity." Most husbands, not particularly introspective, simply dismiss the notion that their marriage might have been a monumental error.

Husbands on the other end of the spectrum—those who suspect that their marriage might have been a mistake—offer many reasons for that feeling. Some say they are sexually incompatible, others that they married too young. Some believe that their wife focuses on the children too much, or they sense that the marriage is getting worse over time. A few even insist that their wife is too good for them.

Sexual incompatibility is a demoralizing and upsetting development in any marriage, and many men confess that this is one of their main problems. "I feel like a roommate and not a husband" is the way Terrell, twenty-eight, from Texas, puts it. A full-time student who also works as a secretary and is in the Army Reserve, Terrell doesn't have a lot of chill-out time, but he wishes that "my wife had more of a sex drive and that she'd show some affection towards me. For once, I'd like to have quality sex instead of very controlled and bland sex," he explains. "It would also occur more than twice a month and I would not have to stop asking because I am so tired of being turned down." A fifty-nine-year-old chemist from Morgantown, West Virginia, has been married just three years to his second wife, but he feels the same way as Terrell. "Before we got married, we had a vigorous sexual relationship, but that's turned into a much more conservative one," he says. "I would like for my wife to be more open to sexual exploration and to initiate the act of making love."

This is one of the most common husbandly complaints, the gradual and unforeseen reduction in the frequency and quality of marital sex. They are disappointed and shocked by what is actually a near-universal phenomenon. Take this forty-nine-year-old Manhattan husband who feels frustrated with his superior wife's lack of sexual desire: "I wish my wife would be up for having sex at all times of the day, not just at night. She'd be more adventurous sexually and wouldn't mind waking up just for sex. And she wouldn't require the whole house to be asleep first."

Such men have apparently been sheltered from widespread revelations about the most common of all marital transformations, the no-more-sex phenomenon that fuels late-night comedy jokes and barroom banter and hair salon gossip. Here's the news they've missed: as marriages and spouses get older, sex gets scarcer. Almost all sex researchers find that after the first few years of marriage, the frequency of sexual intercourse declines slowly but very steadily over time. This happens to *all* couples in *all* marriages, generally speaking. Experts even have a name for the phenomenon: they call it "the honeymoon effect." This means that sexual frequency is highest during the first three or four years after the wedding, then goes into an inexorable downward plummet every year thereafter.[22] This sexual malaise in marriage is almost as unavoidable as death and taxes. But it's also true that being in a superior wife marriage can make for an even less active sex life, as I'll discuss in chapter 6.

Husbands who sense that they may have married too young, before they had matured enough to know what they wanted in a wife, also become disillusioned. "We married for reasons of security," says Jake, thirty-five, a college administrator in Pennsylvania, "but I probably should have married someone who had more in common with me." Jake and his superior wife have been married for twelve years and have two children. "I know I should connect with my wife more, but sometimes I don't feel anything for her," Jake says. "I know I should be right there, supporting her and telling her something encouraging, but I just can't do it." Another too-young bridegroom, Darrin, thirty-five, is a factory foreman in Toronto and has been in a Booster marriage for eleven years. "We were young when we married, and we struggle financially and never get time to ourselves, away from the kids," he says. That's exactly how Jamal feels, although he's one of the very rare superior husbands. "We were not ready to get married when we did," says Jamal, a police officer in North Carolina with four children. "I pay all the bills, I make sure the kids have what they need, and I cook and clean and shop for food." If he had it to do over again, Jamal would wait a few years and not get married at the age of twenty-two, he says.

Men whose wives pay a lot of attention to the children can also feel excluded from the family, as if they've been banished from the marriage altogether. "It seems that after our two children were born, I have become a forgotten man," says Ben, thirty-four, a small truck salesman from Oswego, Illinois. "She gives so much to the children that I have to ask her to make time for us, but that never seems to happen, as if it's not important enough to her," Ben explains. His Captain and Mate marriage is an unhappy one, he says, and sometimes he feels that it was a mistake. So does Marc, forty-one, an advertising salesman in an Even-Steven marriage from Spokane, Washington. "Having children changed the dynamic of our marriage," Marc says. "Before, it was about us and our relationship, but now it's all about the kids. There's no time for adult conversation, even when we have a date night. I am a bit resentful about this."

It's husbands like Ben and Marc, no doubt, who eventually begin to feel that their marriage is on a downhill slope, getting worse and worse as time goes by. "In the last thirty years, we have grown in different directions," says Richie, fifty-four, a manager for an international missile defense company who lives in Saudi Arabia with his Hungarian wife. "She is sometimes jealous of my career, and I envy the free time she has to socialize and exercise," he says, adding that he sometimes believes that his marriage was a mistake. Mitch, forty-one, has been married for only ten years, but he feels the same way. "I sense that we are more like roommates or business partners rather than the soul mates we once were," Mitch says. A public relations executive in Detroit, Michigan, Mitch dreads hearing his cell phone ring, worried that it's a call from his wife. "I immediately feel nervous," he says. "What is it this time? What did I do? What did I forget to do? What did the kids do? It seems that as soon as something goes wrong, she calls me. What am I supposed to do about it? She expects me to handle the discipline over the phone, because she can't handle it," Mitch complains, adding that it feels good to vent about problems he never discusses openly with his wife.

Occasionally a rare husband will claim that he believes his marriage might have been a mistake—not because the marriage is flawed but because his wife settled for less by marrying him. It was a mistake for her, although not for him. "Not a day goes by that I don't think that my wife could do better. I want her to be happy, giddy, skipping-about happy. But I believe she is less happy than she could be because she's married to me," says Grey, forty-two, a computer programmer from Cleveland, Ohio, who suffers from mild depression. "Though she might protest, it's clear that our marriage was a mistake for her. She's better than me by miles, and she takes more responsibility. I want to be a perfect husband, man, employee, son, brother, uncle, and everything else. But because I can't be perfect, I feel like a failure." Though not nearly as gloomy, Bart, forty-six, says that he too often wonders if his wife "could have done better, since she's amazing and I am not." An evangelical pastor who works eighty hours a week, Bart believes that his Even-Steven wife may have married beneath her. "My wife works constantly to see that our family is healthy and happy, and she keeps the house as clean as anyone could, with five kids, two dogs, an aging father, and a busy husband. She rises early in the morning, before I do, and doesn't stop working until evening. She is better than me, she listens well, she is wiser than I am, and she is more attractive than me too. Her eyes twinkle, especially when she grins," he says. If there was any marital mistake, Bart says, it was on his wife's part, not on his.

Still, shrinking-violet hubbies like these are in the minority, and not many husbands spend time reflecting on their marital mistakes. But many, many wives tend to agonize and obsess over such mistakes, both minor and major ones. In the next chapter I'll explore the "she said" half of the "he said/she said" story of superior wife marriages.

5

I'm Always Right: How Superior Wives See Themselves

What's it like on the estrogen-infused side of the superior wife marital divide? Both similar to the male side but also radically different.

Like their husbands, many wives engage in playing dumb, they get nagged by their spouse, and they sometimes feel a sense of marital regret. Superior wives, though, are quite distinct from other wives by being even more likely to play these conjugal games and by feeling deeply unhappy with their lives and with their marriage.

It's clear that superior wives suffer for their superiority.

I am not saying that such wives are victimized by their husbands or that they are martyrs to their marriage. On the contrary, I believe that superior wives can be stubborn and self-righteous about their convictions and rigid about taking the stance that they always know best. As a result, superior wives often end up feeling self-pity, resentment, anger, and sometimes despair about their situation. In addition, they can be overcritical and short-tempered, while also unaware of being superior. In addition, most of these wives don't realize the substantial emotional cost of their superiority. Indeed, over the course of conducting my research, I have come to realize that superior wives are almost always more miserable and more distressed than other wives, mostly because they have chosen the wrong path through the jungle of marital complexity. And this choice has trapped them in a superior wife marriage.

Even worse, most superior wives have no idea that this has happened, since being a superior wife is a subtle, nonobvious condition and most are only vaguely aware that that's what they have become. It's impossible, for instance, to identify superior wives easily: they don't shave their heads or walk two paces in front of their husbands or wear "Superior Wife" caps.

Indeed, my research shows that superior wives aren't on average older or more religious, and they don't work longer hours or earn more money than other wives. It's true that they've been married longer, so it's possible that their superiority is a result of a slow process of evolution, a superior habit that has become an inexorable marital destiny. But it's much more complicated than that, because it's also true that these women hold subtle, highly traditional beliefs about femininity that ensnare them into behaving in ways that ensure their superiority. My research demonstrates that superior wives hold more traditional views about femininity than other wives. In fact, they are significantly more likely to rate being emotional, self-sacrificing, and sensitive as extremely feminine characteristics.

Angie, fifty-five, is one of these superior wives, and to her, femininity means being demure and compliant. A mother and part-time social worker in Los Angeles, Angie doesn't believe it's possible for wife and husband to share responsibility without something going amiss. "Usually the kids suffer, or the wife," she says. "The few cases I've seen where the husband does as much as the wife, she has a more powerful job or makes more money, so the husband is forced into the 'mommy' position because she doesn't have enough time or energy for the kids. But men don't think the same as mothers," Angie says, "and therefore can't successfully replace them." What Angie doesn't realize, though, is that it's this conviction that is dooming her own marriage. It's no coincidence that Angie is not very happy about her superior wife marriage or that she "gets tired of saying the same things over and over for twenty years," as she puts it, "to try to get him to pick up the slack for a change."

With beliefs like Angie's, conscious or not, wives trap themselves into a superior situation so that their rigid and old-fashioned gender ideas force them into doing too much at home, regardless of how many hours they work or how much money they earn or how much they expected their husbands to share when they were first married.

Leah, forty-seven, is a perfect example of a superior wife who has woven herself into a tight web of superiority, much to her own dismay and disgust. Leah is an Alpha wife and a Vermont lawyer who earns more than her husband. Yet she reports that she also "manages the house, the school affairs, the medical appointments, the finances, the emotional crises, the playdates, and everything else. I married an eternal youth who never grew up, even after we had children. He earns very little and relies on me to be the breadwinner, but he doesn't take responsibility for doing any household chores. He wants a millennium wife in the workforce, but a nineteen-fifties housewife at home," Leah says. And that's what he gets, since Leah agrees to be both breadwinner and housewife, in part because she's convinced that being self-sacrificing and emotional are womanly traits, an ideal to which she aspires. So Leah colludes in the construction of her own superiority trap, although it's a constant source of resentment and ill will for her.

By definition, superior wives like Leah do more of everything. More of them than other wives feel they have control over the family: 86 percent say so, compared to 53 percent of other wives. Significantly more superior wives than others are the family expert on nine out of ten tasks, such as socializing with friends and taking care of the house. More superior wives keep track of the family money, more of them make important decisions, more of them organize the family, and more of them supervise the children. More of them than other wives say that they're the spouse who gives much more, and more say they alone are in charge of what happens at home.

Superior wives live their lives under a banner of more and more and more.

Perhaps because they tend to wield an iron fist over hearth and home,

Nonsuperior Wives Are Happier Wives

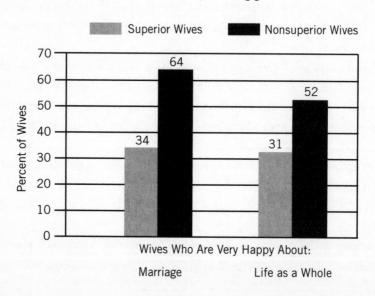

more superior wives admit that they are the primary nagger in the marriage: 56 percent, compared to 42 percent of other wives. More of them also believe that their marriage may have been a mistake, and finally, more of them are deeply unhappy. More superior wives than others say they are unhappy with their marriage, with their sex life, and with their life as a whole. All three of these differences are statistically significant, which means that they occur not by chance but because there are very real and very important disparities between superior and other wives.

Listening to the voices of frustrated and puzzled and despondent superior wives, I hear the same story over and over again. They're in charge but miserable; they're the boss but distressed; they're superior in many ways but irritated. It's as if they have taken over, but reluctantly and with sorrow. Wistfully, they long for their marriage to be otherwise, but they have no idea how to transport themselves into that other, less superior and better way of life.

Etta, forty-eight, is a superior wife in Palo Alto, California, who hungers to be a wife of another stripe. At first glance, she would seem to be as different from Vermont Leah as water from fire, but they are actually sisters under the skin. Etta doesn't work outside the home, so she supervises her children's health and education and transportation, and she's also in charge of the emotional health of everybody in the family. "I could have had a career," Etta says, "but I quit when my husband proved incapable or unwilling to help with the children and household." Because her husband earns all the family income, Etta defers to him, even when she's convinced that he's slightly crazed. "My husband is an electronics engineer, and he's obsessed with using the correct phone lines and access codes to avoid extra Internet charges," Etta explains. "He is oblivious to dirt, trash, and junk in the house or yard, but he will get fixated over a small mark on his cars, blemishes on his electronics test equipment, or small imperfections in anything that is 'his.' He keeps equipment he will never use or sell in a two-thousand-square-foot storage space, but if I complain about the cost of all his stuff, he just won't listen." Despite all this, Etta has convinced herself, just as Leah has, that it's feminine to be sensitive and self-sacrificing and emotional, so she follows that self-imposed rule like a prayer. She has become a superior wife under the delusion that it's the most feminine alternative. It's not surprising, then, that Etta admits that her marriage is an unhappy one.

Compare Etta to Connie, thirty-six, an Alpha wife from Boston, Massachusetts, who is not the least bit superior. "There was a time, at the beginning of our marriage, when I did more than my husband, and it frustrated me no end. When we talked about it, he would always be receptive and respond right away," Connie says. "I came to realize that my husband has to be told what to do, that he will happily do anything as long as I tell him what to do and how to do it. He just needs direction. Our responsibilities at home started balancing out as soon as I asked him to chip in, because as long as I wasn't speaking up, he assumed everything was hunky-dory. So now I just lay it on the line, and I communicate frankly," Connie says. For Connie, being aggressive and ambitious and strong are traits that are both masculine and feminine; for her, a feminine woman is not one who defers and does it all but one who speaks her mind and gets her way.

Jordana, forty-eight, is also a reformed superior wife. She's the director of a children's science museum in Oregon, with two children and a husband who earns more than she does, though both work forty hours a week. "For a long time, I carried the total burden of our family, because my husband was a workaholic who was traveling constantly," Jordana says. "But then he sold his business and began to work out of our home. It has been an incredible role reversal, because now I'm the working professional and he's the at-home dad. I understand now why he was preoccupied before, with so many other things besides us and the children. When I come home from work, I collapse and have no energy for anything. I defer to his decisions some of the time, but we truly share equally in our responsibilities for the family." She'll never go back to the way things were, Jordana adds, because she realizes that being superior wasn't fair—to her or to her husband. (In chapter 7 I'll examine nonsuperior wives like Jordana in greater detail, exploring the ways in which they have avoided superiority.)

What Wives Want

Superior or not, most wives are united in their great expectations for marriage and for the man they have chosen to be their life partner. For many women, marriage is the be-all and end-all; it's the focal point of life. Marriage is the hub at the center of the female wheel of existence, the point where all the spokes originate; it is the source of friendship and love and passion, of companionship and family and children, of safety and comfort and security. To most women, marriage is what makes all of that possible, as well as giving them identity and a sense of purpose. Women want it all from marriage, and they are determined to get it all, at least at the beginning. As soon as they become brides, women expect complete emotional connection, they want equality in decision making, they want domestic fairness, and they want relief from stress. While these wishes are often unspoken, they are also powerful, though not granted to many wives.

Wives want their husband to be a best friend, someone who is kind and supportive and who will always stand by them, no matter how much weight they gain after pregnancy or how irritable they get while menstruating. They want to feel loved and appreciated and understood to their very core. They want to receive affection and compassion and gentle consideration. They want a marital bond as lasting as a childhood friendship, as powerful as a mother's feelings for a newborn baby, and able to leap all run-of-the-mill stresses and problems. And they expect, indeed demand, that all of these benefits should be supplied by the man they married.

It's a very, very tall order, this wifely expectation invoice.

Wives' views of marriage, and what it should provide, are very different from husbands' notions, since men don't place all their emotional eggs into the marital basket. Marriage simply doesn't carry so many meanings and obligations for men as it does for women. Although wives are more likely than husbands to have strong ties to best friends and sisters and colleagues, they want an emotional bond with their man that's just as fulfilling. For them, that's the whole point of marriage. Wives expect to spend time with their husband, to openly express affection and to receive it, to share intimacy, and not just in bed, and to have meaningful conversations, and not just about what's for dinner or if the car has enough gas. This is the emotion work of marriage, and social scientists say that wives long to have a husband who will engage in such emotion work, but often to no avail. In fact, wives' satisfaction with their husbands' emotion work is the key to understanding their feelings about marriage, researchers say. Wives with husbands who share the emotional effort and who offer affection and compassion are happiest about their marriage. This isn't surprising, since the researchers find that husbands who are more committed to marriage tend to make a greater emotional investment in it. These husbands try harder, so it's no wonder that their wives are grateful and gratified.[1]

While it may seem obvious that wives want affection and attention from husbands, it's not necessarily apparent to their husbands. The fact that women yearn for a strong emotional connection with their mate is a mystery to many husbands, according to psychologist John Gottman, who has been studying the ways in which marriages succeed or fail for several decades. It's in a woman's nature to confront her man when she is emotionally thwarted; it's in a man's nature to avoid such emotional blowups, he says. If she always confronts and he always avoids, these opposing forces almost always push the marriage off track. She wants to talk and probe and discuss problems, like a dentist eager to clean out an infected tooth. But her husband is inclined to evade and avoid and leave, like a dentist-phobic patient. Men are more easily overwhelmed by strong emotions, and they are often flooded by anxiety at the very notion of a disturbing clash. If forced to respond, they will begin to stonewall, and eventually they will either refuse to engage in discussion or become hurtful and mean, doing what Gottman calls "destructive stonewalling." In this way, some husbands come to avoid frank and open discussion in a nasty, upsetting, and vicious way.[2]

Wives can become petty and malicious too, of course, when trying to force an intimate connection with a reluctant husband. Sometimes they do so by nagging, which makes them feel even worse. "I know nagging doesn't really get me anywhere, but I continue to do it because I just have to make my feelings known," says a superior wife from Michigan, trying to excuse her own behavior. Her husband responds to this tactic with utter silence, she says, which is, in its own way, a passive form of criticism, as well as an absolute refusal to become more intimate. Men often retreat into silence and stoicism as a way of refusing to connect or bond with their wives, and many wives resent this enormously. This pattern is most typical of superior wife marriages, I find.

"When times are difficult, my husband does not want to talk about anything," agrees Kay, forty-one, a superior wife in a second marriage from rural Oklahoma. "If I try to force him out of his silence, it turns into a fight, with name-calling and accusations, and nothing is resolved," she explains. "He works, and therefore he thinks that's all he has to do, not lifting a finger at home, even though I earn more than he does," Kay adds. "We can't really talk about our feelings, because it always turns into a fight." It's no wonder that Kay describes her marriage, and her life, as utterly unhappy.

For wives like Kay, an ideal marriage would be an honest marriage—one that's emotionally open and candid, instead of tightly closed, as if seriously constipated. Such marriages do exist, though they are not as common as many brides would like to believe. Betty and her husband are an example of such a relaxed marriage, even forty-three years after their wedding day. "We were only eighteen when we got married, and we didn't know what we were getting into, but we raised each other," she says. A nonsuperior wife from Georgia who manages a plus-size clothing shop for women, Betty says that her marriage has lasted so long because "we share the responsibilities and we have learned to tell each other how we feel. We make decisions together, we talk to each other, and we're a team. We have learned what hurts the other and what makes them cheerful, and we've found out that it's a lot more fun to make each other happy than to make each other upset," Betty explains. "My husband has very little hair left, and he has a potbelly that we are working to get rid of, but I love him, and when I look into his eyes, I see his gentleness, his kindness, and his concern for me." Betty's is an emotionally healthy marriage, one that could serve as an ideal fantasy marriage for many superior wives.

Most wives yearn to have an equal say in marriage, the way that Betty does. This doesn't mean they want to be the boss, like so many superior wives are. Instead, most wives want a man who will be a true partner and coconspirator, one who will collaborate on what to serve for a fancy holiday dinner and when to buy new shoes for the children and how often to get the car serviced. Wives, even superior wives, would prefer not to be marital Zen masters: they want to be egalitarian disciples, half of a dynamic duo seeking a joint path to enlightenment. Or, if that proves too difficult, wives would prefer at least to have a fully cooperative and obviously caring husband.

Is that too much to ask?

Perhaps it is. Social scientists find that the more couples share in decision making, the happier wives are, but that this situation is not the norm. The researchers point out that shared decision making is much more important for wives than it is for husbands, who don't seem to care about it as much. Asking couples which one has "the final word" on decisions, they find that wives who say that neither partner controls the decisions are the happiest.[3]

Practically speaking, then, what seems most important for many, many wives is quite simple: it's fairness. They want to feel that each partner is doing his or her fair share at home. The split doesn't have to be right down the middle either, since women's subjective judgment of what's reasonable is quite lenient, researchers say. A majority of wives consider it fair if their husbands do *just one-third* of the domestic drudgery, according to some research, which is a pretty good deal for men, all things considered.[4]

In addition, researchers find that the more housework husbands do, the happier wives are. It's a simple equation: Husband Does Chores = Wife Grows Glad. While that may not be earth-shattering news, it should be eye-opening for husbands. The greater the share of domestic duties done by a husband, the happier the wife feels about his love and affection, his understanding, his faithfulness, his companionship, his sexual prowess, and his support. A husband who does the dishes and changes the diapers and folds the laundry is one sexy guy, according to his wife. What's sad, though, is that this isn't at all true for husbands. The more husbands pitch in, the *less satisfied* they are with their marriage, according to the same national marriage survey. For men, that simple equation is turned on its head: Husband Does Chores = Husband Grows Mad.[5]

Giving is not, apparently, its own reward, at least as far as husbands are concerned.

By this logic, then, the husbands of superior wives should be the happiest fellows in the world, since their wives take on an inordinate level of chores and duties, letting them off the responsibility hook. But this is not true of the men in my Web survey, at least among those who are willing to admit that their wives are superior. If I factor in the oblivious husbands, the ones who don't recognize their wives' superiority, then it's clear that *wifely superiority does not benefit husbands.* As we'll see in chapter 6, the resentment and unhappiness of superior wives reverberate throughout marriage, echoing in both partners' sexual frustration and general misery.

Yet most wives, especially superior ones, do not ask all that much of their husbands, and they view their domestic arrangements as fair if they receive even a modicum of cooperation from husbands, according to sociologists who study family work. Wives who consider their marital situation as fair are less depressed than other wives and more satisfied with their marriages. It's not difficult to understand why this should be true, of course. In fact, other research shows that the more time women spend doing routine, repetitive housework, the more depressed they are.[6] I'm not sure we needed a scientific study to prove that scrubbing toilets, mopping floors, vacuuming carpets, and changing sheets week after week make women feel sad and gloomy. It's no wonder, then, that experts say that during the past several dozen years there has been a steady and dramatic decline in the number of hours that women and men spend cleaning their homes. By the way, it's also true that American homes are becoming dirtier and more disorganized by the decade, although many women tend to believe that everybody else's house is filthy but their home is just fine.[7] Clearly, then, if it's a choice between mess and distress, many wives prefer to take the mess.

There's a chicken-and-egg problem, though, when it comes to fairness and happiness in marriage. While it's true that wives who believe their husbands do a fair share are happier, it may also be true that wives who have happier marriages are more likely to have husbands whose contributions are fair. Which comes first, the fairness or the happiness? It is impossible to know for sure. But there is some evidence to show that bad marriages can lead to unfairness and that a sense of unfairness can cause marital distress, and that both can happen at the same time.[8] What's most seriously disturbing for wives, and superior wives especially, is that perceptions of unfairness can literally make them sick. The raw sense of injustice that wives feel can get under their skin, and that's not just a metaphor. Researchers find that when women feel victimized by unfairness, in a way that makes them angry but powerless to change the situation, the resulting psychological misery can actually make them physically ill. Their stress hormone level skyrockets and their immune system deteriorates, which can lead to heart disease, infections, chronic illnesses, and a host of other nasty physical problems.[9]

Too much unfairness, then, can be bad for a superior wife's health.

In addition, while everybody gets stressed, women are especially likely to be plagued by extreme stress and to consider themselves unable to cope, according to the latest psychological research. As a result, more women than men complain of psychological problems, such as irritability, anger, sadness, nervousness, anxiety, or feeling on the verge of tears. They're also more often troubled by physical ailments, like fatigue, insomnia, chronic headaches, stomach woes, and muscular aches and pains. More women than men also end up using prescription medications, another indication that their overstressed state is making them sick.[10]

Most Americans understand, of course, that overwhelming demands are a natural part of life, and so is the resulting stress. Indeed, eight in ten Americans admit that they feel stressed by work and worries about money and children and family responsibilities, according to a recent study. But superior wives may suffer even more from the added anxiety of feeling rushed and pressured about not having enough time to do everything that has to be done. Such worries have increased over the past few decades, especially among women, who "feel more pressure to combine a high level of domestic output with paid work hours," researchers say. They note that wives pay what they call "a family penalty," because after women marry and have children, their workload increases tenfold or even more.[11] It's no wonder, then, that superior wives are high priestesses of stress.

"Our finances are getting to the breaking point, and my stress is very high," explains Phyllis, thirty-seven, an administrative assistant from Columbus, Ohio, whose husband recently lost his job. She also runs the household, doing all of the cooking, shopping, laundry, and cleaning. "I work full-time, but I cannot support our family on my salary. My husband is doing construction work to help pay the bills, but that requires him to work strange hours. We have one daughter leaving for college and another still living at home, and I just don't know how we're going to manage," Phyllis says. "Sometimes I feel that I am the grown-up and that my husband is my child. I know he worries about his job situation, but he doesn't ever show it." Phyllis has started taking antidepressants just to help her get through the day, but sometimes the pills aren't enough to do the job.

Games Superior Wives Play

Wives can't always get what they want, whether it's an emotionally fulfilling marriage or a fair marriage or enough time in the day or a temporary cure for stress. When this reality becomes obvious, some superior wives resort to games and other shenanigans to try to wheedle and cajole their way into getting at least some of what they want. Husbands are no different, of course, although men's talent for game playing may be somewhat less advanced.

Pretending to be dumb. Three in ten wives say that they sometimes play dumb to avoid doing things they just don't want to do. Not quite as many husbands believe that their wives play dumb, just 22 percent, so maybe some wives are actually fooling their mates by engaging in this little white ruse. Wives who make a pretense of stupidity do so for very specific reasons. Some say that it's fatigue, that they are tired of being superior. Others hope to inflate their husband's ego. A few insist that they learned to play dumb by watching their husband. And a fair number believe that they must pretend to at least some ignorance, or else they'll never get any relief or assistance, ever.

"I'm getting tired of being the one to do everything," says a forty-eight-year-old superior wife and mother of four in Illinois. "So I've started to blow things off like he does," she explains, taking her cue from her dumb-playing hubby. A superior wife from Minnesota realized only recently that her husband has been pretending not to know how to do most domestic tasks, she says, "so I have begun to play the same game. It works, because then I do not have to do the job, like mowing the yard or cleaning out the dryer vent."

There's a fine line, though, between playing dumb and simply refusing to learn how to do a dirty or annoying or frustrating chore. "There are things I honestly don't know how to do, and I simply refuse to learn," admits a forty-four-year-old superior wife from Nashville, Tennessee, who resists researching car insurance and fixing dripping toilets. "I just call in the experts if it bothers me enough," she says.

A surprising number of wives insist that they play dumb to help their husband feel more manly. They let him master what they call "guy things" so he'll feel good about himself. Surprisingly, these are not wives who've fallen out of a time warp from the 1950s. They are contemporary wives, living right now, but their beliefs about masculinity seem to have been encased in permafrost, like a preserved woolly mammoth. Such women believe that certain tasks are "male territory," including computers and cars, appliance repairs and "handyman stuff," and that such things are his job, not hers. "It's not that I play dumb, but I play weak," says Shannon, twenty-nine, a textbook editor from New Jersey. "Why kill bugs or lift boxes when he's right there? I just ask him to do it, and he does," she explains. "It's easier to act like I can't do something, plus it bolsters his ego," agrees Judy, sixty, a superior wife in Overland, Kansas. "When we were married, in 1965, men did nothing around the house; they were pigs in those days," she recalls. "He's doing much more now, and we both do the shopping and the cleaning. But I watch television while he does the dishes," Judy says, feeling slightly weird about the whole concept. Indeed, Judy still believes in her heart that it's the husband who's supposed to mow the lawn and take the car in for an oil change, because that's what guys are for.

Plenty of wives too admit that they model their dumb playing after their husband's Oscar-worthy dumb act, appreciating its many advantages. "I watch my husband stand perfectly still in the kitchen while I'm a whirling dervish of activity to make lunches, get breakfast on the table, serve him coffee, put away the dishes, make sure the kids go to the bathroom, and try to get out of the house in five minutes," says Vicki, forty-two, a superior wife from New Hampshire. "But he pretends there's nothing he can do to help, so he just stands there!" Inspired by this frozen male tableau, Vicki explains that "I realized his tactic works, though it frustrates the dickens out of me. So I try to do the same. I close my mouth and watch while he tries to figure out why the television or the DVD player doesn't work and why the machine won't fit on the new shelving. I let him deal with it without offering advice, since he wouldn't appreciate it anyway," she says.

Superior wives like Vicki tell me that they pretend not to know how to do a number of traditionally masculine things, including mowing the grass, shoveling the snow, lighting the barbecue, dealing with wildlife, doing electrical work, doing plumbing, engaging in accounting, and dealing with anything and everything related to the automobile. There is even an elite cadre of very clever and very nonsuperior wives who claim to be unable to do traditionally feminine tasks, like laundry, cooking, cleaning, or ironing.

More than a few wives say that mowing the grass is simply "not my responsibility." A few add that neither is "weed whacking" or "edging" or "leaf blowing," or anything that involves yard work and noisy machinery. They say that it's imperative to pretend ignorance of such things, because "if I do it once, it will become my job forever, so I just don't know how to do it," writes a thirty-five-year-old wife from St. Paul, Minnesota, with a self-conscious wink about her magnificent pretense. In winter, she says, she also becomes unable to figure out how to do any manner of snow removal, which in her hometown, is a big deal of dumb.

Wives get creative when it comes to ways in which they pretend ignorance. In addition to faking an inability to light a coal or gas fire, they won't fix broken things, take out garbage, take responsibility for spiders or roaches or ants or snakes, deal with the dead mouse the cat has dragged in, or clean up pet-related waste. "We have a rule that whoever sees the cat barf has to clean it up," confesses a Michigan wife, "so sometimes I pretend not to see it, even if I've already stepped in it."

Handyman chores, like electrical repairs and plumbing, are high on the wifely dumb-playing list. It helps that these jobs support traditional male gender roles, so some wives feel exempt from ever having to master such things. Wives say they are frightened by computer glitches, they are made anxious by electrical wires, and they shudder at the thought of having to figure out the TiVo or the DVD player or the digital video camera. Likewise, they are repulsed by the idea of plunging toilets, they say, or of unclogging any kind of drain. And if their refusal to master such tasks does not impel their husband to step up, they say, there's always another alternative. "My husband expects me to know how to fix leaks, and if I say I don't, he says, 'What happened to women's lib?' I tell him I know how to use the phone to call the repair guy," says a fifty-year-old nurse from Oregon.

In addition to an aversion to electrical shocks and flash floods, a few wives are also allergic to doing taxes, paying bills, or balancing the checkbook. It's not that they couldn't take on these numerical duties, it's just that they prefer not to. "I'm so tired that I have avoided learning how to do the taxes, since I'm homeschooling our four children," says a thirty-seven-year-old superior wife from Cape Cod, in Massachusetts. "I have very little time to spend on thick books and ledgers, the way I used to before we had children. Right now, I just can't add anything else to my workload," she explains.

The most popular of all the wifely arenas for playing dumb, though, is automotive. Many wives who admit to playing the dumb game say that they don't want to do things as simple as pumping gas or washing the car. They prefer not to have to change the oil, check the air in the tires, replace the wiper fluid, or do any automobile maintenance whatsoever. The wifely consensus seems to be "It's not my job." Even superior wives have to draw the line somewhere, and that boundary is often at the front fender of the family vehicle. "It's a man's job," they say, usually without embarrassment. Others point out that they refuse to deal with body shops or car repair guys. "I fear the men there will take advantage of my lack of knowledge," explains a thirty-eight-year-old Alabama wife who refuses to have anything to do with fixing her car. "I give my husband a hard time when he asks me to take my car in to the shop, since it just makes me nervous."

Although a number of wives are intimidated by auto repairs, it's important to remember that they are actually in the minority. An even smaller number of wives, minuscule actually, claim to be unable to do laundry or to cook. They say they can't figure out what needs hot water and what goes in cold, or that they have no idea how long a pair of jeans should be in the dryer. Or they've never gotten the hang of ironing, especially children's uniforms. There's at least one wife who claims to be inferior at cleaning house, though she has a great excuse. "My husband is a much better housekeeper than I am," says Molly, a fifty-nine-year-old wife from Florida. "I will let things slide, but he will get them done properly. The fact that he is a custodian is probably a big factor." Too bad she can't clone him and auction off copies to the highest bidders.

Finally, a handful of wives insist that they just cannot get the hang of cooking. "I have never cooked anything in our twelve-year marriage," says Heidi, thirty-three, an Even-Steven wife from Layton, Utah. "There has to be something that I'm not stuck with doing, at least one thing that's the man's job to do," she explains. Another wife, a sheriff's deputy in Arkansas, confesses that "I hate to cook, though I probably could, but it takes me longer to follow a recipe. My husband is just better at it, and if it weren't for him, I probably wouldn't eat." Wives like these are somewhat gleeful about their purported ignorance, as will become obvious in chapter 7. Playing dumb is how they have cured themselves of superiority, once and for all.

Most superior wives, however, don't have the luxury of playing dumb, since nothing would get done if they did. They abide by a double-negative rule that goes "I'm not allowed to not know." They are matter-of-fact about their superior status in their union; as much as they may resent it, they're the one who gets things done. "I have the most responsibility for everything, since my husband is from Ireland. We met online, and we spent less than thirty days in each other's physical presence before getting married," says Diana, forty-six, a disability claims examiner from Madison, Wisconsin. She admits that this flash decision may not have been the smartest thing she's ever done, since now "I can't pretend I can't do something, because I'm always the one who has to figure out how to do everything." Other wives explain it using the exact same phrase: "If I don't do it, it doesn't get done," and "it" means anything and everything.

Superior wives who don't have the luxury of not knowing how to do something say that they're willing to learn. "I'll tackle anything," says a superior wife from Tennessee, "and there are plenty of how-to books." Indeed, many wives believe that there's nothing they can't do or can't figure out how to do. If they have to, they'll hire somebody, and if not, they'll deal with it. "I had to learn how to pressure wash, take the cars for maintenance, repair toilets and sinks, mow the lawn, edge the lawn, and repair roof shingles, since we can't afford to pay people to do these things," says April, thirty-one, a superior wife from South Carolina whose husband works eighty-hour weeks as a medical intern. "I bought a home-repair book written for women and I've used it to do many chores, since there was no room for me to play dumb," April explains. "I've even purchased some power tools and built two bookshelves. It's amazing what you can learn to do outside of the traditional roles if you are put into a situation where you have no choice."

That's really the bottom line: many wives simply do not have the luxury to play dumb, since it's their job to be superior.

Some wives actually say they like to impress their husbands with how competent they are, and they revel in doing whatever is difficult and complicated and challenging. "I try to blow him away with my abilities," says a forty-five-year-old superior wife and legal analyst from Atascadero, California. Then there's Claudia, forty-eight, a superior wife and yoga teacher from New York, who enjoys demonstrating her prowess. "In the winter I go up on our flat roof and shovel snow for hours at a time, to save the roof from leaking. This week I rented a water pump and set it up in the basement, dragging a garden hose from outside to pump water out, after our washer ran on the fill cycle for three hours and flooded the basement. I also plunged a cap through the bathtub drain so it would work properly, after my daughter had a temper tantrum because she couldn't bear standing in two inches of water saturated with her brother's dirt and germs," Claudia explains.

Finally, there are plenty of superior wives who insist that they don't like playing games, that "life's too short to play dumb," that they are too old to engage in such chicanery, or that they simply ask for their husband's help when they need it. "I'm more handy around the house, and I'm in charge of every financial decision we make, so it never dawned on me to pretend I don't know how to do something," says Misty, thirty, a children's book editor and a mother of two from Florida. Other wives agree about the futility of playing dumb, saying "Why waste the time and energy?" or "I would never do that" or "I just tell my husband, 'This one's yours.'" A twenty-nine-year-old at-home mother and superior wife from Cincinnati, Ohio, explains that her husband would be horrified if she pretended not to know how to do something. "If there's something I don't want to do, I simply say, 'This needs to be done, and I don't feel like doing it. Would you mind taking a turn?' And he does," she says.

While the dumb game may not be all that popular among American wives, nagging is much more so, according to the hundreds and hundreds of women who wrote lengthy essays in response to my question about nagging. Nagging is like an event at an all-female Summer Olympics; it's the Super Bowl of female achievement. Nagging is not only a game, it's a way of wifely life. And that's even more true for superior wives than for others.

The news on nagging. Half of wives agree that they are the primary nagger in the family, and that's exactly what half of husbands say as well. So the wifely nagging norm stands at 50 percent: one in two wives are self-described naggers. Thus, there's some truth to the nagging wife stereotype. Wives nag. But so do husbands, and their nagging is remarkably similar to wifely complaints.

Many wives nag because they can, because they must, because they are frustrated or angry or resentful, though they also realize that their nagging is rarely effective and can backfire, resulting in bad feelings. "Nagging doesn't get the issue resolved to anyone's satisfaction," says a sixty-four-year-old lab technician from Boston. "The nagger feels taken for granted and the naggee feels put upon," she adds.

"Nagging does not get my husband to do chores," agrees a sixty-year-old superior wife from San Francisco. "So I either hire somebody to do it or I do it myself. If it is going to get done, I do it. My husband is a city boy and does not cut grass, wash cars, bathe dogs, do home repairs, or dust the house. He is a scientist and he lives inside an alien bubble," she jokes.

Just like husbands, wives realize that nagging has an ugly side: one wife says it sounds too much like "hag," and several say they prefer to say "rag" rather than "nag." Despite the fact that wives tend to be nagging pros, husbands do their fair share of nagging, and on almost identical topics. Wives report that they get nagged by their husband about subjects that run the same nagging gamut, from A to Z. (See the encyclopedia of nagging, chapter 4.) Each nags the other about earning more money, working fewer hours, having more sex, losing weight, cooking, and spending too much time on the computer. In this small way, then, gender roles almost converge, at least as far as nagging is concerned. In addition, both partners nag each other about the bane of married existence: socks. While wives nag husbands about leaving dirty socks around the house or losing single socks, husbands nag wives when they can't find wearable ones. "My husband is on my case because he's looking for clean socks in the morning while he's trying to get ready for work," says a thirty-nine-year-old wife from Chicago. Her husband, she says, has no socking patience.

In some marriages too, each spouse has a veritable litany of nags, a his-and-her list that if inscribed on a parchment scroll would be as long as a year's supply of mismatched socks laid heel to toe. "He criticizes my hobbies, my education, my television shows, my need to lock the car doors and check the tires, my need to follow the rules, my need to plan for vacation trips, my choice of recreation, how I manage my time, the food I like, my desire to try new things, and that I get angry over what he calls 'nothing,'" says Dot, fifty-two, a superior wife from Longview, Washington. At seventeen she married a man she'd known only four months. "I thought he was a knight in shining armor, but it turns out that he was the horse," Dot explains. She, in turn, nags her husband, she says, "about not listening, not being empathetic, putting others' needs ahead of mine, not being loyal, not being safety-minded, being a slob, peeing on the floor, breaking traffic laws, letting the children do things they aren't supposed to, and endangering my pets."

A twenty-six-year-old wife from Madison, Wisconsin, says she and her husband have their own mutual nag rags. "He gets really annoyed when I don't wash my dishes after using them, even if it's just a single cup or one fork. He doesn't like having overhead lights on, especially in the evening. He also bugs me about getting places on time and how much time I think it will take to get something done versus how much time it actually takes. I nag him about leaving his clothes on the floor, using a germy sponge or cold water to wash the dishes, leaving tissues in his pockets, which make the laundry linty, not telling me when his clothes are stained, leaving messes on the stovetop, not filling the car with gas when it's low, and putting off car repairs," she explains, adding that "he thinks he knows a lot about keeping a house tidy, but he doesn't understand the difference between straightened and cleaned."

It's massive inventories like these that make it nearly impossible to summarize the essence of marital nagging. But I'll try to generalize anyway. Wives nag their husbands about helping out and cleaning up; husbands nag their wives about putting out and cleaning up. Husbands want more sex, better sex, different sex. They also want a cleaner house, a less cluttered house, a better-decorated house. One husband wrote "Dust Me" on their bedroom radio, one wife reports. Husbands are somewhat predictable in what they nag their wives about, and in the end, their nagging is more similar to their wives' nagging than they care to admit. Nevertheless, every so often I find a rare and unusual nag. There's the Massachusetts wife and mother of five who nags her husband "because he buys guinea pigs when I'm away and I can't stop him." There's the husband who nags his wife to stop picking dead skin off her fingers. There's the husband who nags his wife about her morning breath, "as if he expects a mint is going to magically appear in my mouth before I kiss him," she says. And there's the husband in Indiana who nags his superior wife about not burning rice or pasta in the pot and not dropping her cell phone into her latte "because I'm always trying to do too many things at once," she explains.

As alike as spousal nagging can be across the gender divide, there are a few minor differences. Husbands nag wives about having too many pairs of shoes—a topic for which there is no male equivalent. Also, few if any husbands nag their wives about watching too much television or playing too many video games. However, they do nag about child-rearing responsibilities in a way that wives almost never do, since husbands expect wives to "do something" about the kids. Men complain that the children are too bothersome, too noisy, too undisciplined. One such husband, for instance, nags his wife about the state of their tween-age daughter. "He's positive that there's 'something wrong with that girl' and that it's my job to fix her," says a thirty-one-year-old Air Force wife from Tucson, Arizona. "I disagree with him, though. She's weird, because she dresses in purple and has a pink streak in her hair, but that's pretty normal for a twelve-year-old."

Finally, there is a fundamental difference between wives and husbands about what marital nagging means. For husbands, nagging is simply what it is: a wife's to-do list of chores, a series of jobs to complete, an indirect catalog of slings and arrows. But for superior wives, nagging becomes a symbol of all that is wrong with the marriage. It's an indication of deep flaws and hidden faults in the marital psyche, a trove of pent-up frustration, anger, and anxiety, of loving struggles and bitter grudges. Nagging carries secret and subtle meanings for wives, just as interpretations of inkblots contain hidden meanings for psychiatrists. Wives wish that their nagging would persuade their husband to truly hear what they are saying, to listen and to understand and to sympathize. "I only nag him when he asks me something that I've just told him or when he acts like he's not listening to me," explains a fifty-two-year-old superior wife from Connecticut. A superior at-home wife from Long Island, New York, feels that her husband puts his needs first, "and he feels since he's the one who earns the money, he deserves a free pass on all of the other responsibilities that go along with being an adult." She wishes that he would "give from the heart," the way she does, and at least once make her a priority, not his work or his golf game or his private time with ESPN.

More than a few wives sense that their nagging is not effective: it doesn't get them anywhere. They say they are sick of hearing themselves talk, so they try not to nag. Other wives avoid nagging because their husband's explosive temper frightens them and any criticism usually ends in an argument or worse. "I've learned that it's best not to nag about anything, because we always end up fighting," says Michelle, a forty-year-old superior wife from Leesville, South Carolina. "I work forty-five hours a week, but I still come home to cook dinner, clean up the kitchen, take care of the dogs and the kids, and I don't get to sit down until it's time for me to go to bed," she explains, adding that her husband deserves to be nagged about it but that she's afraid to complain. Martha, forty-six, a superior wife from Toronto, learned early in her marriage to "avoid raising issues with him. During the first two years, if I'd ask for help around the house or wanted to talk about finances or when he would find a steady job, he'd erupt into an outburst of anger. The more he wanted to avoid the issue, the louder he would get and the more demeaning of me he would become, hoping that I'd stop nagging him," says Martha. "Over time, his little oversights, like not sharing responsibility, not getting a job, and not helping with the children, became bigger neglects, though he'd try to make me think my complaints were overblown," she adds. His anger didn't work, however, since she and her husband are now separated.

Despite Martha's failure to nag effectively, there are actually some ways in which a wife's nagging can be productive and even helpful to husbands. Psychologists who study couples' health find that wives tend to be more effective than husbands in getting their partner into good physical shape, by getting him to eat better and to exercise more. Wives are also more effective in persuading husbands to see a doctor, to quit smoking, and to take prescription medication. Wives do this by nagging, by modeling the appropriate behavior, and by discussing the issue, techniques that husbands tend not to use, researchers say.[12]

"I nag my husband about health issues," agrees Selena, forty-six, a superior wife from New York. "He never puts sunscreen on, and he burns every time, so I have resorted to just putting the sunscreen on him, as if he were a child. I used to nag him about his horrible diet, since he was obese. He'd get angry and tell me to stop nagging. But it was a health crisis, since he was hypertensive and had no energy. Finally I hired a physical trainer to come to the house, and my husband is no longer obese, he eats right, works out, and lifts weights every day. Instead of just nagging him, I had to do something concrete," she explains, "and it worked."

Like Selena, a few wives have learned the art of creative nagging. Instead of yakking about it, chipping away at a husband, one flaw at a time, they take inventive action. "I find that if I put up a list on the refrigerator, it is a silent reminder of things yet to do," explains a fifty-three-year-old superior wife from Hudsonville, Michigan. "It also helps me remember the things he wants me to do," she adds diplomatically. Another wife makes her husband a to-do list but never with more than three things on it, so he doesn't get overwhelmed and she doesn't have to offer nagging reminders. Finally, Annette, a superior wife from New Rochelle, New York, has learned after twenty-one years of marriage to appreciate what her husband does, rather than get irritated by what he doesn't. "I used to nag him about putting plastic tubs on the bottom rack of the dishwasher, because they sometimes melt. But I realized that the husbands of my friends never even help with the dishes, so I shut up about having to replace the GladWare."

Her Marriage Mistakes

Whether or not wives play marital games, they almost always have very different and much greater hopes and expectations for their marriage than husbands do. Before they marry, a great many women long to find a man who will treat them with kindness and be supportive, according to my Web survey. When, and if, these wishes are not satisfied, wives become much more sensitive to problems and more attuned to the emotional deficits of their marriage. As a result, wives tend to be less satisfied with marriage than husbands are, superior wives even less than other wives. This unhappiness can lead to depression and to the logical view that the marriage might have been a mistake. Such regrets can eventually lead to a decision to divorce, which is much more likely to be made by the wife than by the husband. After they divorce, a majority of ex-wives eventually marry again, giving them an opportunity to be disillusioned by a second husband or a third, as if they have stepped onto a marital merry-go-round.

It used to be the rule that marriage was a state that women longed to enter but men were determined to avoid. A great number of wedding day jokes focused on how adept the bride had been at trapping her groom into matrimony. Indeed, several decades ago, women were more likely than men to say that their ideal life included getting married. But no longer. Now women are the ones unenthusiastic about marriage as an ultimate goal in life.[13] Women are the ones who've gotten cold wedding feet, which is why fewer of them than ever before are currently married, as I mentioned earlier. One of the reasons that this has happened, I believe, is that while women still want and expect a great deal from marriage, they are increasingly aware of how difficult those marital goals will be to achieve. Researchers say that women expect better communication and more affection from marriage than men do, and wives are then deeply upset and disappointed when they don't get the understanding and the respect that they wanted.[14]

These female longings are neither hidden nor discreet, since many wives are vocal about their expectations for an ideal relationship and their resulting disenchantment with the one they've got. Some of the superior wives in my Web survey say that their husband can be "critical and sarcastic," that "he has distanced himself," and that they just don't feel loved. A few are blunt about their despair. "We have very different communication styles," says Jessie, forty-five, a superior wife from Nampa, Idaho. "I'm very direct and he is an avoider, so it can sometimes make life hard to be together." Other superior wives yearn for "the hugs he used to give me during our first few years of marriage" or for any physical display of fondness or warmth, however small. "I hoped for a relationship in which my husband would show his love," says Joann, fifty-two, an Alpha wife from South Dakota. "But when I ask him, 'Do you love me?' he tells me that if anything changes, he'll let me know." She realizes this is just the way he is, but she's sad that he'll never be her Romeo.

Perhaps because wives expect so much from marriage, they tend to be much less satisfied with marriage than husbands are. Just about every major study of marital happiness shows that wives score lower on nearly all measures of marital satisfaction. Wives are less happy about the understanding, love, and affection they receive from their spouse; they suspect their marriage is probably not as good as most others; they sense that their love is not as strong. They say they do fewer activities with their spouse, like eating together and visiting friends. They disagree more often and have more serious quarrels and bad feelings than their husbands say they do. Wives are more likely than husbands to assert that one spouse gets angry, is critical or domineering, gives the silent treatment, refuses to talk, or is easily hurt. And wives are more likely than husbands to say that the marriage is in trouble or that they have considered divorce.[15] The two partners are in the same marriage, but they're seeing *a completely different version* of what's going on inside it, as if they're both in the same multiplex theater but watching two completely different movies.

The majority of wives are not utterly miserable, of course. It's just that when wives are compared to husbands, they are generally more unhappy about their lives. And superior wives are even more likely than others to land on the unhappy end of the spectrum. What's bad for such wives too is that the despondent ones pay a steep penalty for their misery. Experts agree that it's dissatisfied wives who are most likely to be depressed and to abuse alcohol. Their immune system is often impaired by their state of marital distress, and, as a result, they tend to suffer from fatigue, headaches, stomach upsets, infections, flu, colds, and hepatitis. As a result, they see the doctor more often than other wives and are even hospitalized more often.[16]

Being in a bad marriage, then, is a lot worse for wives than it is for husbands, in part because many husbands just don't pay so much attention to the bad stuff. Maybe that's because they wear rose-colored glasses while observing their marriage, happily blind to the bad or difficult or troubling, or maybe they don't examine it all that closely in the first place. Whatever the reason, wives are more highly sensitized to what's wrong with their marriage. In addition, an unhappy wife is a depressed wife. If she has no confidence in her husband's love and support, if she feels that the relationship is shaky and may not last very long, those doubts make her feel sad, hopeless, negative, upset, and generally miserable, even if there's no divorce on the horizon.[17]

As I mentioned earlier, more wives than husbands say they regret their marriage, sensing that it was a mistake: 49 percent of the wives in my Web survey say so, compared to 38 percent of husbands, a significant difference. And even more superior wives—six in ten—agree. Once again, this means that *a majority of superior wives feel their marriage was a mistake.* Such wives are quite definitive about why they feel such twinges of marital remorse and sorrow, and they're much more articulate about it than husbands are. Many wives believe that it's human nature to wonder what might have been, to think about the paths not taken. Asked if they ever feel "as if your current marriage might have been a mistake," several responded, "Doesn't everybody?" or "If I say no, I'd be lying." A forty-three-year-old superior wife from Michigan agrees: "Everyone feels they may have made a mistake at one point, but you work through your problems." A superior wife with four children admits she wouldn't mind what she calls "a do-over." Another asks herself, every so often, if she simply "settled" for a less-than-ideal husband. These wives suffer from a bad case of the what-ifs, an emotional affliction that causes some melancholy and requires the use of a time machine. "I often wonder about what my life would be like if I had remained single and pursued my dreams before getting married and having a family," says a superior wife and cooking teacher from White Plains, New York. It's only natural for some wives to ask what if: what if they'd finished their college degree, what if they'd taken that job, what if they hadn't gotten pregnant? A superior wife from Tennessee harbors such thoughts. "To be honest, there are times that I just plain wonder what my life would be like if I'd married someone else," she says. "In my opinion, it would be unrealistic never to have entertained this thought at least once," she explains, adding that these ideas are just "fleeting fantasies," since she'd probably marry the same man all over again.

I find that wives give five basic reasons for regretting their marriage: they made a bad choice, the sex is unsatisfying, they've grown apart, they married too young or too soon, or he doesn't do his share. But all is *not* woe and despair and tears on the marriage front, since half of all wives say they have *no regrets*. These wives claim to have found their best friend, their soul mate, the love of their life, the union that was meant to be. First, let's examine the wives with regrets; then we'll inspect the ones who have none.

Bad choice. This is a ragbag category of marital regret, encompassing just about every problem from a lack of communication and not feeling loved to a husband who is bad-tempered or abusive or hypercritical or one who's an alcoholic, a drug abuser, or a philanderer. An Even-Steven wife from Houston, Texas, says that she and her husband lack "intellectual intimacy," since they're unable to discuss their children's problems or things that really matter to them. Another believes that her husband is "reluctant to get emotionally involved," since he won't offer her smiles or soft touches or any of the tenderness that she desires. Even more drastic, of course, are husbands who have affairs, even if it is "a single sexual encounter" that one Kentucky wife describes as "an emotional affair." Another tries to be tactful about it, saying that "one of us has fidelity problems." A regretful wife from Arkansas admits that "my spouse has strayed, emotionally and physically, more than once." Even worse, in some ways, are husbands who are abusive. "My husband has such a bad temper that sometimes I think he is less in control than my toddler," says a thirty-seven-year-old superior wife from Montreal, Canada, who adds that "this is bad for my spirit. He's also very critical of me, and lately, we cannot go five minutes without him making a snide remark. Did I find his baseball cap? Did I buy chips at the grocer or his spaghetti sauce, and if not, how come?" There's a superior wife from Connecticut whose husband's drinking has become such a problem that she asked him to move out for a year, until he is in recovery. A San Francisco wife says that she and her husband were both "heavy drinkers" when they married seventeen years ago but that he's since become an alcoholic, a condition that she tolerates, though just barely.

Bad sex. Some superior wives say they are no longer physically attracted to their husband, or that "we are missing a spark," or that "we are not sexually compatible." Quite often that's because she wants to be sexually active and he's no longer interested. The degree of sexual dysfunction can be mild, as for the superior wife from Colorado who comments that her husband refuses to talk about their sexual problems, to catastrophic, as for the superior wife from Michigan who asserts that "I get no sexual satisfaction, and my husband doesn't want to put forth the effort to help me get there." There's a thirty-nine-year-old superior wife from Massachusetts who says, "I've lost my will to be attracted to him, mostly because he needs to lose sixty pounds." On the other hand, a superior wife from Italy longs to have her husband "desire me sexually, and I'd like to have a man who cares more about his body and does not expect to be sexy while wearing a white tee shirt with big white pants over his big belly."

Grown apart. Sometimes formerly solid partnerships fall to pieces simply because spouses change or discover they have little in common. "When we first met, my husband seemed independent and confident," says a forty-five-year-old superior wife from Providence, Rhode Island. "Once I was hooked, though, he changed. He stopped exercising and gained weight, he quit college and never went back, and he got lazy," she says, somewhat confused about how this terrible transformation occurred. A superior wife in Oklahoma who's in a second marriage says that her husband seems to resent "having to start all over raising kids," because hers were so much younger than his when they first married. "He never said anything, but he got moody and became less and less interested in us as a couple," she says, still upset about the bait-and-switch trick her husband seems to have pulled. Other regretful wives realize, too late, that "we're complete opposites" or "we're poles apart." Their spouses come from different social backgrounds or religions or different parts of the country, or they were raised in very different ways. Or it was only after living with him, for one year or ten, that they discovered they've got nothing in common, "except our children." They say, "I am upbeat, but he is miserable." Or that "we want different things: he wants to make a lot of money and I want to spend time together." Or that "I'm a social butterfly and he's a recluse," as one wife puts it. "My husband and I are so different in so many ways—our sense of humor, what we like to watch on television, the way we think, how we raise our children—that I sometimes wonder how and why I fell in love with him in the first place," says a superior wife from Baltimore, Maryland. Sometimes wives have enough insight to know that their differences are minor and don't really matter. Sheila, sixty-six, from New Jersey, is one of those wives, who understands that she and her husband disagree about everything, "except the big stuff, like moral standards and beliefs and politics. Still, I think we are a mismatch," she says. "He's rigid and different in so many ways. He plays golf and is committed to exercise, but I'm an avid bridge player and I love card games, which he hates."

For a few superior wives, the sense of alienation is so great that they feel a constant sense of loneliness, although they are rarely alone. Their husbands, they say, are almost never affectionate or sexual and seem to be mentally absent even when sitting right there, in a nearby living room chair.

Too young. Some superior wives attribute their marital regrets to having married either too young or too soon after meeting a man. In both cases, they say they should have waited longer. "We met and fell in love too young, when we were seventeen," says a New Jersey wife, now twenty-nine. "But delaying the wedding wouldn't have made it right. We're together, as we should be, but it would have been nice to have more of a life beforehand." Another wife, now in her late sixties, married at seventeen to escape what she calls "a dysfunctional family" and because she thought she was in love. Now though, "I wish I'd waited until I was at least twenty-five," she says. Another admits that "we rushed into marriage, meeting in May of one year and marrying the next, and the whole time it was a long-distance relationship." This thirty-five-year-old superior wife from Georgia claims to have recognized her future husband as a soul mate at first, "but the longer we are married, the more I see that we have different views on many things." Likewise, a thirty-eight-year-old hairdresser and superior wife from Albany, New York, says, "We really didn't know each other that well when I got pregnant," though they now have three children and have been married nearly twenty years.

A variation on the too-young theme also includes women who married a too-young man, as did Juanita, a superior wife in Florida, now thirty-two, with a twenty-four-year-old husband. They've been married for five years—do the math!—and he's out of state with the Army, so he's not around to help with their three children. "I've felt for a while that this marriage was a mistake," Juanita says, "although he's grown a lot in the last two years." Still, when her husband comes home on weekends, "he's in 'bachelor mode' and doesn't do anything with the kids or the household, and I resent the hell out of it."

No help. Juanita's wifely lament is an oldie but goodie: she can't get no satisfaction—or help around the house either. Superior wives resent giving more, suffering financial setbacks, and brooding about unfairness. "Sometimes I get overwhelmed, and I feel like I'm giving and giving and not receiving anything in return," says a twenty-seven-year-old superior wife from Los Angeles. "That's hard, especially with a six-month-old baby to deal with." Problems like this are only compounded when husbands lose their job, refuse to get a job, or go deep into debt. Another wife is tired of "the financial struggle," she says, especially since her contractor husband's clients "try to screw him out of his fees." But it all comes down to what's fair and what's not, about expecting equality and not getting it. "Coming into the marriage, I thought everything would be fifty-fifty, but now I feel like I do almost everything, and I'm not even appreciated for it," says a twenty-five-year-old superior wife and mother of two from Woodbridge, Virginia, who works fifty hours a week. "It's all on my shoulders" and "I can't do it all" and "I thought my husband would be more involved" are the broken-record plaints of so many regretful wives. "I give way too much more than he does" is how a twenty-eight-year-old superior wife from Griffin, Georgia, puts it, summing up the problem with an emphatic zing.

It's important to keep in mind, however, that these disgruntled superior wives are offset by no-regrets wives, who make up a large portion of married women. Wives who don't regret their marriage rarely long for do-overs or time machines to rectify their marital mistakes. They say they have found a friend, a soul mate, or "the love of my life," as a twenty-six-year-old Nevada wife and mother of three puts it. (I'll focus on wives like these in chapter 7.)

As for the rueful wives, the ones who look back on their wedding day with more than a bit of disappointment or sorrow, they're the ones most likely to end up divorced.

Giving Up, Getting Divorced

As a marital solution, divorce is the ultimate do-over. But for superior wives who are truly fed up, it's sometimes the only option left. Still, very few wives take this step without a great deal of agonizing and soul-searching, weighing the alternatives carefully and obsessively before reaching their final decision. While it's true that superior wives may be slightly more likely than others to end up divorced, I can't really tell this from my research. To do that, I'd have to follow the wives in my Web survey to see how many superior and nonsuperior wives end up divorced ten or fifteen years from now. However, it's my guess that superior wives are much more likely than others to end up divorced.

Indeed, because nearly one out of two marriages ends in divorce, marital dissolution can be a predicted for at least half of superior wives who are in a first marriage.[18] While the divorce rate in the United States is the lowest it has been in thirty years, that's only because the marriage rate is also at an all-time low. Fewer couples are getting divorced because fewer are getting married.[19] But no matter how many couples become entangled in the painful and expensive mess of divorce, it's clear that about two out of three of those divorces are initiated by wives, not husbands.[20] This is true, by the way, even of older couples; among couples between the ages of forty and seventy-nine who divorce, two out of three do so because the wife wants the marriage to end.[21] Some experts say women take the lead in divorce because wives know that a relationship is in trouble long before their husbands do. Wives have a better sense of the well-being of their marriage, monitoring it daily, as they would a toddler with a fever. Wives take more responsibility for maintaining the marriage and for curing it, if at all possible.[22] Thus, when that relationship is sick, they know about it right away. Wives are acutely attuned to the nuances of their marriage, while husbands are much less cognizant of a marriage's ups and downs. In fact, in one study of divorced couples, about a quarter of husbands say they were utterly flabbergasted when their wife announced her plans to leave: they had absolutely no idea whatsoever that she was so unhappy.[23]

The reasons wives give for believing that their marriage may have been a mistake is a comprehensive catalog of wifely regrets, as my Web survey illustrates. The examples I've compiled resemble a heap of potential final straws, ready to be stacked onto a camel's back. Any single one of them is probably not enough to tip a marriage into divorce, but two or three or four of them add up, until finally the newest straw becomes the last straw. In some ways, divorce resembles murder, since there have to be motive and opportunity for both. The motives for divorce include all the reasons to leave, and the opportunity for divorce includes the financial ability to leave, along with future alternatives that look better than present reality.

While there are countless reasons that marriages might end, there are a handful of well-known and relatively common ones. Couples divorce for reasons both major and minor, all related to being exploited or being hurt in some way. Wives consider divorce if their husband is physically violent or if he's an alcohol or drug abuser. They ponder divorce if they have prolonged and intractable financial problems.[24] Wives also consider a lack of fairness as a reasonable motive for divorce. One study, conducted over a five-year period, shows that wives who perceive their marriage as less than fair will be more likely to end the marriage several years later. The same isn't true for husbands, though, despite the fact that some husbands feel they do an unfair share of family work. The researchers believe this is probably because the degree of unfairness that wives suffer is much more substantial than that experienced by most husbands.[25]

Wives will also end a marriage if they argue and fight often or if they feel unloved, belittled, or emotionally abused. A superior wife from North Carolina explains it this way: "He built walls and held unforgiveness in his heart toward me, so I left." Another superior wife from Columbus, Ohio, was married to a man who went through two midlife crises, "and he did exactly what he wanted, with little regard for my welfare." This includes the affair he had with a co-worker, "and both of them lost their jobs because of it," she says, "so I call it the world's most expensive blow job." What hurts her the most, she says, is that at first "he was a great guy, but the older he got, the more narcissistic he became." Divorce researchers notice that men's reasons for wanting a divorce seem somewhat different: men who initiate divorce complain that their wives are inattentive or neglectful. Still, these husbands are in the minority, since many husbands are the last to know that their marriage is on the verge of ending.[26]

Psychologists and sociologists aren't the only ones who pay close attention to why couples divorce; so do the lawyers who do the litigation. I spoke to several attorneys who specialize in matrimonial law, and all agree that it's wives who propel divorce to its final, and sad, conclusion. One such matrimonial lawyer, Joy Joseph, is based in a generic-looking office off the exit ramp of a major highway, just thirty miles north of New York City. It's here that she helps couples dissolve their legal bonds. She has been practicing divorce law for several decades, she says, and about two out of three of her clients are wives. "Usually, the women tell me that they are in a loveless marriage," says Ms. Joseph. "They realize they were never in love, or that the love has died, or that they were together only for the sake of the children. Often, they tell me their husband verbally abuses them or that he doesn't support the family emotionally. He's not helping around the house, he's not being a companion, he's mistreating them." One of Joseph's clients, she says, is a wife whose husband called her "a f——ing bitch, a liar, and a coward." Another told her that after her mother died, the husband didn't help her or comfort her in any way and actually scolded her for not being around to cook his dinner. Another client, an African American woman, was married to a Mexican-born doctor, who called her "a stupid, third-world monkey," Joseph recalls, still horrified.

Joseph has been doing divorce law for so long, she says, that she can almost predict in advance the reasons a potential client wants a divorce. "She feels unfulfilled and says that her husband is not meeting her needs," she explains. "Wives tell me they want to leave the marriage in a quest to find something better because women aren't afraid to go it alone anymore." They'd rather be single and in no marriage than be tethered to a man who is unkind and uncaring and unloving. On the other hand, Joseph observes, husbands "almost never leave a marriage unless they already have someone else lined up." They seem to know that, for them, going it alone is not a viable option, especially if the husband is one who's been spoiled by living with a superior wife for years.[27]

"I was responsible for all areas of the family while I was attending graduate school and raising our children," says Lynne, forty-six, a teacher in Smyrna, Delaware, referring to her first marriage. "It was very stressful and hard on my health, which is why we ended up divorced, after being married for seventeen years." Four years into her second marriage, Lynne is thrilled to have found a better partner and to have relinquished her endless-seeming superiority. "My husband prefers to shoulder responsibility so that I don't have to worry about everything," Lynne explains. "He's a kind and caring man who loves his family, and he treats my parents and children with love and respect too, something that my first husband never did." Monica, thirty-two, didn't have such great luck after her divorce, since "there were too many similarities between my second husband and my ex-husband." A superior wife for the second time now, Monica says, "I provide the steady income and the health insurance, because my husband has no predictable job schedule. I had to threaten to leave him so he'd get counseling for his issues, and we had couples therapy, but I still make a lot of the decisions and I'm more responsible for the family. I have chronic back pain too, but I have to beg him to bathe our large dogs and to do anything that requires heavy lifting."

Although she doesn't like to admit it, Monica is afraid that her second marriage may also be headed for a divorce. Because Monica earns her own paycheck, she has the opportunity to divorce. Having a regular paycheck gives wives like Monica the ability to divorce, one that traditional and at-home wives don't share, since they are economically dependent on their husbands. Some social critics make the mistake of believing that it's simply having a job that causes women to seek divorce, a connection that's simply not there. In fact, the process usually happens in the opposite direction: wives who worry that their union might be flawed are more likely to go out and find work, to give themselves a safety net just in case they'll need it someday.[28] They keep that net too, since remarried wives earn more and have a higher average household income than first-time wives.[29]

Actually, other research shows that the more money wives earn, the happier they are with their marriage. Looking at couples over a seventeen-year period, sociologists found that wives whose income increases over time are actually in better psychological health. They are less depressed and lonely than other wives, and they have fewer symptoms of anxiety, like upset stomach and cold sweats. Finally, they are no more likely to get divorced, despite having grown more financially independent.[30] So it's not having money that makes women agitate for divorce; it's having a bad marriage that does the trick.

You'd think that after experiencing a wrenching, emotionally draining divorce, wives might be fed up with marriage altogether, especially those who used to be superior wives. Why do so much for so little in return, when you can do it all just for yourself and your children? That's exactly what a superior wife from Tennessee was thinking just before she divorced her first husband, an alcoholic whose only social activity was "watching television and drinking beer," she says. "I felt that if I was going to be broke and alone all the time, I would rather be broke and alone and not married," she explains.

Still, many American wives believe in redemption, in the possibility of happily ever after, despite any evidence they may have gathered to the contrary. They hope, in their hearts, that even after a home-wrecking, child-traumatizing divorce, they will once again discover the magic of true love and eventually live (almost) happily ever (almost) after. Just because that didn't happen the first time, who's to say it won't happen the second time or the third time or the fourth time?

"I was married before and really got my heart ripped out, and I wonder sometimes if I got married again too quickly, just to reaffirm my belief that marriage is good and that I am lovable and worthy of commitment," says Sheila, an insightful thirty-six-year-old Michigan woman. A superior wife who has been married to her second husband for nine years, she says, "I do ninety-nine percent of the household jobs, and I usually do all of the outdoor stuff too. My husband works a forty-hour week, as do I, but he seems pretty content to sit back on his days off, saying he doesn't have the energy to do the mowing or the car work or whatever," she says. "But I never get the freedom to just not make a meal or not do laundry. I wonder if I am just a martyr to my guilt and sense of obligation."

Remarried wives like Sheila are no more or less likely than first wives to be superior, I find, so they don't seem to have learned from their mistakes. Almost two-thirds of remarried women are superior wives, just as almost two-thirds of wives in a first marriage are superior, according to my research. It may be that superior wives carry their superiority from marriage to marriage, like a broken suitcase or a bad allergy. In my Web survey, remarried wives are on the whole no happier than women in a first marriage, although there are a few notable exceptions.

Take Kaneesha, thirty-two, a former superior wife who had two bad marriages before she hit the jackpot on number three. She is a nurse and mother of two in Dalton, Georgia, and her third husband is a trucker. "Out of all the marriages I've had, this one is the best, and I wouldn't trade him in for anything on earth," she says. "This husband is seventy-five percent better than I am," she says, which means that she is no longer trapped in superiority. "He comes home off the road after being gone for two weeks and won't say a word of how upset he is to see the house in a mess. All he does is come in and clean," says Kaneesha. "Not only that, but one of our two kids is not his, and he isn't at all happy about her being in his house, but you would never know. He treats her as if she is his child," Kaneesha explains, proud to have found a man who gives his stepdaughter love and respect.

One of the greatest challenges of remarriage, according to the superior wives in my Web survey, is dealing with a blended family and figuring out how to handle each other's exes and apportion responsibility for her children, his children, and their children. Several superior wives agree that they use a divide-and-conquer method, saying that "we each take primary responsibility for our own children." They split parental duties right down the biological line, for example, paying household bills out of separate bank accounts. Being a stepmother as well as a superior wife is surely complicated, as well as difficult. In addition, wives who bring their own children to a second marriage are more likely to end up getting divorced again than those who don't.[31] Social scientists call this process *churning*: the increasingly common experience of American women and men who marry and divorce and remarry and divorce again.[32] Superior remarried wives have certainly done their share of churning. It's as if you put hundreds of ex-wives and ex-husbands in a mammoth washing machine all at once, pushed the on button, and shook and agitated them until they emerged in completely different married pairs, like random sets of socks.

Paying the Price for Superiority

Many women expect the stars and the moon and the sun when they marry, as if marriage will be the universal solution for whatever ails them. It's only when they become superior wives, however, that they begin to understand that their private fairy tale may not end so happily ever after. My research shows that superior wives tend to be dissatisfied with their lives and with their marriage, and miserable about their sex lives too, as we'll see in chapter 6. These emotional woes are all part of the superior wife syndrome, a set of negative symptoms and problems that are consequences of being a superior wife. Superior wives are most likely to end up being the wives who nag, the ones who play games, and the ones who sense that their marriage may have been a mistake. They feel anger and irritation with their partner, they feel self-pity for falling into a self-made trap of superiority, and they may be somewhat resentful and bitter about how their lives have turned out. For some, the ultimate outcome of superiority will be poor health, as well as psychological distress, such as feelings of depression and anxiety, misery and malaise. Finally, wifely superiority may ultimately result in divorce.

"Our marriage was very unequal from the beginning," says Celine, forty-six, a marketing manager and superior wife from Perth, Australia, who is now filing for divorce from her husband. "We never fully shared responsibility as partners or as parents, because I always supported the family financially. He rarely did anything unless I asked, and I had to ask many times. We argued a lot because I felt that he was refusing to be a part of our family. My husband relied on his mother for money, and she was willing to help him so she could maintain control over him. She didn't care that he was supposed to be a grown-up, with a need to take ownership and responsibility for himself and the family he created with me," Celine explains. "His mother complained to me about how we were raising our children and other shortcomings of mine as a mother and wife, and my husband sat back and watched. Now he's trying to stall our divorce proceedings, and he seems unconcerned about me and our sons," she concludes, with sadness and regret but with great determination to end her superiority.

Michelle's situation is not as extreme as Celine's—she's still married after twenty-two years and four children—but she too is a longtime superior wife. "I manage and coordinate the children's schedules, my husband's schedule, and my schedule, and all of our activities and our health," says Michelle, forty. "I am the go-to person when something is broken, when there's a problem at work or at school, and when someone is sick." The owner and manager of a small restaurant in Taiwan, Michelle does not resent being superior, since she views it as somewhat of a genetic inevitability. "My husband is a great provider, and I am a great nurturer, and we fulfill our stereotypes, because it's in our nature to do so," she says. "We have learned to be quite patient in expressing our annoyance and irritations with each other, and I only nag him sometimes, mostly about eating sweets," she continues. "He makes more money than I do, but he listens to my advice about how to spend it, because I spend to benefit the family and not myself. I don't buy jewelry, for example, and most of our money goes into raising our four children."

Still, Michelle has frequent stomach pains and headaches, and she's not completely happy with the way her marriage has turned out. Neither are the vast majority of superior wives. Despite the "superior" label, *these women are not better wives*; in fact, superior wives suffer, and so do their husbands.

Superior wives feel resentment and anger about how their marriage has turned out. Superior wives feel depressed and anxious about their situation. Superior wives feel disappointed and upset about their intimacy and their family life and their sex life. Superior wives struggle to overcome these feelings by pretending not to have them, or by carping and nagging about vaguely related topics, or by directing the blame inward, becoming sick and unhappy. Occasionally they face the truth about the mess their superiority has created, but mostly they don't. That's because superior wives rarely realize or understand that it's their superiority that is at the heart of most of their problems. They are blind to the effects of superiority on themselves, on their husband, on their marriage, and on their family. This inability to see superiority for what it is—a self-destructive reaction to men's innate inclination to be lazy—dooms them to a life that is less than it could be.

And it is one that they do not deserve.

Fortunately, being a superior wife is not a life sentence; there are many ways for wives to train themselves out of their superiority, as we'll see in chapter 8. But first, I'd like to explore the sexuality of superior wives and discuss the ways in which wifely superiority can infiltrate, and contaminate, the marital bed. The next chapter examines how superior wives and their husbands, as well as nonsuperior wives and their partners, view their sex lives and their ideal sex fantasies. It will also explore the four types of married sex.

6

Sex and the Superior Wife

Sex life? There's sex after marriage and kids? Why wasn't I told?" a superior wife asks in mock indignation.

She's only half joking, but her half joke is also half true. Superior wives are likely to neglect their sexuality, in part because it makes them so unhappy and so unfulfilled.

There are roughly two million jokes about sex and marriage, and most of them refer to the imaginary nature of marital sex and its ever-dwindling character. "I know nothing about sex because I was always married" is the way former sexpot Zsa Zsa Gabor once put it.[1] "Sex in marriage is like a medicine. Three times a day for the first week. Then once a day for another week. Then once every three or four days until the condition has cleared up" is another way to put it.[2] Multiply these two jokes by one million, and you get the idea.

Sex in marriage is a now-you-see-it, now-you-don't magic trick. Social scientists who study sexual frequency like to say that if you put one marble in a bag every time a couple has sex in the first year of their marriage and then take out one marble for each time after that, the bag will never be empty, no matter how long the marriage lasts. In other words, when the honeymoon is over, it's really over.

We know this because one of the simplest ways that sex researchers have to study sexual behavior is to keep track of how often couples have intercourse, focusing on quantity and not quality. This obsession with numbers is part of a natural human urge, especially a male urge, because it's a simple and objective way to compare ourselves with other people. Many husbands and wives want to know if they're "normal," if they are having sex about as often as everybody else. The answer is that almost all marital sexual encounters fall into the normal category, since the range for what's sexually normal is vast, from zero to a dozen times a week. It's normal for married couples to have sexual relations almost never, and it's normal for married couples to have intercourse every day of the week or even twice a day. The research reveals that married couples make love quite often during the first year or two, but after that, sexual frequency declines, slowly and steadily, over the years. Recently married couples have intercourse, on average, about three times a week. Six months after the wedding, the same couples have sex, on average, about twice a week, according to one study.[3] So it doesn't take long for couples, even newlyweds, to start sliding down the marital sexual decline. That's why those imaginary marbles in that imaginary bag never quite disappear.

Sex researchers have studied sexual frequency quite intensively during the past few decades, and they find that, in general, married couples have sex about once or twice a week. This figure depends, however, on how old the couple is and how long they've been married. Older couples have sex less often, as do couples who have been married longer.[4] Time may heal all wounds, but time also decreases all sex.

There has been some debate among experts as to why couples have sex less often as the years go by. A few researchers believe that the drop in sexual frequency among married couples is due to the pressures of work. They claim that when both partners have jobs, they have less time for sex, which is why such wives and husbands are sometimes known as DINS, or "double income, no sex." But there's no evidence that this is true; in fact, some working couples actually have sex *more often* than those in which only one partner works. Indeed, the drastic drop-off in marital sex is most likely related to a simple lack of novelty. Once the thrill of new sex is gone, couples do it less often, which is why it's called "the honeymoon effect." New sex is great sex; familiar sex is not. Perhaps this is why researchers also find that the longer couples are married, the more likely it is that the husband, but not the wife, will have an extramarital affair.[5]

Still, many couples believe that having a good marriage includes having good sex, and they define good sex as frequent sex. So if they have sex often—which usually means as often as the husband would like—then they view their marriage as a good one. It's as if they use sex as a barometer, one that can forecast clear skies or stormy weather, to keep track of every marital high and every marital low.[6] Many of my Web survey wives and husbands seem to feel this way, with a few notable exceptions, like the forty-eight-year-old financial consultant from New York City, who says, "I don't know any honest couple who, after sixteen years of marriage, claims to have sex regularly. Those who think such couples exist are deluded. The foundation of all lasting marriages is celibacy," he concludes, obviously speaking from experience.

Despite what this husband believes, most long-term marriages are *not* celibate, though as the years pass, both spouses usually notice that they're having sex less often. Husbands are especially likely to be the ones who moan and groan about longing to pick up the sexual pace. The less often they make love, the less happy they are with their marriage, which results in a vicious cycle. Making love less often makes husbands and wives unhappy, and the more unhappy they are, the less often they want to make love. The less often they want to, the less often they do, so they're unhappier.[7] And so on.

In this case, less really is less.

"My wife is rarely interested in sex, and even foreplay is something she doesn't understand," says Todd, thirty-nine, an electronics industry blogger in Los Angeles. "In the first four years of our marriage, we had sex more often, but now we hardly ever do. My wife will not entertain oral sex in any form, and she is staunchly opposed to experimenting with sex toys or anything different," he says. It's not surprising that Todd is unhappy with his sex life, with his marriage, and with his life in general. It's also not surprising that he's married to a superior wife, since those are marriages with relatively inferior sex.

Todd's disappointing sex life is the superior wife rule. Doug's sex life, however, is exceptional, even in a nonsuperior wife marriage. Doug, who has been married for twenty-three years, says, "We have always had sex two or three times a day, and this is been our practice since we got married." Doug, forty-nine, a youth minister in Brent, Alabama, adds that "we have grown closer because we place God first and we usually pray before we engage in sexual activity, since God comes first and then fleshly desires."

It's a safe bet that whatever Doug's secret, many husbands would willingly worship him as a superhero, more amazing than Batman, Superman, Spider-Man, and all of the X-Men rolled into one. Doug is an extreme

example of the idea that good sex makes for a good marriage, but the obvious question is which comes first, the good marriage or the good sex? Does
a good marriage always lead to good sex, or does good sex result in a good
marriage? That's the chicken-and-egg question of the century. Research
shows that couples who are happier about their marriage tend to say that
they're happier about their sex lives too. The reverse is also true.[8] But it's
probably impossible to untangle the effects of having a loving relationship
and having a relationship full of loving.

Married couples have sex because they're supposed to, but it's not that
simple. In fact, women and men have sex for 237 *different reasons*, at least,
according to one study. There are the usual reasons for sex—to experience
physical pleasure, to show affection, to have fun, to please a partner, and to
share intimacy. But people also have sex "to manipulate him/her into doing
something for me" or because they feel pressured or obligated or because
they feel that it's their duty, this research shows.[9]

Sex as a duty is actually one of the four types of married sex, I find, and
it's especially common among superior wives. In addition, some superior
wives are honest about their habit of using sex as bait, as a way to coerce
their husband into cooperating more fully. They view this as just one of several effective, sneaky ways to persuade and cajole and sway their husband to
their way of thinking, whatever that may be. Some superior wives try to use
sex to their advantage, but they aren't particularly happy about it, nor does
it work every time.

How Superior Wives Use Sex

Among superior wives, sex is like connubial money: it's the coin of the marital realm. They can withhold it or bestow it, initiate it or refuse it, depending on how exploited they are or how angry they feel or how manipulative
they want to be. In essence, sex has endless uses. It's a means of procreation
and recreation, of satiation and sublimation, of restoration and remunera-
tion. Sex is a bargaining chip, the biggest and best means of female persuasion known to womankind.

And superior wives are not afraid to use that means, either. Some
are matter-of-fact about it, some are ashamed, but a great many superior
wives dangle the possibility of sex in front of their husbands like a trainer

offering sugar cubes and carrots to a balky horse. It's a cheap trick, but it works.

Nineteen percent of superior wives say that their husband begs for sex quite often, and another 30 percent say that he sometimes does so. "My husband's self-image revolves around sex," says Lois, fifty-one, a superior wife and speech therapist in Louisville, Kentucky. Lois says that "sex works wonders in our marriage. I can get almost anything I want by using sex or paying an abundance of attention to my husband," she explains. "I even got the kids a jungle gym, built with sex," she adds, bluntly. Marilyn, forty-seven, a superior wife in rural Wisconsin, knows just how that technique works. "My husband is constantly asking for sex, because he'd like sex every night of the week, but I'm fine with once a week," says Marilyn, an evangelical Christian. "It's on his mind around the clock, and whenever I talk to him by phone, he's always asking if we are going to have a 'date night' tonight. I get tired of hearing the same question every day," Marilyn explains. "He has to be touching me all the time, and he always has to have a hand on me, somewhere." Marilyn adds that "I'm sad to admit this, but if I really want to get my husband to do something, and he doesn't want to do it, all I have to do is tell him that I'll have sex with him." She's not proud of using this method, she says, but it's effective.

"I hate to say it, but sometimes I use sex to get what I want," agrees Jill, a twenty-eight-year-old superior wife and at-home mom from Eureka, California. "I know that if my husband really doesn't want to do something, nine times out of ten he will do it if I offer sex. It's awful, I know, but it's true." Jill's guilt doesn't prevent her from turning an act of love into an act of negotiation. "I started initiating sex, even when I was exhausted, to get him in a good mood so that I could broach some subject about wanting him to do something," agrees Gloria, forty-five, a dermatologist in Miami, Florida. "I'd wait until the next day or two to ask for what I wanted, and this always worked. I saw a one hundred percent correlation between my husband's sexual satisfaction and his desire to please me. It's my magic formula! I have learned to have sex first and to talk second. The talk is always way more productive if it's after the sex."

Many husbands sense that they are being played for sex, like a double bass in a bluegrass band, and the idea does not thrill them. A twenty-seven-year-old husband from Oklahoma says that in the best of all possible

Nonsuperior Wives Are Sexier

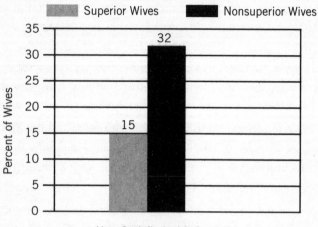

worlds, "my wife would want sex as much as I do and I wouldn't have to ask for it. We would both know that sex was going to happen right then, and I wouldn't have to beg." He still loves her and believes that they complement each other, "since we each make up for what the other is lacking." But oh, not having to beg would be heaven, he adds.

The fact that some superior wives dole out sexual favors generously, like candy to trick-or-treaters on Halloween, or begrudgingly, like jelly doughnuts to members of Weight Watchers, means that their sex lives are somewhat premeditated and contrived. Indeed, superior wives are not as happy with their sex lives as other wives, though most wives are not all that pleased about sex to begin with. Just 15 percent of superior wives say they are very happy with their sex lives, compared to 32 percent of other wives, a shockingly small minority in both cases.

Sex is a sore topic for many wives, superior and nonsuperior, many of whom suffer from a lack of sexual desire. A number of others are also tired of getting nagged about sex by their husbands. Sex is one of the most common reasons for squabbles and spats between superior wives and their husbands, so it can be as great a source of pain and distress as it is of pleasure and intimacy. The truth is that sex is a marital battleground for many couples, with potential for enormous conflict and resentment as well as for love and intimacy. This is especially true of superior wives, some of whom harbor deep and abiding bitterness about the lack of fairness in their marriage and who are not afraid to wield their sexual power as a last resort. They may use the withholding of sex as a tit-for-tat payback. It's in the sexual arena that they can fight for honor, justice, and the superior wife way of life, in an effort to remove a persistent kernel of anger and resentment about the inequities in their marriage. That sense of unfairness, if broad and pervasive enough, undermines their sexual desire and erodes their sense of affection and caring for their partner. As I mentioned earlier, a wife's perception of unfairness in marriage can cause great unhappiness and can even make her sick, so it's only natural that this hostility will seep into her sexual relationship as well.

Indeed, many wives feel that their husband must *earn the right* to have marital sex, that he has to deserve it. Unfortunately, though, most husbands of superior wives don't seem to understand the concept of well-earned marital sex. A few husbands, however, deliberately take on the responsibility for cooking and chores, in the hope that their wives will look upon them with greater sexual favor.[10] The road to sexual favors is, apparently, a two-way street. "I know that if I really want to improve our sex life, I should take on a few more chores around the house for my wife," says a thirty-year-old pastor from Kansas, who classifies his wife as superior and understands exactly how the tit-for-tat sex system works. "Have you ever heard the phrase 'Sex begins in the kitchen, doing the dishes'?" he asks. Just because he's heard the phrase, though, doesn't mean he's heeded it. Likewise, a Georgia husband says that "one of my wife's favorite sayings is that there's nothing sexier than a man doing the dishes." Finally, a forty-year-old architect in Kirkland, Washington, who admits that his wife is superior, says that "I realize my wife would want to have sex with me more often if I could make myself into a more listening, caring, attentive, thoughtful, compassionate, supportive, and loving husband. I let my own moods and low self-esteem rule my life, and I don't give her what she needs to get in the mood." He knows the rules, he just doesn't follow them.

Sex Initiators, Sex Refusers

While it's true that superior wives are more likely than other wives to force their husbands to beg for sex, that difference is minor compared to the enormous differences between the genders on sexual matters. Very generally speaking, *men want sex, women don't*. That's not true for every husband and every wife, of course, but mostly, "men are more carnal than women," as a twenty-nine-year-old Illinois husband says. Another married guy explains that most men are simpleminded: "Women wonder what's on our minds, but that's easy. We wanna beer and we wanna see something naked!" Men think about sex more, they want it more often, they care about it more. Wifely superiority simply magnifies this difference.

"Women need a reason to have sex. Men just need a place," says comedian Billy Crystal, whose well-aged joke reflects an essential truth.[11] But it's not just random husbands and comedians who've noticed this gender disparity in carnality. Research shows that men have a higher sex drive and that this drive is almost certainly fueled by brain hormones.[12]

Neuroscientists say that testosterone, the male sex hormone, fuels sex drive in both men and in women. It's just that most men have between ten and one hundred times more testosterone than most women: voilà, major sex drive gap. In addition, the so-called sex center of the brain is twice as large in men as it is in women, so men, "quite literally, have sex on their minds more than women do," as one neurologist puts it.[13] For men, processing thoughts about sex requires a large section of the brain, like a huge international airport; for women, such processing occupies just a tiny speck of brain area, like a small dirt landing strip.

These differences in biology explain why the sexual gender disparity occurs among men and women around the world. In a study of women and men between the ages of forty and eighty in twenty-nine countries, for instance, experts find that men are more emotionally satisfied with their sex lives and that they get more pleasure from sex than women do. In addition, men rate sex as being much more important than women do. This is true of people who live in places as dissimilar as the United States, Brazil, China, and Taiwan, as well as in Korea and Mexico, Morocco and Turkey, Israel and Thailand, and nineteen other countries.[14] Even in mainland China, men are more satisfied than women with their sex lives. In addition,

Chinese women are more unhappy than their partners with the amount of attention they receive, and they're annoyed that their husbands rarely kiss during intercourse.[15]

Given the large number of countries in which men and women are equal in many ways, this gender stereotype about sex seems dated, but it is also reality. Husbands are sexually assertive, wives are sexually passive. While wives may be struggling to achieve equality in the home and in the workplace, they have ceded their chance for equal sensuality in the bedroom. In my Web survey, for example, it's quite clear that even before they marry, men place much more importance on sexuality than women do. Twenty-seven percent of husbands say that finding a sexually compatible partner is one of the two most important considerations in their choice of a spouse. But just 10 percent of wives use the same criterion for selecting a potential husband.

When twenty-seven-year-old Jamal, the manager of a sporting goods store in Jacksonville, Florida, decided to get married two years ago, he deliberately sought a wife "who desires sex as much as I do." He found one "who is very open to sexual discussion, and we have no problem talking about our sexual desires," Jamal explains, adding that they both agree that "sex is an important part of marriage," and not just for him but for both of them. Although Jamal follows "biblical guidelines on who should be the head of the household," he follows his own sexual guidelines in his choice of a mate, because he values having a well-matched sexual partner.

Jamal was lucky to find such a wife, since sexual compatibility falls seventh on a list of seven for what women consider important in a future husband. Women would rather find a best friend, someone who is kind and supportive, a soul mate, a good parent, someone able to earn a good living, and someone willing to give independence. For women, good sex comes last on the list. It's fourth on the list men make for their future wives.

Gender differences in sexuality become even more obvious after the wedding bouquet has wilted and the honeymoon is over. More than half of husbands, 56 percent, feel that they sometimes or often have to beg their wives for sex. And among wives, about half, 49 percent, agree that yes, their husband does beg for it once in a while.

Husbands are sexual beggars; wives are occasional sexual almsgivers.

Sam, forty-six, lives in St. Paul, Minnesota, where he's in a second marriage to an Alpha wife. They have eight children between them, so it's not surprising that Sam says, "My wife refuses me quite often, because she's tired or 'the boys might hear,' as she puts it." That's why Sam resorts to begging when necessary. "I rub her feet for her at the end of the day, because it means a lot to her," he says. "But I would be a liar if I said I did it for purely altruistic reasons, since it helps warm her up for my advances later on and I have to do less begging that way." Likewise, Phillip, a fifty-year-old government official in Fremont, California, has just about given up begging his superior wife for sex. "I wish she would take as much interest in sex as when we were first married, in terms of new and different experiences," he says. "But now I'm reduced to begging almost all the time, and it's a lot of work and takes time away from other things." Phillip got so fed up with having to beg, in fact, that he has had several affairs over the past twenty-five years, "though that's just as much work, but at least I don't end up having to beg."

While many husbands resent having to plead for what some consider their conjugal right, others are more sympathetic to their wife's point of view. Darrell, forty-two, a sheriff in Alabama with six children, is married to a superior wife. He says, "It's quite simple. The husband always wants more sex, and the wife is just expected to 'put out.' It took me ten years to come to terms with my wife and to realize that when I act like an ass, I don't get laid." As a result of some thought and consideration on his part, Darrell says that "now I get it, that the better and more understanding I am, the friendlier and more willing she will be." Translation: when Darrell remembers to be considerate and kind, he will receive his sexual rewards.

Not nearly as many wives, about 21 percent, say they sometimes feel they are begging for sex; the same number of husbands agree that this is so. In this situation, one in which the normal gender stereotypes have been flipped upside down and inside out, both partners may feel a bit uncomfortable. That's probably because both partners are painfully aware of how unusual they are. A thirty-three-year-old special education teacher in Chicago says she longs for "an overhaul of my husband's sex drive. I want him to desire me more often and to want to have sex more often too." But she's embarrassed to talk to him about it, because she doesn't want to challenge his manhood. A superior Alpha wife from Alabama longs to have sex three or four times a week, which she would thoroughly enjoy, she says. "But we've been married for almost thirty years, and my husband just doesn't seem interested anymore. Still, he's my king and I'm his queen, and we love each other, so I don't mention it."

Even so, my Web survey results confirm that husbands are sexual initiators and wives are sexual refusers. In the survey, I asked this question: "Think back to the last ten times you had sex with your spouse. Who initiated it?" I also asked how many times during the past month each partner had refused the other's "sexual overtures." My results were exactly what you would expect, at least according to the somewhat inflexible bedroom-based gender stereotypes. According to wives, their husband is the sexual initiator seven times out of ten; she is about three times in ten. Superior wives are just as likely as other wives to report this seven/three split, so they follow the general gender rules when it comes to being sexual initiators.

Husbands tend to agree that they are the sexual initiators seven times out of ten, but nearly one in four says that his wife never initiates sex, ever. Fewer wives agree that this is so, just 16 percent. And many women, especially superior wives, feel they have good reason to be sexually reticent.

"Sometimes I feel like my husband is the hunter and I am the prey, which doesn't make me feel very sexual," says a thirty-seven-year-old superior wife and mother of four from Olympia, Washington. "It's like I want to avoid being 'trapped,' because I also feel so angry at him for so many reasons," she explains. It may be her husband's job to initiate, she says, but that's why it seems like it should be her job to refuse, as a kind of sexual counterbalance. He's up and she's down; he wants in and she wants out.

Brandon, a thirty-year-old social worker from Fulton, Maryland, feels as if he's constantly trying to initiate sex, while his superior wife is constantly refusing. "She says it's because she's tired," he explains, "but I don't buy it. I'd love to be awakened by my naked wife riding me or performing oral sex on me at least twice a week, the way it was when we were dating and couldn't keep our hands off each other." Unfortunately for Brandon, it seems that it's become his job to initiate and his wife's job to concede under duress or to just say no. Like Brandon, some husbands say they are tired of being the one who initiates all the time, and they'd be thrilled if their wife were to assume that job, at least on a part-time basis.

Wives seem to have endless reasons for refusing to have sex, as if justifying their lack of sexual passion has become a hobby. Wives refuse their husband's sexual overtures, on average, about twice a month, according to wives. But to husbands, it seems to happen much more often. They say their wives refuse to have sex nearly three times a month. Both husbands and wives are in agreement, though, that husbands almost never refuse sex, not even once a month.

Russell, thirty, is one of the rare exceptions to this rule. An insurance adjuster in Grove City, Ohio, Russell says, "I get nervous about pregnancy, since I have been trained not to get anyone pregnant." Married for three years, he adds, "I've had a condom break, and that scared me, since my wife and I want to wait a few more years before we have children. Unfortunately, this prevents me from fully enjoying the experience of sex, so I sometimes just refuse to start, because I'm scared of making a baby." Again, as a male refuser in the marital sex game, Russell is so rare he's practically an endangered species.

It's almost always wives who refuse sexual overtures, especially superior wives, many of whom feel justified in doing so. "We've had two babies in the past twelve months," says Tara, a superior wife and oil company executive from Spring, Texas, who got pregnant a few weeks after giving birth to her first child. Tara is refusing her husband left, right, and center these days, but not because she's afraid of another instant insemination. "I want to have sex more, but I'm not very interested because I'm sore and exhausted and because I have some resentment about not getting enough intimate contact with no strings attached," she says. "I want more caresses and strokes, without getting the feeling that these are some sort of foreplay and a selfish gesture on my husband's part. I'm also resentful that I never got any back rubs or foot rubs during pregnancy, so I guess I'm a bit, well, angry."

Another superior wife from Wisconsin has to fend off her husband every night, obliging him only once a week or so, she says, "just so he doesn't pester me anymore." She and her husband lost a teenage son in a car accident a few years ago, and she has never recovered her sex drive, she says. "I would like to accommodate my husband more often, but I am tired and just not that interested," she concludes.

Though wives and husbands differ dramatically in how often they initiate or refuse sex, both express similar sexual wishes and desires. Superior wives and their husbands, nonsuperior wives and their husbands—all long to be younger and sexier and more desirable, as well as thinner and more energetic. Husbands believe that their sex lives would be vastly improved by having more oral sex, by earning more money, and by being in greater sexual synchrony with their wives. Superior wives, and others, wish they could derive more satisfaction from sex, which would make them less likely to refuse it so often. Better sex would make everybody feel better.

Top Ten Sex Wishes of Superior Wives

In my Web survey, I asked wives and husbands the following question, which they had to answer in their own words: "If you could wave a magic wand and dramatically improve or change your sex life, what would happen?" Wives were very clear about what they want, at least in the bedroom. And they weren't too shy or too embarrassed to tell me, either. Only a handful of wives and husbands said that this is a private matter, one that they preferred not to discuss. Everybody else, the vast majority, was forthright and honest and amazingly open about their sexual wishes and dreams. A legal secretary from Virginia, for instance, says she'd like her husband to moan and sigh when he makes love, because "he's a silent lover, and I'd like him to be more wild." Wives don't hold back about what intrigues them sexually, what inflames them, or what causes them sexual despair. They tell me that they long to be younger and thinner and sexier; they ache to have a mate who constantly demonstrates his love and his affection, all the time "and not just when he's 'in the mood.'" But most important of all, they have an overwhelming desire to have more sexual desire: they want to want it more than they want it.

Here are the top ten sexual wishes of superior wives.

1. To renew lost desire. The most common sex wish among superior wives is to restore libido, to revive sex drive, "to put it back at the top of my priority list," as one wife says. Another wishes that she and her husband could "coordinate our sexual time zones," since her husband always wants to make love early in the morning, "but for me, it just doesn't work, since I'm not awake enough and I'm usually tired and thinking of all the things I need to do." A lack of desire, day or night, is women's primary sexual problem, and it's one that many wish they could cure. They really do hope to be in the mood again, on a regular basis, and not just once in every other blue moon. Superior wives ache to return from the land of lost desire. One wife says, "I'm waiting for pink Viagra." Another, whose husband is already on the little blue pill, is taking a female sex supplement sold at vitamin stores, and she says, "Thank God for modern medicine." Many husbands complain bitterly about their wives' vanished sexual needs, but many wives are just as upset and disturbed by the shutdown of their sexual generators. They blame the problem on aging and menopause, on the side effects of medication, on disease, on pregnancy, and on having to deal with screaming, nursing infants. Superior wives blame it on their husband's lack of cooperation and helpfulness, which makes them more cynical and resentful than sexy. Whatever the reason for wives' lack of desire, many honestly hope and pray for its eventual return. "I want back the libido that pregnancy, childbirth, and breast-feeding have sucked out of me," says a twenty-nine-year-old mother of a newborn and a toddler.

The loss of sexual desire is an overwhelmingly common sexual dysfunction among all women, not just superior wives. About three in ten American wives say they lack a desire for sex, according to a major national sex study.[16] That number is repeated in similar studies all over the world. A recent global sex survey shows that 32 percent of women over the age of forty in Canada, Australia, and New Zealand, as well as in the United States, lack sexual desire.[17] American wives are clearly not the only ones whose sexuality has waned, nor is the problem an imaginary crisis among wives who answer Web surveys like mine. Instead, it's a universal and international phenomenon—and one that can be attributed, in part, to the effects of wifely superiority, I believe.

Women's lack of desire may have some biological basis too, according to neuroscientists. Women cannot reach orgasm unless the amygdala, the part of the brain that controls fear and anxiety, has been turned off. But men don't need to disable this fear center to enjoy sex, which is why it takes women a lot longer to reach orgasm than men, between three and ten times longer. In addition, "a woman needs to be put in the mood. Before sex, there has to be a soothing and smoothing of the relationship, and she has to be able to stop being annoyed with him," according to Louann Brizendine, author of *The Female Brain*.[18] This is one reason why unresolved anger at one's partner is a major cause of sexual problems in marriage, she adds. Sex therapists also point out that for women, foreplay is everything that happens in the twenty-four hours before the sexual encounter. For men, it's what happens three minutes before.[19] It's no wonder, then, that superior wives are significantly more likely than others to be extremely unhappy with their sex lives.

2. To banish fatigue. Even if they haven't lost their urge to merge, many superior wives complain about the effects of daily exhaustion, saying that they wish they could have increased verve, more energy, and a return to the days when they'd rather have sex than sleep. "If only we could have the vigor and stamina of our youth, with the confidence, experience, and comfortableness we have now," says Anna, forty-four, who runs a lumber company near Decatur, Alabama, with her husband. "We'd embrace each other's imperfect, human bodies and we'd accept each other and ourselves just the way we are, and we'd use our get-up-and-go to get it on for hours!" Superior wives, who are energetic doers and achievers all day long, are especially likely to feel overwhelming fatigue that banishes any and all thoughts of sexuality. They reach a point at which the most erotic fantasy they have is of their head hitting their pillow.

3. To be romanced. Just a bit more cuddling and kissing, attention and foreplay, intimate chitchat and whispered secrets would add essential spice to a bland sex life, many wives say. They want to feel "cherished and respected"; they want him to demonstrate "caring and consideration"; they want to "go on dates, which would be good for my sexual arousement," as one wife misstates, though with heartfelt accuracy. Wives with this sexual wish are quite precise in their sexual improvement fantasies, like a fifty-seven-year-old superior wife and personal trainer from the suburbs of Buffalo, New York. "I would love to have sex that would be exciting and passionate and not just feel like body parts colliding. It would include deep kissing and hugging and lots of touching. My husband would call me after he leaves home and tell me he misses me and that he can't wait to see me. He'd pursue me, rather than saying from twenty feet away, 'Do you feel like doing something?' which means he wants sex. And then he'd say he wants to take me to dinner or to a movie or out for a drink. He'd woo me, and ruffle my hair, and tantalize me with neck kisses and eye kisses, and he'd put me first and

I'd know he cared about me." Because she's a superior wife, though, she's more likely to suffer in silence than to make such specific sexual demands.

Other wives long for what one Connecticut wife calls "romantic foreplay, dinner and candles and music." Married for twenty-nine years, this fifty-three-year-old wife and mother says that her husband has never bought her flowers, "except once he brought me a rose from work. Later he told me that one of the receptionists in his office had received a dozen roses as a birthday gift, and she gave him one to bring home to me!" But, she says, things might be looking up, romancewise. "Last week, my husband and I went on a walk together. I stopped to rest in a shady spot, and he went further. When he came back, he had a yellow flower that he had picked for me. It was really touching, and when he asked me what kind of flower it was, I couldn't bring myself to say the word 'weed'!"

4. *To be thinner and younger.* If only they could lose ten pounds, twenty-three pounds, thirty pounds, seventy-five pounds, they'd feel much sexier. It's this belief in the power of svelte that propels the multibillion-dollar diet industry and underlies the mostly frustrating quest for dream-weight sexiness. "My own personal body issues limit me," says a forty-six-year-old wife in a second marriage. "My husband never makes me feel bad about my body, it's all within me, and I know he'd be ecstatic if we had sex more often," she confesses. It's just that she doesn't feel sexy at her current weight, though there's also no guarantee she'd feel any different if she were to lose twenty pounds. While they're dreaming impossible dreams, wives would also, by the way, like to be younger. "I want to have my twenty-three-year-old body back," says a forty-one-year-old wife. Another wife, who's fifty, wants to be twenty again; others specifically ask to be twenty years younger or to be nineteen again or to simply "turn back the clock." A wife in her sixties would settle for being thirty again. "Younger," of course, is relative to a wife's current age. Thirty looks a lot younger at sixty than it does at, say, forty-three. Wives aren't selfish in their being-better-looking dreams, since a great many also wish their husband would lose some weight and be younger too. A forty-year-old superior wife from Virginia fantasizes that she'd have great sex if she resembled supermodel Heidi Klum and if her husband were the spitting image of actor Matthew McConaughey. That's about as likely to happen as her superiority disappearing completely by next Sunday.

More realistic wives confess that both partners need to lose some weight. "We both need our sexy, youthful bodies back, and if I were fifty pounds lighter, I'd feel sexy again," is the way one wife puts it. A forty-eight-year-old superior wife from Topton, Pennsylvania, is blunt and open about the way she feels about herself. "I am disgusted with my physical appearance, so I'm ashamed to think sexual thoughts or to act out sexually," she says. "I don't fit the mold for a sexy babe, ergo, I shouldn't be having sex, much less enjoying it." This kind of female self-loathing and contempt is far from unusual, especially among superior wives, no matter how young or old, fat or thin they may be. "Since my son was born, I feel flabby and ugly," says a twenty-six-year-old superior wife from Germany. "My husband has a ton of pornography on his computer, and I would love to look even a little bit like one of those women, but my stretch marks have scarred me forever." Meanwhile, most wives over the age of forty or fifty would give anything to have their twenty-six-year-old body back, no matter how stretch-marked. It certainly doesn't help, however, when husbands make disparaging remarks about how their wife looks naked, as does the husband of a forty-six-year-old superior wife in Wisconsin. "I wish I'd feel loved and know that he wants me no matter how I look, but he laughs at my rear and pinches the fat on my thighs," she says, with resignation.

5. *To cure husband's problems.* Wives aren't the only ones who suffer from a lack of desire and other sexual problems. That's why some long to increase their husbands' minimal desire as well. Wives wish they could cure his impotence, his erectile dysfunction, or his inability "to stay awake after nine at night or longer than three seconds after his head hits the pillow." Their husband takes medication that reduces his sexual potency, or he has been treated for prostate cancer, or he drinks too much. "I did not realize that when men hit fifty, the male sex organ becomes smaller and unable to get and maintain an erection," says a sexually frustrated superior wife from Los Angeles. Her job is not only to manage her family and her house and her job but also to cure her husband's erectile dysfunction. It's no wonder that she's perturbed.

Wives suffer when they feel a diminished sexual urge, but they suffer just as much when it's their husband who loses his sexual zing. "If I had that magic wand, I'd wave it over my husband to make his need for beer disappear," says a fifty-two-year-old wife from Pitkin, Louisiana. "All the beer in the fridge would turn back into the money he spent on it, and I would be able to have sex with the person I married and not a drunk," she adds. The husband of a forty-eight-year-old superior wife from Baltimore, Maryland, "has an erectile problem, even with Viagra, because he drinks too much. But he's a denier, so I can explain this to him until I'm blue in the face, but he still refuses to admit it, because he's so stubborn."

6. *To do it more often.* It's true that husbands tend to be the sex initiators and wives the sex refusers, but that's not always the case. There is a small but vocal group of wives who long to have sex more often than they do. Some would like to make love more often than hardly ever; others would like to have sex a lot more often. "I'd like to do it not once a month but three or four times a week," as one wife puts it. Another wants it "daily, instead of every other day," and yet another wants it "twice a day, instead of every day." A twenty-five-year-old superior wife in Port Townsend, Washington, wishes she could have sex more often, but her husband says "he's too tired, because he works really hard and has long hours. The other night, he stayed up playing video games instead of having sex with me. That was a serious blow to my ego," she adds. Because she's superior, though, she views the situation as her fault, which only makes matters worse.

7. *To have more time together.* Wives long to have quality time with their husband, for the benefit of their sex lives, if nothing else. Instead, though, their children get in the way: the kids interrupt, or they're too old or too young or too in-between. Wives want to sneak away from crying babies, nearby teenagers, and demanding toddlers, so that they can pay some sensual attention to their husband. They yearn for weekend getaways or to be "in a fabulous suite looking at the sea in Tahiti," as one desperate housewife fantasizes. "I just want my children to go to bed and fall asleep," says one sexually frustrated wife. "We need time without the kids around, because our teenagers stay up late and always seem aware of what we're doing. We really need an empty house, but we almost never get it," she says. A few of these wives confess that they just don't make enough of an effort to be alone together, although they realize how important that is. "I need to separate my focus on getting tasks done, like grading test papers, making

dinner, coaching my students' soccer practices, and getting ready to go out with friends and instead make time for the two of us to be together," says a twenty-six-year-old wife from Springfield, Oregon. "I know that personal time together should be a priority and that we have to focus on our own life together," she says. Even grannies know that, as does Mary Ellen, fifty-two, a superior wife from Rockford, Illinois. "We need weekends away, for hotel sex, a place where there are no distractions, no pagers, no computers, no children or grandchildren or dogs," she explains. "We used to go folk danc-ing, and we miss it very much, because we always had sex after dancing, because you are so 'high' from the activity," adds Mary Ellen. Because she's a superior wife, it's a good bet that Mary Ellen will take on the job of figur-ing out how to fix her sex and folk dance problems, along with everything else.

8. To be sexually satisfied. Once in a while, it would be nice "if my hus-band would know how to satisfy me and not just look out for himself," several wives say. "I'd prefer less lazy lovemaking, like when he lays on his side right on top of my leg and cuts off the circulation," says a twenty-six-year-old superior wife from Silverdale, Washington. "Maybe then he'd pay some attention to my satisfaction." Says another, "I'd like to get what I need, instead of just fulfilling his small quota of needs, while I am always hungry for more." A forty-seven-year-old wife yearns to "know what an or-gasm is again. I want to feel that I want him, not that sex is a weekly marital obligation, like laundry. I know that sex has to be better than what I'm getting," she explains, "because otherwise, the planet would stop procreat-ing." Superior wives often sacrifice their own sexual pleasure for the sake of marital harmony. But most of them are also unaware that this can sabotage their own happiness, as well as the health of their marriage.

Take Laura, who had been complaining to her husband, Sal, about painful intercourse for more than a year. A forty-nine-year-old superior wife from Rhode Island, Laura says she's very dry down there, so she has to use artificial lubricants. She's tried almost every kind, both gels and liquids, she says, but every one of them burns like crazy. At first they seem okay, but after she and her husband begin touching each other, a fiery sensation be-gins. After a while, she says, "It's as if a little elf has lit a match and started a small oil fire over every inch of my private parts. Not only is it distracting, but it makes getting any pleasure out of sex incredibly difficult." Her only wish is to get rid of the pain during intercourse, so she won't dread the whole thing. "When the burning began, it was just so unpleasant that I wanted to say 'the hell with it,'" Laura explains. But as a superior wife, Laura felt that she had to fulfill her sexual obligations, regardless of her own discomfort.

One day, Laura decided to forget the lubricants and use saliva. Still, to her surprise, "I felt the burning worse than ever. I leaped out of the bed, and then I had a flash of understanding." She realized that Sal's hands were covered with the pain relief cream that he used every day for his sore back. "Every time he touched me, he was getting the stuff all over my vaginal area. I looked at the tube, and right where it says, 'Penetrating Heat Relief Formula,' it also says 'Keep away from eyes and mucous membranes.' I guess he wasn't considering my membranes." Now that she has forbidden her husband to use the pain cream, Laura says, her sex life is much improved, though she's still angry about her husband's complete lack of insight into the side effects of his personal body lotion.

9. To be creative. A few wives want kinky sex, experimental sex, playful sex, aggressive sex. They want to have sex as an indoor sport, rather than as a demure parlor game. "I'd love to have sex at different times, in different ways," says a thirty-seven-year-old superior wife from Mountain View, California. "My husband is a meat-and-potatoes kind of guy who almost invariably wants sex early in the morning, every other day, in the same way. It's really more like routine maintenance or an exercise in hygiene than making love," she concludes unhappily. Says another, "It would be less the same, with more variation," though she's not very specific about the whats or the hows of it. Other superior wives echo the same thought: they fantasize about fabulous and different sex, but they're a bit hazy on the details.

10. To be helped and to be understood. The mantra of superior wives everywhere, this is the sexual secret that so many husbands just don't get. Here it is: if he helped out at home, she'd want sex more often. "I'm usually not interested in sex because I'm too tired," says a forty-three-year-old superior wife from Gastonia, North Carolina. "If he would help with the dishes and the children in the evenings, I'd have more energy, and it would help

me feel that we're in a total partnership," she explains. "I'd also like him to start making overtures earlier in the evening, not when I'm about to fall asleep, and to talk to me for a while, instead of just jumping on top. It would be romantic if my husband would watch our three-year-old every so often and take some responsibility," agrees a thirty-three-year-old superior wife from Michigan. He usually lies on the couch while she bustles around the house working, and that's rarely conducive to getting in the mood, she says. A superior wife from Massachusetts adds that "sexual attraction happens in lots of places besides the bedroom." Like, say, in the kitchen over the dirty dishes; in the bathroom, over bathing a toddler; in the living room, over a vacuum cleaner. Smart superior wives agitate for these kinds of changes, but most resign themselves to the status quo. Either way, their sex lives will not improve dramatically until they rid themselves of their superiority.

Lori, forty-seven, a superior wife and banker in Brentwood, Tennessee, knows this intuitively, though she has yet to take concrete action on that knowledge. "I wish my husband would have a great awakening and realize that sex doesn't start in the bedroom, but it's about how you treat your partner all day," she says. "It's thoughtfulness and kind words and rushing to carry something heavy, or just to say, 'Honey, you go sit down, put your feet up, and I'll take care of dinner,' even if it's just ordering a pizza! It's paying attention during conversations, which means *no damn electronics devices* in the room, and it's sharing a movie or a laugh or a peaceful walk."

Wives long to be "loved and accepted, not criticized," to be understood down to their bones, which would make them eager to trust and to give themselves to their man. But for some superior wives, this happens rarely, if ever. "My husband is so defensive that it's impossible for me to relax and enjoy an intimate relationship with him," says a thirty-five-year-old wife from Brawley, California. "We almost never have a meeting of the minds or the feeling that we're in this thing together. He's so focused on his genitals that he fails to realize what's going on in my head, and he doesn't care either," she concludes.

Superior wives have sex wishes and dreams, but those fantasies are rarely fulfilled, in part because such wives are reluctant to make demands or to threaten the stability of their marriage, no matter how unsound it really is. That's why many superior wives suffer sexually.

Husbands' Top Ten Sex Wishes

Men's sexual longings tend to be simpler than women's, more closely focused on frequency and technique. For husbands, ideal sex revolves around *more sex:* they want more, more, and more. Also, more. They have no problem imagining what to do with a hypothetical magic wand that would drastically improve their sex lives; a few even imagine that the wand would become their own personal, and magical, organ. Flush with notions of watching porn and using sex toys, one husband fantasizes, double-entendre style, that "my magic wand would get a real workout." Most husbands find it relatively easy to cook up sexual fantasies, with appropriately erotic bells and whistles, most of them involving the word "more." A few, though, despair of even a miracle-working stick helping their sex life. "I try to have sex with my wife many times a week, and she refuses, for one reason or another, so I'm at the point of giving up," says a forty-nine-year-old husband from San Diego, California. "I might save the power of the magic wand and use it to solve world peace, since world peace might be easier to achieve."

A forty-five-year-old composer from Chicago wishes that his sex life were simpler, with less fuss and bother. "I wish my wife would be more adventurous and that she'd want to wear different things and get turned on easier, without all the foreplay. But sometimes," he explains, "a man just wants to 'hit it' and 'quit it,' without all of the pregame show and postgame commentary." For him, marital sex might as well be a sporting event, and he's doing the scoring.

Here, then, are the top ten sex wishes of husbands.

1. *To have more creative sex.* A large number of husbands want sex that's more adventurous, more spontaneous, more flexible, and more innovative. They'd also like sex that's rougher and wilder, please. These husbands would like to get out of the marital sex rut, and many of them can vividly imagine just how they'd do that. Some of their ideas: "lights on," "leather," "have Internet sex on camera," "anal," and "have another woman in our bed." They'd prefer to find "different places in the house," "to have more fantasies," and "a lot more variety." One clever husband says he'd like "to turn my wife into twins." These guys are not shy, that's for sure. "If I could

wave a magic wand, the two of us would each have our own little harem of boys and girls that we fool around with," says a thirty-six-year-old librarian (!) from New Jersey. "Then we'd come back to our own bed and regale each other with scandalous stories of our extramarital seductions," he adds. His wife is superior, he says, and also the more responsible one, "but I like to think I help her open up and explore new things." Another husband wishes that he and his wife "would have oils and lotions, vibrators and other sex toys, and we'd watch porn together. We'd have handcuffs and other restraints, and mirrors too." More than a few husbands also say they'd like more spontaneous sex, "to spice it up," though they haven't a clue how to do that, exactly. One man longs for the day when his wife "would be more accepting of 'quickies,' and more into adventuresome positions and different places in the house." Another husband would like it if he and his wife could run around the house naked and have sex outdoors, though he admits that his wife "would have to feel a lot better about her body" for this dream to come true.

2. To have sex more often. Husbands want more sex more often, period. "I'd get Sex On Demand, like Movies On Demand from Time Warner Cable, except it would be sex with my wife," says an inventive twenty-nine-year-old husband from Austin, Texas. This is a repetitive and endless male litany: he wants more sex, more often, but she doesn't. What's amusing is that it doesn't really matter how often these husbands have sex, they just want more of it. Husbands who have sex once a month want it once a week. The ones who have it once a week want it twice a week. The ones who have it three or four times a week want it every day. The ones who have it every day want it twice a day. There's never enough marital sex for some husbands, no matter how often they are doing it. "If our sex life could magically improve, I'd expect the frequency of intercourse to double or triple from our average of about three times a month," says a thirty-year-old husband from Harrison, Tennessee. But he admits that both he and his wife are busy with work, "and at least one of us brings a laptop or paperwork to bed every night, and oddly enough, that's not conducive to frequent lovemaking," he admits. Like many other husbands who yearn for more sex, it's his fault as much as hers that it's just not happening. This longing is not limited to horny thirty-year-old men either. A sixty-five-year-old husband from Pennsylvania who answered my Web survey wishes that he and his wife would have sexual relations "five or six times a week."

3. *To increase wife's desire.* Husbands want their wives to want them; they wish she'd lose her inhibitions, get rid of her back pain, her hot flashes, or their children. They'd also be grateful if she'd climax faster, easier, better. They want her to get her desire back, the way it used to be when they were first married, or before. "I wish my wife would let go of her inhibitions," says a thirty-four-year-old software engineer from Oregon. "We've been married for nine years, but there are things she won't do, because they are too embarrassing or too weird for her," he explains, with some irritation. If only she'd feel as much sexual craving as he does, they'd be able to have more sex, and better sex, he claims. Husbands wish they could find "a Viagra for her" or that "my wife's sex drive would magically match mine, and she'd want to have sex as often as I do. Once a day would be terrific," says a hopeful thirty-five-year-old engineer from Rhode Island. "I wish it could be more fun for her and less of a task," says a considerate husband who'd also like more sex more often. Because they sense that it would be difficult, if not impossible, to ramp up their wives' sexual desire as high as their own, these husbands tend to be melancholy about their chances, at least without a magic wand to wield. (And not the built-in wand that's already attached.)

4. *To be more fit.* Like their wives, husbands too wish they could be younger and slimmer, though this longing is not nearly as common among men, and they think of it as a desire to be "more fit" instead of "less fat." Husbands who wish to be more youthful and slender tend to be older, since they're the ones most likely to have piled on years and pounds. "I'd like to be twenty-three again," says a forty-year-old. Other guys wish they could "go back fifteen years," or twenty years, or seven years, since it's all relative. If he had some magic, says a thirty-nine-year-old husband, "I wish it could be the way it was eighteen years ago—think bunnies!" As for being more slender, well, husbands are just as likely as wives to gain weight over the years, though not as many of them seem to have noticed. Those who do, however, wish they could be "in better shape" or have "a healthier body" or "be stronger." They want to lose thirty or forty or fifty pounds, and they say that if they lost that weight, they'd enjoy their sexuality more.

5. To have a wife who is more fit and more confident. Some husbands notice that their wives could use some dieting too. If only "my wife could be a size six again, yep, that would do it," exclaims one husband about his most fervent sexual desire. Another guesses that if his wife lost weight, "it would make her more self-confident and more able to enjoy sex." More than a few husbands confess that both partners need to lose weight. If they did, "we'd have more energy and we'd be more able to get into fun positions," says one husband whose magic wand would shave fifty pounds from him and another fifty from his wife. A twenty-eight-year-old husband from Cedar Rapids, Iowa, agrees that both he and his wife "would be fit if we were sixty pounds lighter, and if her breasts were reduced to a B cup." That way, he says, they'd be better able "to try positions other than missionary." More than just body issues, husbands would like to cure their wives' psychological troubles. "I wish my wife would feel as beautiful as she really is and would be less self-conscious in bed," says a considerate thirty-one-year-old new father from Minnesota. "But her low self-esteem always seems to get in the way of her letting go." A number of husbands despair that their wives seem to lack self-assurance about their bodies, despite the fact that the women are actually lovely and desirable and "smoking hot," as one puts it. This puzzle mystifies and distresses them immensely.

6. To have more time together and more romance. If only, husbands say, they could spend more time together, the sexual atmosphere would be more conducive to romance and thus to sexual encounters. Many sexual encounters, preferably. "If only we could spend time enjoying each other," says one husband, "we'd both feel really intimate." Husbands long to have their wife's undiluted passion and her intense sexual interest. A few even long for time "to cuddle, talk, and touch," to "have more of a connection," "to have more physical contact and kissing," and "to snuggle and watch a movie, covered in a cozy blanket." They long for romance with an undistracted, sexually focused, adoring wife. But watch out, because "if there's any annoyance lingering, it's a sex killer," says an observant fifty-five-year-old husband in Garrison, New York. So husbands want to rid themselves of all marital irritants, to recover the thrill of first love. That's what a twenty-nine-year-old Missouri man longs for, explaining that "it would be nice to have it all be fresh again, the newness of discovery, of touch, of making out. I miss the exhilaration that used to come from touching her hand or kissing her neck." A few husbands even wish they could be "swept away by passion," without chores or children or church or sleep getting in the way, as one says.

7. *To have more stamina.* Like women, men also get too tired to have sex, too stressed out, too pooped. "I wish I had more emotional energy, because when I come home after work, I'm tired and my mind is on the problems I had during the day, and it's hard to devote the energy to my wife that she deserves," says a simpatico twenty-nine-year-old husband from New York City. With four children under the age of seven, a thirty-two-year-old husband from Peoria, Illinois, says that both he and his wife are always exhausted. "We need a magic wand to get more energy at the end of the day, so we can be more responsive to each other's sexual needs," he says. Likewise, husbands wish they could "go five times in a row," or they say, "I wish I could last longer, since I can be kind of 'short-fused,'" or, "I wish I could get a decent erection, other than once, in the morning."

8. *To have more oral sex.* "We'd have oral sex in the living room while watching television and in the car while driving," says one husband, who is, presumably, the one doing the driving. When husbands wish for oral sex, it's almost always as receiver rather than giver. "I want my wife to be more aggressive and to give me oral sex" is the blunt way one husband expresses himself. Others simply say they want oral sex "more often," though one admits that he's desperate "for my wife to perform oral sex on me. However, because she chooses not to in our marriage, I have to respect her wishes." A teacher from Merced, California, who's been married for twenty-three years, says he's been waiting a long time for his oral wish to be fulfilled. And still he waits.

9. *To have more money.* A few husbands, for whom money means manhood, believe that their sex lives would be vastly improved if only they had "a better job," "less bills," "zero debt," and "more money to travel for sex." Being financially stable, says a twenty-seven-year-old husband with two children and two jobs, "would make us feel more relaxed about having sex." Another just wishes that "the bills would be paid for one month of no worry, and the kids would be at Grandma's house." Not enough money

means too much worry, which leads to stress and tension and not being in the mood, they say.

10. *To synchronize their sex drives.* "We would both want it at the same time" is one husband's wish, since he and his wife can never get their timing right. "The best thing that could happen would be for both of us to have the desire for sex at the same time," agrees another husband. "Also, if the baby would magically sleep or play quietly, and if our phones were turned off, it would be perfect," he adds.

Men's sexual desires are quite similar to those of their wives, but many of them miss the sexual point completely. Instead of wishing for more sex, or better sex, or oral sex, they should be wishing for a cure for their wives' superiority, something over which husbands have ultimate control. If they were to become more helpful, more aware, more cooperative, and more wifelike, if they were to take on half the family and household responsibility and decision making, they'd discover a new realm of more satisfying and more frequent sex, and it would seem like magic. They wouldn't need to ramp up their wife's desire or willingness to be kinky, since that would occur naturally, as a result of the transformation of their marriage into a fair and equitable one. If husbands would take on some of the burden of worry and caring and sacrifice that most superior wives carry on their own, their wives' sexuality would blossom. It's in this way that husbands would discover the most practical, and most effective, magic wand for marital sex.

Four Types of Superior Wife Sex

There are four major types of married sex: Duty Sex, Old Shoe Sex, Hot Sex, and No Sex. Superior wives experience every type, but they are most likely to practice duty sex and least likely to enjoy hot sex, according to the reports of those who responded to my Web survey. The four types are not mutually exclusive, however, since it's possible to have duty sex most often, for example, but to leap into a hot sex situation on occasion. Likewise, couples who engage in duty sex long enough may find themselves eventually joining the no sex group. And even couples who usually enjoy hot sex may discover that they are stuck in a rut of old shoe sex for a short time.

Duty sex. A significant number of couples view sex as a marital obligation, a duty that wives must fulfill. This is especially true of superior wives, who know what's expected of them—an active sex life—but whose negative feelings about their husband may translate into sexual reluctance or chilliness. On a conscious level, such wives are resentful of how little help and support they get from their mate. They feel disappointed, disillusioned, and dismayed about their situation, but they have no idea how to fix it. On an unconscious level, these sensations can turn into sexual frigidity, like being on a semipermanent sexual work stoppage. It's not quite an all-out sex strike, but it's not labor as usual either.

For many centuries, it has been considered a conjugal right for husbands to be able to have sexual relations with their wives. Ever since the Middle Ages, at least, wives were instructed to submit to their husbands sexually. Indeed, until the late nineteenth century in England, a husband could legally hold his wife prisoner if she refused his sexual advances.[20] Even as recently as the last half of the twentieth century, fifteen popular marriage books and manuals advised that a "considerate wife" was one who would "accommodate her husband's sexual needs," no matter what. A wife's major responsibility was to serve her partner's needs, according to the sociologists who analyzed these documents.[21] Maybe that's why the British philosopher Bertrand Russell wrote in 1929 that "the total amount of undesired sex endured by women is probably greater in marriage than in prostitution."[22]

More than a few superior wives would heartily agree.

"Sometimes I feel like I'm just here to service him," says a thirty-five-year-old superior wife and at-home mom from Reno, Nevada. "My husband expects sex every night, and if he doesn't get it, he makes me feel as if I'm not living up to my part of the bargain." Another superior wife and at-home mother from Calgary, Canada, agrees, saying that her husband "makes me feel like it's my duty and his right to have sex whenever he wants." Yet another superior wife, this one a systems analyst from Long Island, New York, regrets that she views sex as "my wifely duty." She admits that "I am so disenchanted with my husband that I don't even want him to touch me," and this is a constant source of pain and regret for her. Regina, forty-five, a superior wife and high school teacher from Canton, Illinois, knows exactly how that feels. "I sense a lot of pressure to have sex when I'm just not in the mood. My husband pouts when I turn him down, which, I must admit, is often. When he pouts, I'm even more turned off. I feel guilty that I don't want to have sex more often, but once a week is as much as I want to make myself 'available,'" explains Regina, adding that she doesn't enjoy having sex as often as he does, though she doesn't know why exactly. A superior wife from Sandusky, Ohio, is a bit more in touch with the feelings of anger her husband inspires, saying that she wishes she could banish "thirty years of feeling used," a result of her frustration with her husband, who makes her feel "marginal and unimportant."

Husbands too are keenly aware when their sex life falls into the duty sex category. A forty-one-year-old Virginia husband realizes, with dismay, that his wife views their sex life as "a necessary evil." Another husband, from Albany, New York, knows that his wife "views the physical act as a chore or an obligation," although he wishes that it could, instead, "be an affirmation of love." A British husband says that he has to wait until his wife feels the call of her sexual duty, or else "she knocks me back and I feel like a pervert for wanting to be intimate with my own wife." All these husbands, by the way, say that they are not particularly happy with their sex life or with their marriage. And all categorize their wife as superior, which is not a coincidence.

Clearly, duty sex can be a sign of a marriage in trouble or, at the very least, a marriage in which at least one partner is suffering. Still, duty sex is not necessarily bad sex, as Carlotta, a forty-five-year-old superior wife in a third marriage, tells it. "My husband wants sex all the time, but I don't because I'm tired from working," she says. "His thing is 'Let's just start, and if you don't want to, we'll stop, but if you want to go on, we will.'" Carlotta's duty sex becomes transformed. "He always takes me from thinking, 'Okay, I'll let him start and I'll cut it off, because I don't want to do this' to begging him not to stop!" For Carlotta, it's duty sex at the beginning but hot sex at the end.

Duty sex is probably a global affair as well. Chinese women say that most of the time their sexual encounters are initiated by their husbands, and 40 percent say they have sex only to please him. Forty percent also say that they fake orgasm, and one in four adds that she submits to her husband's sexual demands even when she doesn't really want to, according to a recent study conducted in mainland China.[23]

Old shoe sex. Not all superior wives view sex as a duty or a chore, like doing dishes or laundry, only requiring less time and detergent. Some superior wives enjoy sex and look forward to its physical and emotional pleasures, but for them it has simply become routine. Go to work: check. Assemble tray of baked ziti for dinner: check. Pay electric bill: check. Have sex with husband: check. It's not Fourth of July fireworks or the moving of the earth. This is year-after-year, decade-after-decade sex, and it constitutes the most common type of married sex. Like its name, it's not fancy. One wife calls it "meat-and-potatoes sex," another calls it "do-it-in-our-sleep sex." "Our sexual routine is pretty much the same" is the way a thirty-five-year-old lawyer in North Carolina describes his sex life, without embellishment or poetry. A thirty-nine-year-old husband from California, who's been married to a superior wife for eight years, calls his sexual encounters "routine and fast." An Army officer who's been married for six years says that his formerly "very experimental" sex life has become "slightly repetitive," especially since the birth of their first baby ten months ago. And although he's been married only two years, a Texas-based legal secretary says that his sexual re-lationship has already become "controlled and bland." Sometimes, he adds, this makes him feel "more like a roommate than a husband," a situation that distresses and upsets him. The same goes for Bradley, twenty-eight, who's been married to his superior wife for four years and who says that his sex life has become boring and hurried. He and his wife have been reduced to grabbing any chance they can for sex, as long as it doesn't interfere with his rigorous job as an Army officer or the demands and needs of their two toddlers. "I wish we could be more spontaneous, but it seems as if we have to schedule our sex life around everything else, even if one of us is not in the mood at that particular moment," Bradley says.

While superior wives are those most likely to engage in old shoe sex, it's practiced by a majority of married couples, regardless of their superiority sta-tus. That's because routine sex is pleasant and unthreatening and requires little planning or passion. A high level of sexual excitement and creativity is difficult to maintain for more than a few years of marriage. (Though a few couples do just that, as we'll see.) Thus, couples who believe that a good marriage is a sexual marriage will fall into a regular sexual pattern. Year after year, they will make love in roughly the same position, in the same way, in the same amount of time, in the same place, over and over again.

While old shoe sex may be boring, it is also reassuring and predictable, and it keeps the marriage sexual. Most adults view sex as having three very distinct goals, researchers say. Sex is procreational, to produce babies; sex is relational, to encourage love; or sex is recreational, to provide fun.[24] Couples who have had their children and who are no longer in the honeymoon stage gravitate to the relational idea of sex. So they soldier on, having mostly old shoe sex during the high-intensity child-raising years, the car pool years, and the on-and-off marital doldrum years. They do it just to do it—which is exactly how great sex eventually becomes old shoe sex.

Hot sex. Couples who view sex as recreational, however, are more likely to have hot sex. These wives and husbands, a small minority, say that their experience of married sex is "great," "magic," "the best," "awesome," "fantastic," and "hard to beat." These couples tend to be enormously enthusiastic about their marriage. And they are not just newlyweds or twenty-five-year-olds, either. One fortyish wife claims that "sex is the glue that holds us together, and occasionally, the balm that heals us." Another, now thirty-five, says, "We always click with sex." A third wife, married eleven years, insists that "I feel blessed that I found someone who's my best friend, and we have a great sex life." Finally, a wife married for eight years says that the only way her great sex life could get any better would be if both she and her husband could quit their jobs, "so we could have more time for sex." These women and men view sex as a fun, calorie-burning alternative to jogging or biking. And they haven't become jaded or bored with each other, so their all-consuming marital sex is just that—as miraculously fabulous as it is unusual.

Superior wives are least likely to enjoy hot sex on a regular basis, however, mostly because they are unable to overcome the buried hostility and disappointment they feel for their mate. It's difficult for a wife to swoon with ardor over a man who does not feel like a true partner or helpmeet. For this reason, superior wives who have regular hot sex are as rare as an honest politician or a cheap plasma television set.

The rare wives and husbands who describe their erotic life as hot sex have truly beaten the odds, since most sex research shows that married couples have less sex, and less good sex, the longer they've been married. Among married couples, for example, just 7 percent have sex four times a week or more often, studies show.[25]

At fifty-two, Peggy is one of the lucky few who enjoy hot sex. An Illinois software designer married to her second husband for ten years, she says that "the sex is the best I have ever had, and he says the same. I've had good sex, and I've had great sex, but this is better than that. We respect each other, and we never say mean words, because we love being married and we value our marriage." A fifty-seven-year-old wife, also in a second marriage, says that she and her husband "park in the car and act like teen-agers, only now, we're in better cars. I'm fifty-seven and he's forty-seven, so that ain't half bad," she brags. A forty-five-year-old first wife echoes the sentiment, saying that her sex life "is the most unbelievable part of our relationship. I asked him what was different about last night, because the sex was so incredible, and he said he just slowed down, like one frame at a time, instead of going regular slow. It was boring for him, but he said my response to it made it a blowaway for him. He put me first, but he ended up with an intense sexual experience," she adds. None of these wives is superior.

Husbands also rave about hot sex, describing it as "great" and "perfect" and saying that "it keeps getting better the longer we're married." These beat-the-odds guys realize how lucky they are to be having such a wonderfully sexual marriage. "We have a great sex life that is part of our relationship, and sex for us is like breathing," says Fred, fifty-two, an engineer in Cleveland, Ohio, who has been married to his second wife for twenty-three years. "Sometimes it's the way we start the day and end the day, and we feel complete as a result," he adds. Most husbands in the hot sex group believe they've hit the sexual jackpot, if only because they have sex so often. Most other husbands would probably agree, with no small amount of envy. "I married a great woman who desires sex as much as I do," says a fortunate Florida husband, who adds that "she's very open to sexual discussions and she understands that sex is an important part of marriage." Married two years, a Mormon husband from Utah explains that "I can count on one hand how many times we haven't had sex at least once a day." And then there's Jimmy, sixty-five, an evangelical Christian who's not a newlywed— he's been married for thirty-seven years—but who still enjoys what he calls great sex. "Novelty is the spice, especially in the form of travel," Jimmy says. "For my wife, a motel room is a great turn-on, so is romance and affection and intimacy. And whenever we've abstained for a while, the reuniting is truly exciting."

"We have fantastic sex, and we are a team, through good times and bad," agrees a fifty-year-old Indiana husband. "My wife is constantly randy, so I'm content," crows a twenty-nine-year-old Air Force electronics technician from Florida, who counts his blessings every day. A terse husband describes his hot sex marriage by saying, quite simply, that "we have house sex, not just bedroom sex." A fifty-one-year-old Honolulu husband in a second marriage to an Alpha wife says that "my wife is more responsive than any partner I have ever been with. We're awfully good together, and she has bought books and magazines to improve our sex even more, and I know at least one couple who is uncomfortable around us, because my wife finds it so easy to talk about sex." A Michigan husband says that "I think we have a good sex life, because we average at least once a day," adding, modestly, that "it's good as far as we can tell."

No sex. A small but vocal group of wives and husbands have sex rarely, if at all. In nationwide studies, this group represents about 15 percent of married men and women, who report that they have sex a few times a year or never.[26] A large portion of these couples include superior wives, I believe. They are wives who have given up on physical intimacy and pleasure, for a number of reasons. They say their partner has physical problems or that they are no longer interested in giving in the bedroom, after giving all day at work and in the kitchen and in the bathroom and everywhere else that they outwork, outplay, and outlast their husband.

Several superior wives say they haven't had sex in one year or five years or twelve years, which they blame on their mate's lack of desire or their own. "He's not interested," says a fifty-five-year-old superior wife in Missouri, who adds that she is occasionally willing but her husband is not. Another distressed superior wife with no sex life says that "my husband has developed an interest in Internet sex and has left me behind." Other superior wives blame the lack of sex on their husband's medical problems. "My husband hurt his back and our sex life has never been the same," says Melanie, a thirty-five-year-old superior wife from Waycross, Georgia. "Sex seems to be too much of a strain for him, though he's not opposed to oral sex, but only for him. It's as if he's forgotten sex even exists," she says, some-what miserable about the situation. "I don't necessarily need the sex, but a kiss or the holding of a hand would be good for me."

While some superior wives are resigned or relieved to be in an asexual marriage, just as many are distraught and in despair about it. "I take care of my own needs, but it's been a struggle for more than half of our twenty-one years together," says a forty-year-old superior wife from Muncie, Indiana. "Sex is very important in marriage, and without sex it's more of a friendship than a marriage, and definitely not as fulfilling," she says. "If it weren't for our disabled son, I would have been out the door long ago."

Husbands are equally disturbed, as well as resigned, to a life without sex. Some even tell themselves that most long-term marriages are celibate, though that is certainly untrue. A few husbands say that they don't have sex because their wives no longer care, or that they have resorted to masturbation or to taking other lovers. It's possible that one or both partners in these marriages suffer from a sexual dysfunction that leaves them unable to enjoy sex. About 40 percent of women have at least one such dysfunction, as do between 20 and 30 percent of men, according to a recent study.[27] But some researchers say that not everyone who has an inability to derive sexual pleasure is all that worried about it. Their view is that if a woman is not *upset* by her lack of sexual desire or her inability to reach orgasm, then she really doesn't have a sexual dysfunction. By this more lenient definition, then, only one in four women suffers from a sexual problem or dysfunction, another study shows.[28] Still, it's very likely that such wives fall into the no sex category, and a large number of them are probably superior wives.

As bizarre and unlikely as it may sound, however, it's possible that there may be a robotic remedy to sexless marriages. Someday soon, women and men will have sex with robots and will fall in love with them too, according to an artificial intelligence expert. Just as people develop strong emotional bonds with their dogs and cats and virtual pets, and just as they get sexual satisfaction from vibrators and sex dolls and Internet sex, soon they will do the same with realistic humanoid robots, designed to look and speak and make love like real people.[29] When that day comes, reluctantly celibate wives and husbands will celebrate a revival of their sexuality, albeit a mechanized one.

While sex robots might solve some couples' sex problems, they surely won't help superior wives escape their marriage trap. Such wives can, however, learn a great deal from the exceptions to the superior wife rule. I call these women "nonsuperior wives," and in the next chapter, I reveal who these special women are and how they came to avoid superiority.

7

Why Nonsuperior Wives Are Better Wives

This chapter is not about superior wives. It's about the nonsuperiors, the ones who avoid superiority. It's about wives who are exceptions to the superior rule, the ones who are Mothers Nonsuperior. These wives defy biological and social and psychological imperatives by refusing to be the most efficient, most organized, most decisive, and most sacrificing person in their marriage. Because it takes two to do a nonsuperior tango, nonsuperior wife marriages are relatively rare. But when they work, a nonsuperior wife marriage is one that is happier, more fulfilling, more equitable, and more sexually satisfying than any other.

Surprisingly, wives achieve their nonsuperiority in two very distinct and antithetical ways. One way is to develop an equal partnership, just saying no to the six signs of superiority. The second is to be in a mutually acceptable traditional marriage, one in which the husband is so clearly head of the household that there is no room for wifely superiority. Oddly, both types of wives—the truly egalitarian and the truly traditional—are better able than others to avoid the superiority path.

The two routes to nonsuperiority are as distinct as can be: democratic and cooperative versus conventional and subservient, liberal-minded and modern versus conservative and orthodox. There is no guarantee, however, that all egalitarian wives will end up being nonsuperior or that all traditional wives will end that way either. Indeed, my research shows that the majority of Captain and Mate wives, who adhere to old-fashioned, traditional gender roles, are also superior. It turns out that the secret to nonsuperiority is for *both partners* to buy into the man-as-breadwinner, wife-as-homemaker plan, wholeheartedly and without reservation. If either one harbors any doubts or resentment, the scheme goes awry. This happens, for instance, to wives who stay home with children but would prefer to be working, and to husbands with an at-home wife who would rather have a two-income family.

Many nonsuperior wives of both types describe their relationship as "being in sync," as if they and their spouses are on the same wavelength almost all the time about almost everything. Others say that their marriage is one of "sharing equally," of "not keeping score," or of "filling a need when we see it." This is a kind of relaxed egalitarianism; it's not a rigid system in which every "she does" requires an equal and opposite "he does." Instead, it's an unspoken and completely natural sense of fairness that permeates the marriage and the family and the home. Many nonsuperior wives rely on their own strengths for some things and on their partner's strengths for others, but they don't make a habit of keeping track of who's doing what and when. They have no barter system, no haggling or negotiating; the only competition they engage in is to see who can do more for the other, rather than who can do less.

About one-third of wives fall into the nonsuperior category, according to the women who answered my Web survey. Unlike other wives, these women are not the CEOs of the family, they do not get into the driver's seat, they do not step into the breach; they do not use the word "everything" to describe what they do. They don't take charge, and they don't take on a superior role in the family.

The only way that these wives resemble their superior sisters, in fact, is that they share almost identical work patterns: one in four doesn't work for pay, half work full-time, and one in four works part-time. So working for pay has no influence over whether a wife is nonsuperior. These wives differ from superior wives, though, since they draw a line in the sand, right down the middle of the marriage, when it comes to expertise. They do not claim to have all or most of the know-how and proficiency in the marriage. By definition, these wives do not have five or six signs of superiority. They are also much less likely to call themselves the family expert on most tasks and chores. Nonsuperior wives say they aren't necessarily the best one in the family at making social arrangements with friends, at managing finances, or at managing health care, for instance. Unlike superior wives, they do not share a tacit understanding with their husband that they will do all and be all at home. Significantly fewer nonsuperior wives than superior ones

Unspoken Assumptions of Nonsuperior and Superior Wives

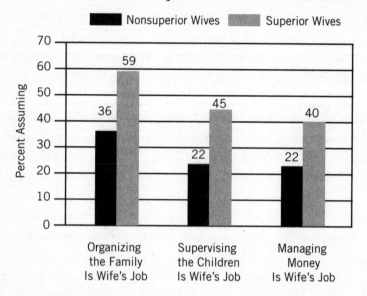

believe that organizing the family is the wife's job, that supervising the children is the wife's job, that managing money is the wife's job, or that making important decisions is the wife's job.

More nonsuperior than superior wives say that both partners give equally in the marriage: 69 percent of nonsuperior wives do, compared to 46 percent of superior wives. Again, even if they hold very strict, traditional values, these wives have a sense of fairness about the marriage and the relationship that other wives simply don't have. In addition, many more nonsuperior wives say that both partners are in charge: 48 percent of nonsuperior wives do, compared to 29 percent of superior wives. Theirs is a share-and-share-alike mentality, or as close to one as is humanly possible.

Sometimes, though, the nonsuperior wife situation is only temporary, such as when wives become sick or disabled. A forty-four-year-old Florida wife has breast cancer, so her husband "does most of the shopping and cooking and cleaning, at least until I feel better," she says. A nonsuperior fifty-four-year-old wife in Arkansas needs a liver transplant; she relies on her husband for everything, she says, "because I have difficulty with memory and can no longer drive, and I don't have the endurance to do the household chores. My husband has stepped up to the need and taken over most of the things I was once able to do, lovingly and without complaint." In marriages like these, however, both partners long to return to the good old days, when the wife used to be superior. I don't consider these nonsuperior wives to be the real thing, since their situation is transitory. Instead, in this chapter I will discuss wives who are in a more permanent state of nonsuperiority.

Long-term nonsuperior wives almost always do less managing and organizing, deciding and arranging than other wives; their husbands, by default, do more than husbands with superior wives. Indeed, these women rate their husbands as being the expert at more domestic and family-related tasks than superior wives do. Their husbands are much less likely to play dumb—three out of four nonsuperior wives say that their husbands don't—compared to just half of superior wives. Fewer nonsuperior wives play dumb themselves, and fewer call themselves the "primary nagger" in the marriage.

"I never pretend not to know something, but I do pretend to not be strong enough," says a twenty-eight-year-old nonsuperior wife from Maryland. "If I'm organizing a closet full of heavy items, I'll wait until he gets home, so I can direct him while he does the heavy lifting," she explains. "I don't feel guilty because he is stronger, and it's easier for him, and in my defense," she concludes, "I am pregnant!" A fifty-year-old nonsuperior wife from Wyoming says, "My husband can do anything, and he expects me to able to do anything as well," so neither one plays dumb. "We have a relatively honest relationship," says another nonsuperior wife, "and I never play dumb. I'd rather have more knowledge than less, so if I don't know how to do something, I'll probably want to learn how to do it."

As for nagging, many nonsuperior wives just don't see the point. "We seem to have reached an equilibrium, since my husband has taken over so many duties at home that I don't want to ask any more of him," says Fran, fifty-two, a nonsuperior wife from Butler, Ohio. "This doesn't mean that there aren't things we would both like to see get done, just that we have chosen to give each other a break from time to time. When we go out together on special dates, we ask each other, 'What can I do differently that I haven't been doing?' and we answer each other honestly," she explains.

"When we discuss this kind of thing in a calm, gentle way, it works for us. One time he told me he'd like me to keep the kitchen work island clear, so he could have a place to sit and have his breakfast. After that, I started to clean it up in the mornings. Another time, I shared that I would like him to be the one who cleans the tub, since it does a number on my back. From then on, he was the one who scrubbed the tub. It helps if two people are determined to make their marriage as pleasant a journey as possible," says Fran, "and we are."

Although she's been married only for two years, Kristin, twenty-six, says that she and her husband "try to avoid nagging. We realize that we both have habits that annoy the other person, but we just try to brush them off. No one is perfect, but our relationship is balanced, in a very back-and-forth kind of way." This attitude is typical of nonsuperiors, who are much less likely than other wives to hold grudges, to keep score, or to focus on their partner's flaws and faults.

While it's obvious that the marriages of superior wives and nonsuperior wives are quite different, it's also true that each group was focused on different qualities when they first set out to find a lifelong companion. Before they were married, more nonsuperior wives were looking for a best friend or a soul mate. Superior wives were much more concerned about finding a man who'd be kind and supportive or who'd earn a good living. It's possible, then, that nonsuperior wives—either by instinct or by deliberate forethought—sought out men who would value true partnership and who would be committed to sharing. Whatever their secret, though, they have clearly discovered a unique and wonderful marital oasis.

Inez, thirty-five, a teacher in a small town in Puerto Rico, had a terrible first marriage, one in which she was supremely superior. She vowed never to marry again unless she found a man who'd treat her as an equal, one who would share the family responsibilities with her. A few years later, she met and married a man who was eighteen years older, but he "treated me with love, patience, and affection," she says. Inez's second husband is having trouble finding work now, "so to compensate, he does things around the house while I'm at work," she explains. He cooks, he cleans, and he takes care of his son from his first marriage and her daughter from her first marriage. A twenty-six-year-old wife from Topeka, Kansas, longed to find a husband who would be her best friend, and she has. "My husband and I always seek to serve each other. We're supposed to take care of each other, and we don't need to be selfish and think only of our own needs, if one spouse is watching out for the other one," she explains. Married just two years, she's convinced she has found the ideal husband because "he's an awesome man who loves me and loves the Lord." Then there's Allie, forty-seven, who's been married for twenty-seven years to a man she met at the age of fifteen. "We dated for five years and got married really young," she says, "because I knew I'd found a man who would be my partner and my best friend." She's an at-home mother of ten children—yes, ten!—and she helps her physician husband operate a free medical clinic in Dallas, Texas. She runs the household when he flies off to Ethiopia to teach medical students, and although he's the one who wins the humanitarian awards, they both know that he could never do it without her.

Perhaps because nonsuperior wives have marriages that are true partnerships, they tend to be more relaxed and contented at home, as well as more successful in life. They don't play games, they are less likely than other wives to view their marriage as a mistake, and they are much happier with their marriage and with their lives as a whole. "We complement each other, and we fill in for each other's weaknesses, and I believe we have a real partnership," says Lupe, thirty-seven, a registered nurse from Tallahassee, Florida. "We started out as best friends, but as soon as we got together, it was as if the passion light got turned on immediately. We never take each other for granted or assume that we know everything about each other," Lupe explains. "Each day is an adventure, and our marriage is the best of anybody I know," she adds. She's not smug, she's just honest.

Helene, thirty, a nonsuperior wife from Hartford, Connecticut, agrees that she and her husband of two years are soul mates, "and nothing will break our bond." In addition, theirs is a true partnership, because "we are equal on so many levels. We knew since the first time we met that we'd eventually be married," says Helene. "We complement each other so much that we often finish each other's thoughts and sentences. Neither of us gets upset if one does a little more, because we want to, and not because we have to. And we appreciate even the smallest things," she adds. Helene is blissfully happy with her marriage and her sex life, and she can't imagine that it will ever change, even after she has children.

Listen to these wives long enough, and they begin to sound so sappy and sentimental, it's as if they're living in some kind of marital fairy tale, a wifely Disneyland. Indeed, to many superior wives, such a marriage seems a near impossibility, one that's too good, too perfect to be true. Still, nonsuperior wives are real, and although they are in the minority, they are a powerful and exemplary group. They are potential role models for superior wives everywhere, shining possibilities of what could and should be.

Take Linda, a fifty-three-year-old Boston wife, who could be a nonsuperior wife poster girl, a *Vogue* cover model for superior wives everywhere. "This is going to sound like Pollyanna, but my husband and I share everything, including power. My husband is an engineer, so he's very logical and focused. I am a public relations executive with better communication and management skills. So we naturally play to our own strengths and we take on the tasks we're best at. Making decisions is second nature to us, so we do that together. The basis of our thirty-one-year marriage is that we're good friends, and we've weathered ups and downs based on our shared religious beliefs and our priorities, of children, family, and education. We agree on the major stuff, so we can put the petty stuff in perspective," she explains. In her mind, there was no question, from the start, that theirs would be a marriage of equals, partners who would be determined to cooperate and to collaborate, as long as they both shall live.

Linda makes it sound easy to arrange a nonsuperior wife marriage. Unfortunately, it's anything but. Linda can't imagine a relationship in which one partner slacks off while the other takes control, because she's never had one like that. In her mind, it's only natural to be nonsuperior, but the numbers tell another story, since a great majority of wives fall into the superiority trap.

How do wives like Linda avoid this trap? How do they prevent their own slide into doing more, being more, working more, caring more? They do it by marrying the right guy: having a husband who will not tolerate such a situation is what allows wives to be nonsuperior. A *wife cannot will herself into nonsuperiority*, since it takes two to make a wife nonsuperior. Whether a couple has a highly traditional marriage or one that's an egalitarian partnership, *both partners* must agree about their convictions, whatever those beliefs may be. And this agreement must be not only in word but in deed; husbands must not only *believe in* the importance of wifely nonsuperiority, they must also *behave* as if they do.

The Unique Qualities of Nonsuperior Wives

From the moment they say "I do," if not long before, women must be prepared to face the harsh reality of modern marriage, which is that *most of them will end up being superior.* This is a fate that two out of three wives will not avoid, but the ones who do, the nonsuperior wives, will have to work at staying that way, year in and year out. These wives have not managed to avoid superiority by a quirk of fate or extraordinary luck. Instead, they have deliberately chosen to live by their convictions, and they have found a man who will abide by those principles, either highly traditional ones or highly egalitarian ones. This is the key: finding a man who will agree to the rules and stick to them, no matter what. It's a matter of laying out every expectation and hope for what married life will be like, with both partners agreeing on everything, both before and, especially, after children arrive. Many couples make the mistake of entering marriage and simply trying to "wing it," or to "figure it out later," or to "play it by ear," as some wives tell me. They never discuss their own expectations or wishes for how their daily lives will play out, simply assuming that their husband shares their unspoken assumptions. Most men, however, are not psychic about their wife's desires, nor are they inclined to take a position that will result in their doing *more* work and taking on *more* responsibility. Husbands will almost always take the path of least resistance, the path of easiest existence. Because wives tend not to understand this, at least until it's too late, their self-deception and obfuscation invariably lead directly, and unequivocally, into wifely superiority. Most men will opt to have a superior wife if given a choice—and why not, since she makes his life so much easier, so much less complicated, so much nicer?

After all, who wouldn't want a superior wife?

Amy, forty-six, a Web design consultant in Portland, Oregon, certainly didn't want to be such a wife when she was married almost twenty years ago, so she did everything she could to avoid it. And Amy succeeded, since she now describes herself and her husband as "truly equal in our marriage, because we had an understanding that we wanted that to happen. I was not given away by my father to my husband, because I didn't like the symbolism, that I was some sort of property to be handed over. Instead, we entered the wedding hall together," Amy explains. "I kept my maiden name, because it's who I am, and there have been times in the marriage when I've been the breadwinner and he's stayed home with the kids, and other times when I've stayed home and he worked," she adds, though both are now working. The secret to her nonsuperior marriage, Amy says, is that she and her husband make important decisions together and are both committed to fairness and balance in marriage. Perhaps most important of all, none of this changed after they had children.

Amy and her husband abide by the first four of the five rules of non-superiority: being attuned to fairness, having a strong belief in equality, practicing an as-if philosophy, and tolerating imperfection. The fifth rule, accepting a patriarchal marriage, applies only to highly traditional wives.

They are attuned to fairness. Many wives who start out married life determined to blaze a fairness trail, right until the "death do us part" stage of life, are fine at first but run into serious trouble after they have children. For them, motherhood is almost always the straw that breaks the fairness camel's back, as a Canadian mother of three explains with great despair. "I feel that what we agreed upon before we got married has been thrown out the window, and now, even though I'm a student, I'm also a full-time mom and maid," says Colette, twenty-seven. "Before we had children, he promised me that we'd share domestic responsibilities and that he was going to be responsible and reliable, but he hasn't been, at all," she says. "If I had known then what would really happen, I'm not sure I would have gotten married in the first place."

Colette speaks the truth, and far more than she knows. Many, many other superior wives feel the same way. A few superior wives try to persuade themselves that their marriage is fair, no matter how unfair it really is, but they are fooling only themselves. Wives are most likely to become disillusioned with marriage after the birth of a first child, according to psychologists who study couples both before and after they become parents. Wives are especially unhappy about their marriage when they feel that they are doing all or most of the baby work, researchers say. Before they become parents, both spouses may notice that their household duties are allocated somewhat unfairly, but after the baby is born, both perceive that everything becomes even more unbalanced. It's when wives observe, over and over again, how unfair their marriage has become that they are increasingly distressed with the situation, experts say. It's almost always true too that these inequities don't subside but actually increase as the years pass. In one study, psychologists interviewed married couples before they had children, again when their first child was six months old, and a third time six to nine months later. By the second interview, the wives felt increasing resentment about their ballooning responsibilities, while husbands felt guilty or defensive about the arrangement but did nothing about it. Even in this short period of time, wives' perceptions of unfairness had escalated, as had their unhappiness about the marriage. The situation had become worse six months after that, at the third interview. The researchers conclude that wives are "underbenefited" when they become parents, while husbands are "overbenefited."[1] In other words, women get cheated and men get rewarded.

Indeed, it's quite clear that parenthood can be hazardous to marriage, as just about all the research over the past few decades has shown. Parents are more unhappy about their marriage than nonparents, and mothers are more unhappy than fathers, according to psychologists who reviewed nearly one hundred different studies about how parenthood changes marriage. In addition, the more children they have, the more miserable couples tend to be. Mothers of infants are most unhappy of all, probably because they're constantly exhausted, they're worried about gaining weight, they feel guilty about nearly everything, they're afraid about not being perfect moms, and they've lost their freedom. Once again, researchers say that because the burden of child care almost always falls on women, it's no wonder that wives are more distressed than husbands after becoming parents. If the distribution of parental responsibilities between spouses were more fair, women might be more satisfied with marriage, they conclude.[2]

No kidding. And if life and love and calories were 100 percent fair, there'd be no superior wives, and women would lose their pregnancy weight instantly and forever.

It's clear that most of the old-fashioned, traditional gender rules about who should do what seem to favor the male side of the equation. Wives are supposed to deal with children, cook the meals, clean the house, and organize everybody and everything—all tasks requiring hours of time every single day. Husbands are supposed to take out the garbage, mow the lawn, and service the car. These chores take from three minutes to an hour, and none has to be done daily. Thus, comparing a wife's traditional tasks to a husband's is not like comparing apples and oranges, it's more like comparing apples and French fries. A recent addition to these somewhat antiquated gender rules is that wives are also supposed to work for pay, which requires eight or nine hours a day, plus commuting time. This is probably why many superior wives are so disappointed by the unbalanced and unfair trajectory their marriage has taken. Before they were married, six in ten wives expected to share household chores with their husbands, but fewer than half that number actually do. It's no wonder, then, that so many superior wives still can't quite believe the situation they have gotten themselves into. They didn't predict they'd be doing so much, it just kind of happened, and most of them don't understand exactly how or why.

This situation is precisely what nonsuperior wives don't tolerate: they refuse to give in to the tyranny of mother knows best, wife does all. And their husband doesn't expect them to. Nonsuperior wives who respect fairness will not tolerate inequity in marriage, whether they are parents or not. If they've chosen their partner carefully, neither will their husband. "We have a very balanced and fair relationship, because my husband is stereotypically 'womanish' in terms of worrying and overthinking and being able to multitask," says Candy, thirty-seven, a nonsuperior wife and mother of two from Teaneck, New Jersey. "We share all the jobs relating to finances and medical decisions, investments and bill paying. We're both totally involved," she adds, "and I wouldn't have it any other way."

They have a strong belief in equality. Nonsuperior wives infuse their marital relationship with a sense of balance. They take pride in the equality and parity they've fostered by freeing themselves of gender-specific rules and regulations about who should do what. They refuse to settle, refuse to justify, refuse to maintain inequality at home. But the key to a wife's becoming nonsuperior is that her husband fully shares these egalitarian beliefs. It's only when *both partners* hold such views that their marriage will include a nonsuperior wife. Psychologists call this belief system *gender ideology,* which is simply a person's intuitive sense of the unspoken rules, the ways in which he or she defines "a woman's work" and "a man's job." It's when both partners believe that real women fix toilets, manage money, and rotate tires and when both partners think that real men do dishes, bake cookies, and change diapers that they will be more likely to share and share alike. Although this notion may seem like common sense, it's also supported by the results of a massive national study of married couples, which shows that husbands who do a significant amount of domestic labor are the ones who hold egalitarian beliefs about who should do what at home.[3] In other words, husbands will probably not succumb to nagging about pitching in unless they *already* believe that it's their job to share equally.

Psychologists sometimes measure egalitarian beliefs by asking husbands and wives how strongly they agree or disagree with these general, but somewhat loaded, statements:

- A woman should not be employed if jobs are scarce.
- The husband should be the primary breadwinner, even if his wife works.
- A husband should earn more than his wife.
- A woman's most important job in life is to take care of children.
- An employed mother cannot create as good a relationship with her children as a full-time homemaker.

The more strongly men and women *disagree* with these very traditional beliefs, the higher their score on the test and the more egalitarian their beliefs.[4] This may not be a particularly deep or sophisticated way to measure such a vital and important conviction, but it's one of the best methods that social scientists have found to assess gender ideology. And it's reliable too. If both wife and husband score high on this test, they're egalitarian and likely to have a nonsuperior wife marriage. Likewise, if both have low scores, both hold traditional views about gender ideology and may also be in a nonsuperior wife marriage. Such wives neither expect nor desire equality in marriage, and they firmly believe that it is *not their place* to be the superior member of the union. It's when couples agree and feel equally strongly— about being very traditional or very egalitarian—that they are most likely to include a nonsuperior wife.

It's rare for partners to concur about egalitarianism, however, since wives are more likely than husbands to hold such views. And although men are becoming more open-minded about gender ideology, they still lag far behind women when it comes to having strong feelings about marital equality.[5] As a result, an equal-minded husband is extremely hard to find.

But that didn't stop Kathi, a thirty-three-year-old Virginia wife, from shopping for one when she decided to get married, about ten years ago. "I wanted to find a man who'd be committed to making this thing work, but with me as a truly equal partner, not as a secret, second-class citizen," she says. "It took me four years to find one like that, but I did. My husband and I work in tandem with each other, and he puts me first and I put him first," Kathi adds. Her husband does what needs to be done, without her having to ask, because "we have a one-for-all-and-all-for-one perspective," she explains. They are the Two Musketeers, a duo who share a belief in an even-steven rule of household management and domestic money earning.

But keeping the egalitarian faith, as Kathi does, is extremely difficult, and while many couples assume at the beginning that they are completely and utterly committed to sharing, that's not necessarily what happens. For some husbands, especially, that commitment lasts about as long as a manufacturer's grocery store coupon. One way to tell how dedicated a man is to having an equitable relationship is to find out how much he's willing to sacrifice for it. While women are trained from birth to be sacrificial—they are the sultanas of self-sacrifice—men tend to be much less so. At the very beginning of their love affair, most couples say they are willing to sacrifice for each other: for example, "I'd give my life for her!" and "I'd do anything for him, anything!" But for a relationship to last after the initial burst of sexual excitement wanes and the thrill of newness fades, both partners need to see themselves as a team, not as two separate people. In fact, studies show that the more husbands are willing to sacrifice for their wives, the longer their marriage will last and the healthier it will be.[6]

A willingness to sacrifice, then, is a key ingredient for believing in marital equality. "On a spiritual level, I believe there are karmic reasons for two people being in a relationship, so I am willing to give up what I want for her sake," says John, a fifty-one-year-old husband of a nonsuperior wife from Camden, Maine. "We have both always operated from the premise that creating and raising a family is a joint venture, and tradition and gender roles be damned," he adds. John is the epitome of a self-sacrificing, strongly egalitarian husband, and he's also one who has a nonsuperior wife.

They practice an as-if philosophy. It follows that if a wife and a husband really hold egalitarian beliefs, they will not follow strict gender rules about who should do what. They will not believe that only the wife "knows best" how to cook a beef stew or put the toddler to bed or clean up dog vomit. They will not believe that only the husband knows how to check the oil in the car or repair a light switch or decide where to invest extra money. When gender rules like these are banished, a wife has the luxury to become a practitioner of the art of as-if. She can behave as if the house and the children and the social life and the medical insurance and the bills were not her sole responsibility. She can behave as if she has a fever and can't do too much. She can behave as if she cannot manage on her own. This is not the same as playing dumb, it's simply using an as-if operating system, one whose default mode is that "I can't do it all and I can't do it alone." It's not about being a helpless female; rather, it's about an insistence on being a dependent *partner*, one who needs cooperation and support and help in order to function.

It's about *not being superior*.

"In our marriage, we do the tasks we enjoy most, not what we think we're supposed to do," says Vicki, a forty-four-year-old wedding planner from San Francisco, California. "My husband prefers to do the cleaning, so I act as if I just can't do those things, but that's because I really don't want to," she explains. "But he's also the one who volunteers at our children's school, and I'm the one who replaces the garbage disposal, so we surprise ourselves sometimes," Vicki adds. "If I'm too busy to do something I usually do, then he'll do it, and other times, if he's too busy, then I will do his job. If we're both busy and it doesn't get done, that's okay too." Vicki is a firm believer in having an as-if mentality, but that's because her husband is ready and eager to fill in the gaps and even take over for her completely, in a way that many husbands are not. As a result, she appreciates his special qualities. "He does household tasks cheerfully and willingly, and he washes the dishes and cleans the kitchen and bathrooms every night," Vicki says. "He also does laundry and picks up the house, but I don't remind him or have to ask, he just does it." Vicki knows how lucky she is, but she also points out that she would never tolerate a husband who was not an equal partner in the business of marriage.

Another woman with an as-if mind-set is a thirty-year-old wife from Fort Myers, Florida, who has always thought this way, she says, because she was "raised with maids, so I am a bit lazy with chores and other things around the house." Her husband is the more efficient, more organized one, and their marriage revolves around the assumption that both partners will help each other figure out what needs to be done and when. Casey, also a nonsuperior wife, is a thirty-two-year-old social worker from Penfield, New York, who says that her husband has obsessive-compulsive disorder and therefore has much higher household cleaning standards than she does. "He ends up doing stuff that I won't, like scouring the shower walls and putting away the dishes just so and straightening every hanger in every closet," she says. Casey behaves as if meticulous housekeeping is beyond her ability and interest because it really is, and therefore her as-if approach is genuine. That's why, Casey says, "we balance each other out."

Veronica, a twenty-eight-year-old nonsuperior wife from Houston, Texas, puts her as-if beliefs in the starkest terms of all. "At first, my husband assumed that I would be Miss Molly Homemaker, but we both have labor-intensive jobs, so I slacked off on the chores because I was not getting any help. Now my husband does what it takes to get us by, and I am flat-out lazy. He enables me, because I refuse to enable him," she explains. "We pitched in together recently, by setting up a cleaning schedule so that both of us can do chores." When they have their first child, though, they'll have to negotiate a completely different household treaty, she says.

They tolerate imperfection. Wives who employ an as-if operating system also tend to be imperfectionists; they are rarely sticklers for doing it "my way or the highway." Instead, their motto tends to be "My way is good, but yours is fine too." An ability to tolerate what she considers imperfection is essential for a wife to achieve nonsuperiority, since she must rely on her husband's dishwashing ability and laundering acumen and car pool driving skill. This acceptance is especially difficult, of course, for obsessive and somewhat neurotic wives, those who insist that their children be dressed just so, that the kitchen counter be eternally crumb-free, that the dog be fed exactly three tablespoons of wet food a day. Nonsuperior wives aren't purists about household tasks, since they don't view that kind of domestic nit-picking as worth their time or effort.

"My husband and I made a conscious decision to be equitable partners in our marriage," says Tammy, thirty, a magazine editor in Tampa, Florida. "He is just as involved in raising and caring for our son as I am, and I don't boss him around about how to give our son a bath or how to cook the pork chops," she explains. "This is not the norm with our friends, who tend to think it's the wife's job to provide care for the children and for the dad to just pop in for dinner now and then and to make an occasional appearance at a sporting event. That's not us. We shop together and we clean the house together, and we don't view either one of us as being the only expert at something, since we both are."

Other nonsuperior wives echo Tammy's belief that there's no single "right" way to care for children or to do chores. "My husband is the kind of man every girl dreams of, since he cooks, cleans, does laundry, repairs the plumbing and electrical work, and does car and computer maintenance," says a thirty-five-year-old nonsuperior wife from Wisconsin who's in her second marriage. "He's also sweet and a good talker and listener, and I would never, ever tell him that he's doing something the wrong way," she adds. "Actually, I would never think it either!" A reformed nonsuperior wife from Denver, Colorado, says that "I used to be a perfectionist, until I realized that I needed to just let go. If my husband buys one wrong box of cereal at the grocery store or puts the light laundry in with the darks, the world truly won't come to an end." Another nonsuperior wife, a family doctor from Boston, Massachusetts, says that her husband "likes everything neat and tidy," but she doesn't really notice what he's cleaned or how he's cleaned it, just that doing it makes him happy. And that's fine by her, since "I'm laid back about how the house looks and I'm too busy with my medical practice to bother about it."

Finally, a thirty-six-year-old nurse from Oak Ridge, Tennessee, had premature twin boys who needed special care when they came home from the hospital. "My husband made me teach him the monitors and the parameters, even though I was the one with medical training, and he pulled many night shifts with them so that I could sleep," she says. She never corrected his attempts to care for their preemies or directed him to do things her way, she says. "I realized early on that if I wanted to keep sane, I had to give up hovering all the time and let him do things his own way," she says. "And I've never regretted it, since now he cooks dinner a few times a week, does the laundry, bathes the baby, cleans the kitchen at night, helps with homework, and coaches the boys' football team." She could never have raised three children and gone back to work without his help, she concludes.

They accept a patriarchal marriage. The fifth attribute of nonsuperior wives is completely unrelated to the other four, since it guarantees that these wives have nothing in common with egalitarian couples. Although equally nonsuperior, these wives are grateful and content to be performing old-fashioned, traditional gender roles. They enjoy being mistress of the manse. They don't mind being the one who cares for the children, cooks the food, arranges the social life, pays the bills, and tends to the breadwinning husband, as if he were a weedy but bountiful summer garden. These wives are comfortable playing second fiddle to hubby, because that's what they view as their rightful role. They adhere to a simple value system that requires few choices or challenges or decisions. Their religious beliefs often dictate how they behave, and as long as their husband holds the same opinion, both partners tend to be comfortable about their strictly proscribed roles within the marriage.

"According to the Bible, husband and wife are unequal, because God gave the husband more responsibility for the family, providing physical and spiritual needs and being the 'captain,'" says Brandi, twenty-seven, a nonsuperior wife from Bishop, Georgia. Her religious faith dictates the way she runs her family, and those beliefs provide little room for improvisation or doubt. "The husband is to love and cherish his wife, no matter what she does, just as Christ loves and cherishes the church," Brandi says. "The wife, however, is given the responsibility of birthing and nurturing the children, as well as submitting to the husband. But the wife is the best adviser, besides God, that a husband can have," she explains. With such clear-cut, unbending rules, Brandi doesn't need to question her husband's motives or nag him about helping around the house, because she prefers to abide by gender-specific principles. He earns the money; she cooks and cleans and raises the children. No muss, no fuss, no superiority necessary.

In a way, wives like Brandi have the most stress-free nonsuperior wife life of all, since they rely completely on stringent gender rules that have been imposed from above. They don't need to agonize over decisions or problems because their belief system is so comprehensive and so clear-cut, requiring little introspection and almost no personal choice. Such wives assert their belief that "the husband is the head of the household" or that "he has the final word on things," and that's all there is to it. A fifty-year-old wife and social worker from Nacogdoches, Texas, praises her husband for holding their family together and for doing "far more than I do. He believes that God has given him the role of head of the household and it is not one that he takes lightly. Because he is father to five children, he feels that everything he does for me reaches down to the children as well. He works for a religious organization, and sometimes when he comes home, he'll cook or help homeschool our children. There is no way I could even fantasize about having a better husband or father," she adds. Nor would it be her place to harbor such a reverie, since she also feels that she and her husband "were made for each other." This kind of certainty and conviction is relatively rare, but it makes for an unquestioning and highly idealized nonsuperior marriage.

Not all nonsuperior traditional wives are necessarily ultrareligious. Jeannie, a twenty-five-year-old wife and mother from Fulton, New York, who says she doesn't go to church very often, explains that "my husband is best at taking care of our family, and he works very hard to make sure we have a roof over our head and that we are warm and dry. He is my protector and my lover. I never have to worry that something bad will happen, as long as he's here to watch out for us and take care of us." Jeannie works full-time, though, and makes almost as much money as her husband does, so it seems that her patriarchal view of marriage may be a fairy tale she tells herself to fend off anxiety, like a magical mantra. After all, she's paying for that roof too.

Still, wives in patriarchal marriages frequently mention Christianity as a central reason for their nonsuperior marital arrangement. "My husband does his best to take care of our family," says a forty-four-year-old mother of five from Florida. "We can't do it without each other, husband and wife and Jesus, as the strong center of three strands wrapped together. If either one of us starts to put too much 'self' in this relation 'ship,' that ship will take on water and sink," she says, gathering handfuls of metaphors to explain herself.

Almost all nonsuperior wives in marriages like this would probably agree with Stacey, twenty-eight, a nonsuperior wife from Oklahoma who thinks of her husband as "the leader." She married him, she says, "because I knew he knew how to lead me." Crystal, twenty-nine, a Mormon wife from Utah, surely would concur, since she describes her husband as "the patriarch and the head of the house." She says this is so despite the fact that she works full-time and her husband has been gone for five months, training for a new job. During this time, Crystal says, she's learned "to be more self-reliant, since I had to sell our house and pack and store our things, so we can start our new life in a new state." Nevertheless, Crystal still views herself as a traditional, nonsuperior wife, one who is beholden to her husband, the master of the household. It seems as if Crystal is wearing blinders, because she refuses to perceive her own independence and competence; having a traditional marriage is so important to her that she'd rather ignore her own proficiency and strength for the sake of appearances.

Nevertheless, it's wives like Crystal, women with husbands who hold equally traditional values and who behave according to those rules, who are happiest about their marriage and who have strong feelings of love for their husband. Research shows that if couples hold traditional attitudes about gender but share chores at home, they end up fighting more often and feeling less love for each other. This is probably because their beliefs are at odds with their behavior. It is the traditional wives and husbands who pair their attitudes with an equally traditional separation of chores and responsibilities who do best.[7]

Such marriages can go bad, however, if the wife's views undergo a radical transformation, as Judy's did. Judy, fifty-one, a dairy farmer's wife from Indiana, began her marriage assuming that her husband would run the farm and make the important decisions and that she'd raise the children and help out on the farm, just as her parents and grandparents did. Over the years, though, her views about the benefits of a traditional marriage "have changed completely," she says, "though my husband's have stayed the same." She no longer relishes the idea of being like June Cleaver, the epitome of the 1950s uptight homemaker, whose house is always spotless and whose children are always polite. Over the years, Judy raised the couple's four children, worked part-time for pay, and did the morning and evening milking every day. Looking back now, she realizes that she fooled herself into believing that her traditional, superior wife marriage was satisfying, since she received little support or appreciation from her husband. As far as Judy is concerned, she's fed up with being in that kind of relationship and wishes she could throw out those old-fashioned assumptions and start all over again. Judy's husband, though, thinks their marriage is hunky-dory, she says, and he sees no reason to send it to the mulch pile.

Judy serves as a warning to wives everywhere: it is a serious mistake to believe that a superior wife can remake herself as nonsuperior, regardless of what her husband believes and wants. That is never, ever the case. The key to wifely nonsuperiority is, almost always, the husband: who *he* is, what *he* believes, and how *he* behaves.

Husbands of Nonsuperior Wives

A nonsuperior wife is not born, she's made—right there at the altar, dressed in her bridal gown—since she'll never achieve nonsuperiority unless she marries a man who will encourage and assist her in nonsuperiority. No matter how much a woman yearns for a shared partnership, she won't reach that goal if she doesn't have a husband who thinks almost exactly the way she does. And such men are surprisingly difficult to find.

Many men are simply unwilling or unable to trade in their old-fashioned gender rules for newer ones, which require active and equal participation in family affairs. The old rules, dating from the post–World War Two era, dictate that men should earn a living and tinker in the backyard and that women should do everything else. Such marital laws seem to have been written in stone, poured in concrete, and fashioned in steel, at least as far as many men are concerned. That's not so surprising, since these decrees are in their favor: having a traditional wife renders a husband's life remarkably easy and relatively stress-free, whether she works for pay or not. Gender-based marriage rules are so ingrained in American men that they are almost impossible to dislodge, even when men think they believe otherwise. A great many men are reluctant to give up on the norms of the good old days, the days when father knew best and father did less.

Today more women than men long for truly egalitarian marriages. Indeed, research shows that men are more conservative on gender issues than women are, and their attitudes about them are changing more slowly too.[8] Because men with sincere egalitarian beliefs are in such short supply, there aren't enough of them to go around for the large number of women who want to marry one. Thus, more and more potential brides are postponing marriage or avoiding it altogether. Indeed, legal experts believe that the current decline in marriage rates is a direct result of women's unwillingness to marry men who expect them to become superior as soon as the wedding bells chime. These experts believe, in fact, that the decline in marriage rates will not change until more men become willing to accept new and radically different gender roles.[9] As a disillusioned superior wife from Illinois says, "I tell my daughters they should not get married, because it's not worth it. They'll end up being glorified slaves with a 'Mrs.' in front of their names."

When a wife is not superior, it doesn't follow that her husband is. In most nonsuperior wife marriages, *neither partner is superior*. In fact, according to wives who answered my Web survey, the number of superior husbands is so small as to be virtually nonexistent. If I define superior husbands the same way as I define superior wives, those who have five or six signs of superiority, then not even 1 percent of men are superior, wives say. Even among husbands, whose standards for themselves are more forgiving, only 7 percent describe themselves as superior. There are so few superior husbands, in fact, that I can't really analyze or discuss them, since any comparisons would be based on numbers too small to be statistically valid. But I did find a few to examine, mostly out of curiosity.

Mark, fifty-one, is a superior husband with a nonsuperior wife and proud of it. His marriage, he says, "has brought me more joy than I thought possible." His wife does not work for pay, and he describes her as being "made by God just for me." He's extremely happy about his marriage and his life, despite the fact that he does more than his wife in just about every way. She is an empress of the as-if philosophy, he says, "because she lacks any domestic common sense, and she says she can't cook, shop, clean, do laundry, or manage money. As a result, I am sole support for eight people and I do all the cooking, the shopping, the laundry, the yard work, the house maintenance, and the finances. I whine about it sometimes, because society set my expectations not to have so much domestic junk to do. But it's really not that hard," he adds. "I just do the grunt work to free up my wife to do the important stuff, like caring for the emotional and spiritual well-being of the family, since she's the glue that holds us all together." Mark is a god among men, a paragon of superiority that most wives would give several pints of blood or a finger or a toe to find.

If superiority is so bad for wives, it should also be bad for husbands, even Mark. Still, I can't help but feel optimistic about finding a potential trove of superior husbands. After all, such guys would help balance the marital scales, if only temporarily. Women have taken on the superior role in marriage for so long, it's time for men to take a turn, to see how the other half lives. After a while, we can all enter an era of truly egalitarian, mutually satisfying marital bonds.

Alas, Mark is a one in half a million husbands, almost as rare as a polar bear in Jamaica. In general, there are probably several dozen different types of husbands, based on their beliefs about gender and how they behave at home and how they define their own sense of masculinity. Roughly speaking, however, there are just three basic husband types in nonsuperior wife marriages: the Caveman husband, the Team Player husband, and the Intersex husband.

Caveman Husband. This man is in a mutually agreeable traditional marriage, and he views himself as the king of his castle, the master of his domain, the cock of his roost. He makes many or most of the family decisions, especially those related to money and finances, because both he and his wife believe that the man should be the master manager of the household. His nonsuperior wife sees herself as mistress of the children and the cooking and the cleaning. If both partners agree on these matters, the marriage is smooth and successful; if not, it's likely to be in shambles. About two in five nonsuperior wives have a Caveman husband, one who takes control of and responsibility for his family, a man who believes that it's his right and duty to be in charge. One nonsuperior wife with a Caveman mate says that "in my marriage, I am the neck but he is the head; since he's the man, he makes major decisions, and he has the final say." Others agree, saying that "by nature, women are caretakers and men are earners," or "my husband is the wage earner, the rock." Many, but not all, Caveman husbands have wives who don't work for pay, since the ideal traditional marriage is one in which the husband earns the money and the wife stays at home. True Caveman husbands, and their wives, obey these clear-cut gender roles religiously, especially since many of them are religious.

One such wife is Erika, thirty-four, an at-home mother and nonsuperior wife in Waterville, Maine, who homeschools her children. She is immensely pleased to be married to a Caveman husband and to be able to stay at home. "My husband says that his role is to make sure that I get to be the best me that I was created to be. He takes care of loads of details, like finances, insurance, and retirement savings. He used to get up with me when I nursed our babies and read aloud to me from some of our favorite books. Sometimes," she adds, "we take time for ballroom dancing classes, so we can play together." As far as Erika is concerned, her nonsuperior wife life is blissful.

Likewise, a forty-two-year-old nonsuperior wife from Texas says that "we live out our faith, which says that the husband is in charge of the family and the wife is submissive to him. We feel that it's a wife's obligation to submit to her husband." She adds, perhaps further clarifying her point of view, "I am also brain-injured from a car accident."

A thirty-eight-year-old Caveman husband, owner of a moving company in Columbus, Ohio, says that "my job is to be the sole provider and protector of the family. As long as I make sure money comes into the house, my wife makes sure everything else is taken care of." He takes control, because he makes the dole.

Some Caveman insist that they are rulers but not dictators and that their wives are submissive and obedient out of love, not fear. "We share marriage responsibilities, and my wife is my helpmeet, and our duties are to God," says a forty-seven-year-old Alabama husband, who adds that he doesn't think he's better than his wife, just that "the wife completes the man, and we have grown closer to the Lord being together." Another Caveman husband, a thirty-two-year-old Web technician from Illinois, is married to a nonsuperior wife who stays home with their five young children. He explains that "we consult with each other about what we do, and we feel that God putting us together could not have been a mistake." For this reason, they rarely argue or fight about who should do what, since she's in charge of the children and he earns and manages the money, the way they believe God intended it.

Caveman husbands guarantee their wives' nonsuperiority, since the basis of their relationship is that the man is in charge.

Team Player Husband. Other nonsuperior wife marriages, those in which both partners reject traditional role and rules, must include a husband who insists on equality at home. About two in five nonsuperior wife marriages include a husband who truly believes in being a team player; he thinks that both partners should give the same amount and that both should be in charge. These men are fervent about fairness, relentless in their pursuit of marital equality. It's almost as if they view their marriage as part of an offensive line in a football team, or as the two leadoff batters on a baseball team; they're obliged to share and share alike for the good of the marriage team. Although these husbands may be thinking in sports metaphors and behaving as if they were part of a domestic athletic event, they are actually tacit feminists. Team Player husbands believe that women have equal rights, that women aren't obliged to defer or kowtow to their husbands. Many of these men, and even their wives, might not admit to being feminists, since the stereotype is that feminists are ugly or single or lesbian or all three. But men who support feminism have a stronger and healthier relationship with their wife, and they share a greater ability to confide their feelings to each other, to laugh together, and to feel close. Such men may even have better sex lives, according to a recent study of married feminists.[10]

Marcia, fifty-seven, is married to a Team Player husband ten years younger than she is. They run a restaurant in Alaska, and she says that he is just as competent at organizing and cleaning and deciding and sacrificing and supporting and being efficient as she is. "There's nothing my husband can't fix with baling wire and duct tape, while I deal with the books and the personnel and making everything balance in the long run. There's nothing we don't share or do together, and I wouldn't want it any other way, and neither would he," Marcia says.

In Marcia's house, there is no such thing as a "wife's job" or a "husband's job"; it's all "our jobs," which can change from day to day and week to week. Nonsuperior wives like Marcia spout endless reiterations of the phrase "share equally," because that's what they really do. And they are very, very happy about it too. Wives flourish in egalitarian marriages, and that's true all over the world, apparently. A study done in Lebanon, for instance, shows that the more involved husbands are in housework, the more psychologically healthy wives are and the happier they are with their marriage and with their lives. The Lebanese researchers defined housework as a series of twenty-five chores, everything from doing laundry and cooking to managing expenses and buying gas, to doing errands and cleaning the kitchen and bathroom. "Involvement of a husband in housework is strongly associated with the psychological health of his wife," they say, having conducted the first-ever such study in the Middle East. And the first ever, surely, to reach this very feminist conclusion.[11]

Wives with Team Player husbands seem to prance and preen as they describe their mate: they adore him for permitting them to enter into the exclusive sorority of nonsuperior wives. "I could not ask for a better life partner," says Wendy, forty-seven, a nonsuperior wife from rural Tennessee. "We have always shared chores, and he changed diapers and ran errands and now we own an insurance agency together, so we are even closer than ever." They are team players at home, and now they're team players at work too. Many wives like Wendy use the word "team" over and over again when they describe their marriage, including a fifty-two-year-old nonsuperior wife from Santa Barbara, California, who refused to answer the survey questions that required her to choose which partner was best at a series of tasks because "in our marriage, we truly share the responsibility for everything. We're a team and we work together on whatever needs our attention." Even when they barbecue, "it's a team effort, all the way around. We plan the menu together, we grocery shop together, we prepare the food together. We are a team from start to finish of nearly every day," she says. They are even on the same bowling team, she adds.

Dana, forty-four, a nonsuperior wife from Milwaukee, Wisconsin, also has a tough time explaining who does what around the house, since she and her Team Player husband divvy up everything. "He does almost all of the cooking and shopping," Dana says about her husband, "but I will cut up vegetables and clean the fridge and nudge him to plan dinner. I do all of the financial stuff, but he will argue on the phone about a bill or negotiate a better cell phone plan. Yes, he leaves the car a pigsty, but he also does the car maintenance and has spent up to twenty hours a week driving my elderly parents all over and bandaging their gangrenous wounds." Dana explains her way of thinking about her nonsuperior marriage by saying that "it's really easy to buy into the b.s. that you are the victim and that your partner is the bad guy, and then to distort all the facts to support that egotistical point of view. But when you let go of that dynamic, you realize that you both give, and you both appreciate the other."

Husbands who are Team Players also have difficulty when asked to pinpoint who's the better partner at various tasks. "We are both experts on most subjects, and that's because we both make an effort to be involved in every aspect of the family," says Aaron, twenty-nine, a Team Player husband with a nonsuperior wife from Kahuku, Hawaii. "Being a husband is about becoming one with the wife in taking care of the family," he says, adding that "in our marriage, things are shared equally because we forget about ourselves and look to help and serve the family unit as a whole. The day you say 'I do,' it changes to 'We do.' I expect to share an eternity together with my wife and children, so I need to share in the tasks, work, decisions, and responsibilities of the family right now."

I have a feeling that if Aaron's wife put him up for sale on eBay, she'd get plenty of offers for him, and far above her asking price too.

"'Equal share' ought to be an option on this survey, since we have a partnership," insists a twenty-nine-year-old Team Player husband from Ohio. He and his nonsuperior wife have no children yet, so things could change, but right now, he says, "she handles some chores, and I take care of the ones she doesn't like, such as dusting, vacuuming, and cleaning the kitchen. I also do most of the cooking, since she enjoys the quality of the food I put on the table." He and his wife are still in school, and he notes that "we want to help each other grow into the fullness of our potential."

Many Team Player husbands are in relatively new marriages and have no children. For them, it seems simple and logical to share in a nonsuperior wife marriage, though that may change drastically after their first baby is born. A twenty-seven-year-old handyman in Minnesota has been married a little more than a year, but he says that "we are a team, and that's the way it will always be." His wife probably hopes that's true too.

It's not just young and childless husbands who are Team Players, however. Brian, forty-nine, is an engineer and a Team Player from Michigan with a nonsuperior wife. "Life is a balancing act and working mutually together," he says. "Think of a hand: the fingers are strengths, the gaps between are weaknesses, but put our hands together and the gaps are filled. Both of us are responsible for everything, and we back each other up. It's not about what I do or what she does," he concludes, "it's about what we both do together." Brian has four children, and both he and his wife work full-time. But into the chaos of their family life, more than a little teamwork must fall, and Brian is the one who makes it happen.

Likewise, Shane, thirty-three, has been married to a nonsuperior wife for five years. They have a fourteen-month-old baby, and both are graduate students in central Florida. He resents answering what he considers "loaded questions" that force him to decide who does what, since "it seems to be a dominance survey. Modern families with two working spouses are becoming equal," he says, with great sincerity and more than a little naiveté. "We break down the chores every night, and one of us cleans up after dinner, picks up the house, and prepares lunch for the next day. The other one gives our son a bath, gets him ready for bed, reads to him, and tucks him in. We switch off when we feel like it," he explains. Both of them work the same hours, both earn about the same amount, "and even our offices are next to each other." As far as Shane is concerned, Team Player husbands are here to stay: they're the wave of the conjugal future, and he's leading the charge.

Elliott, thirty-nine, an elementary school principal from Decatur, Illinois, is also a Team Player husband. He says "we work wonderfully well together as a team in our marriage, and my wife says the same. In the past three years, we've dealt with her near-fatal illness, two births, the building of a house, and a change in careers for both of us. Despite these hardships and challenges, we worked through them, by being a team."

Team Player husbands ensure their wives' nonsuperiority by believing in the importance of equality just as strongly as their wives do, if not more.

Intersex Husband. These husbands also share chores and responsibilities with their wives, but their rationale for doing so is quite different from that of Team Player husbands. These men, about one in five husbands of nonsuperior wives, truly give and sacrifice as much as their wives do, if not more. They are not part of a team so much as they are clones of their wives, as if they've been mind-melded together. I named these husbands after the unusual bass that have appeared recently in the Potomac River in Virginia. These fish are male but also female, since some male bass now produce eggs in their testes, according to the United States Geological Survey. The researchers have dubbed the creatures "intersex" fish.[12] Similarly, the Intersex husband contains the best of both gender worlds. He internalizes domestic chores and doesn't need to be reminded or nagged to "help out." In fact, he doesn't consider it helping, he considers it part of his job. His family's needs and desires are always in the back of his mind, no matter what, just as they are for a superior wife.

Intersex men are difficult to find, but they aren't quite as rare as those fish. Dean, forty-six, is an Intersex husband from Benson, North Carolina, who says, "I do more of the manual labor at home. I cook, I clean, and I do the dishes every day. I take care of the house and the lawn, the dogs and the car, and I do at least half of the baby feedings. I am fifteen years older than my wife, and I was a Benedictine monk for twenty-one years, so I am accustomed to serving others." This man was trained to be Intersex; he is über-Intersex.

Marcus, a forty-year-old computer network engineer in Pittsburgh, Pennsylvania, was forced to become an Intersex husband, mostly because he's hopelessly in love with a woman whose feelings for him are fading. "I am more involved with our kids' school, homework, soccer, and activities, since my wife has a new job. I've always done the laundry and the yard and the house cleaning. I also pick up the kids from school, cook dinner, help them do homework, clean a little, and get them ready for bed," he says. "When my wife comes home from work, her food is warm in the oven, and everything has been taken care of," Marcus says. It's almost as if he hopes that by making such an enormous effort to be a good wife, he will earn his nonsuperior wife's undying love and devotion.

That's not a problem for Chad, a thirty-year-old Intersex husband and chemistry graduate student in Tucson, Arizona. "We are perfect together, and she is my better half, due to the encouragement and unwavering support she gives me every minute," he says. "We split chores or we do them together. Our life with two young children is hectic, but we've learned how to manage and share responsibilities." For Chad, there's simply no question that whatever's going on at home is just as much his concern as his wife's.

Husbands like Chad are celebrated and revered by wives as almost too good to be true. Indeed, a group of women founded what they called the Cambridge Women's Pornography Cooperative a few years ago. They published a book comprising a collection of photographs of handsome men vacuuming and cooking and serving cups of tea, while fully clothed. The group is only half tongue in cheek, but their huge book sales are surely no joke.[13]

Wives who've managed to snag a pornographically suitable Intersex husband rarely take him for granted. "Usually we're in sync with our tastes, opinions, and needs, so decisions and responsibility haven't been a source of conflict for us," says Kayla, twenty-four, a nonsuperior wife and mother from Maryland. "At home, we have no set roles, we just gravitate to what we do best. I do the cooking and cleaning, and I manage the finances; he does the organizing and decorating and baby care. He does all of the decorating of the house, because he's the one who cares about bed shams and curtain valances and swags. We don't take turns or keep track of who changes diapers; we both just do what has to be done."

Intersex husbands ensure their wives' nonsuperiority by becoming just as competent and loving and efficient as a wife's wife should be.

Secrets of the Nonsuperior Wife Marriage

Nonsuperior wives avoid superiority through their own hard work, their own firm beliefs, and their own wisdom in selecting the right partner. Likewise, nonsuperior wives who are in traditional marriages have chosen a husband who enjoys being the sole breadwinner, a man who's both able and eager to be the head of the household. This is the easier path to nonsuperiority, because it's the route of least resistance. Wives in highly traditional marriages are sometimes defensive about their choice, however, because they are moving against a rising tide of wives and mothers who are working for pay. Those who truly embrace their traditional roots are most likely to be nonsuperior and proud of it.

Nonsuperior wives in egalitarian marriages, those who try for an even balance of power and responsibility and emotional effort, have plotted a course that requires not only courage but a great deal of thought about *what not to do*. These wives don't fall into a superiority trap, one in which they view themselves as the chief executive officer and their husband as a midlevel manager. They don't operate as if they are the master and he's the apprentice. They don't function as if they are the supervisor and he's the helper. In these marriages, wives and husbands do not automatically return to the gender role defaults for household tasks and chores: he's not the one who has to do the yard work, she's not the one who has to bake the pies. They do not view domestic duties as the wife's job, and she does not feel guilty if the house isn't clean enough or if the yard isn't well maintained or if the children's clothing doesn't match. Neither partner worries about being judged by other people, nor do they judge themselves for not living up to the gender stereotype rules that are floating around in the cultural atmosphere. In addition, neither partner feels that there's a "wrong" way to do chores, whether loading the dishwasher or bathing the baby or roasting a vegetable, unless it causes bleeding or broken bones or sets the house on fire. In general, an equal marriage is one in which couples divide tasks as equally and as fairly as possible. It's one in which partners view each other as true equals and believe that they are equally committed and supportive. And it's one in which partners view each other's careers as equally crucial and have an equal say in decision making.[14] An equal marriage is like the relationship between co-owners of an Italian restaurant or two doctors sharing an obstetrics practice, only with a lot more love and intimacy and tenderness attached.

For these rare couples, arranging a nonsuperior wife marriage takes an enormous amount of effort and planning and determination. Some non-profit groups have even sprung up to offer advice on coparenting or equal parenting and other ways in which couples can learn to be successfully nonsuperior. The premise is that women can't do this on their own, that they need guidance and backup and constant consultation.[15] Surprisingly, one of the best models for a marriage in which gender roles are almost irrel-evant is lesbian and gay partnerships. Among lesbian couples, for example, both partners are women, so the rules about what a wife should do simply don't apply. Many lesbian couples have truly equitable relationships, and they fight less often and have more satisfying and intimate bonds than het-erosexual couples do, according to one study.[16] It would be ironic indeed if the couples who have the most trouble legalizing their unions are the ones who actually have the strongest, most egalitarian, and most satisfying mar-riages of all.

Among heterosexual couples, it's nonsuperior wives who are most likely to say that their marriage is open and honest and that they don't need to manipulate their partner if they want to persuade him to do something. "This sounds sappy, but I never 'get' my husband to do what I want, like Lucy did to Ricky," says Peggy, a fifty-four-year-old art gallery owner from Pittsburgh, Pennsylvania. She's referring to the 1950s television show *I Love Lucy*, about the trials of a traditional wife who was constantly try-ing to trick her husband so that she could get her own way. "If two people care about each other at all and are reasonably mature, there's no need for

manipulation," she explains. "If I had to use a 'method' to 'get' my husband
to do something, I'd be pretty unhappy. We're not blissful every minute of
the day, but we work well together. He was telling me about a co-worker
whose wife had spent five hundred dollars to buy a laptop computer for
their nine-year-old son, and the guy was mad at her about the expenditure.
My husband and I realized that we couldn't think of a single time we'd had
a fight about money!" Peggy says, surprised at her discovery. "My husband
likes to gamble, and I love shoes, but we're always able to restrain ourselves
from excess, and we agree on priorities," she explains. "If I want my husband to do something, we just talk about it, and we figure it out, together."

Another nonsuperior wife doesn't balk at the notion of husbandly persuasion, but she does insist that she never nags him or puts him on formal
notice that "'we need to talk,' since nothing frightens him more than that.
I make sure that we are sitting face-to-face, looking in each other's eyes,"
explains Angela, forty-five, an at-home mother from San Diego. "And I
make sure that both of us are present in the time and place, that we are
really paying attention. My husband respects logic, so I try to present him
with the facts and the alternative solutions as I see them. I use a method
that makes him feel comfortable, of being unemotional, logical, and pre-
senting a range of solutions and a generous time frame for making the
decision, since he hates being rushed," she says. "Sometimes he'll come up
with an off-the-wall solution, but other times he comes up with something
brilliant, that I haven't thought of, and I'll kiss him and tell him that's why
I love him," Angela concludes, proud of the depth of her understanding her
Caveman husband is able to show.

Several nonsuperior wives with Team Player husbands use the same
method, employing logic, lists, and careful planning to convince their
mate. "It's a matter of approaching him with an idea slowly and allowing
him to blow off steam about it," explains a forty-seven-year-old nonsuperior
wife from Wisconsin, who studies her husband as carefully as a medical
student pores over an anatomy textbook. "I give him time to mull things
over, and he almost always comes around. To be able to prove that we have
enough money to do the plan in question is a big plus," she adds. Another
wife agrees that her Team Player husband "responds well to logic," which
is why she constructs "lists of pros and cons, and we take the route with the
most advantages, as determined by our list." A wife from Las Vegas, Nevada,

doesn't like to gamble when it comes to marital negotiations, which is why she always gives her Team Player husband time to think. "He should feel he has a choice and that he's not being manipulated into doing something, since we don't do that to each other," she says. "We're straightforward with each other, and we like games, but only on the computer."

Many nonsuperior wives who have Team Player husbands say that they're not only teammates but also that "he's my biggest fan," as Carol, forty-two, from Newtown, Pennsylvania, puts it. "He's a great friend, and I am grateful for his companionship and his love every single day," she boasts. "If I want to convince him to do something, I introduce the idea, and if it's a biggie, I make sure I have all the facts about how it will work. Then we discuss it and do research so we can make the best decision together," Carol explains. "It's the same in our sex life, since he's eager to try anything I ask, and he's a real sport in that department." That might also be a very good clue as to why Carol's husband is the president of her fan club: the secret to a man's nonsuperior heart might be through his other part.

Team Player husbands offer similar explanations for how they negotiate their way through marital bliss. "My wife is good about doing things I want, and I try to do what she requests," says a forty-one-year-old husband with a nonsuperior wife in Virginia. "We both try to use reason and principles in our decision making, which often helps," he explains. "If we start to argue, I try to remember all the things she does for me, and I give in to what she wants." Blake, twenty-seven, a Team Player husband from Michigan, is married to a woman who earns about the same as he does, and he maintains that "the idea of equality in relationships has worked out well for us." As far as methods of persuasion, Blake says that they both listen, evaluate, and then compromise, since "no methods of manipulation will ever work, because in the end, it breeds resentment. The most important thing in a marriage is to learn that what you want doesn't matter and that finding out what the two of you want is the key."

An Intersex husband from Maine, who's also an at-home father, says that he always deals with his wife "from the heart." That way, he adds, "I speak openly and directly to air my needs and desires, and I find that listening and truly hearing what my partner has to say is critical to having a successful relationship." A thirty-nine-year-old Intersex husband from Georgia recoils from the idea that he'd force his wife to do anything. Still, he says,

"I try to make sure that she has what she needs when she needs it. For us, love and support at all times is of the utmost importance."

Finally, a Caveman husband admits that he occasionally violates his strict gender role for the sake of marital harmony by becoming "the kitchen fairy," as he calls it. "I clean the kitchen every morning. I am talking spotless, and I grind fresh coffee and brew it so it's waiting for my wife when she wakes up," he says. "This starts her day on a positive note, and she's truly thankful for it. I know, because she brags about it to her friends all the time." He makes a point to bring home flowers and to tell her that he loves her cooking, so there's never a problem bringing her around to his point of view, when necessary.

As it turns out, one of the most essential secrets of the nonsuperior wife is that she has no secrets. She does not need to use special tactics to get her husband to cooperate with her, since collaboration and teamwork are the foundation on which her marriage rests. She doesn't need to make her husband think an idea is his so that "he puts new siding on the house, Sheetrocks and paints it, thins the trees, buys a new bed and a new kitchen sink, and builds a dog pen," as one superior wife crows about tricking her mate. She does not need to wait until he has had a few drinks before broaching a touchy subject. She does not need to bargain by offering sexual favors or by using reverse psychology or by pretending not to want something that she really does want. She doesn't need to cry, or yell at the dog, or employ any of the dozens of tricks that superior wives say they use on a regular basis to influence their husband. (Though such methods can be effective, as we'll see in the next chapter.)

It's not really a superior wife's fault that she needs to resort to such underhanded and almost embarrassing methods of persuasion. After all, the majority of marriages are arranged unfairly, which is why so many wives take on a superior role, as my research shows. This progression occurs despite the fact that superior wife marriages are bad for wives and bad for husbands and bad for marriage in general. The superior wife marriage is more of a curse than a blessing, more of an encumbrance than a strength. For this reason, nonsuperior marriages must be the wave of the future, at least if the institution of marriage is to survive and thrive.

The best marriages either adhere strictly to gender roles or toss out those rules completely; they're at opposite extremes. Indeed, it's the in-between marriages, those that include some obedience to traditional roles with a dash of egalitarianism and a confusing bit of reluctant chore sharing, that seem doomed to misery and distress. Such marriages, those that include a superior wife, can seem like an imitation of marriage, a shell of what should and could be. The real tragedy of these marriages is that *both partners suffer for it*—wives and husbands—although husbands may believe they reap the benefits from having a wife who does everything. In truth, neither partner in a superior wife marriage gets the intimacy and the connectedness, or the partnership and the caring, that they deserve. They are robbed of the emotional benefits that flow from a loving bond when both spouses feel like partners in a shared enterprise. Instead, they get recrimination and resentment, irritation and nagging, sexual refusal and begging. *It's not really a bonus for husbands, or for their wives, to be in a marriage in which she does everything.*

Still, there are many superior wives who spend years pretending that everything is fine, that they are happily married, that their life is not really all that bad. It's the pervasive American belief in the power of positive thinking—if you believe it's good, then it will be—that fools so many women into imagining that although they are superior, their marriage is as good as it can get. But this is a delusion, a false optimism, and a refusal to see what's staring them in the face.

A superior wife marriage is an inferior marriage.

Darlyn, forty-seven, a Michigan mother of two, has been a superior wife since her wedding day, twenty years ago. She works part-time and does everything at home, "because even when I'm sick," she says, "my husband will not interrupt his routine to help out." He treats her job "as if it's a hobby for me," she says, adding that she'd like "to ask him for more emotional support, but I'm afraid to." She feels neither appreciation nor respect from her husband, yet she asserts that they communicate "often enough, and we divide some responsibilities," and she calls her marriage "somewhat happy." On the other hand, Darlyn was seriously depressed a while ago, and she admits that "nobody in my family even noticed that a year of my life was spent just getting through the day. As long as the laundry was finished and dinner was on the table, the dogs were walked and fed, and the grocery shopping was done, no one noticed that I was going through hell." If she ever asks her husband to step in to discipline their teenage children, "he isn't caring or sensitive, he's explosive." As Darlyn tells one story after another about how alone and uncared for she feels, she confesses that "it sounds like my marriage is pretty awful." But she refuses to see it that way, insisting that it isn't as bad as it seems, since "we enjoy each other's company, we share activities with the family, though not with the same enthusiasm, and our vacations are great, though mostly planned by me." Darlyn is a superior wife wearing rose-colored glasses, a giant sun hat, and a huge hood, all to block her view of what's staring her right in the face: an unhappy, unfulfilling, and unrewarding superior wife marriage.

Darlyn, and millions of wives just like her, deserve much better. They deserve to appreciate how the other third lives, those nonsuperior wives who have marriages of like minds, marriages of full hearts, marriages that withstand the tests of time and temptation and babies. The next and final chapter explores ways in which superior wife couples can find their way to nonsuperiority and a greater sense of marital harmony.

8

How to Fix a Superior Wife Marriage

Imagine this: an awards ceremony is being held in Hollywood, California, to select one woman for the highly coveted honor of Best Wife in a Superior Role. Thousands of superior wives from across the country and around the world compete for the title by telling the story of their marriage. They clamor to prove who is the most overworked and underappreciated, who is the most supremely competent, who is the most organized and efficient. They want to establish themselves as the epitome of a wife whirlwind, the most superior wife in the history of wives. The judges, women who are themselves expert superior wives, convene to render a decision. When the winner is finally announced, she thanks both the Panel of Superiors for choosing her and especially her own husband, for making it all possible. "He's the one who falls asleep every night at nine. He's the one who takes me for granted. He's the one who expects me to be his maid and his mom, his lover and his social director," she sobs. "I raise our children, cook his food, bring home a second paycheck, and run his house. I could never have done it without him."

How's that for a pathetic fantasy?

But it's not as far-fetched as you might think. Plenty of superior wives revel in their superiority. They feel superior about being superior, because it's their only source of power and control in a marriage gone wrong. That's why so many of them bristle when they hear their situation described this way, because without their superiority, they have nothing. That's why they refuse to acknowledge their own complicity in their marital gloom. They have no clue that being superior is harmful, or that a marriage can be otherwise arranged, or how a superior wife can transform herself into a nonsuperior one.

Ridding a wife of superiority is a difficult process because the habit is so ingrained and often seems so much easier than the alternative. It's just too annoying and complicated and time-consuming to explain to your husband how to _____ (fill in the blank here), so you might as well do it yourself. But that rationale is wrong, because it's the first step down into a deep pit of superiority. I'm not saying that your husband will ever become as domestically sophisticated as a food network chef or even as savvy as the man I met in the baking aisle of the grocery store, who explained the importance of adding tapioca to a blueberry pie recipe. But maybe, just maybe, you can get to the point where your husband will be the one who offers to shop for the berries and the lemons and who watches you bake so that he can try it himself next time.

Whether it takes pints of blueberries or mountains of miracles or both, the idea is for wives to relieve themselves of superiority once and for all.

It's crucial for superior wives to realize that being in a superior wife marriage almost always takes a toll on both partners, with the greatest detriment for the wife. Researchers find that when wives are in an unhappy marriage, it's the women who have more health problems and more psychological woes than the men. This is true even among middle-aged and older couples, those who've been married for at least fifteen years, experts say. Wives are most miserable, they find, because it's the wife's job to confront painful problems in the relationship. She's the one who is supposed to try to heal what's broken in the marriage, and when she can't, she's the more devastated.[1] But make no mistake: husbands in bad marriages suffer almost as much as wives do. They lose the chance for love and support, their sex lives are unsatisfying, and they are likely to end up divorced. Being in an unhappy, superior wife marriage is a lose-lose situation for both partners.

That's why it's crucial for such couples to go on a marital crusade, to save the superior wife from her superiority. She has to admit her condition, accept the need for change, and then make those adjustments. This chapter will offer superior wives almost two dozen alternatives for renouncing superiority. The idea is to transform a superior wife marriage into its opposite incarnation, to force it into a parallel marital universe, one in which the wife is not superior and in which her marriage is therefore vastly improved.

It's no easy task, of course, to figure out exactly what it is that makes a good marriage good or how successful marriages really work, other than the fact that they should not include a superior wife. But it is clear that *there is no one marriage type that is best or most rewarding.* There are nonsuperior wives in traditional marriages to Caveman husbands who are happy. There are nonsuperior wives in egalitarian marriages to Intersex husbands who are doing well. And there are nonsuperior wives in Even-Steven and Alpha Wife marriages who are equally content.

Tara, thirty-one, is a nonsuperior wife in a traditional and successful second marriage. An at-home mother of two, she's happy to be "in charge of the home front" while her husband serves as an Air Force officer near their home in Tucson, Arizona. Just as it's his job to inspect and maintain jet fighter engines, it's hers to figure out when to serve lasagna and how to clean smears of finger paint off the kitchen table. She willingly does everything at home, "because this is my place as a housewife, since he's bringing home the paycheck." Both Tara and her husband are comfortable with this arrangement, which is the main reason she calls their marriage "amazingly strong," one that leaves her "absolutely in a state of bliss." She's a Captain and Mate wife, he's a Caveman husband, and their beliefs in the rightness of that situation are perfectly matched.

Carmelita's marriage is the exact opposite of Tara's—she's an Alpha wife with an Intersex husband—but she too is truly happy about her union. "I am the breadwinner, so my husband stayed home when we had a child, since I was the one who could make more money," says Carmelita, forty-six, an electrical engineer from Huntington Beach, California. "I feel very lucky that we were able to do this, since my husband is an excellent father, very engaged and sensitive and loving. Also, he does most things better than me," she says, stating her case in a matter-of-fact, taken-for-granted way. "We support our family in different ways, and because of our circumstances it's not in the normal ways, but that doesn't really bother us," she concludes. Like Tara, Carmelita is a nonsuperior wife in a good marriage.

Finally, Sylvia, sixty-four, is an Even-Steven wife with a Team Player husband from Lynn, Massachusetts, but she's also a nonsuperior wife who's happy about her situation. "I believe we are equally represented in the marriage," she says. "I do things I care about, like cleaning, finances, laundry, and investing, and he does the things he cares about, like arranging family visits, organizing, and shopping. Neither of us does the things we don't want to do, like wash the cars or mow the lawn. We eat out a lot, and we live in a condominium, so it all works out."

There you have it: three very different types of nonsuperior wife marriages, but all of them close to ideal.

What Makes a Good Marriage Good?

You can't identify a good marriage simply by looking at who makes the dough and who bakes the dough. Unfortunately, there is no single factor, like earning power or marriage type, that automatically signals healthy marriage. There are many crucial components in a great marriage, and they must all work in tandem to inspire marital success. Some are based on common sense and fairly obvious, though remarkably difficult to achieve. In a good marriage, for instance, both partners try to be polite and respectful. Both try to see the other person's point of view, and both are considerate rather than critical, helpful rather than nagging. All of these factors are apparent, and all are much easier said than done.

But marriage is not like an electric clock, a device that plugs into a socket and runs for decades with little or no maintenance. Also, you can't listen for the regular *tick-tock* of a marriage to know if it's functioning well. Even so, marriage researchers have spent the past few decades interviewing and observing and videotaping couples in an effort to figure out the complicated inner mechanisms of modern marriage. They want to be able to predict who will stay married and who will end up divorced, which is somewhat like trying to figure out which clocks will break and which will keep on ticking. Although this is enormously difficult, some experts have come close to figuring out which couples are which. There are probably dozens, or even hundreds, of specific features that characterize good marriages—and bad ones too, for that matter. Here are just a few of them—five keys to having a successful, nonsuperior wife marriage—all of them based on recent psychological research, as well as on my Web survey. First, a good marriage includes a capacity for forgiveness; second, it requires an ongoing sense of novelty and excitement; third, it requires the ability to fight and argue well; fourth, it balances anger and screaming with jokes and tenderness; fifth, it demands careful attention to disagreements about money.

In the thousands and thousands of years that women and men have been living together as couples, every husband and every wife has, at least on occasion, hurt or offended or betrayed the other, in some small or not-so-small way. Given that certitude, both partners *must be able to forgive each other*, no matter who said what or who did what, if the marriage is to last. Wife and husband must learn to let go after being hurt or wronged, whether the transgression is as minor as forgetting a birthday or criticizing a Thanksgiving dinner or as major as lying or cheating. To get through such a crisis, wives and husbands have to fight their impulse to feel righteous indignation and to retaliate in anger. Indeed, if a wife feels benevolent toward her husband, even after being wronged, then the marriage will be stronger and more resilient, according to psychologists who've studied forgiveness. Likewise, the husband must not withdraw into anger if he is to help resolve the couple's conflict. Most of the time, these psychologists say, wives are the ones who confront a wrong or a hurtful incident head-on, while husbands tend to avoid and duck, like a boxer desperately trying to dodge a knockout punch. If couples wish to overcome their problems, though, they have to head off the husband's creative evasions before it's too late.[2] They need to persuade him to stay and to confront and to forgive.

It helps in situations like these, of course, if at least one partner is a forgiver. It's relatively easy to figure out if you are the one most likely to forgive. Think of something your partner did during the past year or so, an incident in which you felt hurt or wronged, and then calculate how badly you were hurt, from a very little pinch of pain to the deepest injury you have ever experienced. Make sure that the hurt you're thinking of was significant enough that it still stings. Now try to recall how you responded to that injury. When my partner wronged me:

- I accepted my partner's flaws and failures as part of being human.
- I took the first step toward making up with my partner.
- I thought of several ways to get even.
- I wanted to make my partner regret what s/he did.

How much do you agree or disagree with each of these statements? You're a forgiver if you strongly agree with the first two statements and strongly disagree with the last two.[3] If you are truly a forgiver, your marriage has potential for success and long life. If not, then you may need to take some lessons in forgiveness. Learn from a fifty-year-old nonsuperior wife from Los Angeles, California, who is a true forgiver. Just thirty days after she found out that her husband, a powerful chief executive at a major entertainment company, had been having a yearlong affair, she was ready to forgive him. Since then, "we have been making love every day. I am trying to be kind and loving, and I am always calling him 'honey' and 'darling,'" she says. "I am not getting mad at him, and we are going to counseling." Her ability to forgive was boosted by her fear of wrecking the marriage and losing her husband in the process, she adds.

Forgiving a deed as terrible as infidelity is not easy, but it is crucial to preserving the marriage. So is *the ability to inject novelty and excitement* into marriage, no matter how many hours or days or years a couple has been together. This doesn't mean that they have to spend "quality time" together or that they have to "communicate," a piece of jargon so overused that it has almost no meaning. It means, rather, that couples who are able to make their lives feel new and first-time-ish tend to have the best marriages, researchers say. This doesn't mean that the wife and the husband go off and have sex with strangers, as in some bad 1970s movie about swingers. It's actually much simpler than that. To inject novelty into a marriage means that you go out to eat in a different restaurant every so often, or you do something you've never done, like see a play or attend a country music concert, take a ballroom dancing lesson or play a round of golf. The key is to reignite the love sparks by increasing the flow of brain chemicals that respond to novelty, which are the same ones that engage love hormones.[4] Newer is sexier, as far as the human brain is concerned.

It's practically a cliché by now, but *it's not whether a couple fights, it's how they fight that matters.* It's a near impossibility for two people always to agree about everything, unless one is of them is either a liar or a clone of the other one, so it's a given that couples will argue on occasion. Arguing can even be good for a marriage, because it helps to clear the air and fosters new approaches to problems. Happily married couples do get angry and they argue and disagree, but they don't withdraw or give up during those fights, marriage researchers say. Husbands are more likely than wives to withdraw, but the more often either partner refuses to engage, the greater the odds that the marriage will end in divorce. Men are generally more defensive and prefer to keep their emotions on an even keel, so when their wives confront them about problems, they tend to curl up into their own fortress of solitude, refusing to enter any kind of discussion, which further infuriates the troubled wife.[5] If this pattern persists, and if it recurs often enough, experts say, the couple will be extremely likely to divorce after the first seven years of marriage.[6]

Nevertheless, getting angry isn't necessarily bad for marriage, as long as the couple breaks the tension with jokes and distractions and the easing away of hurtful comments. Couples who are happily married make sure that their *angry and negative expressions are outweighed by positive and loving comments.* Successful marriages include negative feelings, but these are almost always counterbalanced by five times as many positive ones. Happily married couples yell and scream; they get annoyed and become contemptuous and defensive. But they also touch and smile and compliment each other, and they laugh together five times as often as they berate and curse.[7] They don't consciously keep their loving-to-angry ratio at five to one, of course. It's just that they have an intuitive sense about the importance of balancing negative with positive, bad with good, hurtful with loving.

Finally, couples are most likely to fight and get angry about one topic more than all others combined. They argue about their in-laws; they clash over the children; they disagree about what to watch on television and where to go on vacation and what kind of car to drive. But most of all, *couples clash over money.* There's something about finances and budgeting and credit card spending that's like a marital red flag: it incites wives and husbands to become raging bulls. When couples battle over money, they are especially likely to be negative and combative and to engage in the confront-and-withdraw dance that can be so harmful to marriage. Perhaps it's the power and privilege and control that money represents that makes many wives and husbands lose their minds a little bit. This is especially true, by the way, among those in a first marriage, who are more likely than remarried couples to engage in money fights. Couples in second marriages end up fighting more often about children than they do about money, researchers say. (Probably because such wives and husbands tend to be financially independent but often have to deal with unrelated sets of children.) When couples fight about money a lot, with no holds barred, many also begin to fantasize about divorce, researchers say.[8] So it's a good idea to keep your financial fights in check if you want to preserve your marriage.

Twenty-one Ways to Fix
a Superior Wife Marriage

It's clear that if a marriage includes a superior wife, it will probably not be a particularly good one, though there are occasional exceptions. Superior wives with absentee husbands might consider themselves happily married, especially if their partner is serving in the military, travels often, or is seriously ill or permanently disabled. Such women have no choice but to be superior, since they are in a kind of one-person marriage, through no choice of their own.

For most superior wives, however, ridding themselves of some or most of their superiority will greatly improve their marriage, from their own point of view and from their husband's as well. Simply put, a superior wife must reboot her marriage; she has to hit the restart button on it.

Obviously, this is a lot easier to say than to do. It is especially exasperating for a superior wife, since she can't initiate any marital change without the express cooperation of her husband. If she doesn't have that, she might as well be trying to use a computer while the power is off or to talk on a cell phone in a dead zone. For a wife to transform a wife-dominant, wife-supreme marriage into one that more closely resembles a partnership of equals, she's got to enlist her husband in the program. This rehabilitation plan has the potential to turn into a disastrous mess, since many husbands tend to be resistant to change or to confrontation of any kind. This male tendency is so predictable that many marriage experts call it *demand and withdraw*, a shorthand reference for what happens when wives try to change their husband's behavior. She requests change, he yanks himself out of the discussion and then out of the room. She becomes frosty and resentful, and nothing is resolved. This is the dynamic duo of demand and withdraw, which might also be termed *nag and run* or *plea and flee*. Whatever it's called, the routine occurs because wives are usually the ones trying to fix what's wrong with the relationship, while husbands are the ones cowering in fear at the prospect of an emotional upheaval. Even worse, wife-demand and husband-withdraw is *most* likely to occur when the wife is unhappy about her husband's contribution to housework, because he wants everything to stay just as it is and she doesn't.[9] She believes in the possibility of negotiation and compromise; he believes in the power and beauty of the status quo. And so they arrive at an unwinnable stalemate.

Although discouraging, this is not a deal breaker for superior wives who yearn for change, since plea and flee can be overcome. Most couples do the plea-and-flee dance at least occasionally, experts say, and it's not always detrimental to marriage. Researchers find that traditional couples may be a bit more rigid when they become wrapped up in a demand-and-withdraw scenario, and their marriage can suffer for it if they don't figure out a way to avoid hurting each other. Partners in egalitarian relationships, though, tend to be more flexible and more understanding of each other's positions.[10] Such couples are therefore less likely to get locked into a situation in which she's screaming that he should show more affection and he's running out the door to mow the lawn.

But fixing a superior wife marriage goes far beyond dealing with various types of wifely pleas and husbandly withdrawals. It's not a simple parlor trick, like getting a puppy to roll over or teaching a two-year-old to sing "The Star-Spangled Banner." Fixing a superior wife marriage requires a major change in the husband's approach to marriage and to life and an alteration in the way a superior wife looks at her world and her family. This change will not happen overnight either, since a profound transformation such as this takes time. You can't have a superior wife marriage one week and a perfect nonsuperior wife marriage the next. The transformation, if it happens at all, will be a gradual process, one that requires a slowly developing sharing of power and responsibility and family management.

Your task in undoing your superiority, should you choose to accept it, is to take a few small steps toward moving your marriage forward, onto a more equal, less gender-biased path. This kind of equality in marriage is hard to find, difficult to maintain, and easy to take for granted once established. It may even be tricky to recognize. There are many wives and husbands, in fact, who delude themselves into believing that they've got an equal relationship without a superior wife when they have nothing of the sort. Using denial and rationalizing, evading and pretending, they end up convinced that they have a fairy-tale perfect, politically correct, egalitarian union.[11] Such couples disguise their adherence to traditional gender roles by saying that the only reason she does so much is that she's better at cooking and doing housework than he is, but that they really share everything and she's not superior. Or that he's better with facts and figures, which is the reason he makes all of the financial decisions, but that otherwise they share everything and she's not superior. Or that he has the longer commute or works a few more hours a week, so he should do less at home, although they share everything and she's not superior. Couples use many complicated, self-deluding strategies to avoid looking their superior wife marriage reality in the eye and seeing it for what it really is: grossly and dramatically unfair to the wife.

Lynn succumbed to this faulty logic years ago, so she sincerely believes her own lies when she claims, "I'm lucky to have a very egalitarian marriage, with a husband who is a wonderful friend." Now fifty-two, Lynn is married to an endocrinologist and lives in Spring Valley, New York. She is a self-proclaimed superior wife, yet she also insists on maintaining that "we work as a team. I'm the one who keeps the calendar, organizes family events, shops for food, cooks, and makes the holidays. I take charge of everything around the house, like decorating and gardening and cleaning, even though I work. My husband handles the finances, since I have no head for numbers, and sometimes he fixes things," she concludes, not understanding that her marriage is as far from egalitarian and nonsuperior as could be.

Like so many other superior wives, Lynn needs to work on curing her superiority, but first she needs to acknowledge it. The reluctance to do so is what prevents so many superior wives from improving their marriage and their lives and themselves. Such women refuse to see themselves as doing more, knowing more, owning more of what it takes to be a mature and high-functioning member of a modern family. Sometimes they don't recognize their superiority until the children leave home and they find themselves living with a man who is incapable of caring for himself. Or it's only when they are bedridden, with colitis or cancer or a broken ankle, that they realize that there's nobody else who can run the household. Or it's not until they write everything down, while taking a Web survey such as mine, that they see in black and white how much they do for their family, as several wives have told me. It's sad to say, but most couples "fall into unequal relationship patterns without their conscious intention or awareness," as several family therapists put it.[12]

Most superior wives, I believe, need a wake-up call to their own superiority. And then they need to wake up their husbands too. Admitting superiority is not easy, so once again, here are the six signs of superiority. Ask yourself this: are you the one in your marriage who

1. can do more than one thing at a time?
2. organizes and plans most family events and schedules?
3. makes most of the family decisions?
4. is the most efficient person in the marriage?
5. shows the most support and affection to family and friends?
6. is likely to sacrifice his/her own needs for others in the family?

If you answered yes to five or six of these, you are probably a superior wife, whether you know it or not. It will be difficult to cure yourself of the problem, though it is eminently possible. To do so, you will have to work first on your husband, then on yourself, and then on both of you, as a team. I've therefore arranged the following twenty-one suggestions for banishing wifely superiority into three groups: the his, the hers, and the theirs. Think of these groups as if they were items on a Chinese restaurant menu; you can pick and choose as many as you want, as long as you try several. It's possible that if your husband is already amenable and you are acutely aware of your superiority problem, you can skip right to the final section of this chapter. Otherwise, you'll have to focus on your husband, and then on yourself, before you attempt to make your partnership less reliant on your own superiority.

Rebooting the husband. It's not completely the husband's fault if his wife is superior, so there's no point in blaming him, although the blame game can be entertaining. As in, he's a grown man, and he can't figure out how to bake cookies? From refrigerated cookie dough? As in, he's a grown man, and he can't have a heart-to-heart talk with his teenage son about birth control? As in, he doesn't notice when the kitchen ceiling is falling down, or when the dishes are dirty, or when the dog has pooped on the rug? As in, he doesn't realize that his wife does everything? Wives may forgive husbands, in advance, for not having the insight to recognize the superior wife trajectory their marriage has taken, since they themselves may also have refused to acknowledge it. But once wives notice the situation, they are obligated to enlighten their husband and to ask for his help in rectifying the situation.

Here are seven ways for a wife to convince her husband of the merits of her case for ridding herself of superiority.

1. Just ask. If it's true that many wives are oblivious to their own superiority, then it is doubly true that husbands are as well. Even when wives admit to their superior state, they must share that information, since their husband is probably not psychic. "When we were first married, I expected my husband to anticipate what I wanted and then to do it. I quickly came to realize that men need to be told bluntly, because they are not mind readers and they can't even take a loud and clear hint," says a twenty-nine-year-old nonsuperior wife from Utah. "Now I make sure that if I want my husband to do something, I'm very clear about what I am asking him to do." She's quite typical, since the number one method that wives use to persuade their husbands to do something is to ask. Many say that they make a point not to bellyache or to plead but simply to ask, wary of crossing the line into nagging. "If I were to whine or beg or ask meanly, my husband would not cooperate," says Holly, a thirty-year-old nonsuperior wife with a Team Player husband from Connecticut. "Because I am respectful of him, he's willing to do things for me." She is wary, because he's afraid of any expression of anger. "If I start to raise my voice, or yell, he just shuts down and tunes me out." As a result, when she's negotiating with him for any kind of change, large or small, "I ask calmly and evenly, in a low tone of voice," Holly says, noting that she trains her husband to behave as if she were dealing with a skittish puppy.

Superior wives who want relief from that condition will, first and foremost, have to *ask their husband for assistance.* The shortest distance between two points is a straight line, so it can't hurt to try to get to the heart of the problem by asking for his help to begin a new way of thinking and behaving. If wives want to be like Holly, they'll have to ask with great tact and skill, using their knowledge of their husband's anxieties and quirks to figure out the best way to do so. Get your husband used to responding to small requests and gentle favors first, so that he will be ready for the big, whopping demand of helping to cure your superiority. A twenty-six-year-old wife from Oregon struggled for a while with her need to be self-sufficient and a reluctance to ask her husband for anything. Gradually, though, she understood that she was doing a disservice to herself and to her husband by being afraid to "inconvenience each other," as she put it. "One day I was really tired from work, and I didn't want to ride my bike home. I called my husband, but I couldn't get out the words to ask for his help. Finally, I blurted out, 'I'm so tired, and I'm so hungry.' Then I got up the nerve and asked outright, 'Can you come and pick me up?' He just said, 'Sure, what time?' It was that simple," she recalls, still somewhat amazed. "Ever since then, we've been working on asking for our needs to be met in simple ways, like me bringing him a cup of coffee or him carrying something downstairs for me. It's been great for our understanding of each other," she says. It also broke her slow drift into superiority, which she and her partner no longer permit.

Another wife, trying to work her way out of superiority, says that she sits her husband down every so often, "and I tell him why something is important to me, and then I ask him to be my equal partner." It works every time, she adds.

So remember, if you don't ask, you don't get.

2. Use logic. Many wives learn through experience that their husband responds best to logic and reason. Men are willing to alter their thinking and their behavior if they can view a spreadsheet or look at a PowerPoint presentation, something that includes lists and details, charts and graphs. They want an emotion-free tutorial that is not accusatory or demanding but factual and well thought out. Don't get caught up in your own feelings of desperation and injustice and anger, since he probably won't respond to your emotional anguish as easily as he will to cool reason and common sense. Of course, only you know if your husband would be most comfortable with this method. If so, then by all means use it. Present the costs to him of not changing, as discovered by family therapists who say that husbands in unequal partnerships—or those with superior wives—tend to be less open, they lose a sense of intimacy, they're unhappy with their marriage, and they have lousy sex lives. In addition, their wives tend to be hostile and depressed and to suffer from low self-esteem.[13] Who wouldn't want to fix a marriage like that? It's obviously not a happy one, and you don't need a spreadsheet to figure that out.

Among traditional couples who deliberately try to transform themselves into equal sharers, both partners become highly sensitized to what's fair and what's not, psychologists find. In marriages like these, that begin on a traditional path, the wife is often the one who initiates change, in an attempt to make the marriage more evenly balanced and to turn it into what the researchers call a *postgender marriage*. One such wife did so by designing elaborate schedules for every member of her five-person family, with chores like cooking and cleaning and driving planned for every minute of every day of the week. Among such couples, wives and husbands stop comparing what the wife does to what other wives do, or what the husband does to what other husbands do; instead, they begin to compare themselves *to each other*, a much fairer and much more gender-neutral type of evaluation.[14]

I found a few postgender wives in my Web survey, including a former superior wife who says she uses Post-its on the refrigerator, on the bathroom mirror, on the bedroom door, and wherever else she thinks her husband will see them, as reminders of what he needs to do. Another considers lists part of her "arsenal," because they are "doable and concrete, and I never ask my husband to do things that I know he can't," says a forty-six-year-old New York wife. "My husband hates nothing more than criticism, so if I want him to be a more equal partner, I cannot tell him he's doing a bad job as a husband. I have to show him a list, comparing my duties to his, so he'll see that we are really out of balance. And I do it over and over again, week after week, because I am a pit bull when it comes to what really matters to me," she says.

A sixty-one-year-old husband from Missouri confesses that his wife's logical and organized requests really did work on him. "We moved to a larger home, and my wife informed me that she would no longer be doing all of the housework herself. She typed a list on the computer of what she does and what I do, and I could see the huge difference. So I asked her what she likes to do least, and she said, 'Clean the bathrooms.' I said, right away, 'Okay, that's my job. What else?' She was flabbergasted that it was so easy," he says, laughing at the memory of his wife's utter surprise at his willingness to cooperate.

3. **Consider sexual bribery.** It sounds low down, dirty, and downright mean, but plenty of wives confess that when it comes to persuading their husband to do something, there's nothing that works better than a little sexual bribery. I am not suggesting that you use this method on a regular basis, turning yourself into a sexual harpy. Instead, I mention it as a kickoff technique; use it once or twice, right from the start, so that you get your husband's attention and so that he understands how serious you are about

your new, antisuperior stance. Variations on this type of persuasion include offers of massages, back rubs, and foot rubs. In my Web survey, sex is the second most common method of husbandly persuasion. Wives use sex as a carrot by offering to initiate it, to do it, to give it orally, or to give it at some future date, with the use of what one wife calls "sex coupons." They also use sex as a stick by threatening to withhold it. Several women refer to this as using "womanly wiles, which makes it easy to ask for help when he's at his weakest," according to a forty-six-year-old wife and mother of five from Folsom, California. "A man who's happy in the bedroom is more likely to consider helping in the kitchen," she observes. And using sex on this kind of hubby is somewhat like using Kryptonite on Superman: it may not be kind, but it is certainly effective, as long as it is used wisely and sparingly.

A twenty-five-year-old wife from Mississippi calls herself "a big proponent of bribery," probably since it's so effective when she uses it on her three-year-old son. "But my husband has begun to catch on to that fact, and he slightly resents it. Still, I always try offering sex or some material thing he may want, to get him to cooperate," she concludes. Because so many husbands want more sex more than anything else, this method can be quite effective, husbands agree. A forty-one-year-old husband from South Carolina is not ashamed to admit that he willingly gives in when his wife "bribes me with sex, because that's what I want."

Using sex as a bargaining tool will go only so far, however. It's a useful method in the short term—for convincing a husband to cook dinner on Thursday nights, say, or to spend more time with the children on Saturday afternoons—but it will probably not be effective in the long term. Persuading your husband that your superiority is bad for you both will take more than sexual promises and payoffs. Still, you might mention the scientific research that shows that the more the husband does around the house and the more concerned he is about fairness, the better the couple's sex life.[15] Some wives refer to the sexual allure in a man's cooperation as "choreplay," but whatever you call it, it's highly effective. Still, you're not just hoping to get him to do a little bit of this and that around the house; you're trying to get him to view everything as his responsibility as much as it is yours.

4. **Resign your duties.** Though it can be voluntary, many superior wives can't face this option until they have no other choice. When they get sick, for instance, their husband has to relieve them of their superiority if the

family is to function. Norma, now sixty-one, had always been a superior wife while raising four sons and working full-time as a sales manager at a Kansas City food company. But five years ago she had a heart attack, followed by a stroke and a brain tumor. "My husband picked up the slack and basically started to do everything, because I just couldn't," she confesses. Now that she's somewhat recovered, though, her husband "still does most everything," Norma says, "because he enjoys it. He does all of the laundry, and he'll reload the dishwasher if I try to do it, because he says I don't do it right." She laughs at the idea that her own husband is more of a superior wife than she is. She was happy that he helped her out when she was so sick, and she admits that "I was surprised, because I really didn't expect him to be able to do all that." It was not how she would have chosen to cure her superiority, Norma says, but now that it's happened, she would never wish it undone.

A forty-eight-year-old wife in Atlanta says that when she was diagnosed with breast cancer, her husband became the superior member of their union. Later, when he broke his leg, she began to take over again. Ever since then, they've achieved a balance, she says, both taking "equal responsibility," which came in handy when their ten-year-old twins were bedridden with meningitis. It was all this adversity, she believes, that allowed her to give up her superior status on a permanent basis.

A financial crisis can also spur a husband into alleviating his wife's superiority, especially if he loses his job and she becomes the sole breadwinner. Though some wives might bend over backward so as not to "emasculate" an unemployed husband, others decide to seize the moment and relinquish their superiority. "I love my work, although I would rather not have to deal with pumping milk every two hours, but my husband was downsized, so he's the one who stays at home," says a former superior wife from Mountain View, California, who is now her family's sole breadwinner. "My husband organizes and maintains our lives, and if I plan a menu, he will shop and cook. I'm also in control of the finances, because he's forgetful and he doesn't pay bills on time, but he's totally in charge of our two children. He plans their activities, feeds them, clothes them, and takes them to school, since I can't control any of this from my office," she adds. When they were both working, she was a superior wife, but now that she's the one who's out of the house all day, her husband has taken on almost all her chores and responsibilities. And she's somewhat amazed and amused, she says, by how good at them he's become.

A fifty-two-year-old wife from Cambridge, Massachusetts, has achieved the same result by going back to get a master's degree and being gone most weeknights and one full weekend every month. "My husband assumed all of the household duties without a whimper," she says. "He saw it as a chance to get closer to his children, because it was just the three of them, and they got more bonded than when I was around." Now that she's back to work, they've agreed on a new way of life, one in which both of them do a little of everything and neither one is superior.

5. **Apply peer pressure.** Nonsuperior wives are relatively rare, so it's not as if a superior wife can look to a neighbor or a cousin or a best friend as an example of how marriage should be. There just aren't enough nonsuperior wife role models to go around. Still, some wives try to prod their husbands into being more supportive by getting friends to point out how exploitive he is, how unappreciative, how just plain wrong. "If I really want my husband to do more around the house, I get our good friends to ask him, since he never says no to them," says a forty-three-year-old Iowa wife. She's not proud of exerting peer pressure, but her husband seems to be able to judge his behavior more objectively and rationally when he sees it from a point of view that's not hers.

Other wives say they use this tactic to induce guilt, a time-tested method of moms worldwide. While it may not be successful in the long term, well-placed guilt can be a strong catalyst for change, just enough to nudge a husband out of his complacency. "I'm ashamed to admit it, but I use guilt a lot, as a reminder of how he would feel if he were in my shoes," says a thirty-eight-year-old struggling superior wife from Davis, California. "That usually works, though I realize he's more likely to want to please me if I make him feel good. So I always temper the guilt with jokes and kisses and compliments," she says, adding that "I keep a little stash of guilt in my back pocket, just in case."

6. **Set the example.** A few wives are aware that the best way to get is to give; the best way to be pleased is to please. It's a form of modeling, imitating the behavior you want to inspire. "Farmers plant the seeds of the crop they want to reap," says a fifty-two-year-old nonsuperior wife from Hot Springs, Arkansas. "And the same method works in our marriage. When I

want more attention, I give more attention. When I want more cooperation, I give more cooperation," she says, noting that this is her second marriage, one that she entered with the unwavering intention of *not* being the one in the driver's seat.

A fifty-year-old-wife from Moravia, Iowa, recalls that "my husband and I both realized that pleasing the other person is a way of pleasing ourselves and that cooperation is the only thing that will make our marriage work, especially with five children at home. When my husband came back from the first Gulf War, he realized that it was only fair to do as much as I did, since both of us were working a full day. It was only by leaving home and contributing nothing that my husband figured out how much he had missed us and how much more he should be doing," she says, adding that it was in this way that their marriage grew into a "true partnership."

Another mother of five, this one from Kingwood, Texas, says that hers is a "democratic marriage" because they share just about all the responsibility. She achieved this, she says, by using clever tactics, such as "asking my husband to show me how to do a job that he'd normally do. He doesn't want me to show him up, so he ends up doing it. But we always balance each other. No husband or wife wants to be led around like an animal on a leash, always being told what to do, and I think you'd lose yourself if you let your spouse make all of the decisions," she comments, adding that this never happens in her family.

7. Get mad. This is a method of last resort, to use only when all else fails, and only on a husband who can take the heat. That's because anger can spin out of control if it's not rationed carefully. To convince a husband of the benefits of nonsuperiority, apply tempered anger, as if you were a farmer starting a small fire to replenish a crop field. But be careful, since wives who vent their anger can end up feeling even angrier unless they have a sympathetic listener who gives them encouragement and support. Obviously, anger will work only on a husband who is not intimidated by frank or harsh emotionalism, which excludes many men. Still, anger can be the catalyst that inspires action and a deeper understanding of a wife's frustration. Marriage experts agree that a wife's anger can be helpful, but *only if* her husband respects and understands her feelings. For this reason, counselors sometimes advise husbands to "embrace" their wife's anger by trying to figure out what's really upsetting her. Husbands should not view this rage as hormonal bitchiness or female demonic behavior but only as a sign of a desperation that needs to be assuaged, they say.[16] That too is very much easier said than done.

A forty-five-year-old California wife, an employee of the state's Department of Mental Health, is constantly getting angry so that she can renegotiate the terms of her third marriage. "We both go through an angry phase, which always includes a 'f——you' and a 'f——you too,' which I imagine most couples don't do," she confesses. She's embarrassed to admit to these episodes of marital rage, but it's the only way her husband will comprehend the depth of her feelings, she claims. Another mental health worker, this one a counselor from Lewisburg, Pennsylvania, says that she uses her temper to get what she wants because it's the only way she can convince her husband that having a true partnership is best for their marriage and their family. So she yells and cries and grits her teeth, and eventually he understands how upset she really is. Finally, a woman who's worked hard to maintain her nonsuperior wife marriage says that she doesn't ever use harsh words or pleading or yelling when she gets angry. Instead she gives him what she calls "the Look," because "that's when he knows I mean business. The Look seems to strike enough fear in his heart to get it done!"

Reconfiguring the wife. It's not just the husband who has to see the error of his ways in order to cure his wife of her superiority. Wives too must recognize the symptoms of their own superiority and realize that it indicates a serious and chronic marital disease. Then they have to be willing to fight it off. Here are seven ways for wives to do just that.

1. **Be less than you can be.** This modified United States Army motto sums up what a superior wife must do to cure herself. She must be less, do less, think less, worry less. She needs to learn to limit her proficiency at all things domestic and family if she wants her husband to take on a fair share of the work. The fact that she may be better at doing the cooking and the housework and the child care doesn't mean that she should be doing it all. Indeed, if she seesaws down by doing less, then her husband must seesaw up by doing more. To accomplish this, wives need to adopt the as-if philosophy that I mentioned earlier. They need to act *as if they can't* do the dishes at night, *as if they can't* drive the children to practice, *as if they can't* do all the grocery shopping after work. So many wives are tempted to prove

their femininity, and their power, by being über-wives, even when they work full-time, that they lose sight of the toll this behavior takes on them, on their husband, and on their marriage. And make no mistake, it takes a heavy toll. Although some wives may claim to feel exhilarated by doing so much for so many so often, superior wives harm themselves and their marriage with their insistence on being ultracompetent. For them, being less is truly being more.

2. **Silence your inner critic.** Many superior wives maintain an all-day-long internal monologue about how moronic, how inept, how insanely incompetent their husband is. This seems to justify their need to do everything, because they are so much better at just about everything than he is. Superior wives often wonder how they managed to marry such an idiot, castigating themselves for not having predicted their husband's monumental and inevitable ineptitude. And though this idea may contain a kernel of truth, it can only further solidify their superiority, the exact opposite of what a superior wife should be hoping to achieve. For this reason, superior wives need to squelch that inner critic and to stifle that criticism, since it will almost certainly become a self-fulfilling prophecy. If you constantly remind yourself how inept he is, you will always take over and never give him a chance to care for children or do chores or make efficient choices. As a result, he will get no practice doing such things and will become even less skilled. Then you will criticize him for being so hopeless. It's an infinite loop and one that almost guarantees a husband's endless failures and a wife's endless superiority.

Instead, refuse to listen to your own inner criticisms. They are your thoughts, after all, and you control them, so just say no to disparagement. If you learn to tamp down the monologue of censure that you focus on your husband, you'll be less likely to succumb to the feelings of frustration and anger and resentment that it inspires. Try to replace that inner discourse with a feeling of *hopefulness* about the possibility of teaching your husband how to do what you do, like sorting the laundry or preparing a spaghetti dinner. Teach him, let him do it on his own, and then let it go. Allow him to do it his way, right or wrong, good or bad. Don't follow up with continued criticism; instead, think optimistic thoughts about how quickly he learns and how much better he'll get at it, with time. Consider this a parallel to the idea that if you force yourself to smile, you'll feel happy.

Psychologists find that if they tell a woman to smile, she'll feel suddenly happier, since the act of smiling itself can induce happiness.[17] Likewise, any small token of cooperation from your husband will make you feel that much less superior. It's also probably true, by the way, that the less often you *think* critical thoughts, the less often you'll *voice them out loud* and the less critical you will feel. And that's a good thing, because there's evidence that the best marriages are those in which the wife rarely expresses negative emotions to her husband, like aggression, alienation, defensiveness, contempt, and yes, criticism.[18]

Finally, try to interpret the hidden meaning of your criticism. If he barely lifts a finger to prepare a meal or to clean up after dinner, are you critical because you wish the two of you could go out more often? Or do you wish that he'd work alongside you in the kitchen, the way he used to do when you were dating? If he seems to ignore the children, do you long for him to be close to them in the way you were with your father, or rather in the way your best friend's husband is with theirs? Look at the layers of meaning underneath your criticism to discover what it is that you really want from your husband.

3. Be kind, don't mind. A corollary to quieting your spousal disapproval is to relax your standards of household cleanliness and efficiency, just a notch. Or maybe even two notches. I'm not saying that it's okay to live with filthy toilets or dust balls the size of large cats, only that you will have to reach some kind of compromise with your husband about what's acceptable. You will also need to understand that your way of doing things is not necessarily the only correct or appropriate way. This means ridding yourself of defensiveness, as well as the kind of self-righteousness that ensures the continuation of your own sense of superiority. A twenty-eight-year-old wife from Fort Worth, Texas, had to conduct a defensiveness-removal operation on herself after she was hit with chronic fatigue syndrome and was forced to rely on her husband to do more and more of what she could not do herself. "I've learned to let some things go and not to remind him every five minutes about what he needs to do," she says. "I try to do nonconfrontational reminders and to keep negative emotions out of what I'm saying, by being calm and gentle instead." Her illness meant that she had no choice but to let go, to learn to not mind so much if her husband wanted to do things his own way.

A twenty-seven-year-old Canadian wife relaxed her defenses completely, she says, after she realized that "I used to be concerned with keeping score about who was doing what and how well we were doing it, so my husband wouldn't take advantage of me. These days I've come to see that it doesn't really matter how I do something or how he does something else, just as long as we're working together as a team. Now I'm filled with joy when I focus on sharing with him, instead of bossing over him."

4. **Expand your friendships.** One of the best ways to reduce pressure on a marriage is to rely on it less, like taking the lid off a pot so the boiling water won't overflow. Superior wives who have difficulty feeling close to their husband will suffer more if they have nowhere else to turn. Their superiority problem is compounded if that relationship is the only one on which they can rely, if it's their only intimate bond, because it's not really all that intimate. Married couples are much better off, both happier and healthier, if they have at least two really close ties, and not necessarily with a spouse, according to a recent study by psychologists in Michigan. "For people with a best friend," they conclude, "having a high quality relationship with a spouse is not necessary for psychological well-being."[19] Superior wives must therefore look outside their marriage for closeness, while also trying to repair the marital bond. If they can find at least one other intimate tie, that will serve as a model for the one they could and should have at home. A twenty-seven-year-old wife from Atlanta, Georgia, has come to realize that this is exactly what she's missing. "We rarely go out, and we make the ultimate sacrifice because we have no friends," she says. She knows this is bad for her and for her marriage, which is why she adds that "I am working on changing it."

5. **Focus on work.** Most wives consider their marriage to be the most important part of their lives—the heart of how they view themselves and the core of what makes them happy or miserable. But they also need to focus on other parts of life, on paid work or on a cause or on a tennis game, or whatever else they have that gives their lives a sense of meaning and purpose, *apart from marriage.* Successful families are those that include two partners who both derive meaning from their work, according to a study of happily married couples with children and jobs. These well-adjusted couples enjoy their work because it gives them energy and enthusiasm, as well as pride in being able to earn a living for their family, but they are also

careful to maintain boundaries around their work, believing that family is their highest priority.[20] Thus, while it's important to keep work in perspective, it's still an essential part of who you are and how you view yourself. Traditional wives have no such option, of course, since they don't work for pay. But they can find meaning in unpaid work, by volunteering at a church or a day care center, at a hospital or a library, at a soup kitchen or a shelter for battered wives. There are endless opportunities for at-home wives who would like to devote themselves to the doing of good deeds. This alone won't cure them of their superiority, of course, but it will help distract them from superiority sorrow.

6. **Develop manly skills.** If you want your husband to do more of what you do, then try to do more of what he does. Make a point to switch gender roles as a therapeutic exercise, for a few hours or days or weeks, if possible. You can be the one who mows the lawn or takes the car in for an oil change; he can do the planning and shopping for all the meals and drive the children on weekends. Because you expect him to make drastic and uncomfortable changes in his life, show him that you're willing to do the same. It's somewhat like switching seats at the kitchen table. In most families, everybody tends to sit in the same place for every meal, so if you and your children all sit in different chairs, it can feel weird and uncomfortable. This is just a small preview of the way the husband of a superior wife may feel when he starts doing all the things his wife used to do for him. To prevent his perplexity from turning into outright rebellion—as in "I won't do it, I can't do it"—prove that you're willing to make a few equally distressing personal changes. A Michigan husband says that his wife sometimes takes over his coaching job for their son's soccer team when he's out of town, a gesture he appreciates. She also goes duck hunting with him, as a token of love, although she despises it as an overly macho activity. Because she's willing to step out of her normal gender duties, he says, he's willing to do the dishes every night and launder the sheets and towels every week.

7. **Contemplate insurrection.** Extreme measures are necessary sometimes, especially if a superior wife feels that she's not making any progress in her plan to desuperiorize herself. Waging a small rebellion is a measure of last resort, one that might be appropriate for a superior wife who's made several attempts to change her husband or herself, without success. If that's

the case, you may need to announce consequences for noncooperation. If you truly want to reduce your superiority, your husband must understand how important this is to you. He will need to know that you are not just talking the talk but planning to walk the walk. You will need to issue an ultimatum or two and promise unpleasant outcomes for noncooperation. Tell him that you will stop doing the laundry, that you will no longer buy his favorite beer or soda, that you will go out with friends on Wednesdays without preparing dinner in advance. You will need to provide specifics for what he needs to do to get out of the doghouse, with clear-cut instructions. You'll take him back into your affections after he does the dishes every night for a week; you'll buy the beer after he has figured out how to pay three of the monthly bills and done so. This tactic requires a degree of relentlessness and dispassion, so be prepared. But make sure he understands that it's a sign of your desperation.

Several former superior wives say they made the ultimate threat, to walk away from the marriage, unless their husband cooperated by making significant marital changes. "I realized that I had to do something drastic to catch my husband's attention, so he'd know that he had to show some respect for my feelings," says a forty-eight-year-old former superior wife from Albany, New York. "I'm not an aggressive person normally, but I had to tell him if he didn't shape up, I'd leave him. And he finally got the message." A twenty-seven-year-old wife from Fort Worth, Texas, says that it became clear to her a year after she married that her husband was "outright lazy. We both work forty hours a week, but that's all he does, while I do everything at home." While she doesn't really want to be a single mother, she has threatened to leave, adding that "when I get really fed up, my husband swears he will change." So far, she's made the threat twice, and it has worked in the short term but not for the long haul. At this point, she says, she's considering a trial separation, just to prove how serious she is. A California wife also uses the I'm-leaving-you threat, but she combines it with a weeklong silent treatment. "It's working now, and he's a bit more affectionate," she says, but she realizes that ridding herself of superiority will be a slow process, like fighting a jungle war in monsoon season.

Restarting the marriage. After you've worked on your husband and on yourself, it's time to work on your marriage. Think of it as joint repair work, an effort that will require substantial planning and insight, as well as considerable cooperation and compromise.

1. Ignore the bad. The basic premise of behavioral psychology is that you should ignore behavior that you don't want to see repeated. If your toddler whines and complains for attention, for instance, you are supposed to ignore him until he stops. If you scold him or hit him or try to explain to him why whining is not what big boys do, you are rewarding his behavior and encouraging future crying and moaning and groaning. If your dog barks for treats, you are supposed to ignore her, so she doesn't learn that barking gets her what she wants. And if your husband insists on clutching the remote and staring at the television all night, resist the urge to nag or to criticize him. Instead, try to ignore him. This will, of course, be quite difficult to do. But if you pair it with the next tip, it's almost guaranteed to change his behavior. This method applies to any behavior that fuels your superiority by entrenching his position as the least efficient, least organized, and least helpful member of your marriage. Be strong: you can prevail!

2. Reward the good. Along with ignoring your husband's bad behavior, it's crucial that you reward him for doing well. Every time your husband washes a dish, reads a bedtime story, does the grocery shopping, plans a vacation, or asks if you need any help, shower him with praise and affection and gratitude. The idea is to reward the behavior you want to encourage, the same method that trainers use to teach seals and dolphins to do tricks. In that situation, trainers ignore unwanted behavior and reward correct behavior until they are able to shape the animals' natural tendency to do flips and tail slaps. Eventually, those actions become the hoop-diving and ball-balancing tricks you see at the aquarium. Likewise, a human male does, on occasion, perform an act that merits a reward. When you see him picking up a pair of dirty pants from the floor, give him coos and kisses. When you see him making a shopping list, thank him profusely. When he decides to organize the front closet, tell him he's a great guy. But when he's watching ESPN while you're preparing dinner, ignore him completely.[21] This may require nerves of steel on your part, but eventually his behavior will change. At that point you'll be ready to work on changing his attitude by convincing him that keeping you as a superior wife is not to his benefit. You'll be that much closer to convincing him of this theory if you've already changed his behavior. A twenty-five-year-old Maryland wife says that when her husband does something that pleases her, like changing their baby's diaper or coming home early to watch the baby so that she can give a piano lesson, she thanks him using her "cute little girl voice, because I know he likes that fake shy and quiet approach." This mini act is his gift for cooperating with her, she says. A forty-year-old wife from Manila, in the Philippines, says that she makes a point to show her husband affection, with a kiss or a pat on the rear or a hug, every single time he pays attention to their four children. She also rewards him when he listens to her carefully or when he agrees to stay at home while she works extra hours at the tourist shop she owns and operates. "I have had to teach my husband about what it means to have an equal marriage, but he is, for the most part, a willing learner, thank God. I believe this is because he really loves me," she explains.

3. Commence creative chatting. That married couples need to talk to each other is more than obvious. But some husbands don't like to have face-to-face discussions, especially if they are sensitive about confrontation or emotionality. For this reason, some wives who are seeking to undo their superiority have to invent new ways to stay in touch with their mate. Some prefer to write old-fashioned notes, the way a fifty-year-old wife from Miami, Florida, does. "If I'm upset by his behavior, I write everything down for him. Putting it in thoughtful black and white, rather than emotive complaining or yelling, works way better. Sometimes he'll take notes on what I write and then write me back!" she says. Other wives email their husband to clue him in to the state of their discontent or to proffer small rewards for good behavior. One wife senses that her husband responds more quickly, and more rationally, when she emails him her complaints. "He takes me more seriously if I send him a calm and thoughtful email about what's bothering me," she says. (Likewise, when her teenage daughter is upset about a curfew or a punishment, she too prefers to email her mom.) A husband loves it when his wife emails him, he says, because that's her preferred method of praise. "Every so often, my wife sends me an email telling me I'm hot," he says, quite pleased with himself. That's all it takes, he says, to get him to follow her lead. A twenty-nine-year-old Texas wife likes to text her husband, because she feels "it's gentle and not overly demanding." This too is a good way to let your husband know how you feel or to reward his good behavior without being intrusive. Just make sure the habit doesn't turn into text nagging, a twenty-first-century, electronic expansion of stereotypical wifely harassment, as in "don't B late" or "go 2 store now" or "call me." You can also arrange face-to-face chats with written notes, emails, texts, or instant messages, to prepare your husband for a live, personal discussion.

4. **Tag team the tasks.** You can use texting and IM-ing to organize marital tag teaming, a way to do tasks together. For this, you will have to be very specific about what gets done and by whom. Several wives who used to be superior explain that they never insist that their husband do a specific chore; instead, they give him a choice. "I say, 'Do you want to clean the two-year-old's potty accident or finish putting away the groceries? Because I can't do both,'" says a thirty-four-year-old wife from Indiana. "That's always the way I get him involved. When we're home at night together, I'll ask him, 'Do you want to do her bath or clean the kitchen? Because after she's down and the kitchen is clean, we can watch a movie.'" It may seem primitive, but it usually works. A high school teacher from Chaska, Minnesota, uses the same method after seeing how well it works on her tenth-graders. "I ask him, 'Would you rather clean the garage or the kitchen?'" she explains, and then he does one or the other.

Tag teaming means that both partners work together on family work, thinking of the responsibility as a joint undertaking, rather than as an amalgam of her jobs (many) and his jobs (hardly any). When couples get in the habit of true sharing, they will begin to cooperate on more than just dishes and children and chores. They will also begin to share the emotion work in the marriage, which means having a deep sense of concern for the health of their partnership and the success of their marriage.[22] They will nurture each other as they nurture their children, and they will tag team nearly everything that a superior wife used to do on her own. Such postgender marriages, those in which there are no gender rules for who does what, should be the ultimate goal for superior wives.

5. **Explore coparenting.** It may sound like science fiction, like a futuristic fantasy about a galaxy far, far away, but some couples have begun to practice what they call *coparenting*. This is when both partners believe and behave as if neither mother nor father knows best. Instead, they make sure that both parents are equally responsible for everything that matters about child rearing. Experts say that this is one of the best ways to guarantee true relationship equality, by simply forgetting all the old rules about

what moms and dads should do, tossing out all those former "shoulds," and starting over. When couples coparent, they support each other's skills in dealing with children rather than undermining each other, they hold the same values about child rearing, and they have a nearly equal division of labor, researchers say. Compared to most parents, mothers who coparent have a much easier adjustment after giving birth for the first time, they are happier about their marriage, and their child's emotional health and social competence are vastly enhanced. Thus, the benefits of coparenting extend not only to the wife, the husband, and the marriage but to their children as well.[23] If superior wives could institute coparenting, that would put a large dent in their superiority, perhaps even ending it altogether. To do so, they have to relinquish their sense of self-righteousness about being the better parent, but that's a rather small price to pay for a superiority cure.

Coparenting is not for the weak of heart, though: constant vigilance and attention are needed to avoid backsliding into bad old habits. "My husband and I just started to try equal parenting," says a nonsuperior wife from Illinois. "We're both working forty-hour weeks, and we try to spend the same amount of time every day with our children. We alternate baths and book reading, meal preparation and driving to day care, but we don't always remember who did what when." They are trying this as an experiment, she explains, since their old method seemed so unfair. "I was exhausted from doing so much with the kids," she says, "and my husband felt that he hardly knew our boys. Both of us were desperate for a change, and so far, it's a real improvement."

6. Get counseling. On occasion there's nothing a superior wife can do that will shift her husband into nonsuperior wife territory. He's an immovable object, impermeable to suggestion, impenetrable to any and all persuasive techniques. If this sounds like your situation, either you will have to force your mate to read this book or you will need to get marriage counseling. Some husbands, those who are used to seeking professional help for emotional problems, will not have a problem with this. For others, though, it will be like trying to lead a buffalo to water and make him drink. When Michelle, forty-nine, an Even-Steven wife from Houston, wanted to have a second child, her husband refused, so they went to counseling to work it out. "We needed to do that," she says, "to determine how important

having another baby was to me and how important staying married was to him. He agreed to have another child, and I agreed that he could have a vasectomy afterward, despite the fact that I wanted to have four children." Even though that worked out, she says, "I'm a firm believer that you can't make a man do something he doesn't want to do, you can only try to convince him that he really wants to do it." Gabby, an Oregon wife, says that she and her husband used to "scream bloody murder" at each other, until they went to counseling. "Now we understand each other much better and we recognize the reasons that we disagree," she says. "It was an important step for our marriage, and we're a lot better off as a couple because of it," Gabby adds, explaining that her level of superiority was reduced by at least 75 percent after attending six sessions of marriage counseling. Some men are comfortable with the notion that a paid stranger will help solve their marital problems, and others would never try that in a million years. You probably know which kind yours is.

7. **Recognize defeat.** There is a time to keep and a time to cast away, and sometimes you need to know which is which. There may come a moment when you will know that it's time to throw in the towel. Even marriage counselors, who believe that nearly every possible marital problem has a potential solution, recognize that there are some unions that just can't be saved. These marriages are beyond repair, which usually means that the wife or the husband or both cling to anger and bitterness. Such spouses refuse to make any changes; they relish the harboring of hostility and the memory of pain. In such cases, counselors advise, the marriage is over, and there's nothing to do but to end it.[24] Of course, this may take a while to recognize and some painful years along the way. If you are wondering whether this describes your own marriage, ask yourself these key questions. First, if this were your daughter's marriage, what advice would you give her? Distance yourself from your own superiority problem, and figure out how you'd feel if it were happening to someone else, to someone you love. If you'd tell her to end the marriage, maybe that's what you should be doing. Second, as you look back on your marriage, do you have regrets? If you could, would you undo your marriage instantly, even erasing the children you've had? If your answer is yes, that's a fairly good indication that the marriage is beyond repair. Finally, do you feel you will never be able to forgive your husband or love him the way you used to? Has your heart

hardened to him so much that there is no room for anything other than rage and resentment? If so, then it may be time to pack it in.

The Marriage Revolution

I don't want to end on such a sour, pessimistic note. Most marriages, even superior wife marriages, can be saved, with the proper combination of intention on the wife's part and effort on the husband's part. It's simply a matter of making sure that *both* partners realize that it is to their benefit to eradicate the superior wife from their marriage, since she has an almost mystical ability to ruin the relationship. A superior wife marriage is more of a curse than a blessing, more of a weakness than a strength. Couples need to understand the importance of purging and eliminating all remnants of wifely superiority, like ridding themselves of a nasty case of food poisoning. This kind of comprehensive cleansing has to happen one marriage at a time, couple by couple, wife by wife, husband by husband. The process will be slow and painful and private, which is the opposite of the way it should be. If life were fair, the method of curing superior wives would be a public process, and women would not have to wage such an important battle on their own. Ideally, women everywhere would have social and legislative and cultural support for curing their superiority. There would be a general understanding, as a universal imperative, that wives should not be superior. There would be a broad and legal assumption that it is unjust and unreasonable to expect wives to be superior. It would be a given that husbands have a social and moral obligation to do half of everything, to share equally and fairly, without being credited for their open-mindedness or liberality or sainthood. It would be implicit and expected that both partners should do everything: they *both* decide and delegate, they *both* multitask with great efficiency, they *both* sacrifice and organize.

In the best of all possible future worlds, wifely superiority would be vanquished utterly and forever. If that were to occur, then every new bride would long to be a good wife, but so would every groom. Men would consider it the epitome of masculinity to be tender and supportive, caring and efficient, nurturing and well organized. Every marriage would contain two partners who wanted to be the other one's wife; each marriage would be a dual union of wives. The word *husband* would be reserved for one simple meaning—a mate and a breeding partner. All men would long to be good husbands, of course, but they would also yearn to be good wives.

Ideally, people would be horrified to hear about a marriage in which the wife did it all. They would assume that there was something very wrong with both partners if a woman insisted on managing the household with no help from her husband. They would blame the man, and he would be publicly shamed into doing his part, horrified at the idea that he did not live up to the manly bargain of being a good wife to his wife. No one would question such a belief, since nearly everybody would hold the same view. And lifelong traditional marriages would be viewed as a relic of the past.

Ideally, couples would take it for granted that it is a husband's job to share the grocery shopping and the meal planning, the cleaning and the child care, whatever needs doing. All men would not only know that they are *supposed* to share, but they *really would* share. They would be just as likely as their wife to take parental leave after the birth of a child; they would be just as likely as their wife to decide to work part-time or to job-share; they would be just as likely to take a day off from work when a child is sick. They would be just as likely to be the kindergarten class parent or to chair the performing arts committee at the high school.

Ideally, almost all marriages would become truly equal partnerships, or else they would be temporarily traditional, with a working husband and an at-home wife. Or temporarily nontraditional, with a working wife and an at-home husband. This situation would last only as long as the children were at home and would revert to equality as soon as the children were launched, as a matter of fairness and balance. Ideally, even traditional couples would recognize the value and importance of marital equality, and they would aim to achieve that goal.

I am revealing a personal bias here, by calling for a future filled with egalitarian unions and devoid of traditional, father-knows-best marriages. Although I don't believe that the so-called traditional marriage will ever vanish, I do believe that this arrangement is not to a woman's benefit, since it guarantees her a lifetime of subservience and inferiority. A marriage in which the husband is the supreme head of the household is a pact made at the expense of a wife's independence and self-reliance and self-confidence. In the best of all possible worlds, then, every marriage would be one in which both partners take responsibility, in which both are equal.

Ideally, corporations and government would support both wives and husbands in their attempt to have a balanced family life. They would make it easy for one or both partners to take parental leave, regardless of gender. They would offer flextime and job sharing to both partners, and neither would be punished professionally for leaving work early on occasion or for taking family leave or for requesting to work at home one day a week.

Arlie Hochschild proposed a few of these ideas twenty years ago, to help resolve what she called the "stalled revolution," the arrangement of domestic married life that forced so many wives to perform a second shift of work at home. But there is still no universal right to paid parental leave in the United States, the way there is in Sweden. There are no profamily policies in the United States worth talking about. There are no tax credits for developers who build affordable housing near workplaces that have day care centers.[25] Sadly, Hochschild's plans still seem woefully unattainable, dreams that will never come to pass.

These social changes should have happened over the past few decades, but they did not. They should be happening now, but they are not. They should be happening very soon, but they will not. Instead, this is what will probably happen to help superior wives change their status: nothing.

No social or governmental cure for the superior wife is likely to arise, simply because it would be too inconvenient for men. The marital status quo is ostensibly in their favor, and on the surface, it seems to make their lives easier. So men will continue to pay lip service to the idea that they should be equal partners, but they will try to get by with doing as little as possible. They will resist entering a truly egalitarian marriage, or changing the one they have, for as long as possible. They will do this automatically, because they can and because it's easier: it's the path of least resistance. They will do so because they do not understand the many ways in which having a superior wife can be emotionally and physically and sexually detrimental to men.

Likewise, women will continue to enter marriage fully expecting to earn a living and to share household responsibility, only to find themselves doing the first but not the second. They will long for a truly egalitarian marriage but discover early on that theirs will never be a truly equal partnership. They will continue to be superior because they will feel that they have no alternative. They will resign themselves to not having the full and voluntary cooperation of their husband in all things. They will come to view this situation as "normal" and as their natural lot in life. They will eventually give up on curing themselves of superiority.

Over time, these individual changes will inevitably lead to broader social changes. As each generation of young women observes more and more superior wife marriages, women will become discouraged about the possibility of finding a man who is truly willing to share. This may convince more young women to avoid long-term relationships, for example, or it may cause a dramatic uptick in the number of single women having children on their own. Most likely, over time single women will continue to postpone marriage or to avoid it altogether. Their rationale, although they may not think of it in these terms, will be to avoid wifely superiority and to safeguard their own well-being. Thus, the age at which women marry for the first time will rise even higher than it is now, eventually approaching thirty. In addition, the proportion of never-married women will continue to rise, especially among professional and career women. Women with the advanced education and training necessary to earn a substantial living will be less likely to see the need ever to marry, especially after they realize they are destined to fall into a superiority trap. Traditional and religious women will be the only exceptions to this rule, because by accepting a submissive marital role, they make superiority irrelevant. They will continue to marry young and to consider it their duty to obey their husband, who is the head of the household.

Meanwhile, as more single women realize that the pool of marriageable men willing to enter an equitable union is small, some may lower their expectations for marriage. They will no longer hope to find a husband who is a soul mate and a best friend and an equal partner; instead, they will accept a spouse as a companion, as long as he is willing to share the breadwinning and whatever portion of household responsibility and decision making he can be persuaded to take on. These marriages will not be ideal, but they will be realistic. Still, many of them will result in superior wife marriages, despite the woman's diminished expectations.

As a result, the divorce rate will hold steady or even rise over the next few decades, as many superior wife marriages come to an end. More and more of these wives will see no point in remaining in a marriage in which they must function as if they live alone. Some will begin to adopt a fed-up-

and-not-taking-it-anymore mentality, especially younger wives, who entered marriage convinced that theirs would be a truly equal and sharing partnership. When it becomes clear that such an ideal marriage remains an elusive illusion, many will throw in the towel on their superior wife union. It's even possible that there will be a rise in domestic violence against husbands, as more superior wives begin to act on their frustrations.

All this may come to pass simply because nonsuperior wife marriages are so difficult to achieve. Attitudes are easier to change than behavior. It is clearly easier to say you *believe* in something than to *do* it, especially if the behavior proves to be particularly inconvenient or onerous. People know they should eat a low-fat diet, for example, but they persist in gorging on ribs and burgers and cheese dip. They know they should save 5 or 10 percent of their income, but they spend it all, and more, racking up charges on their credit cards. And they know they should exercise almost every day, but they don't get around to it that often, if ever. Likewise, many men know that they should share equally at home, in chores and decisions and management, but they try to slide by with minimal effort instead, doing much less than a fair share.

That gap—between men's attitudes about sharing and their actual behavior—will not change until it becomes socially unacceptable to be so hypocritical. When men are made to feel embarrassed and humiliated for not complying with the nonsuperior wife norm, that's when their beliefs and their actions will become one. Only then will husbands finally behave according to their egalitarian beliefs. It will happen when having a superior wife makes a man feel as if he'd worn a skirt to work or forgotten to shower for a month. It will cause him such intense social opprobrium that he will change his behavior quickly and permanently and never relapse again.

How long will it take for such an anti–superior wife movement to become a modern standard? Surely it will take years. Such revolutionary changes do occur, but they almost always transpire slowly, across three or four or seven generations. African Americans and women eventually got the right to vote, but only after decades of social upheaval and protest. Likewise, recent economic and social changes have made working wives and mothers the family rule, rather than the exception to the rule. But this was after fifty years of fighting against social standards that deemed it socially unacceptable for mothers to leave their children and join the workforce.

Now that a majority of wives are working for pay, women are able to take advantage of the benefits in a good economy, and when it's bad, they suffer just as much as working men.[26] And that's only fair.

The era of true fairness in marriage, when wives no longer feel obliged to be superior, is also coming, but it is a long way off. Someday, over the foreseeable horizon, in the hazy and not-quite-imaginable future, there will be no superior wives and most couples will not think twice about sharing everything. In the meantime, women will have to create their own marriage revolution, one marriage at a time. They do not have the time or the luxury to wait for massive social change to make it easier. It is possible to change, and it's never too late to change either. If you've been married for two years or twenty-two years or forty-two years, there's still hope that you can alter your marriage for the better, that you can become the nonsuperior wife of your dreams.

The time is now.

ACKNOWLEDGMENTS

I could not have written this book without the help of thousands of wives and husbands who answered my Web survey. To all of these nameless volunteers, a very grateful, and very private, thank you.

And I could never have conducted all my elaborate Internet schemes without the help of the Web wizard Mark Watkins, at TxWorld, or without the graphic designs of Greg Galloway, at WebSight Marketing. In addition, without the Web marketing genius of Scott Edwards, I would never have figured out how to persuade so many husbands to answer my marriage survey. Finally, I could not have conducted the complex statistical analyses required by my survey design without the help of social psychologist S. Adil Saribay.

My agent, Neeti Madan, gave me more help putting this book together than it is possible to imagine. And my editor, Trish Todd, was a paragon of editorial cool and precision. Not only that, but she's an editor who can really edit.

Also, thanks to Julie Anello, Sue Apuzzo, Penelope Cassar, Deborah Doyle, Harriet Fier, Kay Brown Grala, Sarah Kahn, Teri Levine, Kate Stone Lombardi, Sue O'Connell, Carol Silverman, Jeanne Silverman, and Beth Zolkind. Also, big thanks to my mother, Trudy Rubenstein, my sister, Joann Neufeld, my brother, Steven Rubenstein, and also Ken Neufeld and Laura Spitzer. Plus Lenore and Andrea Glickhouse, and Harvey too.

Finally, thanks to my husband, David Glickhouse, and to my children, Rachel and Jonathan, and to my dog, Kippy.

The Marriage Web Survey

Who Does More?

Who's in Charge in Your House?

Help me conduct my research by answering, and you'll be eligible to win: a Wii Game System, an iPod, and other great prizes. Just complete this survey, and write honest and convincing answers to the essay questions at the end. If you want to win, you'll have to include your telephone number and email address, so I can contact you. All of your answers are anonymous and confidential, even if you win.

Thanks for your help, and good luck!

A. Who Are You?

1. How old are you?

_____

2. Are you:
❏ Female
❏ Male

3. Are you:
❏ White
❏ African-American
❏ Hispanic

❏ Asian
❏ Other

4a. What is your current marital status?
❏ Never married
❏ Married, first time
❏ Remarried, once
❏ Remarried, twice
❏ Remarried, three or more times
❏ Divorced, separated
❏ Widowed

4b. How long have you been married to your current partner?

_____

5. Do you consider yourself:
❏ Protestant
❏ Evangelical Christian
❏ Catholic
❏ Jewish
❏ Muslim
❏ Other

6a. How many hours a week do you work for pay?

_____

6b. How many hours a week does your spouse work for pay?

_____

6c. What kind of work do you do?

_____

7a. About how much did you earn last year?
❏ No income
❏ Less than $20,000
❏ $20,000 to $39,999
❏ $40,000 to $59,999

❑ $60,000 to $74,999
❑ $75,000 to $99,999
❑ More than $100,000

7b. About how much did your spouse earn last year?
❑ No income
❑ Less than $20,000
❑ $20,000 to $39,999
❑ $40,000 to $59,999
❑ $60,000 to $74,999
❑ $75,000 to $99,999
❑ More than $100,000

8. In your family, which of these statements best describes your financial situation?
❑ Husband earns all income, wife is not employed
❑ Husband earns more, but wife is employed
❑ Both husband and wife earn about the same amount, within 15 or 20%
❑ Wife earns more, but husband is employed
❑ Wife earns all income, husband is not employed

9. What's the highest level of education you have completed?
❑ No high school degree
❑ Graduated high school
❑ Some college
❑ College degree
❑ Some graduate school
❑ Graduate degree

10. How many children do you have?

___

B. Your Marriage

11a. In your marriage, which spouse has THE MOST control over and responsibility for the family's needs and problems? Please choose one of the following:
❑ Wife does
❑ Husband does

11b. Please explain.

_____

12. Which partner is usually the one who:

	Wife	Husband
Can do more than one thing at a time?	❏	❏
Organizes / plans most family events & schedules?	❏	❏
Makes most of the family decisions?	❏	❏
Is the most efficient person in the marriage?	❏	❏
Shows most support & affection to family / friends	❏	❏
Is likely to sacrifice own needs for others in family	❏	❏

13a. In your marriage, who is the family expert on:

	Wife	Husband
Cooking a decent meal	❏	❏
Earning money	❏	❏
Maintaining cars	❏	❏
Managing finances	❏	❏
Managing health care	❏	❏
Taking care of the house	❏	❏
Talking about feelings	❏	❏
Seeing relatives	❏	❏
Socializing with friends	❏	❏
Supervising children	❏	❏

13b. Why do you think this situation happened?
❏ It's natural, probably in our genes
❏ Society teaches us what we should do
❏ It's all related to who earns more money
❏ It's based on the wife's need to please
❏ I have no idea

14. When you got married, which TWO of these were most important to you in your choice of a spouse? I wanted a partner who would be:
❏ Able to earn a good living
❏ Kind and supportive
❏ A best friend
❏ Willing to give me independence

❑ Sexually compatible
❑ A good parent
❑ A soul mate

15a. When you were first married, who did you expect would do the household chores?
❑ I thought the wife would do most of the domestic work
❑ I thought both partners would share the domestic work
❑ I thought the husband would do most of the domestic work
❑ I didn't really think about it

15b. When you were first married, what did you expect to do about earning a living?
❑ I thought only the wife would work for pay
❑ I thought both partners would work for pay
❑ I thought only the husband would work for pay
❑ I didn't really think about it

C. Your Opinions

16. For each of the following six traits, type in any number between 1 and 9, according to how masculine or feminine you think they are.

Really Masculine   Both   Really Feminine

1	2	3	4	5	6	7	8	9

16a. Aggressive

_____

16b. Ambitious

_____

16c. Emotional

_____

16d. Self-sacrificing

_____

16e. Sensitive

_____

16f. Strong

_____

17. Do you and your spouse have any of these understandings—spoken or unspoken—about how your marriage works? Check ONLY the ones that are TRUE for your marriage.
- ❏ The children are mostly the wife's job.
- ❏ Earning a living is both partners' job.
- ❏ Organizing the family is the wife's job.
- ❏ Making important decisions is the wife's job.
- ❏ Keeping track of family finances is the wife's job.
- ❏ The husband should earn more than the wife.

18a. Does your spouse ever play dumb, pretending not to know how to do something to avoid doing it? (Doing the laundry, say, or cleaning the bathroom, pumping gas, or bathing a baby?) Please choose one of the following.
- ❏ Yes, often
- ❏ Yes, sometimes
- ❏ No

18b. Please explain.

_____

_____

_____

_____

_____

19a. Do you ever play dumb, pretend not to know how to do something to avoid doing it? Please choose one of the following.
- ❏ Yes, often
- ❏ Yes, sometimes
- ❏ No

19b. Please explain.

_____

_____

_____

_____

_____

20. Which best describes your marriage?
❑ Husband gives much more
❑ Husband gives more
❑ Both give the same amount
❑ Wife gives more
❑ Wife gives much more

21a. Do you ever feel as if your current marriage might have been a mistake? Please choose one of the following.
❑ Yes, quite often
❑ Yes, sometimes
❑ Yes, rarely
❑ No, never

21b. Please explain.

_____

_____

_____

_____

_____

22. In your marriage, who is the primary nagger?
❑ The husband
❑ The wife
❑ Both
❑ Neither one

23. What does your spouse nag or criticize you about most often? Also, what do you nag or criticize your spouse about most often?

_____

_____

_____

_____

_____

_____

_____

_____

_____

24. In your marriage, who's in charge?
❑ Husband
❑ Wife
❑ We say both, but mostly the husband
❑ We say both, but mostly the wife
❑ Truly, it's both

D. Your Sex Life

25. Do you ever feel as if you are begging your partner for sex?
❑ No
❑ Yes, sometimes
❑ Yes, quite often

26. Do you ever feel as if your partner is begging you for sex?
❑ No
❑ Yes, sometimes
❑ Yes, quite often

27a. Think back to the last 10 times you had sex with your spouse. Who initiated it? If appropriate, write in "0." I initiated sex _____ times out of the last 10.

27b. Think back to the last 10 times you had sex with your spouse. Who initiated it? If appropriate, write in "0." Partner initiated sex ____ times out of the last 10.

28a. Think back over the last month. How often have you or your partner refused each other's sexual overtures? If none, write in "0." I refused sex ____ times during the past month.

28b. Think back over the last month. How often have you or your partner refused each other's sexual overtures? If none, write in "0." Partner refused sex ____ times during the past month.

29. If you could wave a magic wand, and dramatically improve or change your sex life, what would happen?

_____

_____

_____

_____

_____

_____

_____

_____

_____

_____

E. Judging Your Life

30. Taking everything together, how would you describe your marriage?
❑ Very unhappy
❑ Somewhat unhappy
❑ Neither unhappy nor happy
❑ Somewhat happy
❑ Very happy

31. How happy are you with your sex life?
❑ Very unhappy
❑ Somewhat unhappy

❏ Neither unhappy nor happy
❏ Somewhat happy
❏ Very happy

32: How happy are you with your life as a whole?
❏ Very unhappy
❏ Somewhat unhappy
❏ Neither unhappy nor happy
❏ Somewhat happy
❏ Very happy

F. In Your Own Words

33. In your marriage, do you feel that one spouse is better than the other, doing more work, making more decisions, and taking more responsibility for the family? Please explain why or why not.

_____

_____

_____

_____

_____

_____

_____

_____

34. In general, how do you get your partner to do what you want? Do you have any methods that really seem to work?

_____

_____

_____

_____

_____

_____

_____

_____

_____

35a. In what U.S. city do you live?

_____

35b. In what U.S. state do you live?

_____

35c. Other (if you live elsewhere)

_____

G. If You Want to be Eligible to Win the Contest, Please Give:

36. Your first name:

_____

37. Your telephone numbers:

_____

38. Your email address (required):

_____

NOTES

Introduction

1. Colette Dowling, *The Cinderella Complex: Women's Hidden Fear of Independence* (New York: Summit Books, 1981).
2. Arlie Hochschild with Anne Machung, *The Second Shift: Working Parents and the Revolution at Home* (New York: Viking Press, 1989).
3. Moderata Fonte, *The Worth of Women: Wherein Is Clearly Revealed Their Nobility and Their Superiority to Men*, edited and translated by Virginia Cox (Chicago: University of Chicago Press, 1977).
4. H. L. Mencken, *In Defense of Women* (New York: Alfred A. Knopf, 1922).
5. Ashley Montagu, *The Natural Superiority of Women* (New York: Lancer Books, 1953).

1. Six Signs of Superiority

1. Bruce Eric Kaplan, *New Yorker*, August 25, 2008, p. 52.
2. Sam Roberts, "51% of women are now living without spouse," *New York Times*, October 16, 2006; also see Stephanie Coontz, "Too close for comfort," *New York Times*, November 7, 2006.
3. Mike Luckovich, *New York Post*, January 20, 2007.
4. Hiromi Ono, "Women's economic standing, marriage timing, and cross-national contexts of gender," *Journal of Marriage and Family* 65, no. 2 (May 2003): 275–86; for European statistics, see www.eurohealth.ie/newrep/socio.htm, retrieved September 2008.
5. Andrew J. Cherlin, "American marriage in the early twenty-first century," *The Future of Children* 15, no. 2 (Fall 2005): 33–55.
6. U.S. Census Bureau, "Households, families, subfamilies and married

couples: 1980 to 2006," retrieved from www.census.gov/compendia/statab/tables/08x005.pdf, January 2008.

7. Pew Research Center Report, "As marriage and parenthood drift apart, public is concerned about social impact," July 2007, http://pewresearch.org/assets/social/pdf/Marriage.pdf, retrieved April 2008.

8. Arland Thornton and Linda Young-DeMarco, "Four decades of trends in attitudes toward family issues in the United States: The 1960s through the 1990s," *Journal of Marriage and Family* 63, no. 4 (November 2001): 1009–37.

9. From my analysis of the General Social Surveys, 2004, conducted by the National Opinion Research Center (NORC), data obtained from www.norc.org/GSS&Website/Data&Analysis/, retrieved January 2008.

10. I infer this from the Pew Report, 2007.

11. Pew Report, 2007.

12. Ibid.

13. Stephanie Coontz, *Marriage, a History: How Love Conquered Marriage* (New York: Viking Penguin, 2005).

14. Proverbs 31:10–31.

15. Fonte, *The Worth of Women*, quotes from pp. 47, 68.

16. Ibid., p. 38.

17. This story and information on the history of marriage are from Coontz, *Marriage, a History*, quote from p. 34.

18. Jane Austen, *Pride and Prejudice* (New York: Pocket Books, 1976), p. 413.

19. Charlotte Perkins Gilman, *Herland* (New York: Pantheon Books, 1979), quote from p. 59.

20. Mencken, *In Defense*, quote from p. 30.

21. Ibid., p. 21.

22. Montagu, *Natural Superiority*, quote from p. 129.

23. Nineteen percent of white wives were working in 1920, compared to 43 percent of nonwhite women. James P. Smith and Michael P. Ward, "Time-series growth in the female labor force," *Journal of Labor Economics* 3, no. 1 (January 1985): S59–S90.

24. Margaret F. Brinig and Douglas W. Allen, " 'These boots are made for walking': Why most divorce filers are women," *American Law and Economics Review* 2, no. 1 (Spring 2000): 126–69.

25. Thornton and Young-DeMarco, "Four decades."

26. Cherlin, "American marriage."

27. U.S. Census Bureau, "Estimated median age at first marriage, by sex: 1890

to the present," www.census.gov/population/socdemo/hh-fam/ms2.pdf, retrieved December 2007.

28. Ibid.

29. From the World Values Survey, which includes about eighty countries; see Stephanie Seguino, "Plus ça change? Evidence on global trends in gender norms and stereotypes," *Feminist Economics* 13, no. 2 (April 2007): 1–28.

30. In the Pew Report, 2007, 62 percent say "sharing household chores" is "very important for a successful marriage," while 41 percent say the same about children.

31. National Survey of Families and Households, my analyses, www.ssc.wisc. edu/nsfh/home.htm, retrieved January 2008.

32. From a 2001 Gallup Poll conducted for the National Marriage Project, cited by Cherlin, "American marriage." Among unmarried adults aged twenty to twenty-nine, 94 percent say that a spouse should be a soul mate; 16 percent agree that the main purpose of marriage is to have children.

33. Paul R. Amato, Alan Booth, David R. Johnson, and Stacy J. Rogers, *Alone Together: How Marriage in America Is Changing* (Cambridge, Mass.: Harvard University Press, 2007).

34. Ibid.

35. From an April 2007 survey of 1,062 mothers conducted by BizRate Research for Shopzilla, www.shopzilla.com/12T_-_rel--216, retrieved January 2008.

36. Coontz, *Marriage, a History*, p. 310.

37. David Leonhardt, "A reversal in the index of happy," *New York Times*, September 26, 2007.

38. The survey was accessible on several Web sites, including DrCarin.com and WhoDoesMore.com.

39. Having had several decades of experience doing survey research, I knew early on that wives would be more motivated than husbands to answer a series of questions about their marriage to gain personal insight into the matter. For this reason, I offered prizes to entice reluctant husbands to think about married life.

40. My book, *Beyond the Mommy Years: How to Live Happily Ever After . . . After the Kids Leave Home,* was published by Springboard Press in New York in August 2007.

41. Stephanie Rosenbloom, "On Facebook, scholars link up with data," *New York Times*, December 17, 2007.

42. U.S. Census Bureau, "Estimated median age at first marriage."

43. Average age of wives in my survey is 42; average of husbands is 41, a difference that is not statistically significant. Wives have been married an average of 15 years, compared to 13 years for husbands, a gap that is significantly different. Eighty percent of husbands are in a first marriage, as are 78 percent of wives; 15 percent of each have been remarried once; 5 percent of wives and 3 percent of husbands are remarried two or more times; 2 percent of wives and 1 percent of husbands have divorced or separated. None is widowed. Other demographic breakdowns:

Race

	Wives	Husbands
White	85%	86%
African American	5%	3%
Hispanic	6%	5%
Asian	2%	3%
Other	2%	3%

Age group

	Wives	Husbands
25–29/27–29	20%	12%
30–39	22%	35%
40–49	30%	29%
50–59	25%	20%
60+	3%	4%

Religion

	Wives	Husbands
Protestant	25%	24%
Catholic	22%	16%
Evangelical	15%	18%
Jewish	9%	8%
Muslim	1%	1%
Other	28%	33%

Education

	Wives	Husbands
High school graduate or less	12%	8%
Some college	27%	22%

College graduate	31%	34%
Some graduate school	9%	9%
Graduate degree	21%	27%

Work status

	Wives	Husbands
None	24%	7%
2 to 20 hours/week	14%	2.5%
21 to 34 hours/week	9%	2.5%
35 hours or more	53%	88%

Personal Annual Income, in 2007 dollars

	Wives	Husbands
None	17%	2%
Less than $20,000	23%	7%
$20,000 to $39,999	25%	22%
$40,000 to $59,999	18%	22%
$60,000 to $74,999	6%	12%
$75,000 to $99,999	6%	13%
$100,000 +	5%	22%

Annual household income, in 2007 dollars

	Wives	Husbands
None to $37,000	8%	8%
$38,000 to $60,000	18%	19%
$61,000 to $80,000	17%	14%
$81,000 to $100,000	14%	14%
$101,000 to $140,000	31%	30%
More than $140,000	12%	15%

Number of children

	Wives	Husbands
None	11%	10%
One	17%	23%
Two	44%	38%
Three	18%	17%
Four or more	10%	12%

44. From U.S. Census Bureau, American Community Survey, "Income in the Past 12 Months," 2007, http://factfinder.census.gov/servlet/STTable?_bm=y&-geo_id=01000US&-qr_name=ACS_2007_3YR_G00_S1901&-ds_name=ACS_2007_3YR_G00_, retrieved December 2008. This figure may seem high, but it includes many dual-income families; indeed, half of married-couple families earned more than $73,000 in 2007.

45. Asking sensitive or embarrassing questions by telephone or in person often results in inaccurate and misreported answers. See Roger Tourangeau and Ting Yan, "Sensitive questions in surveys," *Psychological Bulletin* 133, no. 5 (September 2007): 859–83.

46. For the final version of the marriage survey, see p. 309.

47. From telephone interview with Suzanne M. Bianchi, January 24, 2008.

48. Suzanne M. Bianchi, John P. Robinson, and Melissa A. Milkie, *Changing Rhythms of American Family Life* (New York: Russell Sage Foundation, 2006).

49. Made by Slipper Genie, it's available at www.bedbathandbeyond.com/product.asp?order_num=1&SKU=14896147, retrieved June 2008.

50. Paul Stoneman, "The sociology and efficacy of multitasking," Chimera Working Paper, www.essex.ac.uk/chimera/content/pubs/wps/CWP-2007-05-Soc-Eff-Multitask-Final.pdf, retrieved January 2008.

51. Olli-Pekka Ruuskanen, "More than two hands: Is multitasking an answer to stress?" from http://64.233.179.104/scholar?hl=en&lr=&q=cache:-sBugM_BxAOJ:petral.istat.it/timeuse/paper/paper33.doc+Olli-Pekka+Ruuskanen, retrieved January 2008.

52. Bianchi, Robinson, and Milkie, *Changing Rhythms*, p. 136.

53. From telephone interview, January 2008.

54. Rebecca J. Erickson, "Why emotion work matters: Sex, gender, and the division of household labor," *Journal of Marriage and Family* 67, no. 2 (May 2005): 337–51.

55. Jean Duncombe and Dennis Marsden, "Love and intimacy: The gender division of emotion and 'emotion work,'" *Sociology* 27, no. 2 (May 1993): 221–41.

56. Robin W. Simon and Leda E. Nath, "Gender and emotion in the United States: Do men and women differ in self-reports of feelings and expressive behavior?," *American Journal of Sociology* 109, no. 5 (March 2004): 1137–76.

57. Carin Rubenstein, *The Sacrificial Mother: Escaping the Trap of Self-Denial* (New York: Hyperion, 1998). I conducted the survey for *Family Circle*

magazine by sending questionnaires to a random sample of subscribers; 600 husbands and wives answered, 245 pairs of whom were couples.

58. Kaushik Basu, "Gender and say: A model of household behaviour with endogenously determined balance of power," *Economic Journal* 116, no. 511 (April 2006): 558–80.

59. Only 4 percent of Americans agree, according to the 2005 wave of the National Survey of Families and Households, www.ssc.wisc.edu/nsfh/wave3/NSFH3%20Apr%202005%20release/Nsfh3main04202005new.CBK, retrieved January 2008.

60. Bianchi, Robinson, and Milkie, *Changing Rhythms*, p. 93.

2. The Biology and Psychology of Wifely Superiority

1. Jill B. Becker, Arthur P. Arnold, Karen J. Berkley, Jeffrey D. Blaustein, Lisa A. Eckel, Elizabeth Hampson, James P. Herman, Sherry Marts, Wolfgang Sadee, Meir Steiner, Jane Taylor, and Elizabeth Young, "Strategies and methods for research on sex differences in brain and behavior," *Endocrinology* 146, no. 4 (April 2005): 1650–73.

2. Louann Brizendine, *The Female Brain* (New York: Morgan Road Books, 2006). See also Katherine Ellison, *The Mommy Brain: How Motherhood Makes Us Smarter* (New York: Basic Books, 2005); Simon Baron-Cohen, *The Essential Difference: The Truth about the Male and Female Brain* (New York: Basic Books, 2003).

3. Helen Fisher, *The First Sex: The Natural Talents of Women and How They Are Changing the World* (New York: Random House, 1999), quotes from p. 12.

4. Brizendine, *The Female Brain*, pp. 4, 14.

5. Baron-Cohen, *The Essential Difference*, p. 47.

6. Ina V. S. Mullis, Michael O. Martin, and Pierre Foy, "IEA's Timms 2003 International Report on Achievement in the Mathematics Cognitive Domains: Findings from a Developmental Project," see http://timss.bc.edu/PDF/t03_download/T03MCOGDRPT.pdf, retrieved March 2008.

7. Jennifer Connellan, Simon Baron-Cohen, Sally Wheelwright, Anna Batki, and Jag Ahluwalia, "Sex differences in human neonatal social perception," *Infant Behavior and Development* 23, no. 1 (January 2000): 113–18.

8. C. Sue Carter, "Developmental consequences of oxytocin," *Physiology & Behavior* 27, no. 3 (August 2003): 383–97.

9. Andreas Bartels and Semir Zeki, "The neural correlates of maternal and romantic love," *Neuroimage* 21, no. 3 (March 2004): 1155–66.
10. From telephone interview with Kelly G. Lambert, March 18, 2008.
11. Brizendine, *The Female Brain*, p. 122.
12. Ibid., p. 127.
13. Baron-Cohen, *The Essential Difference*, p. 30.
14. Carolyn Zahn-Waxler, Marian Radke-Yarrow, Elizabeth Wagner, and Michael Chapman, "Development of concern for others," *Developmental Psychology* 28, no. 1 (January 1992): 126–36.
15. Susan Pinker, *The Sexual Paradox: Men, Women, and the Real Gender Gap* (New York: Scribner, 2008), p. 103.
16. Ibid., p. 24.
17. Ibid., pp. 26–27; see also Tamar Lewin, "At colleges, women are leaving men in the dust," *New York Times*, July 9, 2006.
18. Alan Finder, "Giving disorganized boys the tools for success and multitasking," *New York Times*, January 1, 2008.
19. From telephone interview with Kelly G. Lambert, March 18, 2008.
20. Shelley E. Taylor, Laura Cousino Klein, Brian P. Lewis, Tara L. Gruenewald, Rega A. R. Gurung, and John A. Updegraff, "Biobehavioral responses to stress in females: Tend-and-befriend, not fight-or-flight," *Psychological Review* 107, no. 3 (July 2000): 411–29.
21. Stacy J. Rogers and Paul R. Amato, "Have changes in gender relations affected marital quality?" *Social Forces* 79, no. 2 (December 2000): 731–53.
22. National Survey of Families and Households, my analyses.
23. Suzanne Bianchi, Vanessa Wight, and Sara Raley, "Maternal employment and family caregiving: Rethinking time with children in the ATUS," www.atususers.umd.edu/wip2/papers/Bianchi.pdf, retrieved March 2008.
24. From Current Population Survey, U.S. Department of Labor; www.bls.gov/cps/wlf-table4-2007.pdf, retrieved March 2008.
25. Jay Stewart, "Male nonworkers: Who are they and who supports them?," *Demography* 43, no. 3 (August 2006): 537–52.
26. See, for instance, Rogers and Amato, "Have changes in gender relations . . . ?"
27. Margaret Mead, *Sex and Temperament in Three Primitive Societies* (New York: Morrow, 1935).
28. Deborah L. Best and John E. Williams, "A cross-cultural viewpoint," in *The Psychology of Gender*, Anne E. Beall and Robert J. Sternberg, eds. (New York: Guilford Press, 1993).

29. Lewis Terman and Catherine Cox Miles, *Sex and Personality* (New York: McGraw-Hill, 1936).

30. Inge K. Broverman, S. R. Vogel, D. M. Broverman, F. E. Clarkson, and P. S. Rosenkrantz, "Sex-role stereotypes: A current appraisal," *Journal of Social Issues* 28, no. 2 (Spring 1972): 59–78.

31. Sandra Bem, "The measurement of psychological androgyny," *Journal of Consulting and Clinical Psychology* 42 (1974): 155–62.

32. Best and Williams, "A cross-cultural viewpoint."

33. Amanda B. Diekman, Alice H. Eagly, Antonio Mladinic, and Maria Cristina Ferreira, "Dynamic stereotypes about women and men in Latin America and the United States," *Journal of Cross-Cultural Psychology* 36, no. 2 (March 2005): 209–26.

34. Gustavo Carlo, Silvia Koller, Marcela Raffaelli, and Maria R. T. de Guzman, "Culture-related strengths among Latin American families: A case study of Brazil," *Marriage & Family Review* 41, no. 3/4 (Fall 2007): 335–60.

35. From telephone interview with Silvia Koller, March 28, 2008.

36. Paul T. Costa Jr., Antonio Terracciano, and Robert R. McCrae, "Gender differences in personality traits across cultures: Robust and surprising findings," *Journal of Personality and Social Psychology* 81, no. 2 (August 2001): 322–31.

37. John Mirowsky and Catherine E. Ross, "Sex differences in distress: Real or artifact?," *American Sociological Review* 60, no. 3 (June 1995): 449–68.

38. Ibid., p. 465.

39. Thomas A. Widiger and Kristen G. Anderson, "Personality and depression in women," *Journal of Affective Disorders* 74, no. 1 (March 2003): 59–66.

40. Timothy J. Loving, Kathi L. Heffner, Janice K. Kiecolt-Glaser, Ronald Glaser, and William B. Malarkey, "Stress hormone changes and marital conflict: Spouses' relative power makes a difference," *Journal of Marriage and Family* 66, no. 3 (August 2004): 595–612.

41. Lisa A. Uebelacker, Emily S. Courtnage, and Mark A. Whisman, "Correlates of depression and marital dissatisfaction: Perceptions of marital communication style," *Journal of Social and Personal Relationships* 20, no. 6 (December 2003): 757–69.

42. Andrew Christensen, Kathleen Eldridge, Adriana Bokel Catta-Preta, Veronica R. Lim, and Rossell Santagata, "Cross-cultural consistency of the demand/withdraw interaction pattern in couples," *Journal of Marriage and Family* 68, no. 4 (November 2006): 1029–44.

3. The Four Marriage Types

1. See, for instance, Donald M. Fish, "American labor in the 20th century," www.bls.gov/opub/cwc/print/cm20030124ar02p1.htm, retrieved April 2008; also see Monthly Labor Review, February 16, 2000, "Changes in women's labor force participation," www.bls.gov/opub/ted/2000/feb/wk3/art03.htm, retrieved April 2008.
2. Mencken, *In Defense*, pp. 65, 71.
3. Ibid., p. 7.
4. U.S. Bureau of Labor Statistics, "Women in the labor force: A databook," www.bls.gov/cps/wlf-databook-2008.pdf, retrieved December 2008.
5. From telephone interview with Sara Raley, April 24, 2008.
6. Pat Regnier and Amanda Gengler, "Men, women and money," *Money* 35, no. 4 (April 2006): 90–98.
7. Jay L. Zagorsky, "Husbands' and wives' view of the family finances," *Journal of Socio-Economics* 32, no. 2 (May 2003): 127–46; also see Jay L. Zagorsky, "Do individuals know how much they are worth?," *Financial Counseling and Planning* 10, no. 1 (2000): 13–26.
8. Carrie Yodanis and Sean Lauer, "Managing money in marriage: Multilevel and cross-national effects of the breadwinner role," *Journal of Marriage and Family* 69, no. 5 (December 2007): 1307–25.
9. Zagorsky, "Husbands' and wives' view."
10. From telephone interview with Jay Zagorsky, April 21, 2008.
11. Carolyn Vogler, "Money in the household: Some underlying issues of power," *The Sociological Review* 46, no. 4 (November 1998): 687–713.
12. Sara B. Raley, Marybeth J. Mattingly, and Suzanne M. Bianchi, "How dual are dual-income couples? Documenting change from 1970 to 2001," *Journal of Marriage and Family* 68, no. 1 (February 2006): 11–28.
13. Melissa A. Milkie, Suzanne M. Bianchi, Marybeth J. Mattingly, and John P. Robinson, "Gendered division of childrearing: Ideals, realities, and the relationship to parental well-being," *Sex Roles* 47, no. 1/2 (July 2002): 21–38.
14. Bianchi, Robinson, and Milkie, *Changing Rhythms*; see p. 218 for detailed table.
15. W. Bradford Wilcox and Steven L. Nock, "What's love got to do with it? Equality, equity, commitment, and women's marital quality," *Social Forces* 84, no. 3 (March 2006): 1321–45.
16. Julie E. Press, "Cute butts and housework: A gynocentric theory of

assortative mating," *Journal of Marriage and Family* 66, no. 4 (November 2004): 1029–33.

17. Jane Riblett Wilkie, Myra Marx Ferree, and Kathryn Strother Ratcliff, "Gender and fairness: Marital satisfaction in two-earner couples," *Journal of Marriage and the Family* 60, no. 3 (August 1998): 577–94.

18. Steven L. Nock, "The marriages of equally dependent spouses," *Journal of Family Issues* 22, no. 6 (September 2001): 755–75, quote from p. 758.

19. From telephone interview with Sara Raley, April 24, 2008.

20. Julie Brines, "Economic dependency, gender, and the division of labor at home," *American Journal of Sociology* 100, no. 3 (November 1994): 652–88; also see Michael Bittman, Paul England, Nancy Folbre, Liana Sayer, and George Matheson, "When does gender trump money? Bargaining and time in household work," *American Journal of Sociology* 109, no. 1 (July 2003): 186–214.

21. Sarah Winslow-Bowe, "Work-family intersections," *Sociology Compass* 1, no. 1 (September 2007): 385–403.

22. Suzanne M. Bianchi, "Maternal employment and time with children: Dramatic change or surprising continuity?" *Demography* 37, no. 4 (November 2000): 401–14.

23. Bianchi, Robinson, and Milkie, *Changing Rhythms*.

24. Raley, Mattingly, and Bianchi, "How dual are dual-income couples?"

25. Ibid.

26. From telephone interview with Sara Raley, April 24, 2008.

27. Robert T. Brennan, Rosalind Chait Barnett, and Karen C. Gareis, "When she earns more than he does: A longitudinal study of dual-earner couples," *Journal of Marriage and Family* 63, no. 1 (February 2001): 168–82.

28. Veronica Jaris Tichenor, "Status and income as gendered resources: The case of marital power," *Journal of Marriage and the Family* 61, no. 3 (August 1999): 638–50, quote from p. 643.

4. What, Me Oblivious? How Husbands See (or Don't See) Wifely Superiority

1. From the 2004 General Social Survey, my own analysis of data available at www.norc.org/GSS+Website/Data+Analysis/, retrieved May 2008.

2. U.S. Bureau of Labor Statistics, "Married parents' use of time: 2003 to 2006, May 8, 2008," from www.bls.gov/news.release/pdf/atus2.pdf, retrieved May 2008.

3. Yoshinori Kamo, "'He said, she said': Assessing discrepancies in husbands' and wives' reports on the division of household labor," *Social Science Research* 29, no. 4 (December 2000): 459–76.

4. Yun-Suk Lee and Linda J. Waite, "Husbands' and wives' time spent on housework: A comparison of measures," *Journal of Marriage and Family* 67, no. 2 (May 2005): 328–36.

5. Coontz, *Marriage, a History*, p. 282.

6. Steven F. Maier and Martin E. P. Seligman, "Learned helplessness: Theory and evidence," *Journal of Experimental Psychology: General* 105, no. 1 (March 1976): 3–46.

7. Victoria Roberts, *New Yorker*, March 6, 2006, p. 62.

8. Bureau of Labor Statistics, "Married parents' use of time."

9. Marybeth J. Mattingly and Suzanne M. Bianchi, "Gender differences in the quantity and quality of free time: The U.S. experience," *Social Forces* 81, no. 3 (March 2003): 999–1030, quote from p. 1020.

10. Bianchi, Robinson, and Milkie, *Changing Rhythms*.

11. Kei M. Nomaguchi and Suzanne Bianchi, "Exercise time: Gender differences in the effects of marriage, parenthood, and employment," *Journal of Marriage and Family* 66, no. 2 (May 2004): 413–30.

12. Fisher, *The First Sex*.

13. David Dunning, Chip Heath, and Jerry M. Suls, "Flawed self-assessment: Implications for health, education, and the workplace," *Psychological Science in the Public Interest* 5, no. 3 (December 2004): 69–106.

14. John Bartlett, *Familiar Quotations*, fifteenth edition (Boston: Little, Brown, 1980), p. 484.

15. David Dunning, Kerri Johnson, Joyce Ehrlinger, and Justin Kruger, "Why people fail to recognize their own incompetence," *Current Directions in Psychological Science* 12, no. 3 (June 2003): 83–87, quote from p. 85.

16. From telephone interview with Joyce Ehrlinger, May 29, 2008.

17. Benjamin Franklin, "Advice to a friend on choosing a mistress," letter written on June 25, 1745, www.bibliomania.com/2/9/77/124/frameset.html, retrieved May 2008.

18. Robin W. Simon, "Revisiting the relationships among gender, marital status, and mental health," *American Journal of Sociology* 107, no. 4 (January 2002): 1065–96.

19. Linda J. Waite and Evelyn L. Lehrer, "The benefits from marriage and religion in the United States: A comparative analysis," *Population and Development Review* 29, no. 2 (June 2003): 255–75; see also Ross M. Stolzenberg

and Linda J. Waite, "Effects of marriage, divorce, and widowhood on health," in *Work, Family, Health, and Well-Being,* Suzanne M. Bianchi, Lynne M. Casper, Rosalind Berkowitz King, eds. (New York: Lawrence Erlbaum Associates, 2005).

20. Kristen Taylor Curtis and Christopher G. Ellison, "Religious heterogamy and marital conflict," *Journal of Family Issues* 23, no. 4 (May 2002): 551–76.

21. Amato, Booth, Johnson, and Rogers, *Alone Together.*

22. Tom W. Smith, "American Sexual Behavior: Trends, Socio-Demographic Differences, and Risk Behavior," GSS Topical Report Number 25, March 2006, www.norc.org/NR/rdonlyres/2663F09F-2E74-436E-AC81-6FFBF288E183/0/AmericanSexualBehavior2006.pdf, retrieved May 2008.

5. I'm Always Right: How Superior Wives See Themselves

1. Wilcox and Nock, "What's love got to do with it?" They interviewed 5,010 couples.

2. John Gottman, *Why Marriages Succeed or Fail . . . and How You Can Make Yours Last* (New York: Simon & Schuster, 1994).

3. Amato, Booth, Johnson, and Rogers, *Alone Together.*

4. Scott Coltrane, "Research on household labor: Modeling and measuring the social embeddedness of routine family work," *Journal of Marriage and the Family* 62, no. 4 (November 2000): 1208–33, quote from p. 1226.

5. Paul Amato, David R. Johnson, Alan Booth, and Stacy J. Rogers, "Continuity and change in marital quality between 1980 and 2000," *Journal of Marriage and Family* 65, no. 1 (February 2003): 1–22; also see Russell A. Ward, "Marital happiness and household equity in later life," *Journal of Marriage and Family* 55, no. 2 (May 1993): 427–38.

6. Coltrane, "Research on household labor."

7. John R. Robinson and Melissa A. Milkie, "Back to the basics: Trends in and role determinants of women's attitudes toward housework," *Journal of Marriage and the Family* 60, no. 2 (February 1998): 205–18.

8. Nancy K. Grote and Margaret S. Clark, "Perceiving unfairness in the family: Cause or consequence of marital distress?" *Journal of Personality and Social Psychology* 80, no. 2 (February 2001): 281–93.

9. Benita Jackson, Laura D. Kubzansky, and Rosalind J. Wright, "Linking perceived unfairness to physical health: The perceived unfairness model," *Review of General Psychology* 10, no. 1 (March 2006): 21–40.

10. "Stress in America," American Psychological Association, www.apa.org/releases/stressproblem.html, retrieved January 2009; see p. 12.

11. Marybeth J. Mattingly and Liana C. Sayer, "Under pressure: Gender differences in the relationship between free time and feeling rushed," *Journal of Marriage and Family* 68, no. 1 (February 2006): 205–21, quote from p. 217.

12. Megan A. Lewis, Rita M. Butterfield, Lynae A. Darbes, and Catharine Johnston-Brooks, "The conceptualization and assessment of health-related social control," *Journal of Social and Personal Relationships* 21, no. 5 (October 2004): 669–87; also see Charlotte N. Markey, Jessica N. Gomel, and Patrick M. Markey, "Romantic relationships and eating regulation," *Journal of Health Psychology* 13, no. 3 (April 2008): 422–32.

13. Coontz, *Marriage, a History.*

14. E. Mavis Heatherington, "Intimate pathways: Changing patterns in close personal relationships across time," *Family Relations* 52, no. 4 (October 2003): 318–31.

15. Amato, Booth, Johnson, and Rogers, *Alone Together.*

16. Ibid.

17. Sarah W. Whitton, P. Antonio Olmos-Gallo, Scott M. Stanley, Lydia M. Prado, Galena H. Kline, Michelle St. Peters, and Howard J. Markman, "Depressive symptoms in early marriage: Predictions from relationship confidence and negative marital interaction," *Journal of Family Psychology* 21, no. 2 (June 2007): 297–306.

18. R. Kelly Raley and Larry Bumpass, "The topography of the divorce plateau: Levels and trends in union stability in the United States after 1980," *Demographic Research* 8 (April 2003): 245–60, www.demographic-research.org/volumes/vol8/8/8-8.pdf, retrieved June 2008.

19. Betsey Stevenson and Justin Wolfers, "Marriage and divorce, changes and their driving forces," Institute for the Study of Labor, Discussion Paper Number 2602, February 2007, http://papers.ssrn.com/sol3/papers.cfm?abstract_id=969354, retrieved June 2008.

20. Brinig and Allen, " 'These boots are made for walking.' "

21. Elizabeth Enright, "A house divided," *AARP The Magazine*, July & August 2004.

22. Tim B. Heaton and Ashley M. Blake, "Gender differences in determinants of marital disruption," *Journal of Family Issues* 20, no. 1 (January 1999): 25–45.

23. Enright, "A house divided."

24. Laura Sanchez and Constance T. Gager, "Hard living, perceived

entitlement to a great marriage, and marital dissolution," *Journal of Marriage and the Family* 62, no. 2 (August 2000): 708–22.

25. Michelle L. Frisco and Kristi Williams, "Perceived housework equity, marital happiness, and divorce in dual-earner households," *Journal of Family Issues* 24, no. 1 (January 2003): 51–73.

26. Heaton and Blake, "Gender differences."

27. From personal interview with Joy Joseph, March 17, 2008.

28. Coontz, *Marriage, a History.*

29. Stevenson and Wolfers, "Marriage and divorce."

30. Stacy J. Rogers and Danielle D. DeBoer, "Changes in wives' income: Effects on marital happiness, psychological well-being, and the risk of divorce," *Journal of Marriage and Family* 63, no. 2 (May 2001): 458–72.

31. Jay Teachman, "Complex life course patterns and the risk of divorce in second marriages," *Journal of Marriage and Family* 70, no. 2 (May 2008): 294–305.

32. Stevenson and Wolfers, "Marriage and divorce."

6. Sex and the Superior Wife

1. See www.quotationspage.com/quote/26221.html, retrieved June 2008.

2. Sources cited in William H. James, "The fecundability of U.S. women," *Population Studies* 27, no. 3 (November 1973): 493–500.

3. James K. McNulty and Terri D. Fischer, "Gender differences in response to sexual expectancies and changes in sexual frequency: A short-term longitudinal study of sexual satisfaction in newly married couples," *Archives of Sexual Behavior* 37, no. 2 (April 2008): 229–40.

4. F. Scott Christopher and Susan Sprecher, "Sexuality in marriage, dating, and other relationships: A decade review," *Journal of Marriage and the Family* 62, no. 4 (November 2000): 999–1017.

5. Chien Liu, "A theory of marital sexual life," *Journal of Marriage and the Family* 62, no. 2 (May 2000): 363–74.

6. Sinikka Elliott and Debra Umberson, "The performance of desire: Gender and sexual negotiation in long-term marriages," *Journal of Marriage and Family* 70, no. 2 (May 2008): 391–406.

7. Christopher and Sprecher, "Sexuality in marriage."

8. Ibid.

9. Cindy M. Meston and David M. Buss, "Why humans have sex," *Archives of Sexual Behavior* 36, no. 4 (August 2007): 477–507.

10. Elliott and Umberson, "The performance of desire."
11. See www.quotationspage.com/quotes/Billy_Crystal/, retrieved June 2008.
12. For a report on Richard A. Lippa's research, see Natalie Angier, "Birds do it. Bees do it. People seek the keys to it," *New York Times*, April 10, 2007.
13. Brizendine, *The Female Brain*, quote from p. 91.
14. Edward O. Laumann, Anthony Paik, Dale B. Glasser, Jeong-Han Kang, Tianfu Wang, Bernard Levinson, Edson D. Moreira, Alfredo Nicolosi, and Clive Gingell, "A cross-national study of subjective sexual well-being among older women and men: Findings from the global study of sexual attitudes and behaviors," *Archives of Sexual Behavior* 35, no. 2 (April 2006): 145–61.
15. William L. Parish, Ye Luo, Ross Stolzenberg, Edward O. Laumann, Gracia Farrer, and Suiming Pan. "Sexual practices and sexual satisfaction: A population based study of Chinese urban adults," *Archives of Sexual Behavior* 36, no. 1 (February 2007): 5–20.
16. Edward O. Lauman, Anthony Paik, and Raymond Rosen, "Sexual dysfunction in the United States: Prevalence and predictors," *Journal of the American Medical Association* 281, no. 6 (February 10, 1999): 537–44.
17. Gerald Brock, Edward Lauman, Dale B. Glasser, Alfredo Nicolosi, Clive Gingell, and Rosie King, "Prevalence of sexual dysfunction among mature men and women in USA, Canada, Australia and New Zealand," www.pfizerglobalstudy.com/Posters/GSSAB%20AUA%202003_poster_FINAL.pdf, retrieved June 2008.
18. Brizendine, *The Female Brain*, p. 82.
19. Ibid.
20. Coontz, "Too close," p. 170.
21. Dennis Brissett and Lionel S. Lewis, "Guidelines for marital sex: An analysis of fifteen popular marriage manuals," *The Family Coordinator* 19, no. 1 (January 1970): 41–48, quotes from p. 45.
22. Bertrand Russell, *Marriage and Morals* (New York: W. W. Norton, 1970), quote from p. 153.
23. William L. Parish, Shirley Yee, and Edward O. Laumann, "Going along to get along: Female sexual submission in urban China," www.src.uchicago.edu/prc/pdfs/parish02.pdf, retrieved June 2008.
24. Edward O. Laumann, John H. Gagnon, Robert T. Michael, and Stuart Michaels, *The Social Organization of Sexuality: Sexual Practices in the United States* (Chicago: University of Chicago Press, 1994).
25. Ibid.

26. Ibid.

27. Ronald W. Lewis, Kersten S. Fugl-Meyer, R. Bosch, Axel R. Fugl-Meyer, Edward O. Laumann, E. Lizza, and Antonio Martin-Morales, "Epidemiology/Risk factors of sexual dysfunction," *Journal of Sexual Medicine* 1, no. 1 (July 2004): 35–39.

28. John Bancroft, Jeni Loftus, and J. Scott Long, "Distress about sex: A national survey of women in heterosexual relationships," *Archives of Sexual Behavior* 32, no. 3 (June 2003): 193–208.

29. David Levy, *Love and Sex with Robots: The Evolution of Human-Robot Relationships* (New York: Harper, 2007).

7. Why Nonsuperior Wives Are Better Wives

1. Nancy K. Grote and Margaret S. Clark, "Perceiving unfairness in the family: Cause or consequence of marital distress?," *Journal of Personality and Social Psychology* 80, no. 2 (February 2001): 281–93.

2. Jean M. Twenge, W. Keith Campbell, and Craig A. Foster, "Parenthood and marital satisfaction: A meta-analytic review," *Journal of Marriage and Family* 65, no. 3 (August 2003): 574–83.

3. Theodore N. Greenstein, "Husbands' participation in domestic labor: Interactive effects of wives' and husbands' gender ideologies," *Journal of Marriage and the Family* 58, no. 3 (August 1996): 585–95.

4. Items adapted from Jiping Zuo, "Shifting the breadwinner boundary: The role of men's breadwinner status and their gender ideologies," *Journal of Family Issues* 25, no. 6 (September 2004): 811–32.

5. Teresa Ciabattari, "Changes in men's conservative gender ideologies," *Gender and Society* 15, no. 4 (August 2001): 574–91.

6. Scott M. Stanley, Sarah W. Whitton, Sabina Low Sadberry, Mari L. Clements, and Howard J. Markman, "Sacrifice as a predictor of marital outcomes," *Family Process* 45, no. 3 (September 2006): 289–303.

7. Shelley M. MacDermid, Ted L. Huston, and Susan McHale, "Changes in marriage associated with the transition to parenthood: Individual differences as a function of sex-role attitudes and changes in the division of household labor," *Journal of Marriage and the Family* 52, no. 2 (May 1990): 475–86.

8. Karin L. Brewster and Irene Padavic, "Change in gender-ideology, 1977–1996: The contributions of intracohort change and population turnover," *Journal of Marriage and the Family* 62, no. 2 (May 2000): 477–87.

9. Ira Mark Ellman, "Marital roles and declining marriage rates," http://papers.ssrn.com/sol3/papers.cfm?abstract_id=1018141#PaperDownload, retrieved June 2008; also see Amy L. Wax, "Bargaining in the shadow of the market: Is there a future for egalitarian marriage?" *Virginia Law Review* 84, no. 4 (May 1998): 509–672.

10. Laurie A. Rudman and Julie E. Phelan, "The interpersonal power of feminism: Is feminism good for romantic relationships?," *Sex Roles* 57, nos. 11–12 (December 2007): 787–99.

11. Marwan Khawaja and Rima R. Habib, "Husbands' involvement in housework and women's psychosocial health: Findings from a population-based study in Lebanon," *American Journal of Public Health* 97, no. 5 (May 2007): 860–66, quote from p. 865.

12. "Intersex fish are found at high rate in a region," *New York Times*, September 7, 2006.

13. Diane Mapes, "Gals make passes at guys who wash glasses," www.msnbc.msn.com/id/23015839/, retrieved June 2008.

14. Susan C. Rosenbluth, Janice M. Steil, and Juliet H. Whitcomb, "Marital equality: What does it mean?," *Journal of Family Issues* 19, no. 3 (May 1998): 227–44.

15. Lisa Belkin, "When Mom and Dad share it all," *New York Times Magazine*, June 15, 2008; see www.nytimes.com/2008/06/15/magazine/15parenting-t.html?ex=1372046400&en=40ba03d3ab9ec8de&ei=5124&partner=permalink&exprod=permalink, retrieved July 2008.

16. Kimberly F. Balsam, Theodore P. Beauchaine, Esther D. Rothblum, and Sondra E. Solomon, "Three-year follow-up of same-sex couples who had civil unions in Vermont, same-sex couples not in civil unions, and heterosexual married couples," *Developmental Psychology* 44, no. 1 (January 2008): 102–16.

8. How to Fix a Superior Wife Marriage

1. Robert W. Levenson, Laura L. Carstensen, and John M. Gottman, "Long-term marriage: Age, gender, and satisfaction," *Psychology and Aging* 8, no. 2 (June 1993): 301–13.

2. Frank D. Fincham, Steven R. H. Beach, and Joanne Davila, "Forgiveness and conflict resolution in marriage," *Journal of Family Psychology* 18, no. 1 (March 2004): 72–81.

3. Adapted from ibid.

4. Arthur Aron, Christina C. Norman, Elaine N. Aron, Colin McKenna, and Richard E. Heyman, "Couples' shared participation in novel and arousing activities and experienced relationship quality," *Journal of Personality and Social Psychology* 78, no. 2 (February 2000): 273–84.

5. Gottman, *Why Marriages Succeed*.

6. John Mordechai Gottman and Robert Wayne Levenson, "The timing of divorce: Predicting when a couple will divorce over a 14-year period," *Journal of Marriage and the Family* 62, no. 3 (August 2000): 737–45.

7. Gottman, *Why Marriages Succeed*.

8. Scott M. Stanley, Howard J. Markman, and Sarah W. Whitton, "Communication, conflict, and commitment: Insights on the foundations of relationship success from a national survey," *Family Process* 41, no. 4 (December 2002): 659–75.

9. Esther S. Kluwer, José A. M. Heesink, and Evert Van de Vliert, "The division of labor in close relationships: An asymmetrical conflict issue," *Personal Relationships* 7, no. 3 (September 2000): 263–82.

10. David L. Vogel, Megan J. Murphy, Ronald J. Werner-Wilson, Carolyn E. Cutrona, and Joann Seeman, "Sex differences in the use of demand and withdraw behavior in marriage: Examining the social structure hypothesis," *Journal of Counseling Psychology* 54, no. 2 (April 2007): 165–77.

11. Carmen Knudson-Martin and Anne Rankin Mahoney, "Language and processes in the construction of equality in new marriages," *Family Relations* 47, no. 1 (January 1998): 81–91.

12. Carmen Knudson-Martin and Anne Rankin Mahoney, "Moving beyond gender: Processes that create relationship equality," *Journal of Marital and Family Therapy* 31, no. 2 (April 2005): 235–58.

13. Ibid.

14. Barbara J. Risman and Danette Johnson-Sumerford, "Doing it fairly: A study of postgender marriages," *Journal of Marriage and the Family* 60, no. 1 (February 1998): 23–40.

15. Rudman and Phelan, "The interpersonal power of feminism."

16. John M. Gottman, Julie Schwartz Gottman, and Joan DeClaire, *10 Lessons to Transform Your Marriage* (New York: Three Rivers Press, 2006).

17. Paul Ekman and Richard J. Davidson, "Voluntary smiling changes regional brain activity," *Psychological Science* 4, no. 5 (September 1993): 342–45.

18. Richard W. Robins, Avshalom Caspi, and Terrie E. Moffitt, "Two personalities, one relationship: Both partners' personality traits shape the quality

of their relationship," *Journal of Personality and Social Psychology* 79, no. 2 (August 2000): 251–59.

19. Kira S. Birditt and Toni C. Antonucci, "Relationship quality profiles and well-being among married adults," *Journal of Family Psychology* 21, no. 4 (December 2007): 595–604, quote from p. 602.

20. Shelley A. Haddock, Toni Schindler Zimmerman, Scott J. Ziemba, and Lisa R. Current, "Ten adaptive strategies for family and work balance: Advice from successful families," *Journal of Marital and Family Therapy* 27, no. 4 (October 2001): 445–58.

21. Amy Sutherland, "What Shamu taught me about a happy marriage," *New York Times*, June 25, 2006.

22. Risman and Johnson-Sumerford, "Doing it fairly."

23. Mark E. Feinberg, "Coparenting and the transition to parenthood: A framework for prevention," *Clinical Child and Family Psychology Review* 5, no. 3 (September 2002): 173–95.

24. Gottman, *Why Marriages Succeed.*

25. Hochschild, *The Second Shift.*

26. Louis Uchitelle, "Women are now equal as victims of poor economy," *New York Times*, July 22, 2008.

INDEX